JOURNALISM OF THE HIGHEST REALM

FROM OUR OWN CORRESPONDENT

John Maxwell Hamilton, Series Editor

Illuminating the development of foreign news gathering at a time when it has never been more important, "From Our Own Correspondent" is a series of books that features forgotten works and unpublished memoirs by pioneering foreign correspondents. Series editor John Maxwell Hamilton, once a foreign correspondent himself, is dean of the Manship School of Mass Communication at Louisiana State University.

Previous Books in the Series

Waugh in Abyssinia

The Memoir of **EDWARD PRICE BELL**

Pioneering Foreign Correspondent

for the *Chicago Daily News*

JOURNALISM OF
THE HIGHEST REALM

Edited by **JACI COLE** and **JOHN MAXWELL HAMILTON**

Foreword by **JAMES F. HOGE, JR.**

LOUISIANA STATE UNIVERSITY PRESS

BATON ROUGE

Published with the assistance of the V. Ray Cardozier Fund.

Published by Louisiana State University Press
Copyright © 2007 by Louisiana State University Press
All rights reserved
Manufactured in the United States of America
First printing

The memoir of Edward Price Bell is copyrighted by the Newberry
Library, Chicago, and is reproduced by permission.

Designer: Barbara Neely Bourgoyne
Typefaces: Minion Pro, text; Helvetica Neue, display
Printer and binder: Thomson-Shore, Inc.

Library of Congress Cataloging-in-Publication Data
Bell, Edward Price, 1869–1943.
    Journalism of the highest realm : the memoir of Edward Price Bell,
pioneering foreign correspondent for the Chicago daily news / edited by
Jaci Cole and John Maxwell Hamilton ; foreword by James F. Hoge, Jr.
        p. cm. — (From our own correspondent)
    Includes bibliographical references and index.
    ISBN 978-0-8071-3285-2 (cloth : alk. paper)   1. Bell, Edward Price,
1869–1943.   2. Foreign correspondents—United States—Biography.
I. Cole, Jaci, 1983–   II. Hamilton, John Maxwell.   III. Title.
    PN4874.B3694A3 2007
    070.92—dc22
    [B]

                                            2007013870

The paper in this book meets the guidelines for permanence and
durability of the Committee on Production Guidelines for Book
Longevity of the Council on Library Resources. ∞

Contents

Foreword by James F. Hoge, Jr.   ix

Acknowledgments   xiii

Introduction   xv

Note on Editorial Method   xliii

Author's Preface   3

Prologue: "I'm Going to Be a Newspaper Man"   5

I The Early City Period, 1882–1898

1. Half a Writer at Last   9
2. My Work for the *Democrat*   18
3. On the Road for Another Job   27
4. I Head an Editorial Autarchy   35
5. As a Country Editor Saw It   41
6. A Great Infidel Turns Christian   46
7. I Meet a Girl in Black Pigtails   53

II The Chicago Period, 1898–1900

8. Blown Out of My Home Town   63
9. War and Oratory on Leech Lake   70
10. I Learn I'm a "White Nigger"   80
11. Dug It Out of Barrel Houses   90
12. I See "Democracy" in Action   101
13. An Epochal Idea Oddly Born   108

III The Foreign Period, 1900–1922

14. Life Opens for Me in London   117

15. More of Life's "Little Gleam" Abroad   130

16. Our Fight for Side-Light News   144

17. Luminaries of the British Press   154

18. Northcliffe in My Own Finder   165

19. I Go to Tea with Royalty   177

20. Historic Pageantry of the News   185

21. Two World-Rousing Interviews   192

22. When My Hair Grayed a Bit   202

23. The Six Letters to *The Times*   212

IV The Great War, 1914–1919

24. Flying in the Great War   225

25. What I Saw in the Ypres Salient   236

26. A Lively Day on Vimy Ridge   246

27. In the Thick of It at Bapaume   256

V The Peace-Seeking Period, 1919–1941

28. From War Trail to Peace Trail   269

29. Peace-Seeking on Three Continents   276

30. I Push On to the Far East, Economics,
       and Latin America   285

31. I Bring MacDonald to America   295

32. My Final Interviews for Peace   306

33. War Again after Twenty Years   315

Epilogue: Where Are Our Plans Built?   322

Appendix: "What, in Your Opinion,
    Is the Matter with the Service?"   325

Sources   331

Index   341

Illustrations

Bell in his thirties   xxiii

The lavish London office of the
   Chicago Daily News   xxvii

Bell at his typewriter   xxxv

Merrywood, Bell's home upon retirement   xxxviii

Foreword

For most of the twentieth century, the foreign news service of the *Chicago Daily News* was one of journalism's jewels, recognized in the United States and abroad for the enterprise and style of its highly skilled correspondents. The service was created at the end of the nineteenth century and syndicated widely by the *Daily News*'s great publisher, Victor Lawson. And it was Lawson who defined the special characteristics of the service that competitors were to imitate—original reporting and analysis that supplemented the spot news filings of the Associated Press and other basic wire services.

If Lawson provided the means and the objectives, it was Edward Price Bell more than anyone who shaped the service. Bell ran the operation for its first twenty-two years and set the standards for other correspondents by his own energetic performance as head of the London bureau. Even after returning to Chicago in 1922, Bell traveled the globe interviewing world leaders until his retirement in 1932.

Bell was one of the earliest celebrity journalists, known widely among statesmen, generals, and reading publics in this country and Europe. As his engaging memoir makes clear, the qualities that set him apart were evident early on. Bell was still a teenager when he began his journalistic career in the rural Midwest. Too poor to afford a college education until later in life, Bell made the most of his native intelligence and uncommon resourcefulness. He regularly scooped competitors as he climbed from small newspapers to medium-sized ones and finally to the big-city press. Bell also became highly skilled in the cutting-edge technologies of his day—shorthand, typesetting, and telegraph deciphering.

The high standards of Bell and Lawson remained the hallmarks of the *Daily News* foreign service long after Lawson's death and Bell's retirement. But over time, after World War II, the *Daily News* steadily reduced the number of overseas correspondents. By 1978, thirty-five years after Bell's death, the last correspondents were retired or returned to the home office, leaving the *Daily News* dependent on basic and supplementary wire services. Closure of its distinctive foreign news service and other cutbacks were not enough to keep the *Daily News* in business beyond 1978. Like most urban afternoon newspapers, the *Chicago Daily News* was a victim of changing lifestyles and advertising preferences in the television age.

The pressures that killed the *Daily News* have steadily grown to affect all established media, not just PM newspapers. Thus when the cold war ended at the beginning of the 1990s, the major broadcast networks cut back on foreign bureaus and on air time devoted to international coverage. Cost pressures and low public interest led newspapers and news magazines to follow suit. They eliminated bureaus, cut space allotted to foreign news, and reserved prime play only for armed conflicts and other high-profile crises.

In this era, fresh retrenchments are underway as cable channels and the Internet divert more consumers and advertisers from newspapers. In 2007, the *Boston Globe* closed its remaining three foreign bureaus in Israel, Germany, and Colombia. By doing so, the *Globe* joined the *Philadelphia Inquirer, Baltimore Sun, Newsday,* and *Dallas Morning News* in eliminating overseas correspondents. In short, nearly all newspapers and broadcast stations are focusing their staffs on local news and relegating foreign coverage to syndicated services and occasional trips by home-based reporters. Besides syndicated services, only a few elite newspapers—the *New York Times* and the *Washington Post* to name two—still station correspondents overseas. A recent study of the newspaper industry showed only one bright spot. While average daily circulation of U.S. newspapers has declined since 1987 and advertising has followed suit, community weeklies and dailies with circulations of less than 50,000 are prospering on a diet of strictly local news.

In today's fragmented media, foreign news increasingly is to be found in a number of electronic and print niches. For example, the BBC and Bloomberg, the *Economist* and *Foreign Affairs,* are thriving. On the Internet, reports abound on countries, regions, and particular topics, and bloggers comment on just about everything. The audiences for these diversified sources are important but small compared with the general audience of major broadcast

Foreword

For most of the twentieth century, the foreign news service of the *Chicago Daily News* was one of journalism's jewels, recognized in the United States and abroad for the enterprise and style of its highly skilled correspondents. The service was created at the end of the nineteenth century and syndicated widely by the *Daily News*'s great publisher, Victor Lawson. And it was Lawson who defined the special characteristics of the service that competitors were to imitate—original reporting and analysis that supplemented the spot news filings of the Associated Press and other basic wire services.

If Lawson provided the means and the objectives, it was Edward Price Bell more than anyone who shaped the service. Bell ran the operation for its first twenty-two years and set the standards for other correspondents by his own energetic performance as head of the London bureau. Even after returning to Chicago in 1922, Bell traveled the globe interviewing world leaders until his retirement in 1932.

Bell was one of the earliest celebrity journalists, known widely among statesmen, generals, and reading publics in this country and Europe. As his engaging memoir makes clear, the qualities that set him apart were evident early on. Bell was still a teenager when he began his journalistic career in the rural Midwest. Too poor to afford a college education until later in life, Bell made the most of his native intelligence and uncommon resourcefulness. He regularly scooped competitors as he climbed from small newspapers to medium-sized ones and finally to the big-city press. Bell also became highly skilled in the cutting-edge technologies of his day—shorthand, typesetting, and telegraph deciphering.

The high standards of Bell and Lawson remained the hallmarks of the *Daily News* foreign service long after Lawson's death and Bell's retirement. But over time, after World War II, the *Daily News* steadily reduced the number of overseas correspondents. By 1978, thirty-five years after Bell's death, the last correspondents were retired or returned to the home office, leaving the *Daily News* dependent on basic and supplementary wire services. Closure of its distinctive foreign news service and other cutbacks were not enough to keep the *Daily News* in business beyond 1978. Like most urban afternoon newspapers, the *Chicago Daily News* was a victim of changing lifestyles and advertising preferences in the television age.

The pressures that killed the *Daily News* have steadily grown to affect all established media, not just PM newspapers. Thus when the cold war ended at the beginning of the 1990s, the major broadcast networks cut back on foreign bureaus and on air time devoted to international coverage. Cost pressures and low public interest led newspapers and news magazines to follow suit. They eliminated bureaus, cut space allotted to foreign news, and reserved prime play only for armed conflicts and other high-profile crises.

In this era, fresh retrenchments are underway as cable channels and the Internet divert more consumers and advertisers from newspapers. In 2007, the *Boston Globe* closed its remaining three foreign bureaus in Israel, Germany, and Colombia. By doing so, the *Globe* joined the *Philadelphia Inquirer, Baltimore Sun, Newsday,* and *Dallas Morning News* in eliminating overseas correspondents. In short, nearly all newspapers and broadcast stations are focusing their staffs on local news and relegating foreign coverage to syndicated services and occasional trips by home-based reporters. Besides syndicated services, only a few elite newspapers—the *New York Times* and the *Washington Post* to name two—still station correspondents overseas. A recent study of the newspaper industry showed only one bright spot. While average daily circulation of U.S. newspapers has declined since 1987 and advertising has followed suit, community weeklies and dailies with circulations of less than 50,000 are prospering on a diet of strictly local news.

In today's fragmented media, foreign news increasingly is to be found in a number of electronic and print niches. For example, the BBC and Bloomberg, the *Economist* and *Foreign Affairs,* are thriving. On the Internet, reports abound on countries, regions, and particular topics, and bloggers comment on just about everything. The audiences for these diversified sources are important but small compared with the general audience of major broadcast stations and newspapers. A large majority of that general audience cites TV as its source for foreign news even though there is significantly less such TV news available than heretofore. As for the cable commentators who have risen to prominence, many of their observations are viewed by the public as being politicized along political fault lines.

Syndicated coverage of overseas developments is better than nothing. But much of it is cursory and episodic, delivered without historical context or keen analysis informed by lengthy overseas experience. Moreover, the reporting is now often provided by stringers, whose training and affiliations can be questionable. And pressure from governments on stringers to slant the news is difficult to counter. Why care? One potent reason is that in a democracy the conductors of foreign policy are ineffectual in their efforts without public understanding and support. And since public attitudes about international issues are largely shaped by media, the quality and quantity of foreign coverage can be critical.

Reading Bell's memoir reminds us that nostalgia can paint too rosy a picture. The era of plentiful, resident foreign correspondents had its problems as well as its strengths. Editors worried about reporters "going native" and reflecting the bias and interests of their host countries more than those of their readers. And all the experience in the world did not ensure wise judgment. Bell himself was so prone to attributing "great man" vision to those in power that he attributed unwarranted virtues to Hitler and Mussolini. There were mundane issues as well. Staff-produced foreign coverage was even then expensive, leading to constant wrangling over the cost of cables.

So it is well to remember that the high quality of the *Daily News* foreign service was rooted in Lawson's commercial skill as well as in his will power. Lawson made the *Daily News* profitable and then used those profits to sustain a great newspaper. Without that kind of proprietor support, Edward Price Bell and his colleagues could never have created the foreign news service that became the model of excellence for all others.

JAMES F. HOGE, JR.

Editors' note: James F. Hoge, Jr., is the editor of *Foreign Affairs*. His many distinguished positions include editor-in-chief, then publisher of the *Chicago Sun-Times*; editor-in-chief of the *Chicago Daily News*; and publisher of the *New York Daily News*.

Acknowledgments

We are especially grateful to the Newberry Library in Chicago, where Edward Price Bell's unpublished memoir has reposed for years. The Newberry has a superb collection of materials relating to Bell and the *Chicago Daily News* and a gracious staff dedicated to accommodating scholars who come to use it. On our two visits to peruse that collection for material employed in the book's introduction as well as another volume on foreign news gathering, the staff was unfailingly helpful. We thank especially Martha Briggs, associate curator of Modern Manuscripts, who arranged the library's permission to quote from its collections and to publish Bell's memoir, which we gratefully acknowledge here.

MaryKatherine Callaway, the director of Louisiana State University Press, was quick to see the possibilities of this book when we presented it to her. Rather than stopping with Bell, she conceived the idea of a series of volumes like it. She has never lost an opportunity to be enthusiastic about this book. We also enjoyed working with Catherine Kadair and Laura Gleason at the Press.

By extraordinary coincidence, Bell retired not far from Baton Rouge, where we live, to Pass Christian, Mississippi. By good luck, his elegant little home, Merrywood, shielded by a Wal-Mart, survived Hurricane Katrina in 2005. When we learned the house still stood, we arranged a visit through its delightful owner, Ouida Tanner. She and her daughter, Dawn Nelson, gave us a personal tour of the house and grounds, where Bell's memory was kept alive. Alas, Wal-Mart's rebuilding program will probably crowd the sturdy building out of existence by the time this book appears in print.

We also thank our agent, Wendy Schmalz, who lets nothing get by her and yet is ever cheerful; the LSU Foundation, which sustained our research with the Hopkins P. Breazeale LSU Foundation Professorship awarded several years ago to one of us; Angela Fleming, for help on this and other research projects; and Gina Hamilton, for food for thought.

Lastly, we thank each other for the mutual enjoyment of working together on this book.

Introduction

"See that glint!" exclaims a character in Sir Arthur Conan Doyle's 1928 short story, "When the World Screamed," a tale of a mad British scientist's secret drilling in Sussex to reach the earth's life force.[1] "That's the telescope of the *Chicago Daily News.*" In looking for a newspaper known for scouring the planet for news, Doyle could have selected the *New York Times,* which had an outstanding foreign service. He also could have chosen the *New York Herald Tribune,* created in 1924 with the amalgamation of two venerable newspapers, both of which had a history of sending notable foreign correspondents abroad dating from the nineteenth century. But for good reason it was the *Daily News* that came to Doyle's mind.

The *Daily News* virtually invented the American ideal of a newspaper foreign service. It was the first U.S. newspaper to put a thoroughly professional corps of American correspondents permanently abroad in peacetime and syndicate their reporting widely. During World War I, the London *Chronicle* called the *Daily News* "by far the best evening newspaper in the world."[2]

If this were not enough to commend the *Daily News* to Doyle, there was Edward Price Bell. In 1900, shortly after *Daily News* owner Victor Freemont Lawson conceived his foreign service, he stationed Bell in Britain. The Indiana-born Bell was the anchor of the newspaper's overseas coverage, the correspondent who more than any other brought it to life. Before returning home to Chicago in 1922, he was considered dean of the entire foreign press corps in London.

For all this, Edward Price Bell is forgotten. Ask foreign correspondents to list the best of their breed, and he does not collect a single vote. It is doubtful more than a few working journalists today, let alone scholars, can even identify Bell as a foreign correspondent. It doesn't help that the *Chicago Daily News,* which folded in 1978, is fading from collective journalistic memory. The *Herald Trib-une,* which went under eight years earlier, has a fine biography. The *New York Times* story is told over and over. No one has written a history of the *Chicago Daily News.*

Bell received a brief biographical monograph in 1979. It drew heavily on his unpublished memoir, written a few years before he died in 1943. Bell might have fared better if his autobiography, more interesting and better written, had been published instead. Along with a trove of other papers relating to the *Daily News,* the memoir was interred in the Newberry Library—until now.

In addition to telling the story of his rise from Indiana farm boy to jour-nalistic champion of world peace, Bell's autobiography illuminates the early history of the *Daily News*'s famed foreign service. That foreign service began as a great experiment whose outcome was uncertain. Bell's story offers a broad context for understanding the challenges of creating and maintaining quality foreign correspondence, challenges that transcend his own lifetime. The *Daily News* was a model for excellent foreign coverage and is an object lesson in the fragility of even the best foreign services.

§

The *Chicago Daily News*'s foreign service began as an experiment within an ex-periment. Victor Lawson's strides on the international front were apiece with his efforts to create a high-quality daily newspaper.

Lawson got into big-city journalism by happenstance. He was twenty-five when his father, a Norwegian-born immigrant who made a fortune in Chi-cago real estate and other investments, died. Beginning in December 1876 Lawson rented a little space in one of his buildings to the start-up newspa-per of a high school classmate, Melville Stone. When Stone's fellow investors lost interest in their struggling *Daily News,* he turned to Lawson. In the deal they struck, Lawson acquired financial control and became business manager. Stone remained editor. The now thriving *Daily News* took over the building, and Lawson began the higgledy-piggledy process of breaking through walls to make use of adjoining structures. In 1881 he started a morning edition that was later given a separate name, the *Chicago Record.*[3]

The *Daily News* started out as a penny paper, and like penny papers of that time built readership through entertaining news. "All of our fine theories would be of little avail," Stone observed, "unless we could compel attention of the public."[4] The newspaper nurtured good writers with a literary flair (in the twentieth century its staff arguably constituted the best collection of writers ever gathered on one newspaper staff). Stone also found ways to stir up news. In one exciting adventure, he personally tracked down a local financial malefactor who fled to Canada and Germany. In little more than a decade of its creation in 1876, the *Daily News* had the second largest daily circulation in the United States.

Despite the *Daily News*'s enthusiasm for fires, earthquakes, murders, and scandals, it did not let the sensational divert it from respectability and genuine public service. Stone eschewed "the silly so-called 'human-interest stories' of cats born with two heads" and favored reliable news on a range of serious subjects. So did Lawson, who became both editor and publisher in 1888 when Stone sold him his interest in the morning and afternoon papers. "We do not want to fool our readers with sensational stories that have little or no foundation in fact," Lawson admonished his editors during the Spanish-American War.[5] While editors of yellow papers clamored for war stories, Lawson insisted his editors be conservative with headlines, illustrations, and the number of "extra" editions.[6] Lawson also used his pages for enterprising stories that exposed government corruption and promoted progressive civic causes. Unlike many publishers of the era, Lawson was not flamboyant or desirous of personal political power beyond that of running a good newspaper.

Lawson brought this high-mindedness to the business side and made it pay. He charged one rate to all advertisers, rather than making side deals the way other publishers did. He rejected advertisements that promised more than they delivered. This enhanced the credibility of the newspaper to readers and made it more attractive to advertisers. Lawson also was sharp about collecting what was owed to him and avoided waste. Among his schemes along this line, he required his newsdealers to pay in advance for the newspapers they distributed. This ensured not only that he was paid promptly but also that distributors did not take more copies of his newspaper than they could really sell.[7]

Lawson's independence and commercial acumen gave reporters just what they wanted—a large audience and absolute freedom to pursue the news, still a newspaper rarity when Lawson and Stone joined forces. No publisher stood higher when it came to making journalism a respectable business. When Adolph Ochs wanted to promote himself as an ideal buyer for the *New York Times* in 1896, he sought a letter of recommendation from the rectitudinous publisher.[8] After Lawson died in 1925, eulogies poured into the *Daily News,* which filled its pages with them. Over and over the tributes said the same thing: Lawson stood for "clean" journalism.[9]

Lawson showed an early, if episodic, interest in foreign news. In 1879, he introduced regular foreign news round-ups. A decade later, he experimented with gathering news in less well covered regions of Latin America, Australia and New Zealand, and Sweden. William E. Curtis, Washington correspondent for Lawson's *Record,* went to Russia in 1887 and sent home a series of articles, "The Land of the Nihilist, Its People, Its Palaces, Its Politics."[10] It was just the kind of enterprising reporting for which the *Daily News* became celebrated, but in these early years, Curtis's piece and others like it appeared irregularly.

The Spanish-American War marked a turning point. In December 1896 Lawson decided to station reporters from his morning newspaper, the *Record,* in Havana. After the sinking of the *Maine* in February 1898, he sent the *Daily News* into the fray, instructing its managing editor to "send all men possible to war reducing number later if advisable."[11] At the height of the conflict, Lawson had fourteen correspondents for the *Record* and the *Daily News* stretched from Cuba to the Philippines. The *Record's* Spanish-American War service had its own news bureau in Key West, where editors received eyewitness dispatches carried from Cuba by the *Hercules,* a yacht Lawson hired. At one point during the war, foreign news consumed more than 40 percent of the *Chicago Record's* news hole.

The *Record* and *Daily News* were the only American newspapers besides a handful of New York dailies—the *Sun, Herald, Journal,* and *World*—to have a real war service as opposed to just sending a few correspondents.[12] Lawson's competitor, the *Chicago Tribune,* relied heavily on the New York newspapers for its war news.

After two decades of hit-or-miss overseas news gathering, Lawson had built a small-scale model for systematic collection of foreign news. That a publisher in the supposedly provincial Midwest did this was remarkable. If Lawson were interested in making money, there were better ways. Foreign news was then, as it is now, expensive to gather. He was already paying for foreign news from the *New York Herald* and the Associated Press, both of which were less sensational than the yellow *New York Evening World* and the *New York Evening Journal.* On top of all that, his staff was diffident about foreign coverage. *Daily News* managing editor Charles Faye, whose interest in news was largely local, thought *Daily News* reporters would not be able to supply "news or pictures, or news of any sort," but only "descriptive matter and pictures different from other papers." Lawson, however, insisted. "We must print enterprising report."[13]

Only a month into the conflict, Faye admitted that the *Daily News* distinguished itself covering the war. "No afternoon paper even approaches News in quantity and quality of matter and pictures," he wrote Lawson, who was traveling abroad at the time. When the newspaper's April circulation figures were high, Lawson cabled home this promotional comment, which he wanted printed in the paper: "These remarkable figures are but renewed evidence of Chicago's recognition of the *Daily News* as an enterprising news gatherer and of confidence in its purpose to print the truth . . . in the excitement of the hour between rumor and a fact, truth and falsehood."[14]

In July 1898, before the hostilities concluded, Lawson announced the creation of a permanent news-gathering operation abroad. Initially, it ran out of the *Record,* although material appeared in the *Daily News;* when Lawson sold the *Record* in 1901, he kept the service for the *Daily News.* This venture was even more remarkable than covering the Spanish-American War itself. War was a natural newsmaker. Covering the world in peacetime was more problematic. Exactly what this service should do and how remained big questions. What sort of news should the service cover? How would it be sustained financially? Who should do the reporting? There was not a good model for a professional corps of foreign correspondents abroad.

Lawson described his foreign service as "largely an experiment." One of his first steps was to ask an editor to collect all the British newspapers he could find in order to see how they did foreign news.[15] His bedrock principles were that the service should serve Americans and not duplicate the Associated Press, which under the guidance of his old partner Melville Stone expanded beyond its lone overseas bureau in London—an expansion Lawson, who was elected head of the AP executive committee in 1894, supported.[*]

Victor Lawson's letters, cables, and other papers housed in the Newberry Library reveal a man filled with uncertainties. The stream of early instructions Lawson sent to his reporters constantly shifted course. In an early directive to his man in Paris, Theodore Stanton, Lawson cabled: "Chicago Record wants brief cable service covering important matters" that did not duplicate the AP:

---

*Lawson's support for the Associated Press did not stop him from being highly competitive with it. The *Daily News* was the first paper to get a story of the Boxer Rebellion out of Peking in 1900. A professor at Imperial University paid a 15-year-old boy to sneak his account, hidden in a beggar's rice bowl, out of a blockaded embassy. When the Associated Press picked up the story without permission, Lawson told them that they "must not take out foreign cables hereafter without our express consent in individual instances."

"opinions statesmen American questions, foreign relations, continental happenings, not more than 300 words daily, much less ordinarily." Six months later, in January 1899, Lawson directed Stanton to send by mail, "two, three or four times a month," the following: "short, concisely written news notes on matters of recent occurrence and special interests"; "short stories on royalty"; "a terse and carefully written letter once a month, giving a general 'bird's-eye view' of matters of most important general interest in the country at date." A year later, Lawson told Stanton, "what I want to emphasize is to be particularly on the lookout for short, bright, novel, interesting bits of news and story-telling gossip of interest to Americans."[16]

Lawson was equally uncertain how to organize his service. He briefly tried a syndicate partnership with James Gordon Bennett, Jr.'s *New York Herald* and equally briefly supplemented his supplementary service with one started by the London *Standard*. In 1902, he explored the possibility of running the service jointly with the *New York Times*. The discussions came to naught, as Lawson was not willing to give *Times* publisher Adolph Ochs the control he wanted.

These partnerships were designed to offset the considerable expense of gathering news overseas. Lawson calculated that in its first full year, 1899, the service cost $122,155.79—$2.7 million in today's terms. He wrote endless letters to fellow publishers trying to sell them on subscribing to the service. "This morning," he wrote to a potential subscriber in Milwaukee, "we printed special cables from twelve cities in Europe—and we shall do even better when we get our correspondents selected in the Orient, Australia and the South American countries." He also tried to entice subscribers with gossipy bits of news about foreign notabilities, which the *Daily News* ran under the headline, "Queer Sprigs of Gentility." By April 1900, Lawson had eight client newspapers, which covered two-thirds to one-half of his expenses.[17] But syndication faltered later that year when escalating prices for newsprint prompted clients to cut costs and withdraw. In October, the subscription service was discontinued. It would take many years before Lawson made a success of syndication. At its high point the *Daily News*'s foreign service was purchased by more than 100 newspapers across the country, including the nation's capital, which enhanced the *Daily News*'s extraordinary influence.[18]

Lawson was animated by the idea that, with the Spanish-American War, the United States had joined the ranks of the Great Powers. The nation, he believed, needed a new kind foreign reporting that reflected its status and helped it assess its global interests. Although American correspondents in the nineteenth century—Henry Stanley with the *New York Herald* and George

Smalley with the *New York Tribune,* for instance—occasionally showed enterprise, correspondents routinely rewrote reports taken from local newspapers where they were stationed. Lawson believed this rehashed news did not serve Americans because it was framed for those foreign audiences. He wanted his reporters to do original reporting for Americans. This approach came to shape his hiring policy.

At first Lawson used a familiar model of hiring correspondents where he could find them abroad. This made him heavily reliant on foreigners not only as stringers—of whom he had some sixty in 1898—but also for the few permanent fulltime correspondents he hired. Many newspapers took this approach because foreigners had an intimate feel for local customs and politics. The approach was so ingrained that in the late 1920s, Wythe Williams noted he was the only *New York Times* bureau chief in a Continental capital to carry a U.S. passport. Over time, however, Lawson decided he wanted correspondents who understood America and Americans and sent reporters who worked on his staff in Chicago. These reporters, he reasoned, could develop foreign expertise on the job and "judge news from the point of view of the average American newspaper reader."[19]

Lawson's first step in this direction was to replace a British journalist in London with one of his top city reporters. "I find it desirable," he wrote the displaced correspondent, "to have a man who knows Chicago, and knows the working conditions of the office, take charge of the London service."[20] That man was Edward Price Bell.

§

Just as the *Daily News* became a model foreign service, Edward Price Bell was Lawson's model foreign correspondent. He was as much in touch with Middle Western America as a journalist could be. And he epitomized what it meant to be an enterprising reporter.

Born in 1869, Bell grew up on a farm in Parke County, Indiana. He worked his father's walking plow, skipped church on Sundays to play cards with his pals, and for three winters attended the village school. As was common in those days, he learned journalism on the job. At age thirteen he talked his way into a newspaper job in Terre Haute. He later moved on to Indianapolis and in 1898 was hired on the *Chicago Record.* In between, he put himself through the small Indiana college of Wabash and visited England and France as a student in 1896.

Bell's independence, courage, and determination as a young man, which come through in his memoir, explain why he found his way to Lawson's newspaper building and thrived in its "local room." Shortly after hiring him, the *Daily News* assigned Bell to big stories. It sent him out of town to cover a skirmish between the Chippewa and the U.S. military in Minnesota, the Wilmington race riots of 1898, and one of Clarence Darrow's labor trials. One of the distinguishing features of his reporting was his ability to get interviews with leading newsmakers, a trait that came to define his reporting abroad. Bell's reporting on local corruption would have won national awards if such honors had been given at the time, recalled Frederic William Wile, a younger Hoosier who assisted Bell overseas. "Bell," Wile said, "was the finest type of the crusading American newspaperman—persistent, resourceful, honest and fearless."[21]

That Bell was sent to take on such a demanding assignment after less than two years working for Lawson was a credit to his abilities and a further sign of Lawson's experimental frame of mind. Bell sensed this. When he stepped off the boat in England, he figured he would go back to Chicago within five years. He began in a small, one-room office, with no assistant. Lawson initially paid him so little that he could not finance his wife's trip to England. (Lawson paid for her passage within a few months.) When in 1901 Lawson sold the *Record,* his primary vehicle for foreign news, Bell and other correspondents waited to be called home; so uncertain was the future of the foreign service.

If Lawson was a genius in sending an American reporter to get the American perspective, he was more brilliant still in leaving Bell on the ground for years. Bell was on the front line of working out what the foreign service should be. He became its co-inventor, along with Lawson.

"What to Send and What to Kill"

The question of what to cover was weighed and argued for years, and even then never fully resolved. Bell went to London with the same kind of ambiguous instructions other reporters had received—cover "emotional," "intellectual," and "exclusive" news. This left wide latitude for interpretation. Dennis, who remained Lawson's principal lieutenant at home for foreign news, sometimes contradicted his boss. Faye, who continued to work for Lawson for several years, sometimes contradicted them both. Lawson continued to contradict himself. Correspondents entered into the often-tempestuous debate. Bell mediated between them and Chicago, in addition to putting forward his own point of view. He continually found himself asking, What exactly does

Bell in his thirties. European head of the *Chicago Daily News* foreign service, Bell presents himself here as very much the British gentleman. *Courtesy Edward Price Bell Papers, Newberry Library, Chicago*

the home office want? "We need all the light we can get," he wrote to Dennis, "on the subject of what to send and what to kill."[22]

One point among the many that generated disagreement was which countries to cover. Lawson originally conceived his foreign service concentrating on the major European capitals, where he placed salaried staff correspondents as opposed to stringers. Faye argued readers of the *Daily News* did not come from London, Paris, Rome, or Madrid. He complained to Dennis that the service's "long daily cables from London and Paris did The Daily News little good." Faye wanted news from Berlin, Vienna, and Stockholm. News from these and other Scandinavian cities would be "of real value to him," Dennis relayed to Bell in 1901. "It so happens that our cables come from places that awaken no responsive thrill in the minds of readers of The Daily News, who are not Frenchmen, Belgians or Russians."[23]

No matter what city news came from, there was still the question, What should be covered? Should correspondents stress serious news? Should they tilt toward entertaining bits of news and information, which might draw a larger audience? When Illinois-bred Paul Scott Mowrer arrived in Paris in 1910, he was a little defensive over Bell's familiarity with "the fascinating intricacies of international politics." Mowrer told the elder correspondent such reporting was fine in London, but not in Paris. "My situation is different," he wrote. "I was educated in features. My eye is trained to them. For a long time I wrote one a day for the front page of the paper in Chicago. Thus I feel I know something about what the *local* management wants in this respect . . . I say we are both right. Let the dignified, enlightening, really-worth-while cables come from London, and let Paris effervesce the freakish, the far-fetched and the fantastic."[24]

Although Mowrer soon came around and embraced Bell's views on the importance of news with political weight, not everyone else did. In 1911 the home office asked for a weekly summary of the best jokes from the European press—a challenge for Mowrer, inasmuch as the funniest Parisian humor was too risqué for the Chicago reader. Chicago editors worried readers perused serious European news "with a yawn or not at all" and, when they did pay attention, wondered "what the deuce it is all about." Foreign political news, Dennis wrote in an outburst of confused prose, "is so much prunella beneath the tentative mastication of the average Chicago reader. He wants to know about the burglary on Blue Island avenue, if it has novel features, rather than about the latest complication in some bundesrath or reichstag or diet."[25]

Lawson policed coverage carefully with these concerns in mind. To correspondents who sent a cable he deemed "worth neither the cost of cabling nor the necessary space in THE RECORD," he sent a form letter: "The great majority of news events in other lands possess no value whatever to the general reader of an American newspaper. It is only the occasional and exceptional event that has general news value in America . . . The attached cable should *not* have been sent."[26] Below the message, Lawson pasted a copy of the errant story. Although Bell remembers in his memoir that Lawson welcomed serious news, not all correspondents shared the same view of their boss. "Mr. Lawson," Berlin bureau chief Raymond Swing concluded, "did not care a hoot about foreign news."[27]

Lawson's injunction not to duplicate the Associated Press was particularly nettlesome to correspondents. They did not like to be waved off the big stories and resented it when AP dispatches took precedence over theirs. Dennis himself was disappointed when his own reporters had to leave important stories to others. The foreign service, he wrote to Bell, could truly become great only if "the big subjects were not denied" to its correspondents.[28] Bell had a different point of view.

Bell saw the value of covering big subjects and encouraged correspondents to score scoops, for which the foreign service was acclaimed during World War I. The *Daily News* scored "more beats on the war in its special foreign service than perhaps any other paper in the world," the trade magazine *Editor & Publisher* said in a special article on the foreign service. But when the service could not top the AP, Bell was happy to leave the breaking news to them and concentrate instead on background and analysis.

To a considerable extent Bell had his way. The AP provided about two-thirds of the foreign news in the *Daily News* during Bell's years in London, and 92 percent of this was spot news. The newspaper's foreign service provided the bulk of the analysis, a trend that became more pronounced over time. In 1901, only 10 percent of staff correspondent stories were in-depth or analytical reports; in 1913 the share jumped to 27.1 percent and five years later to 37.6 percent.[29] To Bell more than any other goes the credit for understanding the idea of a thoughtful supplementary foreign news service and bringing it into being.

"Shillings Melt like Snowflakes"

In 1918, Lawson calculated the foreign service's expenses that year would "considerably exceed $200,000," a substantial sum at the time. This was only partially offset by subscribers to his syndicate. Lawson reckoned the fifteen papers paying for the service brought in between $50,000 and $60,000.[30] This balance sheet was a cause of endless wrangling over costs and affected how correspondents did their jobs.

When it came to paying his reporters, Lawson was, as Bell put it, "way behind the times." Correspondents complained that they needed reasonable incomes or more liberal expense accounts to finance the everyday necessities of gathering news in Europe. "Whenever one begins to move over London and meet a lot of people the shillings melt like snowflakes," Bell wrote. "I need not tell you that it is impossible to travel about London much at an expense of five shillings a day for cab and 'bus fares, to say nothing of tips and incidental outlays . . . tips come as near to being an absolute necessity as anything else I can think of. Without them one simply cannot manage the matter of news-getting at hotels, embassies and all other places where one is at the mercy of pages, porters and flunkeys standing between him and the people whom he is trying to see."[31]

Lawson was tightfisted in paying stringers, too. Some newspapers gave part-timers a monthly fee to cover their work. The *Daily News* paid by the story. When Wile suggested paying their Stockholm correspondent $50 a month, Lawson was "entirely averse to paying any such sum," Dennis wrote: "Arrangement of 10 kroner per cablegram we will abide by, as I have told Mr. Friberg already . . . If Mr. Friberg is not satisfied then, Lord bless him, let him quit." Bell worried that their stringers, some of whom he learned were working for more than one newspaper, gave the best service to the highest payer, sending them stories first or at the same time as the *Daily News*—a problem for a service trying to build its reputation on exclusivity. "Of course, it would be desirable for us to have the services of all our men exclusively," Bell wrote Dennis, "but it seems that many of them are professional journalists and must have more than one connection in order to live."[32]

The most urgent daily financial concern for correspondents was whether the stories they sent warranted pricey cable tolls or should travel by the slower and cheaper mail service. At times limits were placed on the amount of news correspondents could cable. Editors, correspondents complained, treated "mailers" with little respect, sometimes not running them at all or giving them second place to wire stories. When they sent too much by cable or not enough, Bell often took the blame. To him fell the task of sending monthly reports to Chicago of cabling tolls from around the Continent. He wrote countless letters urging correspondents to heed the home office's demands. At the end of a congratulatory letter to Hague correspondent A. F. J. Kiehl, who covered an interesting angle of a big Associated Press story, Bell slipped in a not-too-subtle admonition, all in caps, "PLEASE BE CAREFUL NOT TO EXCEED YOUR WORD ALLOWANCE AS DEFINED BY MR DENNIS."[33]

When correspondents did send by cable, they had to "skeletonize" their stories, cutting them down to bare bones. Often correspondents found their "stylistic peculiarities," as Bell called them, sacrificed in the name of economy. Worse, "cablese" could lead to errors when dispatches were put back into standard English in Chicago. "To-day your industrial societies cable gave me some puzzles," Dennis wrote apologetically to Bell after editing one of his stories, "and I fear I made some silly errors . . . already—it being too late to correct it—I see that what I made 'the worker who is responsible for the unit scheme of production' should have been 'elevates the status of the worker to that of a responsible unit in the scheme of production.'" Bell in turn begged for guide-

The lavish London office of the *Chicago Daily News*. Even though *Daily News* owner Victor Lawson was parsimonious, he outfitted his foreign bureaus in high style, replete with leather chairs, guest book, and newspapers for visitors to read. *Courtesy Edward Price Bell Papers, Newberry Library, Chicago*

lines from the home office. "It seems to me," he wrote Dennis, "that the man who expands cables in Chicago should be able to formulate some general directions to us touching the problem of correct condensation."[34]

One of the most ridiculous attempts at cost saving was when the home office ordered correspondents to eliminate the word *stop* from their cables. This command generated a years-long debate on the relative merits of using the word. Junius Wood complained that excluding *stop* or *period* from cables led to "bad results in printed copy, sentences split, joined together wrongly, entire sense changed . . . Even the U.P. which gets a half page out of a 50 word cable, requires 'stop' in its cables." Bell wrote a three-page defense of the little word. "I would say that the feeling of cable correspondents is strongly in favor of it," he wrote Dennis, before listing the four reasons why it should be allowed. To make sure Dennis was getting the message, Bell added in a letter two months later, "Re the use of the word 'stop' in cables, I have just heard from [Percy] Noel. He says he has suffered 'shockingly' at times from the omission of this word. Indeed he goes so far as to state that in his opinion commas should be cabled."[35]

One of the compensations for the enormous outlay of treasure to support the foreign service was the prestige that came with having it. Lawson was willing to lay out even more money to advertise this prestige. He furnished his major bureaus in London and Paris in grand style. This was common for newspapers, but Lawson's enthusiasm was unbridled. As Mowrer noted, the bureaus were plush. A reading table held the latest home newspapers. Visiting Chicagoans found tourist information, collected their mail, and left their names, which the *Daily News* dutifully published on its front page. "Please remember," Lawson instructed Bell, "to spare no expense to have the decorating and the furnishing and big, outside, gold, wall-sign just as good as money can buy. In the matter of color for wall treatment avoid the dead white and use the white with a light cream tint or an 'old ivory' white, but the latter should not be too dark."[36]

"Many Letters to Write"

Sorting out the everyday issues of gathering foreign news was complicated by the spotty communication among Bell, his editors in Chicago, and the correspondents in Europe. Communication could be so patchy that, in the early years, Bell often knew little about what was happening with the correspondents. This lack of communication could prolong and confuse discussions of cost or coverage. It also brought its own problems for Bell, who found it difficult to effectively lead correspondents whose inclination was to act independently.

Lawson made a couple of long European tours during Bell's tenure, and Dennis came to Paris to help with coverage of the Versailles Peace Conference after the war. But there were no regularly scheduled visits, as is common in overseas bureaus today. Bell, for one, thought such visits could cure many of the ills that naturally affected a system of correspondents who had little communication with one another or Chicago. "If you were here for a time you could spend a few weeks on the continent studying the situation there and substituting good men for poor ones," Bell wrote Dennis in 1901. "Furthermore, you could individualize, energize, Americanize the service." Lawson agreed, or at least told Bell he did. But, his hand on his pocketbook, Lawson suggested that communication should remain "through the post for the present, reserving the more expensive method for a more propitious occasion."[37]

Bell found he had to "engage in a hand-to-hand struggle with our fellows on the continent" with "many letters to write," letters that often went unheeded or unanswered. Especially in his first years as head of the foreign service, Bell's roving, independent correspondents often acted as though London was no nearer than Chicago and less powerful. "Our men generally do not take very seriously the theory that I have any authority," Bell wrote Dennis. "Edgar Mowrer remarked to me on one occasion, with considerably more truth than courtesy (though I did not mind in the least) that so far as he could see he had as much authority as I had."[38]

Coordinating the efforts of correspondents accordingly was difficult. For years the Chicago office complained both Paris and London sometimes sent heavy amounts of cable on the same day and light amounts the next. Dennis insisted Bell should be able to work this out from London. Bell tried. "If I know that an unusually large amount of stuff is moving from France, I shall do my utmost to hold down accordingly here. On the other hand, if I know that France is sending relatively lightly, I shall release more through London," he wrote Paul Mowrer, attempting to work out a system. "Of course, in the existing state of communications we can manage this thing only very roughly."[39]

For all his complaints about other correspondents, Bell himself expected a certain freedom from authority as well. "You will bear with me, I hope, if I tell you that the treatment my mail stuff has been receiving for several weeks strikes me as leaving something to be desired," Bell wrote his chief during 1915, at the height of the service's and Bell's prominence. "Is it right that a man of my experience—I see no virtue in a modesty that is dishonest—should be turned over to some sub-editor—to be 'switched about' or otherwise changed to suit his fancy? I may be wrong, but I do not think so. I wish my stuff could be printed as I send it and let me be judged by the result."[40]

Correspondents' freedom was a blessing in one very important way. Over the years they developed considerable expertise, and the autonomy they enjoyed meant they could make full use of that knowledge and experience. Editors rarely second-guessed their conclusions. Lawson's editorial philosophy, expressed through men like Dennis and Smith, was "the man on the spot is always right." "No argument by cable," said Edgar Mowrer; "no tampering with his copy."[41] This was central to the high intellectual quality and originality of the *Daily News* foreign service.

"Unofficial Envoys"

Bell's papers in the Newberry Library are replete with letters to and from American and British elites, whose names fill this memoir. Becoming an insider inevitably led Bell and others like him to see themselves as playing a dip-lomatic role. "More than any other writer of his time, Edward Price Bell was newspaper reporter on the ambassadorial level," said Junius Wood admiringly. The editors encouraged this. "The right kind of foreign correspondent," said Charles Dennis, "is, in fact, an unofficial envoy who frequently performs ser-vices of value to the American people."[42] But these services sometimes worked the other way. Correspondents became advocates for the people they were supposed to be covering. This identification with the country in which they were posted has come to be known as "going native."

Although many admired Bell as an important interpreter both of Great Britain to America and of America to Great Britain, he was criticized for be-ing partisan. In letters to the *London Times* in 1917, Bell explained to impa-tient British subjects why Wilson was not entering the war but would later. The clear import was that he thought the United States should come to the assistance of England. Concerned Bell's dispatches were too pro-British for the largely stay-out-of-the-war Chicago audience, Lawson chided him: "If the reader thinks the correspondent is a partisan, the correspondent's influence is distinctly impaired, regardless of how faithful may be his presentation of the truth as he sees it."[43]

Behind the scenes in September 1914, Bell sent British newspaperman Lord Blumenfeld a letter arguing Britain should have more active war propaganda in the United States. He also did what he could to give a platform to British leaders. His exclusive wartime interviews with Lord Grey and Lord Haldane were widely reprinted. He allowed both men to review and correct their com-ments before publication. Bell proudly described the interviews as having the status of official state papers.

If Bell was used, he also benefited. His Haldane-Grey interviews were a journalistic coup. He used his relationships to gain reportorial advantages in other ways. He asked Sir Edward Grey to help send him to the war front to balance out the *Chicago Tribune,* which he alleged was pro-German. "You have some knowledge, I think, of how gladly and diligently I have worked for the cause of the Allies throughout the war. Our paper has fought every one of the principal German schemes in the United States. Our contemporary, the 'Chicago Tribune,' which is favoured by the arrangement which is about to be carried out, has been consistently and offensively pro-German." He offered the same justification when asking General Herbert Kitchener, minister for war at the time, for permission to go.[44]

Bell thought this was not only legitimate but obligatory. "I do not think any correspondent has a right to the shelter of a country at war and then to report things which that country regards as inimical to its national interests," he wrote Lawson. "If we in America were fighting for our lives . . . and if certain English correspondents in our midst were sneaking out everything they could get hold of that looked like news, regardless of whether it hurt us or not, I think I know what we should say about them and what we should do with them. I think we should say that shooting was too good for them and hanging just right—and act accordingly."[45]

Although Bell was partisan, he was not the only correspondent who went native—or was perceived that way by the home office. Paul Scott Mowrer was thought to be too much a Francophile. When Frank Knox acquired the newspaper in 1931, Mowrer realized he was under close scrutiny, as were others. Mowrer survived and became editor. Negley Farson, the London bureau chief, quit rather than come home to be "re-Americanised."[46] Bell, too, parted company with the *Daily News* as we will see presently.

§

The *Daily News* was in many respects sui generis when it came to foreign news gathering, but it was not unique. The issues that bedeviled Lawson and his staff continued to bedevil journalists in their quest to bring foreign news home to readers, listeners, and viewers.

The archives of other newspapers brim with memos about what to cover and how. The concern is not simply competing with, say, the Associated Press. Contemporary newspapers have to distinguish themselves from television news, which trumps them in reporting breaking news. The result has been more emphasis on background and context. Also, changing geopolitics have caused news media to shift the focus of their attention. After the end of the cold war, print and broadcast news media alike closed Moscow bureaus and opened more in the Middle East. "Anyone reading the paper has already seen the new demands being placed on correspondents," the foreign editor of the *New York Times* wrote in a 1993 memo to his foreign correspondents. "Reporters have been asked not only to cover bread-and-butter political stories, but to become informed on ecology developments, the history of ethnic friction in many corners of the world, and on economic developments that previously were the exclusive preserve of 'BizDay.'"[47]

The *Daily News* itself continued to evolve. Donald Shanor, a correspondent for the *Daily News* foreign service during the cold war, summed up his method of operation as follows:

> I tried to be aware of the day to day news not to repeat it to my readers but to use it as information for trend and interpretive pieces I would write . . . I was helped enormously in this mapping out of trends by the Daily News' invention in 1967 of Insight, a 2,000 word daily takeout from abroad, Washington, or the nation that began on the front page and jumped inside. I tried to write two of these every week, and to my surprise, almost all were used. The generous wordage allowed me to start out with an anecdote or description of bleak steel town and to sandwich in good evidence in the form of statistics or (usually not for attribution) quotes.[48]

Similarly, the costs of covering foreign news remain high, although the factors in those costs have changed. No longer do editors and correspondents weigh whether or not to pay cable charges for a story. Correspondents file directly on satellite phones or over the Internet. But the equipment correspondents use is expensive, and their living costs have gone up as cities around the world have modernized. These costs remain an important consideration in how many correspondents are placed abroad. As applied in the case of the *Daily News,* the reward for shouldering these costs lies in the prestige that comes with having a foreign service.

Coordinating overseas staffs is an ongoing concern. No one has yet devised the perfect system. Some larger media groups run their foreign services collectively, as Cox Newspapers does. Its correspondents report to its bureau in Washington, D.C. Others like the *New York Times* run their own foreign services. Communications have improved thanks to the equipment mentioned above that permits easier filing of stories. The down side, however, is that easy communication has encroached on the independence of foreign correspondents. In another age, reporters overseas went for months without a phone call from the foreign editor. Now they often have daily phone conversations.

Going native nevertheless remains a concern for editors, who want to rotate reporters, and for reporters, who want to develop expertise and enjoy being abroad. Few consider leaving a correspondent abroad indefinitely as the *Daily News* did under Lawson. The rule is more like the *Washington Post*'s policy, which provides standard tours of three years that occasionally stretch to a fourth year. A second tour in another country is possible as a reward for superior work. A third tour is rare.[49]

In yet one other way, the *Daily News* illustrates the larger pattern of foreign news gathering that emerged in the twentieth century. It is, perhaps, the most important aspect of all—the precariousness of foreign news.

The *Daily News* foreign news service reached a peak under Lawson, who died in 1925, and continued for decades to excel under other owners, who paid record-setting prices to acquire its prestigious name. Walter Strong, the nephew of Lawson's wife and with the paper for years, led a group of investors to purchase the *Daily News* after Lawson's death. He continued the tradition of strong foreign coverage as did Colonel Frank Knox, who purchased the paper in 1931 after Strong's death.

Still, even at the esteemed *Daily News*, foreign coverage was always a work in progress.* No matter how much it was celebrated, correspondents worried that their foreign service might slip off its pedestal, as eventually happened. Paul Scott Mowrer, who became editor in the 1930s, quit shortly after John Knight bought the newspaper in 1944. Knight's editor, Basil "Stuffy" Walters, wanted a new sort of snappy writing that would reinvigorate circulation, which it did. Foreign news was not as high a priority as it had been on the newspaper. Walters' changes, Mowrer griped, were like "putting bobby sox on the Madonna."[50] Under the Marshall Field family, who purchased the newspaper in 1959, there were the usual promises of maintaining tradition that were soon forgotten. The foreign service grew smaller and smaller, although the remaining reporters continued to enjoy unusual access to newsmakers owing to their many years abroad.

The problem was not simply the new owners' lack of interest in foreign news. Other forces worked against the newspaper, forces that had once worked for it. Lawson's *Daily News* was an evening newspaper, which made good business sense in 1900, when Chicagoans could pick up a copy to read on public transportation on the way home. In the last part of the nineteenth century, commuters were driving home to distant communities. Getting newspapers to the suburbs for delivery in the evening was complicated by the heavy traffic and, besides, commuters wanted to watch television news when they sat down in the living room. Furthermore, Lawson had not wanted his newspaper to appear on the Sabbath. Unfortunately, that was a day when readers had more time and, thus, a day when advertisers were particularly enthusiastic

---

*As an example of the ongoing problems with which correspondents grappled, see the appendix, which contains two internal *Chicago Daily News* communications.

about buying space. It did not help, either, that the *Daily News* maintained its progressive reporting. In 1960s Chicago, stories about the plights of blacks irritated the newspaper's largely white, conservative audience.

In an important 1911 series of articles for *Collier's*, "The American Newspaper," Will Irwin singled out the *Daily News*.

> In some respects it goes far beyond any contemporary in allegiance to truth. When the "News" calls a dispatch foreign correspondence, it is just that; it is not matter rewritten in the office from this morning's newspapers. And the "News," according to general report among publishers—who have their own means of knowing—makes $800,000 to $900,000 a year. Even should it change hands, should a get-rich-quick policy destroy its character, the "News" would go on paying for a generation by power of its old honesty.[51]

Sixty years later, when the Society of Professional Journalists presented the *Daily News* with a "historic site in journalism" award calling attention to its having the oldest continuous foreign service, its time was nearly up.[52] The newspaper's circulation was dropping along with revenue. A brief attempt was made to remake the paper, but the remake had nothing to do with bolstering foreign news. The news service folded before the newspaper itself did in 1978.

§

Bell came home from London in 1922 respected and regarded as an expert in European affairs. Esteemed British journalist J. L. Garvin called Bell a "moral hero . . . one who through all the crises and vicissitudes of the last twenty years and more has rendered incalculable services to Anglo-American friendship."[53] Lord Burnham, owner of the *London Daily Telegraph*, deemed Bell fit to be a real ambassador to England, although he thought him more valuable as a correspondent.

The *Daily News* took advantage of this reputation. Lawson made him an at-large correspondent. A large part of his brief was world peace. As Bell recounts at length in this memoir, he spent his last years with the *Daily News* trekking around the world interviewing political leaders, searching for solutions to the troubled postwar world. From these trips the *Daily News* published two books, *Europe's Economic Sunrise* and *World Chancelleries*. The latter had the grand subtitle "sentiments, ideas, and arguments expressed by famous Occidental and Oriental statesmen looking to the consolidation of the psychological bases of international peace." President Calvin Coolidge wrote its introduction.

Bell at his typewriter. This photograph was taken late in Bell's life during the time he was touring Europe, the Far East, and Latin America as a *Daily News* special correspondent interviewing world leaders. "In this sort of interviewing," he told a group of American journalists, "I have been a lifelong believer, and I have practiced it, with such poor intelligence as was mine, in many parts of the world, and for upward of forty years." *Courtesy Edward Price Bell Papers, Newberry Library, Chicago*

Bell was as close to Lawson as anyone on the newspaper. When Lawson had a nervous breakdown on a trip to Europe, Bell stayed with him for weeks. When Lawson died, he bequeathed $25,000 to Bell. Bell's relationship with Walter Strong, Lawson's successor, was also cordial and supportive. Under Strong's editorship, Bell was listed in a promotional pamphlet for the *Daily News* foreign service as its first and most important correspondent, although he was not even permanently overseas at the time. He was now "commissioner for the foreign service on important missions" as well as "weekly commentator on foreign affairs."[54] Today, Bell might be called an associate editor the way Harrison Salisbury was at the *New York Times* after years as a foreign correspondent. Bell was at the height of his career.

Bell's distinguished standing, however, was as fragile as the *Daily News* foreign service itself proved to be. When Knox bought the paper in 1931, he did not even know Bell was the man who had organized the service. Knox assured Bell he had "no sympathy with changing the character" of the foreign service. But only a month later, they had a disagreement that severed Bell's relationship with the *Daily News*. "I had thought . . . we had arrived at an understanding agreeable to us both for your future uninterrupted services as a member of the staff of The Chicago Daily News," Knox wrote Bell in November of 1931. "Since your letter has a tone of finality about it I will not argue further . . . we will be very glad to continue your present salary up to the first of the year, making your retirement effective January 1, 1932." Bell may have been surprised that his resignation was taken so seriously. A month later, he proposed a return to the paper. Knox demurred. "I am sorry to say no to your suggestion of a renewal of active relations with The Daily News," Knox wrote. "I am, as you must know, put to it to keep expenses down sufficiently in these days of lessened revenue so that despite the reduced business we can still show a margin of profit."[55]

We do not know precisely what caused this falling out, although the Great Depression's impact on *Daily News* revenue was not the fundamental cause. Different recollections as well as complicated personalities cloud the circumstances of Bell's departure. One problem, as we have seen, was Knox's concern about reporters going native. We know from this memoir that the American ambassador to Britain, Charles Dawes, a former vice president, crossed swords with Bell over Bell's aggressive effort to engineer a visit to the United States by the prime minister. Dawes may have complained about Bell's meddling to Knox, who was a friend. Bell's biographer, James D. Starrt, offers another reason: Bell resigned on principle. Bell thought Knox, a strong Republican, wanted to turn the traditionally independent *Daily News* into a party paper. Paul Mowrer believed Bell was actually fired outright for an errant report: "Ed predicted, the day before Britain went off gold, that such an eventuality was unthinkable, [and] Knox fired him."[56] We pose another overarching explanation that brings several of the above factors into play.

It was inevitable that Knox and Bell would collide. Bell expected to write as he pleased, as befit a correspondent of his rank and as Lawson and Strong encouraged. Knox, for whom Bell was just another correspondent, was wary of the highly independent foreign service and sought to show his control, which led to the departure of others besides Bell whom he thought were going native. As it turned out, Knox maintained the foreign service at a very high level and acquired a reputation for not imposing his views on correspondents.[57] But even if Bell had stayed, his place in that foreign service would have changed.

He could not look forward to the sort of freedom he had had as an apostle for world peace.

Bell's exit from the *Daily News* under these circumstances was ironic. The man sent abroad because of his skills as a local reporter was separated from the foreign service because he was too independent of the home office and too thoroughly imbued with his foreign subject. No one could miss the fact that he had outgrown his native Indiana. He made close friends in the British upper class and took on their customs. He sometimes hyphenated his name, British-style, to Price-Bell. Junius Wood noted his habit of afternoon tea and his London accent. Whether these were due to "environment or to preference," Wood wrote, "was never entirely clear." Edgar Ansel Mowrer wrote that Bell "felt a truly English diffidence" toward European Continentals. In retirement, Bell built a home on the Mississippi Gulf Coast that he called Merrywood. He wrapped his property in a fence whose design was reminiscent of the British Union Jack. Inside the house Bell and his wife held afternoon teas.[58]

Bell relished the corridors of power wherever he was let in. He approached government leaders almost reverentially, a trait exemplified in the journalistic tool he prided himself in wielding effectively, the interview. Today's journalists believe interviews are a chance to challenge power, and Bell to an extent agreed that journalists had a responsibility in interviews to "execrate insincerity, lying, fraud, deceitful propaganda." But he also saw the interview as "a carefully-constructed transmitting device, a medium, a mirror."[59] As an interviewer, Bell was a scribe.

He often lionized his subjects. When he interviewed Sir Edward Grey, British foreign secretary during the war, Bell wrote, "This is a man of the most civilised type, broad of vision, nurtured in Liberalism, a fly fisherman, a tamer of birds and squirrels, a life-long protagonist of peace." To interview him, he added, was "a unique privilege and honor." He described Benito Mussolini, whom he interviewed in 1924, as "intensely egoistic and quintessentially Italian. Some might call him affected. I put down his mannerism not to affectation but to individuality. He is too serious, too reflective, too sensible of the weight of his cares, too sincere, to be affected."[60] While Bell was not the only American journalist to fall prey to Il Duce, he did not alter his opinion well into the 1930s when the Italian dictator invaded Ethiopia. "Mussolini does not want war," he writes in this memoir; "Hitler does not."

By today's standards, Bell's interviewing techniques are antique. The evolution of journalism has made his focus on the world's chancelleries equally

Merrywood, Bell's home upon retirement. Bell wrote his memoir at Merrywood, a house he built on the Mississippi Gulf Coast when he retired from the *Chicago Daily News*. He wrapped his property in a fence whose design was reminiscent of the British Union Jack. *Photo courtesy of Ouida Tanner*

old-fashioned. The modern correspondent is expected to be more skeptical about leaders and more inclined to cover news about the common man and woman, their hopes and dreams.

Bell's frustration with his diminished status comes through in his memoir. In the beginning he writes with charming self-effacement about his youth. In the final section he quotes himself, enumerates his accomplishments, and recites his famous acquaintances with the assiduousness of the best name-droppers. One senses the let-down that came when Bell lost his affiliation with the *Daily News* and no longer had a platform from which to express his views or mix with the mighty. In these final chapters he grasps to reclaim his status.

Bell lived the final years of his life in relative obscurity in Merrywood, although he tried to project his voice as he had in the past. In a cozy library-cottage built behind his house, he continued to write. He sent articles to various publications, the *Atlantic Monthly,* for example. Rejection after rejection came back to Merrywood: "This paper of yours . . . covers very much the same ground as an article which we have already accepted"; "we have already printed a great deal on the Far Eastern crisis and still have one or two more articles to come"; "the paper you send us is too fragmentary to make its claim insistent enough for us."[61]

Then, from the same *Atlantic Monthly* that had been rejecting his work came a suggestion he write his memoir. When Bell began sending chapters, these, too, were rejected. First, the editors were not interested in the beginning chapters, written in what they called the "when I was a boy" tradition. Later sections garnered replies like this: "Regret that these specimen pages do not seem to us altogether serviceable for the Atlantic in the midst of our present crowded season"; "really does not recommend itself for our purposes, although there is no denying the underlying vein of excitement which runs through it. We are adding it to the other chapters which we already have."[62]

In 1940, Bell found himself where he had started out as a young man. He began sending a weekly article to the *Saturday Spectator,* a Republican newspaper in Terre Haute, Indiana. Cut off from a national audience in the midst of the war, he wrote letters to American and European political leaders, outlining his plans for world peace and arguing that the United States should stay out of the war. His crusade for American neutrality, not in sync with the views of his former colleagues at the *Daily News,* is a major theme of the closing sections of this memoir. Bell died September 23, 1943, at Merrywood.

This was a sad, dispiriting end for a correspondent who deserved better. Bell had much to be proud of. How many correspondents have this to their credit: to be called, as he was by Lord Northcliffe, Britain's most powerful newspaper magnate, "the best American newspaperman London has ever had"?[63] In the early 1930s Northwestern University proposed Bell for the Nobel Peace Prize, a nomination endorsed by journalists and political leaders around the world.

Bell's intentions were noble. At a time when foreign correspondents were finding their way, he helped invent a foreign news service with an elevated sense of purpose about informing citizens of America's growing global responsibilities. "Our men," Bell wrote to Lawson in 1924, "are journalistic intellectuals, with definite personalities, with considerable personal reputations, and charged with duties in the highest realm of newspaper work."[64]

NOTES

1. Arthur Conan Doyle, *When the World Screamed and Other Stories* (San Francisco: Chronicle Books, 1990), 14.

2. "How the *Chicago Daily News* Covers the War," 5–7.

3. Lawson's early years with the *Daily News* are best described in Stone, *Fifty Years a Journalist;* and Dennis, *Victor Lawson.* Also see Lawson's obituary, *Chicago Daily News,* August 20, 1925.

4. Stone, *Fifty Years a Journalist,* 77.

5. Ibid.; Zobrist, "How Victor Lawson's Newspapers Covered the Cuban War," 325.

6. See, for example, Victor Lawson to Charles Faye, April 2, 1898: "Treat subject with all dignity and seriousness in all editorial and news be enterprising but conservative in expression and tone"; Lawson to Faye, April 24, 1898: "Don't call it extra except when character news justifies, and don't promise public startling news every issue but say: 'to meet the possibility of the receipt of important news between the hours the morning papers go to press and the Daily News noon edition, we will issue an early intermediate morning edition regularly so long as conditions seem to require.' Don't destroy public confidence in word Extra by indiscriminate use. Cable daily size of principle [sic] editions and total for day omitting hundreds, also total Record . . . For genuinely important news use double column display heads, including five o'clock edition, using same type as regular single column except one or two sizes larger first line and other lines one size larger, with liberal headings. Don't make heads otherwise blacker." Both letters in Bell Papers.

7. Dennis, *Victor Lawson,* 47, 137.

8. Lawson's letter of recommendation for Ochs is Lawson to Spencer Trask, head of the committee arranging the sale of the newspaper, April 8, 1896, New York Times Archives.

9. *Chicago Daily News,* August 20, 1925, passim.

10. This is from a draft story by Milt Frudenheim, no date, Chicago Daily News, Inc., Records.

11. Lawson to Charles Dennis and Charles Faye, April 26, 1898, Bell Papers. For more background, see Brown, *The Correspondents' War,* 131.

12. Brown, *The Correspondents' War,* 131.

13. Faye to Lawson, April 18, 1898, Bell Papers; Lawson to Faye, April 18, 1898, ibid.

14. Faye to Lawson, April 26, 1898, Bell Papers; Lawson to Faye, April 30, 1898, ibid.

15. Lawson to Theodore Stanton, August 8, 1898, Lawson Papers; Lawson to Dennis, December 31, 1898, ibid.

16. Lawson to Stanton, July 22, 1898, January 26, 1899, January 13, 1900, Lawson Papers.

17. Lawson to A. H. Belo, February 9, 1900, Lawson Papers; Lawson to Edgar W. Coleman, December 22, 1898, ibid.; Lawson to Albert J. Barr, July 26, 1900, ibid. Lawson addressed this last letter to seven other subscribers to his service, hence our conclusion there were eight at the time.

18. Lawson to W. L. McLean, October 12, 1900, Lawson Papers; Shanor, "CDN: What We'll Miss About the Chicago Daily News."

19. Williams, *Dusk of Empire,* 8; Victor Lawson to William J. Tucker, April 21, 1899, Lawson Papers.

20. Victor Lawson to Horace Townsend, January 26, 1900, Lawson Papers.

21. Wile, *News Is Where You Find It,* 38.

22. Bell to Dennis, November 18, 1901, Bell Papers.

23. Dennis to Bell, July 26, 1901, Bell Papers. This ongoing debate is also captured in Dennis to Bell, January 16, 1906, ibid.

24. Paul Scott Mowrer to Edward Price Bell, June 8, 1910, Bell Papers.

25. Dennis to Bell, May 26, 1905, Bell Papers.

26. See, for example, undated form letter from Dennis to Bell, Bell Papers.

27. Swing, *"Good Evening!"* 37.

28. Dennis to Bell, July 26, 1901, August 30, 1901, Bell Papers.

29. Jaci Cole and John Maxwell Hamilton, "A Natural History of Foreign Correspondence," *Journalism and Mass Communication Quarterly* 84 (Spring 2007): 151–66.

30. Lawson to Bell, August 9, 1918, Bell Papers.

31. Bell to Paul Scott Mowrer, March 10, 1913, Bell Papers; Bell to Dennis, January 11, 1902, ibid.

32. Dennis to Bell, November 22, 1905, Bell Papers; Bell to Dennis, June 28, 1901, ibid.

33. Bell to A. F. J. Kiehl, July 1, 1901, Bell Papers.

34. Bell to Dennis, December 13, 1902, Bell Papers; Dennis to Bell, August 24, 1904, ibid.; Bell to Dennis, June 17, 1901, ibid.

35. Junius Wood to Bell, March 15, 1917, Bell Papers; Bell to Dennis, February 26, 1918, April 1, 1918, ibid.

36. Mowrer, *The House of Europe*, 135; Lawson to Bell, February 16, 1909, Bell Papers.

37. Bell to Dennis, April 17, 1901, June 11, 1901, Bell Papers.

38. Bell to Dennis, January 17, 1918, Bell Papers.

39. Bell to Mowrer, January 24, 1918, Bell Papers.

40. Bell to Lawson, February 6, 1915, Bell Papers.

41. Mowrer, *Triumph and Turmoil*, 176.

42. Starrt, *Journalism's Unofficial Ambassador*, 91; Dennis, *Victor Lawson*, 273.

43. Lawson to Bell, July 9, 1915, Bell Papers.

44. Bell to Edward Grey, February 3, 1916, Bell Papers; Bell to Herbert Kitchener, April 14, 1915, ibid.

45. Bell to Lawson, February 6, 1915, Bell Papers.

46. Farson, *A Mirror for Narcissus*, 26.

47. Bernard Gwertzman, "Memo to the *Times* Foreign Staff," *Media Studies Journal* 7 (Fall 1993): 36.

48. Donald Shanor, personal correspondence to editors, September 2006.

49. Interview with David Hoffman, April 14, 2005.

50. Charles Whited, *Knight: A Publisher in the Tumultuous Century* (New York: E. P. Dutton, 1988). The attribution of the "bobby sox" quote to Mowrer is in David M. Nichol to J. M. Hamilton, November 15, 1990.

51. Will Irwin, "The American Newspaper," *Collier's*, July 8, 1911, 15–16.

52. On the honor bestowed by the Society of Professional Journalists, then called Sigma Delta Chi, see *Chicago Daily News*, May 8–9, 1971.

53. J. L. Garvin, "Edward Price Bell," copy of article reprinted from *The Landmark*, April, 1930, Bell Papers.

54. Quotation is from *Chicago Daily News* flyer, no date, but with this comment: "The Chicago Daily News announces a world-famous foreign news service, available for newspapers after January 1, 1930," Chicago Daily News, Inc., Records.

55. Knox to Bell, September 29, 1931, November 4, 1931, December 18, 1931, Bell Papers.

56. Starrt, *Journalism's Unofficial Ambassador*, 167; Mowrer, *The House of Europe*, 595.

57. Knox to Bell, September 29, 1931, Bell Papers; Raymond Gram Swing, "Knox—Publisher into Candidate," *The Nation*, February 19, 1936, 219.

58. Junius B. Wood, undated letter titled "Answering Your Inquiry of Nov. 19, 1951," Bell Papers; Edgar Ansel Mowrer to Lt. Col. George V. Fagon, July 6, 1951, ibid.; interview with Ouida Tanner, August 26, 2006.

59. Bell, "Major Interviewing: Its Principles and Its Functions," address delivered before the American Society of Newspaper Editors, January 15, 1927; published by the *Daily News*, 1927.

60. Edward Price Bell, *A Free Europe: Being an Interview with the Rt. Hon. Sir Edward Grey, Bart., K.G., British Secretary of State for Foreign Affairs* (London: T. Fisher Unwin, 1916), 2; Bell, *World Chancelleries* (Chicago: Chicago Daily News, 1926), 26.

61. *Atlantic Monthly* to Bell, June 29, 1932, April 24, 1933, Bell Papers; Joseph Barber, Jr., to Bell, July 21, 1938, ibid.

62. Joseph Barber, Jr., to Bell, September 8, 1938, October 29, 1938, November 2, 1938, Bell Papers.

63. Startt, *Journalism's Unofficial Ambassador,* xii.

64. Edward Price Bell to Victor Lawson, May 11, 1924, Bell Papers.

Note on Editorial Method

All books need editing, and Edward Price Bell's memoir is no exception.

Although Bell was an excellent writer, his manuscript was never corrected for even simple typographical errors. In addition to doing this, we have edited out large sections of text, most notably those describing his early years, which have little historical interest. These excisions involved whole chapters and parts of chapters. In a few instances, we have rewritten the text to maintain coherence. As these changes are minimal and because we wanted to save the reader from distractions, we run the text without ellipses, brackets, or other editing marks. The Prologue, "I'm Going to Be a Newspaper Man," comes from one of the chapters we eliminated. Chapters have been renumbered to take these changes into account. Bell's original chapter titles remain in all but three cases, in which the titles were changed to better reflect the content of the chapters after editing.

These edits notwithstanding, the bulk of the memoir is published here. Nowhere have we changed meaning, and where possible we have added to it through considerable annotation of names and events that may not have immediate significance to the contemporary reader. This information can be found in footnotes running through the text.

We have also changed the book's title. Bell called his memoir "Seventy Years Deep." That does not do justice to the book. Instead, we have used his own words, *Journalism of the Highest Realm.*

The *Chicago Daily News* offers a valuable but underused laboratory for studying the evolution of daily journalism as well as foreign correspondence. A final bibliographic note suggests some of the resources available for such research, which we hope others pursue.

JOURNALISM OF THE HIGHEST REALM

To my wife

*Who shared all my anxieties and labors
and joys on the long march*

Preface

Diary-keeping as a habit came to me out of the blue when I was a boy on the farm, and it remained with me throughout my life. My journals tell me where I have been, whom I have met, the essence of what was said to me, and something of what I have felt and thought every day for more than sixty years. These diaries, I scarcely need say, have been of great aid to me in writing this book; but they have not been by any means my sole, not even my chief, aid. I write from documents innumerable and from hundreds of pages of printed matter in newspapers, magazines, brochures, and books. Nor is that quite all. My memory, from the earliest years of observation, clung with strange tenacity to everybody and everything entering in any impressive way into my life. An instance of the working of this faculty is found in the case of the long interview with Lord Haldane, and again in that of a similarly long and intricate conversation with Lord Grey.[1] In neither of these cases (nor in scores of others) did I take a single note, yet the reproductions were such as to win the approval of the interviewees in every substantial respect. This I say with no egotistical urge; I say it to assure the reader, if I can, that the book has at least the quality of authenticity.

E.P.B.

---

1. Richard Burdon Haldane was Great Britain's secretary of state for war from 1905 to 1912 and lord chancellor from 1912 until 1915. Edward Grey was Great Britain's foreign secretary from 1905 to 1916. As he will recount later in this memoir, Bell interviewed Haldane in 1915 and Grey in 1916—two of the first interviews any British public official ever gave to a journalist, American or otherwise.

Prologue
"I'm Going to Be a Newspaper Man"

My brother and I were reluctant farmers. Somehow we simply did not fit tranquilly into that Raccoon Valley situation, numerous as were its fascinations and magnificent distinctively as were its moons. Heredity was troubling us. The unfathomable past was in us. Blood, history, a thousand mysteries which science yet has to learn: are they not sovereign? That Valley, to those farm boys in the moonlight in that window, was the alpha and omega of experience, of knowledge. They had been nowhere else. Never had they seen a city except in their minds' eyes. Yet the world continually was talking to them.

"Will," I said, looking at the moon, "we're forever talking about leaving here. What are you planning to do?"

"I'm going to be a surgeon," said Will with a kind of snap of the jaw.

"A surgeon! What do you know about a thing like that?" I cried.

"Don't talk so loud, Eddie. We mustn't worry Mother or Father now. What either of us shall do when we leave the farm is a good way off."

"Eddie," said Will after a pause, "I don't think you'd better leave the farm. You are suited to it better than I am. You love it, I think. You care more for the flowers than I do, and you worship fishing. I've known you to go with sister Meck and fish in Oard Pond in the hot sun all afternoon for mud-cat. I wouldn't have done it for *money*! And I've known you to wander in the woods from morning to night all by yourself on a Sunday catching blue racers, which you drove home on string-reins along the dusty roads. You even love catching rattlesnakes in Nigger Leg Prairie. And you love to drive spiles into the sugar maples, gather the sap in a hogshead on a sled, haul it to the sugar camp, and lie there all night while they're boiling off. You're again and again out with a telescope looking for bee-trees. You're a farm boy all right, I guess. You'll be happier here."

Of Will's judgment, as a rule, I had a high opinion, not so much because he overtopped me three years in respect of age, but because of what I regarded as the usual rationality and solidity of his thinking. But I could not go all the way with him there in the moonlight and night. He had disappointed me indeed. He had not seen into me as I had hoped. He had not discerned that I no less than he had my strong and insistent life-premonition.

"No, Will," I said, "I'll go, too; not so soon as you probably, but before I'm very old. All you say is right. I do love the Valley. I even could stand the hard work. And the loneliness is not loneliness to me. But I've something to do that can't be done here; it just can't."

"What is it, Eddie?" asked Will, facing me frontally. "What're you going to be?"

"A writer."

There was a faint smile on Will's face.

"I'm going to be a newspaper man, a writer, maybe a great writer, maybe not." I continued, slightly vexed.

"Why, Eddie," said Will, still faintly smiling, "you can't *spell*. Writers have to spell."

"I know they do," I admitted. "That's just it. I've got to learn to spell. I *am* learning. Bet you I know a lot more than you think already. Haven't you seen me studying spelling on the roller and when I stopped the horses to rest in the shade? And do you suppose I spend all those Sundays on blue racers and rattle-snakes? I don't. I'm a *reader*. Guess I've read nearly all Dickens' best books, *David Copperfield, Oliver Twist, Martin Chuzzlewit, Dombey & Son,* and others. They're great. Jack Fagin brought them out to me from Terre Haute. Jack's smart. *He* knows the city from A to Z. He knows newspapers and newspaper men and writers of all sorts. And what do you think? He pats me on the back and says I'll get there!"

Will, I felt sure, was hit unexpectedly hard by my little Demosthenic effort. It was by long odds the most illuminating he ever had heard out of me. It wiped the faint smile off his face and put an expression of gravity there.

"So," he said, "you're hell-bent on being a writer?"

"Yes," I replied. "I'd rather be a writer than an angel!"

Will eyed me for some time in silence. Then he said:

"Good! Let's go to bed."

I
The Early City Period, 1882–1898

1. Half a Writer at Last

Spencer F. Ball's piercing black eyes were alight with intelligence and sympathy. He was looking down at me over the counter of the business office of the *Terre Haute Evening Gazette* in South Fifth Street. He was one of the owners of the paper (the other was his older and more lordly brother, William C.), and he was its managing editor. He never had seen me before but I had seen him scores of times. His spare, muscular figure was familiar all over Terre Haute, Indiana, for he was not only managing editor but reporter, advertising solicitor, and highly-popular social representative of the *Gazette*.

So lively was Mr. Ball's smile as he bent his gaze on me that I thought something must have gone wrong with my makeup. My hat was in my hand, and I was standing before the counter just off the street.

"Why don't you say something?" finally laughed the managing editor.

This brought me round.

"Could you give me a job on the *Gazette*?" I asked.

"Are you a writer?" he inquired with gentleness and seeming sincerity.

I told him all about myself, that I'd grown up on a farm, worked in a drug store, gone to business college, learned shorthand, sold papers on the local train, had a lifelong desire to write; the story poured out so rapidly and with such fervor that I had to mop my brow. Very patiently, and with a kindliness which had a quality really new to me, Mr. Ball heard my recital to the end. His smile had softened somewhat but had not gone. His expression was inquiring and deliberative. Did my country schooling amount to much? Had I read any books? Had I actually attempted to write, to tell what I had seen, to describe my feelings? Could I spell? My general answer was that I knew next to nothing and still misspelled many words.

"I have read Dickens," I said. "And I also have read *The Ole Swimmin' Hole and 'Leven Other Poems.*"

Mr. Ball's lips wrinkled oddly.

"Which did you like the better?" he questioned.

"I'm afraid I can't say," I replied. "They're both very wonderful."

"Make you cry?"

"Yes, sir."

"Your name is Edward Price Bell?"

"Yes, sir."

"Well, Edward, I'll tell you what I'd like you to do. Go and write a story for me, any kind of story, truth or fiction, and send it in. I'll let you know without much delay what I think of it."

I went home and wrote a few hundred words, a purely fictional yarn of how a savage dog jumped over a fence from a garden into the street and sprang upon a child. A workingman was passing with a scythe on his shoulder. The story was that of how the man dragged the dog off the child and fought it to its knees, at last driving the point of his scythe mortally into its body. It was rather a hair-raising tale, ending with the doughty son of toil carrying the child safely to its distracted mother's arms.

Several days passed uneventfully, with me almost living in the mail-box. I sat on the porch and watched for the postman. If he put something in the box, I ran for it. If he did not stop, I groaned. Once I chased him and begged him to have another look in his pouch; I thought he ought to have a letter for Edward Price Bell. He humored me, but there was nothing doing. He giggled and said:

"Some day, my boy, maybe."

The next morning I saw an unusually bright look on the postman's face as he came near our porch. He did not go to the mail-box. He walked straight up to me and said:

"Still think you ought to have a letter?"

"Yes!" I cried.

"Sorry," he said, reaching into his pouch. "I can give you only a postcard."

It was from Mr. Ball, written with his own hand, a light, graceful script. He requested that I call upon him at his office any day after 5 o'clock but withheld any intimation as to what he thought of my story. I was sometimes all hope and sometimes all despair. At first I had in mind to rush down to the *Gazette* office straightway, not waiting for 5 o'clock. But I knew that would not do, and I even restrained myself until the next day.

Mr. Ball was in the counting room where I first talked with him. His inimitably bright eyes and his peculiarly fine smile were just as before. He opened a door in the counter and invited me to enter. Then he led the way to a room surrounded by opaque glass and closed the door behind us. We were alone in cozy quarters with a large writing desk and two or three easy chairs. In one of these, at Mr. Ball's invitation, I sat down. He sat in a swivel-chair at his desk and took up a piece of manuscript: my story.

"Edward," he began, "I think you have some writing gift. Your story has color and feeling, sincerity. Sincerity is perhaps the greatest quality in everything, artificiality the least attractive or valuable. You are a farm boy and know the difference between grain and husk: sincerity is like grain, artificiality like husk. You will write one day, I think, but you must first learn to spell. Your spelling is very bad. Have you ever been in a newspaper office before?"

"No, sir," I replied.

"Ever hear of type-setting?"

"Not exactly, but I know of course there is such a thing."

"I'm going to offer you a job at four dollars a week as a starter," said Mr. Ball. "I want you to learn type-setting and to set the markets each morning. For the afternoons I'll assign you to a reporter's route along the Wabash River, at the railroad bridge, at the freight-houses and depots, in the roundhouse, and at the Normal School, where President Parsons, a good friend of ours, will give you the school news. Do you think you'd like that job?"

"Yes, sir; I'd like it very much."

"Excellent," said the managing editor, rising. "Then report here at 7 on Monday morning."

Verging on fourteen I was as I climbed up on a stool and took a printer's stick and rule in my hand for the first time.[1] I speedily learned the type-boxes of my cases (that was years before the linotype) and made quick progress in the art of shifting quads, spacers, and type to the stick. In a week's time I not

---

1. When Bell began setting type at the *Terre Haute Evening Gazette* in 1883, setting by hand was still common. Linotype, the automatic printing method that gained currency in the first half of the twentieth century, was only in its early stages. The *New York Tribune* used an early linotype machine for the first time in 1886. Bell would have operated the *Evening Gazette's* printing machine manually. In this process, the printer placed blocks of type and spaces with one hand in a small tray called a stick held in the other hand. The printer transferred this stick to a longer tray called a galley. He did this line by line until the entire galley was filled with type for one page. See Moran, *The Composition of Reading Matter;* and Huss, *The Development of Printers' Mechanical Typesetting Methods.*

only could set type but could dump it in galleys without pieing. I threw out my chest metaphorically and rated myself a printer. Old man Waring, white-bearded senior of the shop, paused by my stool, desisted for a moment from his quid, watched the steady movement of my right hand from case to stick, from stick to case, and said:

"You do make 'em click, boy! Damned if I ever saw a kid to equal you!"

I felt as if I had been decorated by a monarch.

When old man Waring said anything in that shop, it went.

But printing was only a side-line; reporting was my principal article of trade, and I was working arduously to lose the auxiliary altogether. And Spencer F. Ball was helping me. I sometimes thought he was either more or less than human, and I still recall him with an astonishment balancing my gratitude. Every day I sweated over my route and brought in my news and wrote my copy for the following day. At night, Mr. Ball and I by ourselves in his sanctum, we went over my stories, and he laboriously corrected my spelling, grammar, and rhetoric. I doubt if any other editor ever slaved as Mr. Ball slaved to make a journalist out of a farmer!

And one day I was given my wings. Mr. Ball said to me:

"Edward, today you have graduated from printing. You are a full-fledged reporter and feature writer. I want you not only to search for news, as you have been doing, and doing well, but to gather material for interesting articles for our big Saturday paper. I want you to write of the house-boats and the house-boat life of the Wabash River, those strange and picturesque homes and people unknown to our readers. Steamboats and their captains and crews also will give you copy. And you might write an article about that bridge watchman of whom you have furnished glimpses from time to time. Understand?"

"Quite well, I think," I said.

My new wings bore me first to the bridge watchman. I had been seeing him daily for many weeks by the pumping-station at the bridge and knew he kept a fleet of canoes for hire. He was a sourdoughy old bunch of brindle whiskers whom I liked and who seemed to like me. He asked me if I should like to go with him for an afternoon's canoeing paddle up the Wabash and through some of the backwaters "where the beautiful willows grew." We went, and it was a great trip, my host doing all the paddling, and I doing all the observing in my power. Over us arched the flexible, verdant willows and occasionally a white sycamore for miles. Never before had I seen a place so romantic, a place where the stillness and the lights and shadows got so pleasingly into me. The old canoeist said very little; merely watched the effect on me.

I wrote that story, a descriptive story, and it was played in the *Gazette* as no piece of mine ever had been played in the past. Over it was thrown a sort of banner-head in thick type, and my eyes blinked at my first by-line: "By Edward Price Bell."[2] When I next saw the bridge watchman, he looked at me ambiguously and motioned for me to follow him to the basement of the pumping-station. There on the clean concrete floor by the hot boiler he stopped, pulled a roll (yes, a roll) of banknotes from his pocket, peeled off a ten-dollar bill, and pushed it at me.

"What's that for?" I said, stepping back.

"It's for your write-up," he answered.

Believe it or not, I was mortified. I felt guilty. The old man had broken something for me.

"Take the money," he urged in patently good faith.

"I did not write the article for money," I said sourly. "I don't write articles for money. I write them for our readers. The paper pays me."

The old man stared.

"I know the paper pays you," he said. "But I want to add a bit to your salary. That article will do me good. It will bring crowds here to hire my canoes. I'm no pauper or skinflint. I want to pay for what I get."

"You can't pay *me*!" was my rejoinder, and I ran all the way to the *Gazette* office to tell Spencer F. Ball what had happened.

Mr. Ball seemed intensely amused, and I guessed he was equally pleased. There was an important lesson in the incident, he told me. Newspaper men of all categories were subject to such temptation. The old bridgeman was in-genuous. He was honest. He really wished to pay something for what he knew would benefit him. But I was right, Mr. Ball declared, in declining the money. I had practiced sound journalistic ethics, my sense of principle had been right, for designing men often tried to use money, and did use money, to further their selfish purposes through the Press.

For the clarifying, the morally fortifying, influence of that early experience in the newspaper world I never ceased to feel indebted. It was my *première*, so to speak, in practicality as related to a writer's duty. It jerked me out of what might have been haze into broad daylight. It stepped me up definitely in self-esteem and in appreciation of my profession. I stood a little bit above some people. I had chosen a calling with the dignity of social responsibility. *Noblesse oblige!*

2. In the late 1800s, bylines were rarely awarded, usually only to well-known writers or for big stories.

Strenuousness was truly my *alter ego* in Terre Haute. Of reporting and feature writing I had enough. I made the Wabash and its floating folk my own. I mixed with railroad men of all grades from the greasiest wiper in the roundhouse to the artist who decorated the sleepers and to the high officials who now and then came to town. I made friends with President Parsons of the Normal School and not only got news from him but received his tickets for lectures by journalists like Henry Watterson[3] and actors like the younger Salvini.[4]

I sat with Thomas E. Newlove, who had earlier tutored me in shorthand, to report political speeches by leaders such as James Blaine, William McKinley, and Daniel Voorhees,[5] elated that I had by my right hand as many lead pencils sharpened at both ends as the wizard Newlove had. Moreover, I reported sermons by the dozen, sitting with a sense of great importance at small tables specially provided near the pulpits. So rapid did I become with the "chicken tracks" of Mr. Pitman[6] that my fat English teacher and mentor became, I thought, almost a little jealous.

Nor was shorthand all of it. I went in for telegraphy with similar enthusiasm, and in this my brother Will—with all his mechanical expertness—gave me invaluable stimulus and support. We shared a room at home, and there we installed a key, sounder, and battery. We called in other boys and proposed the building of a private system of telegraphic communication for juveniles. It was built, our wires following tree-tops and barn-gables over miles of the city. The boys equipped themselves with instruments and storage cells, and buckled to

3. Henry Watterson was a journalist, political leader, and public lecturer. He founded the *Louisville Courier-Journal* in 1868 after fighting for the Confederacy in the Civil War and editing a pro-Confederate newspaper. In the early 1870s, he became a leading supporter of the Liberal Republican-Democratic Coalition. He began to lecture publicly in 1877 and continued to lecture into the 1890s on topics from the importance of the Union to the components of the ideal newspaper. See Wall, *Henry Watterson.*

4. Alessandro Salvini was the son of acclaimed Italian actor Tommaso Salvini (see note 1 of chap. 2). Alessandro, also Italian born, was celebrated in his own right for his role in stage productions in the United States.

5. James Blaine was a Republican representative to the U.S. House from 1863 to 1876 and served a brief term as secretary of state in 1881. Blaine ran an unsuccessful campaign as the Republican nominee for president in 1884, during the time Bell was writing for the *Evening Gazette* in Terre Haute. William McKinley (U.S. president from 1897 to 1901) was Ohio's representative to the U.S. House during the years Bell was in Terre Haute. Daniel W. Voorhees was a Democratic U.S. senator from Indiana from 1877 to 1897.

6. "Chicken tracks of Mr. Pitman" is a phrase for shorthand, named after the man who developed the system, Sir Isaac Pitman.

the work of learning the Morse code and practicing it as if the stake were the salvation of the world.

Stirring calls sometimes came to us in the night, dragging us out of bed half-asleep. Will's call and mine was CH, in Morse two dots, space, and one dot, space and four dots. One midnight Frank Boudinot, a boy living half a mile from us, came wildly over the wire: CH, CH, CH, CH. I jumped out of bed and pressed the key: II, II, which meant, "Yes, yes." And Frank ticked swiftly over to me: "The Normal School is on fire!" A moment later we heard the scream of the sirens and the rush of hose-wagons and hook-and-ladder and the swelling blaze, which laid the great building in ashes.

Terre Haute life made me acquainted with several men of note, Colonel Dick Thompson,[7] snowy-haired orator, among them. He told me that when he got mad at a man he went into the woods with a stout stick and beat up the trees. He said it gave one satisfaction and was safer. When the eloquent colonel was made Secretary of the Navy under President Rutherford B. Hayes, his lovely wife was dumbfounded. "Why," she said to her neighbors, "Dick has been appointed Secretary of the Navy, and he can't even swim." Abraham Lincoln and Colonel Thompson never had seen each other until they met in Washington, but so well did they know each other by reputation and photographs that the Terre Haute man walked up to his fellow-lawyer from Illinois and said:

"Hello, Abe," extending his hand.

Lincoln grasped it and replied:

"Hello, Dick."

Our minister to Mexico, Mr. Nelson,[8] was a Terre Haute man of large dimensions, physical and intellectual. He came home on a vacation, and I was assigned to interview him for the *Gazette*. He was most affable, and I asked him many questions about Mexico. He asked me questions too, and I got pretty well steamed up. As I was leaving, he held my small hand in his big one for a moment, and said:

"Young man, you're a philologist."

"Thank you, Mr. Minister," I answered, and then I made tracks to the nearest dictionary to find out what I was!

7. Richard Thompson was a political leader in Indiana who at various times held the offices of U.S. congressman, Terre Haute city attorney, circuit court judge, and secretary of the navy. During the time Bell was writing for the *Evening Gazette,* Thompson was director of the Panama Railroad Company. See Roll, *Colonel Dick Thompson.*

8. Thomas Henry Nelson was U.S. minister to Chile from 1861 to 1866 and U.S. minister to Mexico from 1869 to 1873. He later practiced law in Terre Haute.

Despite the presence of those illustrious personalities restlessness was beginning to trouble me in Terre Haute. The city which had been so big and so
captivating to me when I was ten—the city of my first ravishing banana[9]—
seemed to be getting a shade tight. I had turned fifteen. My brother Will was
almost ready to leave for Ohio Medical, and it occurred to me I ought to be
moving when he moved. We could dismantle our telegraph plant and revive
it if ever we wanted it. I was cocked and primed for adventure but lacked any
specific excuse for giving up my job on the *Gazette.* It was true that the be-
nevolent Mr. Ball—my first and one of my greatest friends in journalism—had
not raised my salary of four dollars a week, but I was by no means sure I could
do better for a while.

Jack Joyce, a clever man, was our city editor, and his pet reporter was a
talented young writer named Insley, spry and handsome. For some reason or
other I had it in my system that neither Jack nor his reportorial darling had
much liking for me. Only one editorial man on the paper aside from the managing editor was really my friend. His name was Doug Smith, and he wrote
high-school notes. He had wavy black hair, huge shining dark eyes, a dark
mustache, a deeply-angled face, and wore in winter the first sealskin cap I ever
saw. I mention him in passing, for we were to meet again.

It came like a bolt from the blue: my excuse to cut the painter in Terre
Haute. I had written a story of a political meeting in which a party clown and
blowhard had made himself, in my opinion, ridiculous. He had stamped and
yelled and ranted and frothed, and I gave him what for: even said such men
were a disgrace not only to their party but to our flag. It was by far the boldest
of all my flights on the *Gazette,* for I was honestly and thoroughly indignant.
I knew of course I was out of bounds, was editorializing shockingly, but I did
not give a damn. Let them take it or leave it.

They left it.

Chancing into the city room shortly after I had turned in my blazing script,
I found Joyce and Insley in convulsions at Joyce's desk. So hysterically were
they tickled that they did not see me. I passed within a few feet of them and
saw their paroxysms arose from my manuscript, which Joyce's blue pencil already had riddled. I called them hard names under my breath, walked straight
out of the office, stormed along the streets to my home, sat down at my table

9. This is a reference to the first time Bell went to Terre Haute with his brother, Will. In an
earlier section of the memoir not included here, Bell wrote, "I saw my first banana and bought it
and ate it. Glory, it was good!"

in an upper room, and penned my resignation. I unbosomed myself of my gratitude to Mr. Ball, told him I prayed we might some day meet again, but said I no longer could work in an office where my spelling was ridiculed and my best writing butchered.

That night, when the office was dark and still, I slipped my note of resignation under the front door of the *Gazette* office, and the next morning at 7 o'clock I was a passenger on an accommodation train to Indianapolis. My sails were set, and my course was outward. I was ashamed to leave Spencer F. Ball in that way, but I had the joy, many years afterward, while whirling him in my car up and down the gorgeous hills of Surrey, England, to hear him say:

"Edward, I understood your resignation perfectly."

2. My Work for the *Democrat*

My first perch and observation post in Indianapolis was a blood-red fire-plug in Washington Street. I sat there to rest and reconnoiter, my rather pitiful hand-bag—bulging with my small possessions—on the curb by my side. I was an extremely serious boy, tired and sleepy and bewildered. I gladly would have turned back, but every bridge behind me was burnt. Hell might lie ahead, but it would be infinitely better now than Terre Haute. I stood up and felt the little wad of bills in my waistcoat pocket and rattled my silver just to be sure they were there.

It was half-past 10 in the morning, and all sorts and conditions of people were crowding by me in both directions, I wondered why they hurried so and what made them look so tragic. Even the children seemed to have something dreadful on their minds. Yet the fall morning was popping with tone, the sun streamed brilliantly down Washington Street, and the sky was azure. I resumed my seat to watch and think further. I had no idea whither to turn. I had no job. I knew no one. I was completely at sea.

A trim-looking bluecoat, clean-shaven and sharp-eyed, a club at his belt, was passing near me. He gave a keen glance at me and my bag and stopped.

"Lost, sonny?" he asked.

"No, sir," I said, "I'm not lost."

"You look it. Where're you from? What're you doin' here?" demanded the policeman.

"I'm from Terre Haute," I answered, "and I've come to Indianapolis to get a job."

The cop smiled wryly.

"What kind of a job?" he wanted to know.

"A writing job," I replied.

"Reporter?"

"Yes, sir."

"Broke?"

"Not quite, sir. Nearly."

The cop smiled more naturally.

"Pick up your bag and come with me," he ordered. Don't get scared. I'm not arrestin' you. I want to show you somethin'."

We walked into a narrow side-street and halted before a huge show-window. Displayed there in gigantic letters was an announcement of the forth-coming appearance of "the Capital's greatest newspaper, the *Democrat*." The editor was to be a man named Comstock, and the paper, "while ardently and always democratic," would "put truth and right above all else." Its writing staff would be made up of "talented men and women fit to write and incorruptible." Mr. Comstock gave his personal pledge that he would seek such writers "from far and near."

"Might get a job there," said the cop, eyeing me benignly.

"You're awfully good to me, Mr. Officer," I said. "I'll try for a talk with Mr. Comstock."

"Fine!" said the cop, laying his hand lightly on my shoulder and turning away.

"Mr. Officer," I cried after him, "could you tell me where I might find a good place to board and room?"

"Yes," he said. "Go east in Washington Street till you come to Meridian. Turn north in Meridian and go eight blocks, keepin' a lookout on your left. You'll see a big frame house with a porch runnin' the width of it and halfway along one side. It's called 'The Ivies' and is run by an honest dame who'll treat you like a mother. And it's not a millionaire's club."

Right there I installed that policeman in my temple of gods. He graces undimmed my pantheonic company today. The "honest dame" at "The Ivies" was honest indeed and motherly too. She assigned me to an idyllic little room with frost-fired leaves rustling at the window and the mellow bells of a near-by church recurrently breaking in. She told me the park was not far away and was "a lovely place to sit and watch the people." Such it veritably was, and many an hour I spent there until midwinter's snowy blasts blew me out.

I waited till the next morning before attempting to see Mr. Comstock. Then I went to the office in the side-street off Washington and asked an elderly, de-mure lady if the editor would grant me an interview. She said she thought he would. In scarcely more than a minute the lady was back from an adjoining room with the word that Mr. Comstock was waiting for me. I found him a short, well-fleshed man with neatly-clipped dark whiskers and a markedly thoughtful face.

"You want?" he suggested.

I told him I wanted a job.

"You're very young," he remarked. "How old?"

"Going on sixteen," I informed him.

"Any experience as a reporter?"

At this I ran over the checkered annals of my career and did not fail to confess that my spelling was not first-rate, though I had "tried very hard to make it so."

"Spelling?" quoth the editor. "No difference at all. Writing is not spelling. Our desk men and printers will be able to spell. You say you know shorthand. How rapid?"

"I'm a verbatim shorthand reporter," I declared with emphasis. "I've reported word for word many speeches and sermons."

"Extraordinary!"

The way he pronounced the word made me feel he was in some doubt.

"That's true," I insisted. "My teacher is Thomas E. Newlove of Terre Haute, and he'll tell you—at least he's told many—that I'm the quickest and best pupil he ever had. He's a great shorthand writer. He's very fast. He can do any kind of reporting. He's an Englishman and a court reporter, and I've reported with him."

Mr. Comstock was laughing.

"I'll write Mr. Newlove if you like," I promised, no longer doubting the editor's skepticism.

"No, no, no," he said, stifling his mirth. "I need no corroboration. I believe every word you say. I'll give you a job as a verbatim reporter if you care to work for fifteen dollars a week."

No one, I suppose, ever accepted an offer with greater alacrity than I accepted Mr. Comstock's. I was in Indianapolis, the capital of the state, a city which made Terre Haute look like a dozy hamlet. I was without the scratch of a pen to tell anyone who I was. I was on my own. I was in the presence of the editor who was to make "the Capital's greatest newspaper," a paper which would be Democratic but would "put truth and right above all else," and I was to help. Where was the sting of the satire of Joyce and Insley? *I* had a job in Indianapolis!

Our paper came out with a bang. It was beautifully printed and full of good stuff, its news columns sparkling and its editorials dignified, scholarly, and forceful. I had nothing in it, was not in action yet, but had the impression of corporate relationship to it. It was, in my feeling, partly my baby. One day possibly I should sit in the news room and see my fellow-craftsmen looking at me as the reporter who had beaten the world. Shorthand men did not work *all* the time. But *sometimes* they swept the board!

Mr. Comstock called me into his sanctum.

"Your first heavy task is approaching," said he with a solemnity which shook me a bit. "We're a Democratic paper," he went on. "Grover Cleveland is coming to town to make a great speech in his campaign for the Presidency. He will speak at 10 o'clock in the morning from the south steps of the State House. We want every word of his speech, and we want it ahead of the competition. We want to be in the streets with it at the earliest possible moment after Mr. Cleveland utters his last word. Do you feel equal to that task?"

"I feel I can do as well as anyone," I replied. "And of course I'll try to do better."

"Will you make all arrangements yourself?"

"Yes, sir. If I need any help, I'll tell you."

"Good."

I hit a lively lick to the State House. Cleveland was not to come for some days, but work to receive him was in noisy progress, sawing and hammering and shouting in the construction of a vast platform and roofed enclosure for the speaker and the distinguished guests. This platform and enclosure were made a kind of extension of the massive stone steps of the south entrance of the great white building. Against the thick wall of the veranda, with its low balustrade, had been built a long table for "the gentlemen of the Press." It was close behind the spot where the speaker would stand. I leaned over the balustrade and tried to agitate a few brain-cells.

Then I went into the main corridor of the State House and had a talk with a wrinkled, grizzled, friendly-visaged cop whom I often had seen patrolling that corridor. He had spoken to me several times and called me "sonny." I asked him if he would be on duty on "Cleveland Day."

"Sure I will," he said. "Of all days."

I had not the faintest doubt I was talking with another policeman-friend. Humanity and trustworthiness seemed to infuse his very tissues. I decided without hesitation to make a confidant of him—and a confederate—if I could. All my cards I laid on the table for his inspection. I was the shorthand reporter for the *Democrat,* I had the assignment to report Cleveland's speech, and I was expected to beat the competition. I wanted to do it.

"Some job, sonny," said the old cop. "You're up against it proper. What ever made you think you could beat the veterans here? Huh! They're the smartest things in the state."

"I reckon you're right," I acknowledged, "but I must try. I'm new to my job and may lose it if I fail. I want you to lend me a hand."

"Me!" spluttered the old man, pressing a blunt forefinger into his chest.

"Yes," I said, forced to smile at the cop's astonishment.

"What in the Savior's name can I do?" he prayed.

"Have you time to come with me to where the men are building the platform?" I inquired.

"Sure I have," said he, stormy with interrogation.

We bent over the balustrade together.

"See the reporters' table?" I said.

The cop stared at it as if he expected some spooky development at any moment.

"I'll have a ticket for that table," I continued. "It's not more than six feet below this balustrade, and you'll note that projection from the stone support just behind the table. Every inch of space in front of and around the platform, as you know, will be packed. There'll be no escape for any reporter, except up this wall and over this railing, until the crowd has broken up. The moment the speech is over, I want to sneak to that stone projection, climb on it, and lift my hands for you to haul me up here. I'm such a kid I don't think anybody at the table will take any notice of me. Besides, I'll be first, and nobody will be up here to help another man."

My friend was amused almost beyond intelligible articulation. His wrinkles contracted into a knot, and his big body shook. Recovering his composure, he said he would be at the coping and would "see." If the coast were clear, he would "crane" me up. His words indicated to me that he would be a good confederate provided some circumstance, such as the presence of a superior officer, were not in the way. That was the best I could do, and I thanked my friend heartily. I fancied he was pleased, really, and I felt morally certain he would play his part both loyally and well.

Bands crashed in the streets and banners fluttered in the crisp sunlit air. Cleveland had arrived. Tens of thousands of people pushed, jostled, and eddied like a flood. Soldiers and police, spick and span, were all over the place, marching, clicking, curbing the crowds. I was at my seat at the reporters' table with a score of others, shorthand writers, descriptive writers, fashion writers. All was arranged at the *Democrat* office: three stenographers and three crack typists awaiting my return.

In front of me was my pink-lined note-book, the paper white and smooth. At my right hand were half-a-dozen "double enders," lead-pencils sharpened at both ends. I had a delightful sensation of readiness. Why? Ask your meta-physical oracle. *My* guess is that it was the calmness of desperation: *I dare not be rattled.* My one apprehension centered on the situation above the balus-trade. The veranda was black with people, as black as the far-spread scene be-fore and on either side of me. And I caught no sight of my fellow-conspirator.

Clap upon clap of thunder burst over me. Horns were blaring, brass clash-ing, drums beating, innumerable human throats screaming themselves to tatters. And all at once Cleveland stood before us, solid, observant, genially reserved. His long double-breasted black coat buttoned almost to his chin. *Character.* That was the keynote of the man: he was character modeled into human shape. Safety, one felt, could be found under the armor of such a per-sonality. I had not the remotest doubt he topped every other political leader I had seen, and I was impatient to hear his voice. Let the Governor and the other palaverers boil it down: we already had *their cut-and-dried* speeches in type! This was "Cleveland Day" in Indianapolis!

He spoke. His resounding words, issuing from that deep chest deliberately, reached very far over that vast, silent audience, spellbound in the sun. Report-ing him was child's play. I could have done it easily if his speech had flowed twice as rapidly. I did it with plenty of margin to spare for glancing at him and giving thought at times to what he was saying. And suddenly he was at the end, and that deafening roar was rolling afresh. The reporters had jumped from their seats and were crowding toward the orator.

My anxious eyes were on the balustrade. Could it be? *Could it be?* I had pushed my notebook and pencils into my pockets. I crept to the ornamented pillar, sprang upon the stone projection, lifted my hands, and shot upward as if in a balloon. That grizzled cop had made good!

"Keep close to me," he directed, seizing my right hand and moving like an ice-breaker through the crowd.

We reached the main corridor, and he let me go.

"Now, boy," he said, "run!"

Straight as a die through that lofty vaulted passage I dashed! At the north end of the State House I bounded to the street, cleared the whole multitude, and gained the *Democrat* office. To the first stenographer I dictated a few hun-dred words, and he began at once to dictate from his notes to a typist. And thus it went to the second and third stenographers, I reserving the conclusion for typing myself. Take by take the printers got the copy, the type clattered into the sticks, the galley-proofs were read, the forms were made up, the presses rumbled, and nearly an hour ahead of our rivals our newsboys were shrieking in the streets:

"Buy the new *Democrat*! Full report of Cleveland's speech!"

In all truth and sobriety, it was a triumph. My hit, with Mr. Comstock and among my colleagues, was hardly less tumultuous than Cleveland's at the State House. I was surrounded, pelted, mobbed, dubbed "The Great Kid," and at last stole off to my idyllic sanctuary at "The Ivies," feeling strangely chastened. I had done it once. Could I ever do it again? I had a secret longing to tear right out of town while my star twinkled at the zenith!

But this emotion I suppressed. Mr. Comstock raised my salary from fifteen to eighteen dollars a week and said he wished me not only to do his major shorthand work (of which there would be a great deal for some time) but to look for "news beats" and do feature articles. A thought occurred to me. Since I was in so good, I would be venturesome. The theater had begun to pull at me. I had seen a number of good plays and envied dramatic critics. Did Mr. Comstock think he by and by could give me a show at dramatic criticism?

He was surprised considerably, I gathered. But there was no rebuff. He was kindly, as ever.

"Ever see Salvini?"[1] he asked.

I said I never had seen the elder actor but had heard his son lecture in Terre Haute.

"Young Salvini is in America now," said the editor, "and he appears at English's Opera House shortly in a melodrama styled 'Storm Beaten.' They say he has some of the genius of his father; I never have seen him, but intend to go to 'Storm Beaten' if possible. You may try your hand at dramatic criticism that night if you choose."

With all my eyes, and I guess with all my soul, I watched the young Italian in the star role of "Storm Beaten." To say the performance was a treat to me is almost to debase language. It was pure rapture. I was not a dramatic critic in the very least. I was not a critic at all. I was a votary. Such simplicity! Such pathos! Such separation from artifice! Such humility and grace! Such subtlety and depth of character-delineation! As I walked out of the theater, I was walking away from the *real* into the *simulative*!

1. Tommaso Salvini was an Italian actor hailed in the United States for his performance of Shakespearean plays including *Othello* and *King Lear*.

Not all my ecstasy went into my brief critique. I cooled off becomingly with reflection and under the sense of what was expected of a critic. Still I put Salvini down as the worthy son of a great father and asserted that in the finer and lighter roles of serious drama he promised to attain the lonely heights of classic acting. To my great joy, the piece got into the paper precisely as I wrote it, and when I saw Mr. Comstock he said smilingly:

"Not bad at all, your study of Salvini. I liked him as well as you did. I'll try you out in the theater again when something worthy comes along."

My next moment of excitement came a few evenings later at the old Denison Hotel in North Meridian Street. I was in the habit of stopping at that hotel now and then, on my way to and from "The Ivies," to examine the register for notabilities from out of town. Once in a while I landed a good interview or news story in that manner. Many times at night I observed an interesting-looking man sitting alone on an upholstered bench under a shaded light in the lobby. Rarely he was reading, but generally he just sat there, smoked a cigar, looked straight before him, and seemed to be in deep thought. He was pretty heavy and his face was a reddish color.

"Tell me," I said to the clerk, a friend of mine. "Who is that man there?"

"Don't you know *him*?" puffed the clerk in a tone of disdain.

"No," I said. "Who is he?"

"That's 'Benjamin F. Johnson of Boone,' the swellest poet in Indiana."

"You mean James Whitcomb Riley?"[2] I whispered.

"That's him."

"I'll speak to him," I said.

"Don't do it! Nobody speaks to him!" shrilled the clerk.

Who was a hotel clerk to issue orders to the chief shorthand reporter and the dramatic critic of the *Democrat*? I hiked across the lobby and planted myself directly in the line of vision of the red-faced solitary. He looked rather hard at me, removed his cigar from his mouth, and shot up his eyebrows.

2. James Whitcomb Riley, who published under the penname Benjamin F. Johnson of Boone, wrote poems about life in the Midwest. Bell read his book of poetry, *The Ole Swimmin' Hole and 'Leven Other Poems*, while selling papers on trains in Terre Haute. The book made an impression on Bell, affirming his conviction to become a writer and leading him to try his hand at poetry. In an earlier section of the memoir not included here, Bell wrote, "I read the booklet from cover to cover. I read it again and again. I read it with my eyes running rivulets of tears, as I read it yet. All I knew of Indiana, all I knew of the human heart was there." For more on Riley, see Van Allen, *James Whitcomb Riley.*

"Mr. Riley," I said, hat in hand, "my name is Bell. I'm a reporter for the *Democrat.* I've read *The Ole Swimmin' Hole and 'Leven Other Poems,* and I read all your verse in *The Indianapolis Journal.* I'm an Indiana farm boy. May I talk with you?"

I hoped the hotel clerk was looking. Mr. Riley was cordiality itself, grasped my hand, pushed some papers off the seat next to him, and bade me sit down. We talked until the office clock struck 12, nearly three hours. Mr. Riley dug industriously into my past, begged me for stories, roared over the way I quit the *Terre Haute Gazette,* and especially over what he termed my "Napoleonic stratagem" in "canning" the competition on the Cleveland speech. At last we parted, the poet rising to bid me good night and to ask me to "stop for a word" whenever I should be passing.

As I strolled homeward, not quite certain whether I actually had talked with the author of *The Ole Swimmin' Hole* or had met him in a dream, my pleasure was mitigated sorely by the realization that I had done the most un-reporter-like thing of seeking an interview and then suffering myself to be drawn into doing nearly all the talking myself. I was downright sad about it but said to myself: "No matter. I'll see him again, and then we'll find out who does the talking." Meanwhile the lovely spirit of the man had entered into me, and I felt enriched.

Fate dropped a bomb before I had an opportunity to see Riley again in Indianapolis. The bomb terminated the existence of Mr. Comstock's pride and joy, the *Democrat.* He awoke to the fact that ideals and energy and professional ability of the highest order are not enough to put a newspaper on its feet and keep it there. "We did our best, dear Bell," he said to me on telling me good-by, "and I think we made a good paper. But our money was lamentably insufficient. I hope and believe you'll get a better job." Through Mr. Comstock's smiles I surmised I saw a disappointment too deep for words.

3. On the Road for Another Job

Unfortunately I had come away from the Hoosier capital without a letter of introduction from Mr. Comstock. Too bad certainly, and very foolish of me, as one might say, but after all I had heard that letters of introduction were "no good," and as a fact I had got several jobs without one. I would not trouble Mr. Comstock. I would not wait. I would re-pack my little bag and hop a train for the big city across the Mississippi, St. Louis. And that is what I did the next day.

He was at the apex of the "Temple of Truth": Mr. McCullough, editor of the *Globe-Democrat*.[1] As I entered the front door, I almost was bowled over by the rush of persons of both sexes coming and going, many of them clearly employees of the paper in all departments. I had got so I could tell them at a glance, editorial writers, reporters, advertising men, secretaries, foremen, printers, pressmen. It was highly stimulating, if a little disconcerting, to watch the passing show. But I must take my courage in both hands and get busy; a few moments of wabbling, and I might be lost.

"Mr. McCullough's office, please," I said to the tough-looking kid in the elevator.

"Top," he said with an oblique glance up and down me.

Evidently he did not recognize me as a native and shared the world's quite general contempt for foreigners. However, he creaked and rumbled with me to

1. Joseph B. McCullough was editor of the *St. Louis Globe-Democrat*. "Temple of Truth" is what McCullough and others called the eight-story building that housed the *Globe Democrat*. McCullough had been a star reporter during the Civil War, a Washington, D.C., correspondent, and was considered the master of the editorial paragraph. Like Bell, he was one of the first to make wide use of the interview. As an editor, McCullough helped move American journalism from partisanship toward impartial reporting. See Clayton, *Little Mack*.

the "top," opened the door, and pointed directly ahead. I got out and paused. I was looking into a small, circular office—a kind of cupola, I figured—through an open door. I could see no one and caught no sound from inside. I stepped into the doorway and at once was facing a smooth-faced, plump man seated in his shirt-sleeves at a roll-top desk.

He looked sour.

Was *this* my worshipful knight of the editorial epigram?

"Mr. McCullough?" I interrogated, doubtfully.

"*Yes!*"

No ambiguity there!

"May I speak with you?" I asked, approaching him haltingly.

"What you want? Be quick!"

It was the same old answer: I wanted a job.

I thought he would faint with a pain in the neck. Instead he bore up nobly to hear my brief and rapid recital as to where I was from and what I had done.

"And you want a job as a reporter?" he said.

"Yes, sir," I admitted.

"Sorry, boy, but you can't have it here. We're chock-a-block with reporters. Go out there and see them soldiering in the news-room. You'll carry away with you a picture of the damnedest bunch of loafers in America. We're overstaffed from cellar to garret. Where the money comes from to pay us all I haven't a notion. I'm expecting the rag to go bankrupt any day. Clear out of St. Louis! It's a rotten town for anyone looking for a newspaper job!"

All the wind, I hardly need say, was out of my sails.

"Thank you, Mr. McCullough," I stammered. "I'm awfully sorry I can't work for you. I read your paragraphs every day. I think they're the best in the world."

I was nearly to the door before the great editor recovered. Then he shouted to me.

"Come back," he ordered. "You're from Indiana?"

"Yes, sir."

"Know anything about those coal miners around Terre Haute?"

"Yes, sir. I was raised with them," I declared.

He scribbled rapidly on a scratch-pad.

"Take this to the cashier on the first floor," he said, handing me a slip of paper. "Do you know those miners are in an ugly mood and have gone on strike? Do you know the Indiana militia have been called out?"

"I saw the news in the *Globe-Democrat* this morning," I told him.

"Do you want to cover the strike for me? It may be long, you know, and there may be trouble."

I said it would please me very much to have the assignment, and I did not care personally how long or how troubled the strike might be. Mr. McCullough gazed at me for a moment or so.

"Then go," he said.

"I'll go direct to Vincennes," I explained. General Will J. McKee was reported to be mobilizing there.

"Go!"

And America's superlative paragraphist crooked himself over his desk.

Dropping down from the Chief's cupola with the distrustful urchin in the lift, I inspected my slip of paper. The urchin ogled me severely. I knew he was dying to get a glimpse of what was on that paper. He did not get it. The paper bore the signature—or rather the initials—of the Chief and requested the cashier to supply the bearer with $150. Even my name was not mentioned.

At daybreak the next morning, with a red wintry sun slowly rising to the Easter hilltops, a young fellow heavy with sleep and carrying a small bag stepped out of a day-coach on a wide board-platform at the railroad station in Vincennes. That was myself. Before me and to my right and left was a long line of stacked rifles with bayonets fixed. All over the platform and as far as I could see swarmed militiamen in full field equipment.

Threading my way among the soldiers, I found the telegraph office and went in to listen to the metallic tongues of the instruments: tongues, it may be remembered, which spoke intelligibly to me. At the counter, tall, gray, and trimly uniformed, stood an officer writing a dispatch. I surmised on the instant that he was General McKee, and I was right. I stood by at some distance. The dispatch was handed to the chief operator with directions that it should be sent at once. I heard it go. It informed GHQ (General Headquarters) at Indianapolis that General McKee was transporting his troops immediately to Farmersburg as a base of operations.

Farmersburg was a small village up the line south of Terre Haute. Already dozens of empty box and flat cars were assembled on the sidings, and I saw the soldiers beginning to unstack their rifles and climb aboard. Two or three locomotives puffed black smoke lazily and now and then threw out hissing columns of steam. Manifestly movement was at hand. I walked up to General McKee, told him I was a correspondent for the *St. Louis Globe-Democrat,* and said I had been assigned specially by Mr. McCullough to cover the coal miners' strike.

His steely gray eyes pierced into me from a singularly humane face.

"McCullough sent you, did he?"

"Yes, General."

"McCullough himself? A great newspaper man, I think," said the General. "We are moving to Farmersburg very shortly. My staff and I will be in this caboose down the track here. Go and get in. Your bag will be all right. I'll join you as soon as the troops are entrained."

All the way to Farmersburg—a journey of only fifteen to twenty miles— General McKee and I were in conversation. It was a slow, bumpy, dusty ride, with many stops for what no one knew, and the sun was well overhead at our destination. The General told me his troops were in fine fettle, disciplined "like regulars," and prepared to preserve law and order in the mining districts.

"We expect no bloodshed, some excitement perhaps, but no bloodshed. Our miners are not bad fellows as a rule, and the soldiers will treat them right."

My first act on reaching Farmersburg was to dive into a two-by-four eating joint for a stomachic counter-irritant. No wolf was ever hungrier. On a stool poking in mashed potatoes and sausage was a dark, fine-looking man of about twenty-five, a newspaper man, I would have gambled. Who could *that* chap be? He glanced up at me and said, "Sit down." I took a stool beside him, dropping my bag on the bare plank floor.

"Newspaper man?" he asked.

I confessed and rounded with:

"You, too, I guess?"

"Yes," he said, extending his hand, "I'm Jim Hornaday of the *Indianapolis News.*"

I shook his hand warmly and told him I was Edward Price Bell of the *St. Louis Globe-Democrat.*

"Capital!" he exclaimed. "I'm awfully glad to meet you. I've heard of you, I think. Worked in Indianapolis, didn't you? Knew Riley? He told me about you, if I'm not mistaken. Said you were a Raccoon Creek boy. You're the fellow, aren't you?"

I said I supposed I was "the fellow."

"I know you are," he averred. "I assume you're here to cover this coal miners' row."

"Yes," I said.

"Fine! Then all formalities are off," affirmed my attractive companion. "I'll call you 'Ed,' and you call me 'Jim.' We'll work together, for we're not competitors; you are morning, and I'm afternoon."

And there in that little none-too-clean country-town hash-house was born a friendship which lasted until Jim died in Washington on Christmas Eve, 1935, honored as one of the greatest correspondents our Federal Capital ever knew, a man to whom journalism was a religion as well as a profession. We covered that strike together, a struggle which ran into and way through the winter and ended only when the Indiana blue-bird and robin were heralding spring. We slept and ate wherever and whatever we could, in tents, on the snow and ice, in railroad telegraph offices by red-hot stoves with tobacco caddies as pillows.

General McKee's forecast was verified: plenty of excitement there was, but no bloodshed. The miners for the most part behaved with restraint, and the soldiers made friends with thousands of them. At the outset of the campaign, I wired to Charles Henry Dennis, managing editor of the *Chicago Daily News,* and succeeded in adding that great editor's morning paper, the *Chicago Record* (Victor Fremont Lawson's pet child), to my St. Louis connection, thus doubling my earnings.

It fell to my lot by accident to be able to turn a trick for Hornaday as the strike wore on. No one knew I was a telegraph operator, and I continually "tapped the wires." How? Everyone knows how thin are the walls of country telegraph offices on railroads. I watched for General McKee to go to the offices to make his nightly reports to GHQ. Then I stood close outside and listened to the ringing sounders. The nights were still, and I could hear every word. It followed that General McKee knew no more than I knew about what he was saying to Indianapolis.

Jim got fed to the teeth at one time. We were at a standstill, the troops bored stiff, the miners merely marking the slow-paced hours. We were in Farmersburg. Jim came to me one afternoon and announced that he was "off for Indianapolis." He was "damned" if he could "stick it any longer." He was going for a haircut and a bath, and to be de-loused, if McKee killed all the miners in Indiana while he was away. He went.

That night the sounders spoke to me. They told me trouble had broken out at Alum Cave, seven miles down a side-track from Farmersburg, and McKee was marching with a thousand men at dawn to take possession of the mining hamlet. I knew the hamlet well, a picture-postcard sort of place in a setting of hills, the population far removed from the outer world and known for its comparative belligerency and turbulence during periods of unrest in the mining districts.

We marched at dawn, and I was there. The weather was cold but bright, and everyone was more than ready to go. McKee and his staff, I trailing, marched on the railroad track. The troops were thrown out in V formation, five hundred men on the right, five hundred on the left, the General and his companions at the apex of the V. This formation disclosed to me the General's strategy: he was dispatching the tips of his wings to move beyond Alum Cave and then swing around to a meeting point, thus surrounding the village. *His* strategy determined *mine*.

Nothing like knowing your terrain, and I had the good fortune to know mine. Within a mile of Alum Cave, I left the superior command on the railroad track and hurried forward immediately behind the right wing. The units of the wing, the individual soldiers, were advancing in a thin line, the distance between them usually from ten to fifteen feet. I came upon two young men I knew, Captain George Biegler and Lieutenant Frank Parks of Terre Haute, both newspaper men when not in uniform.

"Boys," I said, "I want to split the line."

"What's troubling you?" asked George.

"Oh," I replied, "this army moves too slowly. I'm on my way to Alum Cave."

Both the Captain and the Lieutenant seemed puzzled. They exchanged inquiring glances. We were crashing along through thick underbrush beneath forest trees.

"What do you think, Frank?" questioned George.

"Let him go," said Frank, "he can't stop the army."

"He can tip Alum Cave we're coming," said George.

"But I won't," I pledged.

"Then stir your stumps," said the Captain.

Pretty well out of breath, I bumped into the diminutive telegraph office in Alum Cave and sent a flash to the *Indianapolis News* signed "Hornaday." I reported that McKee was marching on Alum Cave with a thousand men in response to calls for help. Then I took a quick walk about the village. Glum-looking, watchful miners in caps, scarves, and short heavy coats strolled along the single street and streamed down the footpaths from the environing hillsides. I returned to the telegraph office while the returning was good, suspecting that at any time it might be blocked. And I wrote a thousand words for Hornaday, holding it until I saw McKee's men appear on the ridges and begin to flow into the ravine behind bristling bayonets. Then I let it go.

Alum Cave, the picture of sullen stolidity, stared, spoke in guttural whispers if at all, calmly surrendered, every rifle, every shotgun, every pistol passing under McKee's control. Speaking to representatives of the miners, the General assured them the soldiers were their friends, not their enemies, just so long as order were maintained. He added that good care would be taken of their weapons and that these would be restored to them the moment peace should be certain. The tall old soldier walked among the people and chatted with young and old. Profound peace fell upon the Alum Cave front.

My main story of the day's events I filed promptly, touching it with all the color truth would allow—and truth allowed a good deal—and then I traveled back to Farmersburg with General McKee and some of his commanders in a caboose drawn by a special locomotive. At the telegraph office in Farmersburg two wires awaited me, one from McCullough and the other from Dennis, each handing me a bouquet, the first of the sort I had received since entering journalism. Even more than ordinarily, I relished my food that night at the little hash-house: I had helped Jim and won the plaudits of two famous editors.

Into the Farmersburg station fizzed and roared the night passenger train from Terre Haute. I was on the platform, as customarily, for observation purposes: often someone got off at Farmersburg. Someone got off that night, a rather forlorn and crumpled young fellow who would have been handsome if he had not looked so sad. It was Jim. We shook hands, and he unbosomed.

"Ed, I'm ruined," he said.

"How's that?" I asked.

"How's that?" he moaned. "Don't ask me. You know damned well. I'm beaten to a custard. If I'd stayed here, McKee *never* would've marched. Some nippy gazebo sent a fine yarn to my paper on what should've been my story. I'll be fired and ought to be."

"Hold your horses, Jim," I said. "You've not been beaten. As a fact you beat the world on the march on Alum Cave. That 'fine yarn' to the *Indianapolis News* was signed 'Hornaday.'"

I thought Jim would go through the boards.

"Ed," he stuttered finally, "did *you* send that story?"

"Sure I did. Why not?"

"Ahead of your own papers?" gasped Jim.

"Well, a little. You're afternoon and I morning, you know. Besides, Jim, I sent only a stop-gap wire to your little sheet. I saved my *big* story for *newspapers*. Look at these telegrams."

He scrutinized them in the dim light of a station lamp.

"They're real," I said. "McCullough and Dennis themselves signed those. They're the only people who know I'm out here."

Jim burst into his characteristic full bloom, and we dawdled over to our shack of a hotel, where the reddish-brown flat boys were bad enough but not nearly so bad as I found them in some places in later life. We talked till the small hours, and Jim told me of his ambition as a journalist: he wanted to go to Washington to live and work for the *Indianapolis News;* he loved the city, and he loved his paper. In Washington I found him years and years afterward. We picnicked in Rock River Park, and he came to hear Charles Evans Hughes (then Secretary of State, now Chief Justice of the Supreme Court of the United States) and myself address the Overseas Writers' Club. After the speeches, Jim sidled up to me and said:

"Why, Ed, you speak like an old-fashioned Indiana orator."

That remark struck me as slightly obscure: I had heard so many old-fashioned Indiana orators who seemed to me utter blatherskites!

"If the war is over, come home."

That message, or its equivalent, reached both Jim and me a few days after the march on Alum Cave. And we parted company for a long, long time.

4. I Head an Editorial Autarchy

Before I had joined the ranks of Mr. Ball's *Evening Gazette* in Terre Haute, I worked as a "butch" selling newspapers on the train. It was there, on the Terre Haute and Indianapolis Railroad, that I met another Terre Hautean—a very remarkable man—who was working on the same line. He was a locomotive fireman. Later he became a wholesale grocery salesman, got into politics, and was elected city clerk of Terre Haute. He had as much go in him as any man I ever saw, was brilliant, and did not know the meaning of fear. He was a great Radical and Socialist and spent his final years in organizing labor, reading Karl Marx, running for the presidency on the Socialist ticket, lecturing, and breaking into jail or the penitentiary.

Debs was his name, Eugene Victor.

I remember him with the liveliest admiration and pleasure, though to me he was not an ideologist in politics or anything else, just a gifted, brave, and lovable man. I used to see him almost every day in his office overlooking Main Street, on the north side between Sixth and Seventh, in Terre Haute. He was an editor then, editor of the *Locomotive Firemen's Magazine,* and his younger brother was his assistant. They gave me news of the railroad world and of the progress of what they called "man's rights" as opposed to "the abominations of avarice."

It was from Eugene Debs I contracted the itch to edit. Swung far back in his editorial chair one day, he gave me a searching size-up with his keen gray eyes. It was the first really close examination I had undergone at his hands, and I wondered what was coming.

"You want to be an editor, don't you?" he finally remarked.

I replied somewhat negatively, saying my ambition, so far, had not risen above the reportorial sphere: I wanted to be a good reporter, as good as any and better than any other if possible.

"Splendid!" he cried with the fervor which was an elemental part of him. "No worker does more for the world, for his fellows *en masse* everywhere, than the good reporter unfettered. He tells the truth, and the truth is mankind's one ineffable blessing. But now comes the rub. Reporters are seldom unfettered. Editorial direction, responding to publishers' points of view, which respond in turn to capitalistic points of view, presses upon reporters all the time. And the greater the pressure the harder the struggle of the truth toward the light. I should read and observe and study, if I were you, to be an editor. Editors, as I have indicated, are not free; no one is wholly free. But an editor of brains, courage, and will-power is apt to be much freer than any but the most exceptional reporters."

That speech I put down practically word for word in my diary. I read and re-read it countless times. It had an effect upon me too large and shadowy for any definition of mine. It gave me a feeling that our world was really very difficult; that there were grave conflicts in it, that idealism, brotherly love, had a hard row to hoe; that men of power were selfish and without Christian principle; that instead of approaching wisdom and peace nations within and without might be heading irresistibly for folly and war.

I was again in the open with my lightning-rod up for currents from the journalistic heavens. I had made up my mind neither to return to St. Louis, where McCullough was "chock-a-block with reporters," nor to beard Charles Henry Dennis in his holy of holies. With both those editors I had closed accounts happily after the long strike of the bituminous miners, and I had quite a wad of the "comical" in my jeans, more than I had had at any time since I quit the hog business.[1] I would be a gentleman for a spell. Mother and Father welcomed me to my old room at home, and there I spent many hours and some days thinking and scribbling.

I wrote, I will not say poetry. I wrote verse, metrical lines, jingle. I had been clandestinely at it ever since I read *The Ole Swimmin' Hole* and met James Whitcomb Riley. But I had offered nothing for publication. Now I poetically would cross the Rubicon. Riley had given up the pseudonym of "Boone" and

---

1. In an earlier section of his memoir not included here, Bell writes of his father's talent for selling hogs, which he did in addition to farming. Bell was set to accompany his father into Indianapolis to sell hogs one morning when his father fell ill, and Bell had to make the journey alone. It was his first time in that city and his first experience with "the hog business."

was writing for the *Indianapolis Journal* under (or rather over) his own name. I would try to break into that fast company. I broke in. I wrote with Riley! Here was my first published rhyme:

HARVEST FOR THE SOUL

In all the country there's a lavish waste of bloom,
All the freighted air is weighted with perfume,
    Every bud and every bee
    Has a word for you and me,
       I assume.

God is speaking in the flowers He has made,
He is speaking in the beauty there displayed;
    Oh, it pays to wander far,
    Where the rarer blossoms are
      Lost in shade.

We shall larger be and nobler for a stroll
By the wonders which the meadows now unroll;
    Not a flower greets the eye
    But will blossom by and by
      In the soul.

And the laughter of the waters which we meet,
Waters wearing crystal slippers on their feet,
    It will sometime laugh again
    In our life, and doubly then
      'Twill be sweet.

Then let us go and garner while we may,
For all the bloom and beauty will away;
    Not the poorest in the land
    But has riches at his hand
      For today.

Since I had found my life-job at last, and was to be a poet, it occurred to me I must soak myself in the great poetry of all ages. And I tried. From the public library round the corner I got quantities of books and dipped into poetry from centuries before Christ—from Homer and Vergil—to Dante, Shakespeare, Milton, Wordsworth, Byron, the Cockney Poets, and the illustrious Americans, not forgetting my own masterpieces, which were bubbling out of me diurnally and nocturnally. Exactly what set off the alarm I do not know, but I suddenly woke up, ceased to somnambulize. *Poetry* had been the bottom cause. It dawned upon me that I was not a poet, only a cymbalist. Great poets there were, and mighty had been their influence upon things which mattered, but I never could be one of them. Possibly I could be an editor.

I had saved up, as you know, a fair sum of money, all my own. I said to myself:

"I'll not wait to be an editor. I'll be one now."

Father heard with great obvious interest my story of Debs's idea. At its conclusion, he inquired:

"And what do you think of doing?"

"I think of becoming a country editor," I replied.

"Where?"

"At Rosedale."[2]

The name brought a reminiscent cast to Father's features.

"How?" he asked.

Father's expression appeared to me humorously quizzical. I conjectured he was trying to see the realization of Debs's big notion in the terms of Rosedale, and I came back with this:

"Remember, Father, Rosedale is only one town in a district. There are also Coxville, Jessup, Bridgeton, Carbon, Lodi, Fontanet, Coal Bluff, and a few others, none tremendously large but all taken together totaling quite a bunch of people. They're working people, mostly coal miners, and I want to live and write among such people. I think they get the worst of it, and I should rejoice in helping them a little if I could. And there is another consideration: as Mr. Debs said, I must learn and grow older before I can do a man's job. My hope would be to go on eventually from country journalism to an editorship in a city."

"Clear and practical, so far," said Father, "but how do you propose to get a paper in Rosedale?"

We were at the nub of the situation. I blurted out unreservedly that I expected Father to come across. I told him my own savings were probably more than he imagined and were ready for the venture to the last dollar. If he would "put in" with me, his interest would not be heavy, I would promise to reimburse him with interest, and we should launch the paper—"a lively weekly"—just as soon as we could buy and transport from Chicago the type, cases, stools, and presses.

"I'll do it," said Father.

2. Rosedale, Indiana, is a small town northeast of Terre Haute.

I myself went to Chicago and made all the purchases. I rented an upstairs room with plenty of light in it at the rear of Lafe Connerly's groggery. Lafe was Rosedale's unmatched exemplar of versatility. He not only ran a liquor-saloon according to the best traditions of such places but was an iceman, undertaker, town marshal, and justice of the peace, besides functioning here, there, and everywhere as the village wisecracker. I will say at once that Lafe speedily became a bosom friend of mine, never losing a chance to magnify me and boost "the paper." With him it was always that: "the paper," as if it were the only thing in the world of the kind.

Another great friend-to-be appeared in my office as I was putting it in shape for my equipment when it should come. I recognized the caller at once. He was the emaciated, sallow, life-battered fellow whose eyes were a constellation of twinkles. He was a retired "butch" who had coached me in that interesting occupation. He was Yank Sullivan, blithe, inventive, dilettante, the busiest and happiest idler and ne'er-do-well I ever saw.

"So you're going to be an editor?" he broke out hilariously, grasping my hand.

"You've got it dead right," I said.

"How'd you manage it?" he guffawed.

I had succeeded very well, I told him, and had saved my money.

"Your Dad help you?" he interjected.

The question struck me as impertinent, and I was inclined to resent it, but no one looking into Yank Sullivan's eyes could resent anything he uttered. He was one of those persons who are absolutely in earnest, who mean precisely what they say, but who appear eternally to be joking.

"Frankly, Yank," I conceded, "Father is helping me financially. But I'm going to pay him back with interest. This paper is to be mine, and I'm going to say what I please in it."

"Bravo!" shouted Yank. "Then we'll have a hot time in Rosedale. Plenty of people will come along to lick the editor. I'm glad I live here now. And, say, 'butch,' you and I are still buddies. I'll always be hangin' round, and I'll weigh in when the goin' looks good. See?"

"Thanks, Yank," I replied, "I'll be mighty glad of your friendship. I like friends."

"So do I," declared Yank, "and all the more because they're so damned scarce."

Immediately after Yank left me, a tall, gangling, brown-eyed young man came in. He had the mien and the air of an educated man, and I could not recognize him as a Westerner. He explained without delay that he was from

New York, was a printer, and would like to work for a time on "the new paper."
His name was Tom Hardy.

"Do job work?" I inquired.

"All kinds of job work, every kind of work in a newspaper office," he said
in a tone of quiet confidence.

"Why are you here?" I asked.

"Well," he said with a faint smile, "I'm what is known as a tramp printer.
I'm not really a tramp printer, however. I'm a college man, and my people are
well-to-do. I'm knocking about the country for pleasure and to pick up some
knowledge of America west of the Alleghanies. I can help you not only as a
printer but as a writer."

I took Tom Hardy on, for I needed a job printer, and of that part of my
proposed work I knew next to nothing.

Convulsive was the reaction of the village when my sensational consign-
ment came. Men, women, and children swarmed to watch the unpacking of
"the press," the first wonder of the kind ever seen in Rosedale. Farmers and
their families also came, and the news spread like wildfire to the farthest hill
and hamlet. Subscriptions poured in for the *Raccoon Valley Independent,* the
paper's name, and in a week's time all was ready for starting to prepare the
inaugural issue, I in the chair of authority, head of an editorial autarchy.

5. As a Country Editor Saw It

Of the nature of a time of feasting was that day (a Saturday late in 1887) when the *Raccoon Valley Independent,* in its fire-new dress, blazed along the streets of Rosedale. I was atomically small among the celebrants. Lafe Connerly, Yank Sullivan, Tom Hardy, and many another particular friend were close beside me, while Father stood a little aloof, missing nothing and gravely smiling. The village was a tumult of residents and rural visitors alight with eagerness to lay their eyes on what never had been anticipated in the Valley: a newspaper of its own.

City methods of newspaper sale I had taken over, and Rosedale rang with the penetrating cries of specially-drilled newsboys. Some of these nimble youngsters flitted away to the country roads and sold papers to in-comers on horseback and in wagons and buggies. West of town a yellow-clay highway curved over a ridge of hills and faded into a forest. On that highway, from my office window, I could see paper-laden urchins scurrying hither and thither flaunting their wares.

Altogether it was a tempestuous and affecting day, sobering even Yank Sullivan and spreading an unwonted sobriety on Lafe Connerly's face. Never before had they seen in the Raccoon Valley public commotion like that. Tom Hardy stated that the *Independent* was "already a success." Father maintained his aloofness and by nightfall wore a look of fatigue rarely visible in him. A nickel was the street-price of the paper, and when Tom and I had to light our pendulant oil-lamps it appeared that we had nickels enough to float a full-rigged schooner. Nor was that all. We were battling with annual subscription-forms and dollar bills which made the *Independent* office resemble a bank.

Pruning a long story drastically, I put my paper solidly on its feet. Tom Hardy did beautiful job work on our fine new foot-press, and our latest-model

Washington hand-press required only prodigies of energy to turn off adequate editions of the *Independent*. By and by Tom left me, the farther West calling, but other itinerant printers came, and I myself attained fair mastery of every feature of our work.

Retrospective from this distance, I must ask affected modesty to yield to stark candor. How I did all I did sends me down for the count. Mainly totalitarian I certainly was. Final command was entirely mine, and not infrequently (no wandering printer drifting my way) the *work* was entirely mine. "*The Raccoon Valley Independent: c'est moi.*" That I very well might have proclaimed. I wrote every editorial, nearly all the news, many advertisements, most of the special articles, and now and then a stanza or so of verse, of which I published a certain amount each week, all of it original and by home talent. In passing I may remark that some of these contributed rhymes were so good as to find their way into the metropolitan Press.

Such laurels were inexpressibly sweet in the Valley!

I roomed and boarded with my sister Meck, who lived with her family on a farm a mile south of Rosedale: another way of saying I was circumstanced happily with reference to food and fresh air and sympathetic fellowship. But, oh, the mosquitoes! They were colossal! And they struck like hornets! Anti-pest screens were unknown to us, and we lay down to sleep in smudges as dense as a London fog, the smudge-pots in the house itself. How did we live? Well, it takes a prodigious lot to kill people: I have seen and crawled on my belly across battle-fields where only men *could* live. Out of our smudges at Sister Meck's we came not only alive but laughing!

Job work too was on my peripatetic schedule. I got orders for letter-heads, bill-heads, printed envelopes, business and visiting cards, posters, hand-bills, any old thing I could convince anyone he wanted in the printing line. Tom Hardy had tutored me so meticulously on the job-press that I could do what he did with such skill: print all sorts of stationery and cards with perfect uniformity and clearness and yet with absolutely no showing of type-indentation on the opposite sides. At first that looked easy to me. I found it difficult.

Work inside the office was much harder, much closer, than that on the road. Left alone, as so often happened, I brought a mid-night snack from Meck's. At these times I was setting type when the sun went down, and I still was at the case when the sun came up. My imposing-stones were black with numerous varieties of type from poster-letters to brevier, minion, nonpareil, and even agate. I set both the jobs and the paper and made up the forms after proof-corrections. On Saturday Father was there to help me at the Washington hand-press as we ran off the edition for the newsboys and the mailing-lists.

Labor?

I will say it was labor, but it was also a kind of joyous inebriety. One had a pleasant feeling of paternalism. One supplied the heterogeneous community with its moral stimulus and its intellectual pabulum, told it what sentiments it should entertain and what ideas it should strive to translate into individual conduct and into citizenship. In my editorials I aimed to embody the liberal political philosophy of Debs in its spirit—that of a social square deal—rather than in its letter: that of a definite form of government. His "extravagances" of doctrine and of rhetoric I, in my superiority, avoided. I prided myself upon my Hellenic moderation and my ice-chaste judiciality.

I was at work one day when Mont Casey came over from Clinton to meet me. Mont was a fellow-editor, a witty writer, a good printer, and an almost un-equaled scrapper. His paper was the *Clinton Clarion* and was renowned for its biting witticisms and its unmeasured pugnacity. He did not attack me, but he fairly took the hide of every other editor in that region and occasionally paid his respects to the most august pen-wielders in the land. I do not know why, but Mont and I, from first to last, were reciprocally gentlemen and scholars. I quoted him, and he quoted me. If either were attacked by some barbarian editor, the other flew at the offender with vituperative abandon.

On this day the editorial gladiator turned up at the *Independent* office, I was alone and awfully busy. It was our first meeting face to face, and he pleased me as much personally as in his paper. Battle-scarred as he was, and having the unmistakable look of a fighting man, he was yet extremely affable, his smile disarming antagonism. I asked him if he would set type for me for a couple of days, and he consented. At noon we lunched together out of my basket. As we were eating, seated on our case-stools, Mont said to me:

"Anybody come yet to lick the editor?"

"Not yet," I replied, "but I'm afraid I'll have some trouble soon."

Casey looked at me with sharp inquiry.

"We have a bad man in town," I told him. "He's a patent-medicine faker who holds forth day and night on the vacant lot back of Baldridge's drug store. Has a bunch of musicians with him and makes a marvelous talk about his 'pain-killer,' which he sells to suckers as fast as he can hand it out. He's got to leave town. I'm skinning him alive in the paper this week."

"Is his medicine a pure fake?" asked Mont.

"Baldridge is a fine chemist," I answered, "and he tells me the 'pain-killer' is nothing but colored water."

"Can you give me a piece of news-print, a spot of red ink, and a few thumb-tacks?" asked Mont, sliding off his stool.

I got what he wanted.

"Have you a weapon of any kind?" he wished to know.

From a pigeon-hole I handed him a hideous old bowie-knife with a strap on the handle.

"Ideal!" he laughed. "Got a hammer and a nail?"

I had them.

"Any objection to my driving the nail in your wall up there facing the door?"

"Go ahead," I agreed.

Casey tacked the piece of news-print—a white sheet two-and-a-half feet square—on the wall and drove his nail in near the top at the center. On the nail he hung the bowie-knife by the strap. Then he smeared the knife with the red ink and blotched the paper at the knife's point with more red ink, a repulsive sketch. Viewing it for a moment, he went over to a case, selected some large letters and printed them in black on a white strip, which he pasted beneath his gruesome delineation. This was his legend:

"FOR THE MAN WHO COMES TO LICK THE EDITOR."

My excoriation of the "pain-killer" man appeared on the first page in dou-ble-leaded type under a head that could be read across the street. Hardly half an hour elapsed after the paper was out when I heard someone ascending the stairs to my office. Mont was with me, and we turned to face the door. A dark-visaged young man came in, starting back just the least bit as his eyes fell upon the bloody bowie-knife and the words below it. I recognized our visitor as the trombone player in the faker's band. He delivered a note to me with the remark:

"Will you kindly read that? It's from Mr. Biffle."

And the trumpeter made his exit before I could say more than, "Thank you, I will."

Mont was spasmodic. He said:

"Did you see him take another squint at that knife as he went out?"

Well, Mr. Biffle was boiling. He would give me "just one more chance." If I never mentioned him again in my paper, he would forgive me, and we should be friends. If I did mention him "offensively" again, he would visit the *Inde-pendent* office and "clean" me. He would not stop at that piece of laundry work; he would "sack the plant." If I were wise, I would "accept an advertisement"

from him—"a perfectly honest man purveying a perfectly honest remedy"—
and allow him to continue business unmolested.

I immediately sent a reply to Mr. Biffle by one of my best newsboys.

"Your 'pain-killer,'" I wrote, "is represented to me reliably as an absolute
fraud. It is declared to be ditch-water. You will not be permitted to go on swin-
dling our people any longer. I shall attack you with all my force in my next
issue. And may I add that every amenity awaits you at this office if and when
you may come?"

Mont read the note without much enthusiasm.

"You were too dignified," he said. "However, you said it. I should've used
plainer words."

"What should you have said, Mont?"

"Nothing. I'd've gone over and swept that lot with Mr. Biffle."

"But the musicians would've jumped on you."

"*Would* they? Possibly. But maybe I'd've had time to make the little dark
fellow eat his trombone!"

Concretely, I learned my elementary lesson with reference to the might of
the pen. My single exposé of the "pain-killer" nomad killed *him* in Rosedale.
Mont and I strolled by his show-ground that night. The music was going full-
blast, but the "pain-killer" was not selling. Before sunup the next day, Mr.
Biffle and his whole shebang had vamosed.

The orange of country newspapering had been sweet and juicy to me, but
I believed I had sucked it fairly dry. I was satisfied, I was grateful, but a bigger
world of endeavor and possibility was appealing to me. Doug Smith, my old
friend of the sealskin cap on the *Terre Haute Gazette,* was starting a new paper in Terre Haute, the *Daily News* (afternoon), to be staffed throughout with
young writers. And he had written me to join the group as night-police and
court reporter, "with the avenue of promotion wide open." I turned over the *Independent,* with all I had in it, to Father and said, "Sell it." He sold it, and many
years later, on a trip home from London, I sat down in the old office, among
the presses and cases and imposing-stones, and talked for hours with my
editorial successor, a courtly Southerner. I recall few happier chats than that.

6. A Great Infidel Turns Christian

We on the *Terre Haute Daily News* were a dashing and intrepid company. Doug Smith, editor-in-chief, was counted the handsomest man in the city, and there appeared to be no limit to his courage. Intellectually too he was outstanding. He had imagination, writing power, immense professional pride, and an energy and enterprise which only a deadly malady could conquer.

Crusading was our common passion under Smith. We were independent in politics and left prudence to timid souls. No court, no lawyer, no police officer, no advertiser, no bully could deflect us a hair's breadth from our chosen course. We dearly loved to lambaste political vaporers and humbugs and to wage war on corruptionists.

Libel suits?

Oh, yes; they came along now and then. But so long as I knew the paper it never lost a suit. It had a way of winning even when it was wrong. Judges and juries seemed to like us, and the best lawyers in Terre Haute welcomed opportunities to defend us. We did not belong to the jam. We were out of the ordinary. We were soldiers of the right, and nearly everyone smiled when the verdicts came our way.

It was truly a grand lark. I never can forget the atmosphere of exaltation in which we lived nor the high spirits of my God-fearing colleagues. I myself worked principally with the police and on the courts, stepping out once in a while to cover a prize-fight (with bare knuckles, as was the custom then), a dog-fight, a cock-fight, a horse race, or a fashionable wedding. I wrote the story of Dexter's thrilling feat when, as a three-year-old stallion, he trotted a mile in three minutes on the Terre Haute race track and brought down upon his beautiful neck the laurels of the world.

How the town screamed and throbbed that night!

And how the foaming lager beer gushed in fountains!

Card-playing occupied numberless leisure hours of mine for the first time since I played with neighbor boys under the apple trees on the farm. Awaiting developments, I often played patience most of the night at police headquarters. Paddy Burke, an amiable giant, drove the patrol wagon. When it was called, and the knowing horses rushed from their stalls under the suspended harness, I leaped to the wagon, Paddy pulled me up by his side, and together we sped clanging through the streets to fires, fights, accidents, raids on gambling dens or bawdy-houses (of both of which Terre Haute had her full share), or whatever form of excitement might be jarring the night.

Our card-game at the *Daily News* office was poker, and the players represented all departments of the paper. We played for beer. Our tables were in the extreme rear end of the composing-room straight above a well-known grog-shop, where a land-office business was usually in progress, a dull babble and roar constantly coming up to us. There was a wide skylight in the saloon. On clear summer nights it was open. We had a bucket on a cord. Out of a window we lowered the bucket through the skylight to the bar, where it was filled with beer and whence we hoisted it for our refreshment.

With that unforgettable body of writers and mechanicians, sustained by a virtually ideal *esprit de corps,* my break came suddenly, a stunning surprise to me. Major Rosencranz, a wealthy plow-maker in Evansville, was starting a morning paper to be known as the *Evansville Standard.* "Public service" was its watchword, and "looters of public money" were announced as "the official scoundrels" whom the gallant Major intended to "hound out of office into the penitentiary." The Major wanted Doug Smith as his managing editor, and Doug wanted me as his city editor.

We buckled on our armor.

I called Herby Jones, a blond Adonis of speed and spunk, from Terre Haute and made him my chief reporter, though he was barely sixteen. His opening performance in Evansville was at the race track. He was flushed with a sense of his growing importance in journalism and aquiver to the sights and sounds of a new city. Early in the afternoon there was a running-race of great public interest. We expected to post the result on our bulletin board in front of the office, and a large crowd was waiting there. No report came from Herby. The afternoon papers burst into the streets with extras. Still no report from Herby. The *Standard,* and especially the city editor, sweat blood. The electric lights began to twinkle, and in walked—or rather rolled—my chief reporter. Leaning against my desk, he put out a moist paw and said:

"Shake hands with me, Ed. I won sixty-five dollars at hieronymus!"

"Yes," I said, "and you're fired!"

"Fired!" he gulped. "I tell you, Ed, I win sixty-five dollars at hieronymus!"

"Exactly," I growled. "And I tell you, Herby, you're stewed and fired!"

But he was not fired. He turned up the next day in his characteristic Adonis form, neat as a pin: new suit, new necktie and hat, new shoes, a sprig of white jasmine in his lapel, and a rattling good news "beat" up his sleeve. He worked on the *Standard* with liveliness and luster until Evansville began to bind, when he darted to Chicago, ran the gauntlet of star reporting there, and passed on to "frenzied finance," became a New York "doughboy."

Those "official scoundrels" whom Major Rosencranz was to "hound out of office into the penitentiary" escaped our net. We did not land one of them, so far as I remember. But we made a terrific noise and must have thrown a scare into every crook in Indiana, another way of saying we did a whale of a job. Our ablest rival, the *Courier* under the Shanklin brothers (politicians and journalists of distinction), disturbed us. It was too intellectual for us. It knew more big words than we knew and could string them together with appalling sonority. We were slipping before a rush of rhetoric. We heard of John T. McEnnis of Chicago, the man who saved McCullough's life one night in the *St. Louis Globe-Democrat* office when a chap named Slayback aimed a pistol at the famous editor's head. It was said McEnnis not only could knock pistols upward as they went off but could out-write any other man in Chicago. Demoting Doug Smith to the news and city editorships, and dropping me into the street herd, the *Standard* did some mighty trumpeting. It was to have a new managing editor, and he was to be "the peerless John T. McEnnis of Chicago."

He came.

He awed us.

He looked like a Hindu prince, huge and black-bearded; we called him the "Rajah." He had a Titianesque wife who was as amply-proportioned as himself. They were big and swell if you like, and charming, the last syllable in dress, manners, and sociability. McEnnis's tactic was to smother the *Courier* with kindness. It was always, in his editorials, "the dear *Courier*," or "our beloved contemporary," or "our good but ill-inspired neighbor," or "that archetype of culture across the way." Everyone reveled in these editorials, and no one more than McEnnis himself. They convulsed him with good humor. His laughing image is before me now, as—his night's work done—he stands at the Vendome bar and tosses down old rye whisky at 3 a.m.

We had a dictator on the staff of the *Standard*. By long years this lady—and she *was* a lady—antedated the British suffragettes and the general modernist attitude and practice of "the female of the species." But modernity in women, in respect of awareness and assertion of authority, has nothing on what we found in Miss Lizzie Roseman, cashier and secretary of the *Evansville Standard*. Even Rajah McEnnis bent the knee to her, particularly when he wanted "a few dollars in advance, Miss Roseman, if you please," while ordinary reporters prostrated themselves before her for a lead-pencil. Christianity lived in her and issued in all she did. Bossy and indomitable as she was, she was the idol of the shop, and not a man-jack of us, I verily believe, would have balked if she had commanded: "Go down and jump into the Ohio!"

Fortunate it was for me, as I appraise the matter, that the Shanklins were such experts in English. Their mastery of the language brought the Rajah to our staff, and the Rajah pushed Smith down the ladder a rung, Smith in turn pushing me back into the firing-line, where I liked to be. But for that chain of events, I might have waited a long time—might have waited a fatally long time—for the experience which determined the main current of my interest and my labor as a journalist.

"The gentleman asks if you kindly will come up."

Speaking to me was a bell-boy in the lobby of St. George's Hotel. It was early one morning in the fall of 1890. My card, a few minutes previously, had gone up to "the gentleman," a large, rosy, clean-shaven, humorous, resonant-voiced man with gray hair almost white. I knew he looked like that, for I had seen him, and heard him lecture on Othello, at the principal theater of the town the night before: a lecture I shall never forget because of its sparkle, its acuteness, and its eloquence.

Ingersoll was "the gentleman's" name, Bob Ingersoll, Colonel Robert Green Ingersoll,[1] unique for a lot of things: power on the political platform (how often after 1890 right up to his death in 1899 I saw him sway vast Republican audiences in the open air at night!); delightful Shakespearean lectures; mannerisms and stories which loosed tornadoes of laughter; depths of seriousness with nothing for it among his listeners but tears; amusing, ironic, all-challenging on-slaughts upon what he deemed the absurdities of orthodox Christianity.

Trembling a little at what the bell-boy said, I strove not to let on; I wanted to appear hard-boiled. That liveried lad led the way at a smart walk, and I followed at his heels, fidgeting with a notebook in my left-hand coat pocket and

1. Robert G. Ingersoll was an influential and controversial lecturer who traveled the country in the late 1800s, speaking in support of issues such as civil rights, artificial birth control, and the influence of science, and against orthodox religion. See Smith, *Ingersoll*.

a freshly-sharpened lead-pencil in my upper right-hand waistcoat pocket: the tools of my trade. I was 21. Fifty-seven was the age of the celebrity I was going to see, though—spacious and smiling on the stage under a huge reading lamp—he had struck me as a robust man ten years older. Youth and age were blended in him strangely. No one who heard his Othello, I fancy, would have dreamed that in nine short years he would bow himself off life's stage.

Doug Smith had become a trifle martinetish. He spoke sharply to us reporters, seemingly just a jot soured by the ascendency of the Rajah. Or possibly he found that a particle of iron in his discipline was good for us. In any event this is how he put that Ingersoll assignment to me: "I want you to interview the old agnostic. I want you to *interview* him. I want you to make him *say* something. I'm sick of 'interviews' without a trace of brains on the part of either the interviewer or the interviewee. Now, mind you! No excuses from the old pot! Come back with the goods!"

Surely that was enough to put the wind up the most leathery journalistic sourdough in the country.

The bell-boy knocked.

"Come!"

I recognized the low, rich voice of the lecture.

The bell-boy opened the door, and before me at a table sat the man who was the *bête noire* of millions of devout religionists and the unadulterated joy of other millions of shameless irreverents. He rose, turned to me, bowed (he was much taller than I), and enveloped my small red fist in his big warm hand. It was a welcome to put anyone at ease. Something about me must have touched his funny-bone. He chuckled as he had a way of doing so effectively on the platform. He placed me in a chair at the table and stood looming over me, a human mountain, I thought, but one with a warm light on its snowy summit.

Out of my pockets awkwardly I drew my notebook and pencil.

"Apparently," smiled the Colonel, "you want an interview?"

"Yes, sir," I replied firmly.

"What about?"

"Really, sir," I said, "I don't know. I merely was told to 'interview Ingersoll' and warned not to fail to 'come back with the goods.'"

Ingersoll shook with laughter.

"Like your profession?" he asked.

"Very much, sir."

"How old are you?"

"Came of age my last birthday."

"How long have you been a reporter?"

"Since I was 13, sir."

Ingersoll gave a low whistle.

"Expect to live and die a journalist?" he queried.

"It looks that way," I said.

"Aren't you going to college?"

"I don't know yet. I may some day if I can save enough money."

The white-haired infidel laid his hand on my head.

"You'll save it," he said.

Then he sat down beside me at the table. He had become suddenly grave, as he did so frequently in the midst of his merriment before an audience. He took my notebook and pencil into his own hands and knit his broad brow.

"Supposing," he murmured, "you ask me this question."

He wrote it in the book and showed it to me.

"How's that?" he inquired.

"Fine!" I said.

"Good. We'll answer the question in this way, shall we?"

Slowly that big hand moved across the page. Again and again it so moved, the rugged face above it all concentration. Finally, drawing a deep breath, the Colonel leaned back in his chair and declaimed his words to me.

"Like that?" he cried with unmistakable pride of paternity.

"Wish *I* had done it," I said fervently.

More and more I was feeling at home with the man in whom were mixed, along with surpassing practical talent, so much childlikeness, romance, and poetry.

"Never mind, my boy," the Colonel remarked, looking into my eyes. "You'll beat me at this sort of thing one day. I'm an amateur. You're on the way to professionalism."

Glancing at his watch—a watch of luminous yellow gold and the thinnest I ever had seen—Colonel Ingersoll began to write more rapidly, question and answer, question and answer. Manifestly he intended I should have an interview, should go back to my news editor "with the goods." It was just on an hour before he rose, handed me the book and pencil and said he hoped the "interview" (his name for it) would "do."

It "did."

I left the Colonel with his "blessing" and with an "interview" which was quoted from sea to sea. I transcribed it secretly from the author's handwriting to the typed page and made Doug Smith's eyes swell. I made even the Rajah's eyes swell. I got a note of congratulation from Major Rosencranz. Miss Rose-man was transported and said I might have all the lead-pencils I wanted. The reportorial crew was stupefied, old Phy Viets, our "Methuselah," pronouncing my achievement a "miracle." Of course I felt a horrible impostor through all this profusion of flowers and deference. Repeatedly I was tempted to break out the facts, but I resisted. I needed all the glory I could get.

And Colonel Ingersoll was in the role of Brer Rabbit: *sayin' nuffin'*. He was doing unto me, I took it, what he would have wished me to do unto him. The great infidel definitely had turned Christian!

Only in outline do I remember what Ingersoll wrote for me. It was broad and beautiful, I know; dealt with large national and international questions; gave music and the drama as great civilizers; named for our worship as a peo-ple the Fathers of the Republic and "Old Glory." It revealed to me what the in-terview might be: a magnificent force for good. Interviewing should be mine. It should be my "Daemon," in Kipling's word. It became such. And through a long stretch of years it has driven me into fascinating experiences throughout the world.

7. I Meet a Girl in Black Pigtails

Four years of high-tension journalistic life in Evansville convinced me of the wisdom of Ingersoll's implied counsel: "Get a college education." Consistently I had risen in my profession according to conventional notions. The Rajah went back to Chicago, Doug Smith returned to the editorial chieftaincy of the *Standard,* and I re-assumed the duties of the city editorship. Then "the dear *Courier*" took Doug away from us, and I was elevated to his vacant chair.

Paucity of education—even such poor education as the brevity of our days enables any of us to get—handicapped me, as I thought, more and more as my responsibilities increased. I had been thrifty. I had not realized Ingersoll's prediction of savings enough for a college education but had prospered sufficiently at least to make a start. I resigned from the *Standard* in August, 1894, and matriculated at Hanover College, at Hanover, Indiana, on the heights above the Ohio River, in September.

Autumnal magnificence bathed those hills and laid its golden touch on that winding flood. Hanover College, even then an old seat of learning (it was founded in 1832), sat like a great bird of quiet plumage on a shady campus in the midst of all the glory. In spite of the Greek and the Latin and the mathematics there—and they were things new and dismaying to me—I was happy. The "higher education" was wonderful. I could feel myself getting smarter every day. The Delta Taus liked me, and I joined them and became the "frat" orator.

One of our delights was to sit on the dry grass at the edge of the campus and gaze down over a floor of blazing tree-tops at the lovely river. I thus was occupied after lunch one day, oblivious to everyone and everything but the view, when a voice at my side attracted my attention. It was a low masculine voice, not unmusical. Glancing round, I saw a tall, dark, kinky-haired young man almost negroid in both complexion and feature. I had seen him before. He was a freshman like myself.

We entered right there and then into a friendship which not only has survived but has ripened with the years. Albert Leroy was the student's name, and he hailed from Pennsylvania. He was not a Delta Tau, not a fraternity man at all. He was a "barb." But he had plenty of fine stuff in him, and we became companion-wanderers among the hills, through the forests, and up and down the river. We became room-mates too and pooled our wits in the stiff struggle with Greek and Latin verbs and the infinite attenuations of algebra and geometry.

Meeting at Hanover, Hanover saw us leave together. We were in that splendid institution only the fall term. I hardly know what caused us to leave. But I think it was a sense of out-of-the-wayness. We felt too cloistered, cloistered in hills and woods, in beauty, in jealousy of tradition. We had heard much of Wabash College at Crawfordsville, Indiana. It somehow seemed to us in closer relationship to the life for which we were endeavoring to trim our sails. Founded as was Hanover in 1832, it was the Alma Mater of many men distinguished in affairs.

Absorbing and stirring and fraught with joy was my three-year period in Wabash, the whole time in close association with Leroy, he an ardent Presbyterian, I irredeemably under the spell of the magic Ingersoll. So divergent in our view of tenets, Leroy and I went all the way in double-harness with reference to the substantials of human behavior. Our likes and dislikes were a strange harmony. We both favored coming to grips with Greek and Latin long before cockcrow and discriminated identically among teachers and taught. Our pleasures ran in a single current.

There was one man in the faculty who stood quite by himself in our eyes. His name was Arthur Bartlett Milford. Pure humanity was his long suit. Books he knew as I used to know the eddies and riffles of the Raccoon River, but human life he knew yet better. He knew that unless he found the *hearts* of his students, he would introduce them to his books, and hold forth on his books, largely in vain. English was his subject, and he incensed and adored Shakespeare, Spenser, Milton; but he was well aware that he must make them simple and real and momentary to us or discuss with little effect *Hamlet, Faerie Queene, Paradise Lost.* Of all the professors I have known in my life, Professor Milford of Wabash was the least professorial, the most human. Going deeply into Shakespeare's most baffling character, he was just as unaffected, just as *living,* as he was when he sat at his own table, his head bowed, his eyes closed, a smile on his face, while his six-year-old, flaxen-haired Dorothy asked a blessing, her flowing curls falling round her plate.

As for the student-body, I could put together another blue book—calendar of the *élite*—on it. But I will mention specifically only two of the fellows: Howard Greist and C. V. Smith, known to everybody as "C.V." Howard I mention because (mark you, I was not insensible to his *many* virtues) he said one night at our debating society: "If there's a poet in Wabash College, Ed Bell is one." That bucked me up incredibly, though I knew it was not so! "C.V." I name because he saved a score of us from starvation for three years and did it for two dollars a week! Do you think we did not eat? We were epicures! We had soup and meat and vegetables and two or three kinds of pie. We had cake. We had the finest ice-cream in town: "C.V." made it himself. I was sorry for him. I expected him to land in the poor house. Instead he pulled down the presidency of a Minneapolis bank!

Hot times were not uncommon at Wabash when Leroy and I lumbered on to the campus. He-manhood was a tradition there. The he-ness of it came out on Washington's birthday. The classes fought then, the seniors and sophs on one side, the juniors and freshies on the other, each line-up doing its damnedest to maim and humiliate the other and drag the opposing colors in the dust. We had cane-rushes in the corridors of the college, busting heads right and left. We bloodied noses on the campus. Our rows spilled over into the streets of the city and involved the police and fire departments. Gown *versus* gown, and gown *versus* town, spread the fame of the "Scarlet of Old Wabash" in a fashion to make the good Dr. Burroughs tear his hair.

So we stopped it. But not before a disgraceful scene in chapel. The seniors and sophs smuggled six or eight pigeons into the room at chapel exercises on the last Washington birthday of the reign of terror. On the necks of the pigeons were tied the things which made all the trouble. The exercises proceeded normally, President Burroughs winding up with one of his inimitably wise and graceful morning talks. He had spoken of the value of the milk of human kindness in human relations, and his last words to us were: "The Lord give thee peace." We all rose, and then the pigeons fluttered noisily up to the overhead beams from the ranks of the seniors and sophs, carrying their hated colors. Bedlam exploded. Stink-balls were hurled. We became a sneezing, coughing, battling mob. The faculty stood on the dais helpless. Only Dr. Burroughs threw himself into the whirlpool, and the last I saw of him he was being borne hither and thither, his open Bible held in his right hand high above the bobbing heads and his white lips uttering cries we could not hear.

I was lucky enough one day to come across Will Smallwood, my old humorist friend of the *Terre Haute Daily News*. Will had got out of journalism into organized charity work. He was secretary of the Terre Haute Charity Organization Society and was going to England to study the methods of Toynbee Hall, in Whitechapel, London, "Mother of Social Settlements."[1] Would I go with him? I said I would if he could wait until the end of the spring term at Wabash. He waited, and in June we both saw salt water for the first time, sailing from New York on the "Aurania," whose 5,000 tons knew the art of rolling and pitching as, I fancy, few other ships knew it on the North Atlantic.

England shook us to the depths right off the bat. Our first night in Liverpool (where we lived for three weeks in a Baptist Home to observe organized work among the poor) surprised and made us anxious. There was a tremendous, surging multitude in St. George's Square, and four men were speaking at once at the foot of the great monument there. All were shouting wildly against the government, spouting the most flagrant sedition, while sedate bobbies strolled about and took no notice. Will and I expected the government and the parliamentary system to tumble about our heads that night. Well over forty years have trotted by since then, and one hears that the Bull Dogs and their Crown and their Parliament still are carrying on.

England, though Will and I had not realized the fact, lies very far to the north, its southernmost point in about the same latitude as the northernmost point of Maine, a circumstance which led English explorer Sebastian Cabot, sailing due west from England to Labrador, to expect warmth and bloom where he found snow and ice. Will and I also expected what we did not find: dawn coming when it came in Indiana. At 2 in the morning, I awoke on my iron cot near Will in the Baptist Home. It was broad daylight. Feeling the hour was not long after midnight, I looked hard again at my watch. What could have gone wrong with the planet? Was the world on fire or coming to an end? I called Will. He blinked, stared, grunted, and fell asleep. I slept no more and learned the next morning how short are the nights in England in summer.

We went out to a small tavern for breakfast. The waiter wished to know if we desired a "plain breakfast," and we said we did, albeit we had not the faintest idea what a "plain breakfast" was. We were served toast, butter, marmalade, and tea, all of it excellent. It gave us an appetite. We sat and sat at the table.

1. Toynbee Hall is a social settlement founded in 1884 in Whitechapel, a poor and working-class area of East London. It was built to provide well-educated, middle- or upper-class individuals an opportunity to live in Whitechapel, witness the social conditions there, and help improve them.

The waiter came in two or three times, looked at us, and went out. At last Will was getting impatient, and when the waiter re-appeared he gravely wanted to know when we were to get our breakfast.

"You've 'ad your breakfast, sir," said the waiter.

Will and I paid and shriveled up as much as possible as we slipped to the street.

Writing was my function, scientific inquiry Will's. My great friend of the strike days (Mr. Dennis of the *Chicago Record* and the *Chicago Daily News*) had agreed to take articles from me on social conditions and problems and on virtually anything else which might interest me, provided I kept off "the theater" and "society," both of which he considered to be "badly overdone." Will and I went to the Lake District,[2] region of witchery and beauty, and I wrote about the poets, Wordsworth, John Ruskin, and Robert Southey. Sweet were those days! How I loved the job: writing of men of genius whom Milford had made live in our bare class-room! And Mr. Dennis published the stuff on his editorial page!

From the Lake District we walked to London, every step of the way, listening to a thousand melodies new to us, gazing with passionate satisfaction at such meadows and hedges as we never before had seen, and lying down at night in farm cottages cool and fragrant. The farm folk were good to us. We seemed to be curiosities to them. Man, wife, and children sat about us, looked at us, smiled at our speech and accent, and asked us numberless questions concerning America, where not a few of them had relatives or friends. And they fed us well: not only that but apologized for taking a "bob" (shilling) for what a "buck-and-a-tanner" (half a crown) would have been moderate pay.

Gone forever, those days?

I doubt it. I suspect a tramp off the beaten path in England (indeed among the simple people of any land) would be much the same today as Will Smallwood and I found it.

At Toynbee Hall, shut up delectably within ivied walls off Commercial Road, East London, Will and I settled in for real work, Whitechapel's ceaseless thunder beating in our ears. We were given monks' cells, clean but tiny and rigorously severe, in Wadham House, students' hostel of Toynbee, and Canon Barnett, Toynbee's great warden and rector of St. Jude's, took us under his comforting wing. We often dined with him and the university residents at

---

2. The Lake District is a national park in England, which contains some of the country's tallest mountains and most beautiful scenery. Wordsworth was born and lived there.

the Hall and quickly took in their ardor for the ideal of educated men helping, and being helped by, the poorest of the poor. For nine months we steeped
ourselves in unexampled East London, roamed that "metropolitan desert" at
night, dodged "Jack the Ripper," and did our best to turn it all to our respective
accounts, giving a great deal of time and effort to the Salvation Army. Then
we worked for two months among the poor of Paris, fascinated by the piquant
and picturesque contrasts between what we found there and what sprawled
before us in East London.

I wrote reams for Mr. Dennis.

And Will charged himself to the brim with the lessons of social service in
Liverpool, London, and Paris.

Back in Wabash for the fall term of 1897, I resumed my intimate comrade-
ship with Albert Leroy, finding him and all my other pals no less attractive
to me than they were before I "expanded," became a modest cosmopolite or
intellectual imperialist. My prestige, I discovered, had grown. More citizens
of substance wanted me to call upon them. I was invited to speak in chapel
and at two or three churches, and the business men's organizations were after
me. But I rather hugged the shore, kept close-hauled for the finishing touches
upon my academic life. The world now was roaring at me indeed. I yearned
for distant strands, the more distant the better.

"But you must join church, Ed," said Leroy one afternoon as we tramped
among the beeches above Sugar Creek.

"Why, Lee?"

"Because it will help you. It will make you steadier and better. It will be a
moral suit of mail for you."

Lee was very earnest, and I made no reply; felt I could say nothing to
please or console him.

"Will you do it?" he persisted in the quiet, persuasive way which always was his.

We walked on, and I still made no reply.

Leroy drew all his sustenance of soul from religion. He attended Christian Endeavor infallibly, went to every prayer meeting at First Presbyterian
Church, taught in Sunday School, did all manner of church work, and slaved
with others to build a chapel in a poor section of Crawfordsville called "Goose
Nibble." All this, and yet he was a thoroughgoing all-round student who either
got respect voluntarily or took it. To stand against him was not easy, so high
was one's regard for his conscience, his intellect, and his sensibilities.

"Lee," I said, "let us put that church proposition aside for the present. I'm
not ready to join church. Its moralities are in what I say and do, I think. I take

off my hat to its ideals and to its approximate fidelity to those ideals. For what some call its mummeries I care nothing. I should feel a bit of a humbug if I stood up before a congregation to be sprinkled."

Leroy smiled and said no more.

Not long after our chat on Sugar Creek, Leroy bumped into our room one night rather excited. He had been to some First Church affair and wished to talk. I laid down the book over which I had been accumulating a headache, *Oedipus Tyrannus* in the original.

"What's warmed you up, Lee?" I asked.

"I have a very special invitation for you," he replied.

"Yes?"

"The prettiest girl in Crawfordsville, and one of the most active workers in our Church, asked me to *beg* you to come with me to our next Christian Endeavor meeting. Note that word *beg*."

"Do I know the girl, Lee?"

"I think not, but she knows you, or at least has seen you."

"What's her name?"

"Mary Mills, Mary Alice Mills. We all call her Mary Alice."

"I believe I've seen her," I reflected. "Only a child, isn't she? Very dark?"

"That's the girl," said Leroy. "She's older than she looks. She's seventeen. She's got the poise and the brains of one twice her age. Take it from me, you'll like her. You'll be mad about her."

"Is she painfully religious?"

"She's religious all right but all the better for that."

Now I must move on to my superlative moment at Wabash. That moment did not occur when I came out of my dog-fight with Greek possessing an honorary Master of Arts. Neither did it occur when Wabash made me a Doctor of Letters. Those were moving moments, I am bound to say, notwithstanding the fact that my degrees (including a Doctorate of Laws from Northwestern University) seemed ever to elicit from the dull world only a glacial stare. I never could understand how things so important could be viewed so unemotionally!

My superlative moment at Wabash—I guess I should say my superlative moment altogether—came when my eyes fell upon the Girl with the Black Pigtails. I had entered First Church with Leroy, his eyes singularly bright and expectant. It was early evening, and the lights were on in the large Christian Endeavor Society room, a gay and talkative assemblage of young folk of both sexes creating a scene which quickened the pulse. I surveyed it all, delighted.

"There's Mary Alice," said Leroy.

Even as he spoke, I saw her and knew her. She was in a white dress with a red rose at her throat. Those lustrous black pigtails fell lower than her belt. Her classic, oval face, accentuated in its whiteness by dark-brown eyes, showed the faintest trace of pink. Her hair was parted in the center and lay flat on her head, madonna-like. Her body was shapely, her hands slender, supple, finely-molded. Her expression was all friendliness and light. Leroy and I were compelled to elbow our way to her, so numerous and importunate were her admirers. And "goggle-eyed" just about told the story for me. I fell in love with that pigtailed goddess on the spot, and something not dissimilar seems to have happened to her. At any rate we "made it," and we have gone over the wiggle-waggles of life together ever since, a span climbing into five decades.

Certainly. I joined her church and stood up to be sprinkled with the most orthodox. She did it. "Mummery," in my interpretation, took on the meaning of "symbolism," and I was satisfied. Even if I had not been satisfied, I doubt if I should have stood obdurate against her great desire. I probably should have climbed the church steeple if she had told me to. Nor do I regret my acquiescent disposition now. Many things in this world cost more than they are worth, but *some* things are worth more than they cost.

II
The Chicago Period, 1898–1900

8. Blown Out of My Home Town

Ours undoubtedly were the *cornucopiae,* though we were broke: Mary Alice Mills and I on that awful winter day in Crawfordsville when a nice parson united us in holy wedlock and sent us out into the blizzard to face the world. The day was December 21, 1897. The sidewalks were impassable, lost in two or three feet of snow. Mary and I walked to and from the parson's warm drawing-room in the middle of the streets, where wagons, buggies, and sleighs had made a sort of road.

Straight to Terre Haute we went on the very train where I had worked as a newsboy. I had a job as reporter and dramatic critic on the *Terre Haute Express* under George Allen, who would have been a handsomer man than Doug Smith (of my earlier newspaper experience) if he had not been so short. His head and face were very fine, his complexion dark and rich, his mind and personality loaded with color.

Fourteen dollars a week was my salary: thirty had been what I drew before I took in my quota of the "higher education." When I said to Mr. Allen that I was married, he looked at me in obvious surprise, not to say astonishment. He was silent so long that I was beginning to be uneasy; I was afraid he might sack me for what he regarded as foolhardiness. On the contrary, he raised my salary: made it sixteen a week!

And he said:

"You've got the right spirit, Edward. It doesn't pay to put off marriage too long. I'll stand by you."

I have said Mary and I were broke. "Worse than broke" would have told the fuller truth. I owed a cold thousand dollars for money I had borrowed to make the academic riffle. I also owed for the contents of the little home I had fixed up for us in South Seventh Street. With this latter operation George Allen had helped me. He had said "Do it" to a well-known furniture store in Wabash Avenue, and the store was to get its pay from advertising in the *Express,* the amount to be deducted gradually from my salary.

So we set sail!

Work for us did not wait upon any honeymoon. It began the first night of our marriage. Arriving from Crawfordsville late in the afternoon, we went to our pygmean palace, looked it over, decided that the kremlin was a lean-to by comparison, snacked on some delicious food Mary's mother had prepared for us, and went to the Opera House to see Minnie Maddern Fiske in *Tess of the D'Urbervilles.* My review of that wonderful lady's great acting I wrote in the *Express* office, Mary at my side, and as we started home arm-in-arm the East was graying, and the music of the presses was sounding from the basement.

One cannot leave George Allen without a few more words. Enterprising and radiant as an editor, he was infinitely touching and amusing as a man. Give him a good story, turn for him a novel and happy phrase, and he would scrape the till for all he could find to hand you on your back-pay. His love of poker and whisky was a classic at Fagin's "Health Office," whither he hied every morning at 3 (after the paper was out) to mingle with the haggard, feverish-eyed gamblers in the upstairs rooms, play a few games himself, refresh his tired nature with old beaded Bourbon, and thus compose himself for bed.

In bone, tissue, and chemistry, George Allen was a journalist. Truth he loved more than he loved even poker and whisky, and he was not afraid to tell it in the paper. Try to bluff him, or in any way to shape his policy against his convictions, and you would get acquainted with George. It was a fundamental of his professional doctrine that the newspaper business was no place for a coward: he could bear more patiently with a knave or a fool.

This delightful editor got into a dispute with the owners of the Terre Haute baseball team. They were not managing baseball decently, according to his views, and he went after them with his choicest philippics. For a time they ignored him. But when George Allen really donned his batting clothes, *nobody* could ignore him for long. The owners of the ball team, scorning to make any reply to the *Express,* suddenly pulled a *coup:* they employed a husky to see that no *Express* reporter should enter the ball park to report a game.

Now that looked nasty, for no newspaper dared go without detailed stories of the ball games: the fans would revolt, and the paper which lost the fans would lose the fight. George Allen, for once, was anxious and in a quandary.

I knew baseball inside out, and an idea came to me. I hastened to Mr. Allen's office and told him I thought I had a solution for his dilemma. He was astounded and confused.

"What solution can *you* have?" he demanded.

"I'm a telegraph operator," I said.

He eyed me as if he thought I was getting crazier with every tick of the watch.

"Spit it! Spit it!" he cried.

I spat it.

Told him of the young "Western Union" we juveniles established in Terre Haute years before, equipping ourselves with sounders, keys, and batteries and stringing wires from home to home over much of the city. George listened but with growing impatience. At last he broke out:

"Yes, yes. But what the hell has that to do with this?"

"Mr. Allen," I said, "have some workmen put up a tall, sound telegraph pole outside the ball park fence near the grandstand with a full view of the diamond, especially the pitcher, the home-plate, and the catcher. Make a small platform or table on the top of the pole and fix a chair on a bracket beneath the table. String a wire from that table to this office. I will get me some climbing-irons and install a telegraph outfit on the top of the pole. There when the games are on I will sit and wire every play and incident into this office. Kibbe (he was our Associated Press operator) can take the reports and you can post them play-by-play before the crowds in the street. And I think you may be sure there will be crowds."

Our scheme worked like a charm. It went far beyond anything we had expected in the way of a humdinger, rousing thousands of people in Terre Haute to their first intimate realization that the *Express* was a newspaper and not just another rag. The grand-standers roared their congratulations at me, seated atop that pole, and the bleacherites went hog-wild with merriment, volleying me with a blend of felicitations and ribald jokes. For a time it looked as if there would be no game, just a popular pandemonium, with the ball players themselves unable to resist the whooping infection. But we finally got on, the game began to pulsate over the wire, and the plays popped out on our bulletin in the city. Denser and denser grew the crowd before our office until the police were forced to clear a way for the traffic.

You readily will guess the upshot. It very shortly became clear to our friends the enemy that they had taken the wrong turning. We were cutting the attendance at the games in two not far from the middle: the street view saved car fare and the price of admission. Into the *Express* office walked a neutral emissary, and he found George Allen complaisant. I came off the telegraph pole with my instruments and climbers, and again our sports reporter took his place in the press gallery of the park. But we did not remove the pole.

"Let it stand there for them to think about," said Mr. Allen.

George soon retired, the *Express* was sold to a group of moneyed men, Bill McKeen (a railroad man and son of the president of the Vandalia system) at its head, and I prepared to hunt for another job: the set-up lacked all magnetism from my point of view. But to my vast surprise they came along to me with an offer of the managing editorship under the new regime. I should be "free" and my salary would be twenty-five dollars a week, not exactly that of an "industrial feudalist" but substantially better than sixteen! The paper had been independent Republican under Allen, and I was assured it would go on in that tradition.

"If any broad question of policy arises," said McKeen to me, "the decision will be in the hands of the board of directors."

"Very good," I assented.

All the old staff remained, editors, reporters, copy-readers, printers, pressmen. The pick of the lot for quaintness was our ginger-haired, crippled joke-smith, Tom Morgan, and he and I were uncommonly close friends. His right leg was bent and stiff at the knee, and he hobbled about town with a heavy blackthorn, a source of interest and pleasure wherever he went, though no one failed to detect something disquietingly peculiar in his smiling brick-red eyes. Rare was the person who chose to essay lance-breaking with Tom Morgan!

I was working for the *Express* when that ugly Cuban shindy began. Cleveland had warned Spain to mind her step. What Wilson later called "the pitiful process of subjugation" dragged.[1] Cleveland went out, and McKinley came

---

1. "That ugly Cuban shindy" is a reference to the beginning of the conflict that eventually escalated into the Spanish-American War (1898). President Grover Cleveland warned Spain to "mind her step" in his final annual message before Congress in 1896: "when a hopeless struggle for [reestablishment of Spanish rule] has degenerated into a strife which means nothing more than the useless sacrifice of human life . . . a situation will be presented in which our obligations to the sovereignty of Spain will be superseded by higher obligations, which we can hardly hesitate to recognize or discharge." More than a year after that speech, Congress authorized President William McKinley to send U.S. troops into Cuba to stop the civil war. For more on the Spanish-American War, see McCartney, *Power and Progress*. For Cleveland and McKinley's policy toward Spain, see Dobson, *Reticent Expansionism*. For Cleveland's address to Congress, see Cleveland, "Annual Message of the President of the United States," 1896.

in. "Butcher" Weyler was busy in Cuba.[2] Yellow newspapers were exaggerating and lying to boost sales. Munition-makers were at their hoary infamy of fomenting war in which they would get rich and not fight. Up went the battleship Maine in Havana harbor, two officers and two hundred and fifty-eight men killed on the instant. Bad as the facts were, the propaganda was worse. The spit-poisons and gold-diggers, the arsonites of every ilk and kidney, had done their work well. From ocean to ocean America was infected and inflamed and shrilling for action. And still McKinley strove to hold in leash the dogs of war.

One o'clock in the morning.

I am in the managing editor's chair correcting the final editorial proofs. Most of the forms are made up, and the rush is on for the press. Someone comes stamping and swearing along the hall past the writers' cubicles toward my room. He bursts through my doorway and strides to my desk, his eyes flashing and his face lowering. Back of him I catch a glimpse of Tom Morgan, watchful and anxious, and back of Tom my wife. Tom gives me a significant look and lifts his blackthorn in a hard grip.

Bill McKeen faces me.

"Bell," he exclaimed between gritting teeth, "Bill McKinley's a coward!"

"I don't think so," I replied.

"You don't?"

"No, sir. I don't."

"I damned well *know* he is!" cried McKeen.

"And I damned well know he's *not!*" I rejoined, getting on my feet.

McKeen was a much bigger man than I. He easily could have tied me in a knot. But I could hear the crippled jokesmith bobbing up and down outside my door. I could hear his blackthorn striking sharply on the bare boards.

Silent for a moment, almost gasping with rage, the chief owner of the paper finally said:

"I want you to publish a double-leaded editorial this morning—*this* morning—slating Bill McKinley as a coward, and a disgrace to this country, and demanding immediate war on Spain."

"I'll not write any such editorial," I said.

2. Spain sent General Valeriano Weyler to quash the Cuban rebellion in 1896. He was governor of the island during the Spanish-American War. Weyler was known for his policy of reconcentration: separating civilians from rebels and placing the former in camps, where starvation and disease were common. This policy earned Weyler the nickname "Butcher Weyler." See McCartney, *Power and Progress.*

"Then *I*'ll write it," affirmed McKeen.

"Yes," I said, "and I'll kill it."

I thought that railroad man would choke. While he was mute, I stated my position.

"I am boss of the paper tonight," I asserted. "I am responsible not to you but to the board of directors. That is my contract. I am bound to obey my conscience and judgment, not yours, however superior yours may be. I think the President is right, and I think he is magnificently brave, to do every honorable thing in his power to avert war. The *Express* will support him as long as I am in this chair. He is a Republican. We are a Republican paper. When you tell me to break with him, to attack him, I think you're off the perpendicular in both your morals and your politics."

Bill McKeen, grimacing, swung on his heel and left the room as roughly as he had entered it. The paper went to press with a leading article saying about the President everything McKeen did not want said. Satisfied within, I was quite conscious of the dubiety of matters without. I found Tom Morgan and my wife waiting for me in the hall in a great state of subdued excitement. Tom was smiling.

"I saw the big stiff to the elevator," he said.

My wife's face was an illuminated interrogation point. She was not scared. But her face plainly was saying, "What shall we do?" We bade Tom good night and walked home as the dawn was coming. We had a pair of new bicycles, brightly sky-blue and gold-striped, proud possessions indeed. Every morning these were our servants as the day broke. We rode side by side under the trees in the silent street. We often went on to the country, out east where the big oaks were and the May-apples grew, and we went thither on this morning after my encounter with McKeen.

We were sitting on a hillside when the sun came up.

"Ed," said Mary, "*we*'ll have to move."

"Yes," I agreed. "It's probable."

We had not long to wait, Mary and I. We were sound asleep in our little home early one Sunday morning, after the usual all-night grind at the *Express* office, when there came a rude thumping on our front door. I got up and saw on the step a liveried boy from the Terre Haute House, the leading hotel of the town. He told me Mr. McKeen wanted me to report at once at a certain room in the hotel. Half an hour later I knocked at the designated door. Bill McKeen opened it. He shook hands with me and was all smiles.

At the other side of the room, standing, I saw a fine-looking man, white-haired, apparently a scholar. He had his eyes on me and was beaming gently. I liked him.

"Mr. Bell," said McKeen as we drew close to the stranger, "let me introduce you to your successor as managing editor of the *Express*."

We greeted each other most amicably.

"This gentleman," McKeen observed, "is a distinguished journalist from Indianapolis. You will be willing, I hope, to help him all you can. He wishes to learn your routine and to meet the staff."

Addressing the newcomer directly, I volunteered to aid him in every way I could and desired to know when we should start. He said, "now, if you please," and I asked for only time enough to telephone my wife. The gentleman from Indianapolis—and he *was* a gentleman, courtesy and kindness themselves—took over his duties that day, and I was free to talk with my wife about the fresh outlook that night. We were at liberty for once to ride our bicycles at sundown instead of sunup, and I honestly can say not the filmiest cloud of misgiving for the future crossed our souls. It is thus with one always, I presume, when one is on thoroughly good terms with oneself.

9. War and Oratory on Leech Lake

Chicago looked big and luminous and billowed like a wild sea to Mary and me. Our stuff in Terre Haute was warehoused, our money was emphatically on the short side, and we had neither a job nor the prospect of one. We rented diggings at West Jackson Boulevard and Western Avenue, and Mary became housekeeper and cook. I marched to the *Record* office, my old friend of the coal-strike days, Charles Henry Dennis, managing editor, saw me at once, and within an hour I was back at the diggings telling Mary I had a job at twenty-five dollars a week.

Frankly, my first nights on the *Chicago Record* were nights of intense mental distress. "If this is the last word in metropolitan journalism," I was saying far down within myself, "me for a quick scuttle!" All my grief came from a large, loose-jointed night editor named Brazleton. Mr. Dennis I liked; he was splendidly big-minded and considerate. Henry Barrett Chamberlin also I liked; *God* had made him a good fellow. He was the day city editor.

But Brazleton had in him seemingly everything which rubbed me the wrong way. His very first survey of me, as I sat down in the place assigned to me on the telegraph desk, had the appearance of saying, "Wonder where in the hell Dennis picked this up?" Of course copy-reading on the *Record* was new to me. The various types for the heads were new to me. Everything was new to me. Brazleton was decidedly new to me.

I was ready to fly off the handle at the lightest touch. And that touch was not long in coming. To me had been turned over the Washington letter of William Eleroy Curtis, a journalistic celebrity; the man who interviewed the James brothers when the Pinkertons were after them and got himself to the front all over America by his investigation of the Ku Klux Klan of the South.[1] I did not stop with writing the heads; I made some changes in Mr. Curtis's copy.

That is where the bus hit me.

Brazleton crashed into the telegraph room from his desk among the lino-typists (we had linotypes in the big newspaper offices by that time), barged up to me, slammed the Curtis script down under my nose, and demanded to know what I meant by "laying hands on Curtis." I was dumb with surprise and the shock of the man's rudeness. Before I could recover, he was gone, and the copy lay there mutely and unintelligibly accusing me. I picked it up and hurried in search of Brazleton, determined to fling it in his face.

I got within a few feet of his desk and stopped. I turned back. I thought of the diggings at Jackson and Western. I thought of my very recent experience in Terre Haute. I thought of the thinness of the partition between Mary and me and a diet of lake air. The chief of our desk, a fat, good-natured old hand, came up to me and said:

"Laugh it off, my boy. Brazleton's bristles don't mean too much. I should've told you Curtis's stuff is 'must-without-a-change' in this office. God Almighty wouldn't be allowed to touch it if Billy Curtis split all the infinitives in the language and spelt Christmas with a K."

All the desk was merry, and slowly my composure came back. Nonetheless I was sensible of the difficulty of my position and worked awkwardly. Just before midnight Mr. Dennis walked in, a picture of dignity. His face, I thought, was a degree whiter than I had seen it previously. I went cold and bent over my task. Had *he* some trouble for the rookie he so readily had enlisted?

He spoke to the Chief.

"I am afraid," he said, "I must take Mr. Bell away from you. Please put someone else in his place."

I rattled in my shoes.

"Mr. Bell," Mr. Dennis continued, "will you kindly come at once to my office?"

---

1. The *Chicago Record* hired William Eleroy Curtis as its Washington correspondent in 1887. Curtis had an interest in foreign affairs and began to travel frequently in 1892, sending foreign news to the *Record*. During this time, he also wrote several books, including *Today in Syria and Palestine* (1903) and *Modern India* (1905). Curtis also interviewed Jesse James, a Missouri outlaw, and his brother, Frank James. The two were infamous for their robberies of stagecoaches, banks, and trains in parts of the Midwest and South. Pinkerton's National Detective Agency began to track the James brothers after they robbed a bank in 1871 and continued to do so unsuccessfully until Jesse James died in 1882.

I lost no time in getting there, screwing up my courage for anything as I went. Mr. Dennis was seated at his desk in his cubby-hole of a room. He was alone, and I noted that the whiteness of his face was due to fatigue. He was working overtime. Supposedly his was a day job. He should have been in bed hours ago. I saw a pile of legal tender near his hand.

"Mr. Bell," he began, "you did good work for me in the coal fields of Indiana."

"Many thanks, Mr. Dennis."

He was smiling.

"We in the office here got to thinking of you as quite a 'war correspondent.' You gave us some very vivid matter and a number of beats. I happen to need a war correspondent at this moment. The dispatches tonight, as you may have noted, suggest a rather serious situation in northern Minnesota in the Leech Lake country. The Chippewas are on the war-path, and General Bacon's army is moving to the scene.[2] I wish you would take this money and reach the seat of trouble at the earliest possible moment. You have *carte blanche* for the story."

It was hard on Mary (I flatter myself) when I broke the news to her at one in the morning and tore off with a small handbag to catch a train at three for Leech Lake. She was plucky if you like, but those trembling lips and dewey eyes tugged at me heavily. Surely this was a sorry mess: this business of having a lovely wife and a war correspondent's job at the same time. But I would see it through, and one day we should have a cartload of double-eagles and a castle on the Nile. Already I could make out its pinnacles against the Egyptian blue!

Never before or since have I been on sharper tenterhooks than entertained me as I traveled northward that night and the next day. For the first time in my life, I "rode a Pullman" and wrestled with the problem of getting my clothes off and on in a berth and so disposing my money as to make as likely as possible its continuance in my possession at the end of the journey. Yes; I had a gun; it was a hang-over from my police days. I fell asleep with it in my hand as I listened to the rapid metallic babbling of the wheels.

But it was morning before my real anxieties assailed me. In the smoking-room I ran upon ten or twelve smart-looking men in sheep-skin jackets and leather leggings. Some of them were youngish, some middle-aged, all tanned

2. Historians commonly look to this confrontation at Leech Lake as the last Indian uprising in the United States, although it was small in size. Fewer than 30 Ojibwe (commonly called Chippewa) Indians living on a reservation in Minnesota skirmished with about 100 U.S. troops. The Ojibwe were frustrated at excessive logging practices on the reservation and a recent clash with law enforcement officials. See Roddis, *The Indian Wars of Minnesota*.

and weather-beaten. Their talk immediately revealed them as correspondents recently home from Cuba and the brief Spanish-American war. They were comrades, they were real war correspondents, and several of them (a few were from the Twin Cities) represented my competition in Chicago.

Enough to worry me, n'est-ce pas?

How could a comparative greenhorn like me go against those fellows? What was Alum Cave to San Juan Hill?[3]

Furtive glances came my way. "Who is he?" I heard that. And I heard a man (Arthur Clarke of the Chicago Tribune he proved to be) say this: "Must be from the Record. Never saw him before." No one spoke to me, and I spoke to no one. I was the outlander and thought gestures of fellowship should come from the natives. But, feigning utter indifference to my surroundings, I kept as wide-awake as I could. In the end—the train all the while gliding swiftly toward the Chippewa country except when it paused at little stations in the midst of crowds of farmers and lumbermen agog about "the new Indian war"—I think those men from Cuba either forgot me or decided I was not a correspondent after all.

In any event they finally talked freely and openly with one another. It was then that I became troubled sure enough. They were discussing "wire capacity" and "quotas" in the wilderness. There was only one wire, and there were many claimants for a share of its capacity. Each fellow was clamoring for an allowance of so many words. The Tribune, my chief competitor, was healthily in the scramble (I never have known it to be otherwise), and I was nowhere, an outlander indeed. Tempted several times to crash the ramparts of the combination, I did not. Perhaps I lacked the nerve, but I let myself think some still small voice was counseling me, "Refrain!"

Night was upon us when we rumbled into a small settlement on the west shore of Leech Lake, a pine-girted body of water, fifteen miles wide and twenty long, in the high hills of Cass County, Minnesota. The place was already alive with General Bacon's troops and cluttered with his arms and stores. At the single hotel—a shell-like rambling structure of two stories—I was admitted to a second-story room to sleep with four or five other men, strangers to me, apparently foresters or the like. The night was frosty, and I did not remove my overcoat. A brawny chap, half asleep, asked me to share a wide bed with him and another man (happily a small man), and I cheerfully accepted, lying down

3. San Juan Hill was the site of a battle (July 1, 1898) of the Spanish-American War. During this battle, Theodore Roosevelt and his famed "Rough Riders" made their charge up Kettle Hill, near San Juan Hill.

with my hands in my overcoat pockets. My left hand gripped my roll and my right the gun, a first-rate six-shooter which I never had used, and hoped I never should use, on anything more sentient than a poker-chip.

Dead-beat as I was, I could not sleep. My room-mates were snoring. From a distance I could hear the noises of the hotel bar, unmistakably the busiest spot in the settlement, and the spot where I had left my exclusive colleagues rejuvenescing. There also I had left General Bacon, who appeared to be rousing his energies judiciously for the campaign. Incidentally we had learned that a skirmish already had been fought between the regulars and the Chippewas, the regulars expending a deal of ammunition but accounting for very few Indians. It seemed to be up to General Bacon to have a bracer.

Something was happening. I lay as still as a mouse. I had been in bed three or four hours, and could see the first hints of day. My companions went on snoring. Tramp and rattle in the street beneath our windows. No doubt about it. I wanted to peep but feared someone would be awakened and shoot. Well, let them shoot if they must; I was a war correspondent; I was there to see. I crept out of bed, tip-toed to a window, and saw field-pieces and ranks of armed men moving toward the lake. Evidently Bacon's bracer was working. Dimly I saw two smoking funnels against the eastern sky.

I took the boat.

I was a molecule in that voiceless movement of guns and men.

We steamed across the lake, swerving a little to the southward to round an island portage (of which I was to have some experience later), and docked at sunrise at the Indian Reservation settlement, a village of one-story unpainted board shacks. Half-a-dozen redskins loitered about, dumbly curious, non-hostile. Landing as quickly as possible, I watched the slow process of disembarkation and unloading, not seeing one of my fellows-of-the-pen. I supposed they were comfortable on the other side of the water. If in reality they were in a hotter spot than I, luck was theirs. That was all. I simply had got tangled up with the troops.

What was to be my line?

Should I stick to the soldiers and bide events, or should I strike out on my own?

Choice between the alternatives was not easy, for a battle might be fought very soon, whereas General Bacon (who had crossed with us at the head of his staff) might take time for a general reconnoiter, and I knew the *Record* wanted copy and wanted it quick. What was the bedrock of this row anyhow? Why had the quiet Chippewas suddenly become aggressive? Coming over I had had a chance to talk briefly with a strapping young officer, Lieutenant Hoover. I went back to him and said:

"Will you go with me into the interior to see the Chief of the Chippewas?"

Laughingly he replied:

"Bet your life, if Bacon says okay. Ask him!"

I asked the General, and he was surly.

"Most certainly not," he growled. "Hoover can't go, and neither can you. What do you think we're here for? Let me tell you, Mr. Reporter. We're here to quiet down these Indians and get a settlement of this quarrel. We want no 'incidents.' If you go poking about beyond our lines, you may lose your scalp, and then there'll be hell to pay; the papers will be in an uproar. Stay right here."

Of course the General's argument was unanswerable, and I made no attempt to answer it. But I held firmly to my purpose to see the Chief if I could. I reported to Hoover on Bacon's ruling, and he giggled.

"Going anyway?" he asked.

"I'd go like a shot," I replied, "if I could sling the lingo of these Chippewas. My thought was that maybe you and I could find someone to take along as interpreter."

"Mum, now," said the Lieutenant. "See those two Indians down the shore yonder by that birch-bark canoe? I heard them speaking English."

Hoover ducked, and I began one of the most memorable days of my newspaper life. Those English-speaking Chippewas knew where the Chief and the main body of his warriors were camped. They could and would take me to see him. He was a "good man," wanted peace, and believed if America knew the "sufferings" of the Chippewa nation it would cry out for an end of them.

Putting out into the lake until we must have been a mere speck as seen from the shore, we turned northward and paddled for some miles. Then the Indians swung their light craft inshore, we landed, the canoe was made fast in a fringe of brush, and we set off through the pines at a lively walk, the Chippewas leading. An armed warrior stepped from behind a tree, rifle ready, eyeing us. One of my Indians rattled some words at him, and he faded from view.

"What did you say to him?" I inquired as we proceeded.

"Told him you pencil-man see Chief," was the answer.

Thus were we stopped and questioned many times, but at last we came upon the tents of the Chief and probably more than a thousand warriors. The Chief himself we found in a wigwam made of whitened deer-skin. He listened with solemnity to my Indians, throwing an occasional piercing glance at me, and grunted amiably. His face was copper-colored and deeply furrowed, his body short and thick. At the close of what my Indians had to say, the Chief spoke to them.

"He says," I was informed, "will you say in the papers what he says and say not what he says not?"

I stated I would report him with all possible accuracy. Then he gave some directions, and we waited, no one speaking further. In a few minutes' time two young braves came into the wigwam and emptied on the ground in front of me two large basketfuls of empty shells. Then they silently withdrew, and the Chief spoke. Interpreting, my Indian who managed English rather better than the other told me this:

"The white soldiers use all these shells and kill no Chippewa. We not afraid. We fight better than white man in woods and lakes. And we care not if we die. But we want peace. We civilized. We can make our food. We can trade. But we not be robbed. We not be wronged. 'Dead and down' ours. It stolen from us."

Followed the Chief's detailed exposition of the Chippewas' point of view. It was lucid and logical and moving, a great argument stated with the simplicity which becomes such an argument. I ate it up. It all hinged upon the depredations of the half-breeds. The "dead-and-down" timber was the property of the Chippewa Indians. It was being stolen systematically and hauled to the railroad for shipment to market, its owners aghast and helpless till they took up arms. Arms they would not lay down till the "Great White Father" in Washington saw justice done.

That was the story!

I was satisfied it was the biggest story likely to come out of the Chippewa rising.

Now for the wire! I shoved some greenbacks into the hands of my guides and interpreters, and you should have seen them paddle that canoe back to the Reservation settlement! It was dark when we arrived, and a strong wind, almost a gale, had sprung out of the West. The last cross-lake boat was gone, and a waste of whitecaps rolled between me and any chance to deliver the goods. Would the Indians paddle me over? They would!

One knelt on a wad of hay in the bow and struck with his paddles first to the right and then to the left. The other sat in the stern and synchronized his strokes with those of his leader. I sat flat on the floor in the center of the canoe, an arm on either gunwale. And so we stemmed the storm. It was tough going. Every probability seemed against us. The odds looked quite too great.

Wave after wave bore down upon us, and at every fresh onset I felt we were lost. And how cold it had grown! The fine spume from the breaking rollers turned to ice in the air. But for those Indians, their grimness, their bravery, their incredible skill, I fully believe I should have passed out. It was *warming* to watch that marvelous fellow in the bow. The poniards of his eyes cut the gloom. As each great wave rose before him, ready to break, he dug his paddle into its base and lifted the canoe's nose clear of its curling crest. But for those magnificent strokes, the public would have been spared one autobiography.

And that island portage of which I have dropped a line heretofore: you will recall it was in the way of the steamer in the morning. It was very far from being in our way that night. As we were approaching it, its dark-topped pines casting deeper shadows upon the waves, I felt water seeping through my trousers and shouted to the steersman at the top of my voice:

"This canoe is leaking."

The Indian made no sign, held his eyes sternly ahead, and *paddled.* We landed on the island, and the Chippewas inspected the canoe in the light of birch-bark flares lit with matches which they providentially had in their shirt-pockets. I stood about disconsolate. What hope could there be? I did not know the Chippewa and what necessity had taught him. Those Indians cut papery strips of outer birch-bark, boiled a sticky ooze from the same source, and mended the leaks in their craft before I really knew what was going on.

Half an hour after landing we had crossed the portage, the Indians carrying the canoe keel-upward on their shoulders, and were again afloat, steering directly into the wind and jumping the foamy ridges as before. Lights burned on the black hills forward. As we went over the waves I saw them; as we sank into the furrows they disappeared. Those hills sheltered us after a while. The quieter water whispered sweetly, and the red steersman, chin dripping, turned to me and smiled. Who adequately shall voice the joy of the sailor as he at last bursts through the storm?

Deaf to my pleadings, those men of the great Algonquian stock, having put me safely ashore, faced their birch-bark "liner" about and set sail for home. They went with fifty dollars of the *Record*'s money in their pockets and were probably the richest Indians in Minnesota. Greedy as I was for the wire, I stood at the lake's rim and looked after them until the night and the waves had swallowed them up. I was not surprised to read many years later that no tribe of American Indians ever had surpassed the Chippewa in its mastery of the canoe.

Yes, it was a beat, and a very big beat: that statement of the Chippewa case from the Chief's own lips. The telegraph office I found unoccupied except for the idle operator. All the stories of the day—merely stories of Bacon's shifting his base from the west to the east side of Leech Lake—were gone. I wrote rapidly and filed sheet by sheet. Entering the hotel, my task finished, I found myself for the first time a phenomenon of great interest to my competitors.

Where in the hell had I been?

"We've been looking for you all day," said Arthur Clarke (afterward a fine comrade of mine in London). "Hope you haven't a wow of a beat up your sleeve?"

"I've *nothing* up my sleeve," I said. "I'm just a little hungry."

The "Great White Father" heard, and he acted. Whether he saw my interview or not I have no idea; I know only that it was carried to the four corners of the country by the Associated Press out of Chicago. General Bacon never moved from the ground where I saw him land. President McKinley sent his Indian Commissioner to Leech Lake, a grand powwow was held in a building in the midst of Bacon's troops, the Chippewa orators and advocates (emissaries of the Chief) stated their case in the presence of the Commissioner and the Press, and very shortly the half-breed thieves were put out of business and the dove of peace returned to the Chippewa ark.

Mahjigabo was the great Indian of that powwow. He headed the Chief's delegation, squatting on the dirt floor at the top of a semicircle of supporters, all in full Chippewa regalia. Mahjigabo and the Commissioner were *vis-à-vis,* the latter in the center of a long table with correspondents to his right and his left, an interpreter standing between him and the Indians. Each of the Chief's delegates spoke, but very briefly, their words crackling like shot in a tin pan and pausing for the rendering in English.

When Mahjigabo rose from his squatting posture and advanced a few steps toward the Commissioner, a deeper hush fell in the room. His nose and ears were prominent but his cheek-bones not so; he had the cheek-bones of a white man. His short hair, cut as the white man's hair is cut today, was parted on the left side. His face, roughly elliptical, was strikingly broad at the center, his forehead insignificant. His black eyes were concentrated and bright, tending to move to and fro between the Commissioner and the "pencil-men." His upper lip was long, and a deep seam curved on either side of it from the nose to the chin. He was bare-headed, his conical, corded felt hat and blanket on the ground near him. His costume, with apron, leggings, and moccasins, was beaded and fringed richly. Except perhaps for the non-brainy brow, he looked his part.

And his speech more than confirmed his looks. Substantially, it hardly went beyond what the Chief had told me. Formally, it was immeasurably more arresting; it had mysticism, pathos, and beauty as well as power. Theologian, metaphysician, logician, orator, poet; he was all those. God, he said, was with the Chippewa people. The invisibilities were with them. Lacking rifles, lacking shells, they would win. Had the Commissioner not seen the Holy Spirit in the trees and the waters and the winds? Had he not seen God's face in the flowers? God was in the Chippewa too. The Chippewas were *Anishinabeg*,[4] men born of cosmos, unconquerable because *justice* was so.

Mahjigabo, dressed as he had been at the powwow, came to see me shortly afterward at the *Chicago Record* office, with him an interpreter. He was *en route* to Washington to talk personally with the "Great White Father" about his people. No similar courtesy ever delighted me more. I introduced him to my *confrères* as the "Demosthenes of the Algonquins."

4. *Anishinabeg* refers to the "first or original people" according to the traditions of the Obijwe (sometimes called Ojibway or Ojibwa). This Native American people shared the Algonquian language and populated parts of the upper Midwest and eventually the northern Great Plains.

10. I Learn I'm a "White Nigger"

Dame Fortune (who turns her wheel, I am afraid, quite as she pleases) was kind to me in the Chippewa country, scene of my first efforts as a staff correspondent of the *Chicago Record*. I returned to Chicago on a night train, reaching the office at 10:30, and found Mr. Dennis still on duty. He said he was pleased with what I had done and was sorry not to be able to let me rest a while before sending me off on another job.

"What is the job?" I asked.

He replied that serious trouble was brewing between the white and the colored portions of the population of Wilmington, North Carolina.[1] Some rioting had occurred, with more or less bloodshed, and the whites were breathing fire and brimstone. The *Record* would like the situation explored impartially.

"Your going at once to the bottom of matters in Minnesota was admirable," said Mr. Dennis. "We felt we knew the *reason* for what was going on, and the reason for developments of importance is always interesting and valuable news. Behind the rioting and the threats in Wilmington there are obviously contentious standpoints of an obstinate nature; men in large numbers do not fight for fun. We want all the news and especially that which explains clearly and fairly what is causing the strife."

"I will start tonight," I said.

1. On November 10, 1898, armed white men marched on Wilmington, North Carolina, a majority-black town, with the purpose of turning over the town leadership from blacks to whites. A coalition of black Republicans and white leaders had held power in the town since 1894. The marchers forced black leaders to resign and used intimidation tactics to scare blacks from voting in the upcoming election. Scholars estimate that they killed from seven to twenty blacks in the town. See Cecelski and Tyson, *Democracy Betrayed*.

"Excellent. You will find expense money waiting for you at Mr. Chamberlin's desk. (Mr. Chamberlin was our city editor.) Best luck!"

Just a few minutes with my wife (minutes given to mutual rejoicing over Leech Lake moderated by doubts as to what my work was to mean to our home life), and I was clattering in a shaky cab to catch a train to Washington. In the beautiful capital on the Potomac I was happy. Its charms were new to me; I had not realized that a great city could be so refined, stately, and quiet. I wondered if Mary and I might not sometime invest our hypothetic double-eagles on the Potomac instead of on the Nile!

Down the Atlantic seaboard I sped on a night train, getting out at Wilmington in the warm splendor of an Indian summer day, the horizon hazy, the sky cloudless. It was nine in the morning, and I expected to see the bustle of a good-sized town. I saw only scattered persons, all men, walking about the streets. Some had rifles or shotguns on their shoulders, some pistols at their belts. I did not see one colored man. Clearly the whites meant business and were in control.

Issuing from the station, I came face to face with a good-looking man of some fifty years. He was armed with a rifle. He eyed me sharply but not unpleasantly and said "Good morning." I stopped, set down my bag, and we had a brief talk. I told him I was a *Chicago Record* correspondent and was assigned to investigate the trouble in Wilmington. Would he kindly tell me something about it?

"It's very simple, if very painful," he said. "In Wilmington we have 11,000 white people and 14,000 negroes. See what that means in the ordinary course of things? It means negro-rule in this town: a negro mayor, council, school authority, police administration, and all the rest of it. Negro-rule is intolerable. It's the rule of shiftlessness, indigence, insolence, ignorance, brutality, and everything else repugnant to decency and civilization."

"And you purpose to end it?"

The man stroked the butt of his gun.

"Look up the street and around you," he said. "See any colored men? See any white men unarmed? See a single business house open? Wilmington far better were burned to the ground than that the negroes should rule here."

"Will the negroes not fight?"

The man's smile was sad, I thought, rather than cruel.

"Do you have any idea," he inquired, "what was happening here when the whites revolted?"

I shook my head; said I had been in the woods of northern Minnesota and had seen no newspapers.

"Negroes had begun to crowd white men, and white women and children, off these sidewalks. You ask if they will fight. My reply is that they will not. They have seen the white man in the mood certain to be created in him wherever he meets the conditions we now face. It's a mood no negro ever has liked or ever will like. The period of the white man's humiliation is at an end in Wilmington."

"Are the white people united in the matter?"

That question brought a hearty laugh out of the witness.

"I see you *are* from the North," he said.

"I'm told you already have had some rioting," I remarked.

"Yes, sir; we've had some."

"Are you likely to have more?"

"I think not, but one can't tell. Everything is contingent on the behavior of the negroes. If they accept the fact that white men, not colored, are to run this community there'll be no further violence."

"May I quote you in my dispatches?"

"I've no objection. I've told you only what all our citizens will tell you. I doubt if any sensible negro in Wilmington would give you a different version of the situation. Their views of the rights and the wrongs of the case they have of course, but they know as well as we what is going to happen."

"Should you mind giving me your name?" I asked.

"Just say a minister of the gospel said to you what I've said," was the answer.

A minister of the gospel patrolling the streets, a rifle on his shoulder, looking for recalcitrant negroes! One needed, as I thought, no further evidence of the intensity and the depth of the feeling of white Wilmington against their more numerous colored fellow-townsmen. Over my consciousness came that sensation of hopelessness which I felt more than a quarter of a century later as I bored into Japano-Caucasian relations in British Columbia and on the West Coast of the United States: the realization that where such racial contrasts meet, ordinary moral conceptions must yield to physical superiority. One cannot argue with destiny!

Bidding the militant clergyman good-by, I walked a short way up the street to a hotel and was escorted to a room overlooking the main thoroughfare of Wilmington. Without loss of an unnecessary moment, I began my systematic inquiries. I talked with J. R. Kenly, general manager of the Atlantic Coast Line; George Rountree, lawyer, member of the state legislature; Dr. Kingsbury, editor of the *Messenger;* William H. Bernard, editor of the *Star;* W. D. McCoy, lawyer; High McRae of the Wilmington cotton mills, and many other white men. To a man they spoke in the temper and with the voice of the minister of the gospel. The negro must submit or go!

As the day wore on there was desultory shooting, and street-cars were stoned, but I heard of no casualties. The state militia had arrived and were quartered in the armory. I went thither—a place of considerable uproar—and interviewed the ranking officer, a blunt but civil fellow of middle age, popping with vigor. I asked him what he intended to do with his soldiers if rioting broke out on a large scale.

"I intend," he said with great good humor, "to lead them out to shoot niggers."

"But," I observed, "in that case will not Uncle Sam send regulars to Wilmington?"

"Possibly."

"And then?" I queried.

"Oh, if the regulars come Wilmington will quiet down till they go away. They can't stay always, and when they go we'll be right back where we were. North Carolina has been a niggers' heaven long enough."

After dinner that night I wandered out into the streets for a general look round. I came upon a small park and a large crowd of white men. Men were standing on the park benches, and hundreds of boys were perched in the trees. At the center of the throng a huge gasoline flambeau spluttered and flamed, and beneath it I saw the white head and the ruddy face of an old man. He was speaking and gesticulating with great vehemence. I asked a man next to me who the speaker was.

"That's Colonel Waddell,"[2] he replied, giving me an inquisitive glance.

"A Wilmington man?"

"Yes, sir. He's an ex-Congressman."

Working my way discreetly through the crowd, I finally reached a point where I could hear what Colonel Waddell was saying. His first words audible to me were these:

"Our elections are coming on. We will not be swamped and ruined by a black tide. Do you think such a calamity mythical? I tell you it is not. We fight or we go under. Negroes are pouring in here from the South. They are registering illegally. They come to make common cause with the blacks here. Will you stand it: *Will* you?"

2. Alfred Moore Waddell was a white supremacist leader who was instrumental in the Wilmington race riot of 1898. Waddell had fought for the Confederacy as a lieutenant colonel in the Civil War. He was North Carolina's Democratic representative to Congress from 1871 to 1877.

Right hand high above his head, Colonel Waddell paused while a thunderous "No" rolled over him.

And then he said:

"I have a friendly word for the black men in Wilmington and their brethren on the way to this town. I remind them that this is an historical port of entry. I remind them that through it, mingling green water with the Atlantic blue, flows the Cape Fear River. I remind them that white men built Wilmington, and I tell them that white men will rule it. I tell them more. If they dare dispute this dictum, this inexorable principle of our lives, we will dam the current of Cape Fear River with black carcasses."

Again the crowd thundered its approval.

Colonel Waddell finished thus:

"Now remember we are not a crazy mob. We are not out for fury for fury's sake. We are sane citizens under a social obligation we cannot evade. Go quietly to your homes. Molest no peaceful negro. Touch no colored man's property. Leave the fate of Wilmington to your leaders, upon whose conscience it rests sacredly."

I certainly had the white man's broad point of view and knew the impetuosity, not to say ferocity, with which he stated it. His condemnation of the negro was all-sweeping: out of place, anything but an artisan or farmer or laborer, the negro was a social disaster, and as even these he was a man whom the South would lose with limitless rejoicing. He was a monstrous clog on the wheels of progress. His defects could not be corrected. White men had erected a model village for him in a pretty place outside Wilmington, and he was only a little time in making of it a "loathsome piggery." He had no business ability, no property to speak of, and paid no taxes.

"Let those without knowledge hold their tongues!" admonished Oliver H. Dockery,[3] candidate for Congress, referring to "self-holy patter up North." He added the pregnant observation (its pregnancy struck me with full force only long afterward when I had some intercourse with *a priori* statesmen) that "no fool can be guilty of greater folly than a daring idealist who doesn't *know*." Mr. Dockery declared with every indication of sincerity: "White men will win this fight for a white South or the negro ultimately will teach the North why the hardware men of Wilmington today have no more firearms to sell."

---

3. Oliver H. Dockery was a political leader in North Carolina who served the Confederacy for a brief time during the Civil War. He withdrew and became an outspoken Unionist. After the war, he served as Republican representative to Congress from 1868 to 1871.

That was true about the firearms, as I learned by personal investigation. I learned also that from the beginning of the crisis no negro had been able to buy a weapon of any kind: the principle of white supremacy had stopped him at the ironmonger's door. Firearms in considerable quantities had been smuggled into Wilmington at night by the colored men (or such was the story), but no black man dared to appear armed in the streets. That act would have meant instant suicide.

Not a chance for the negro vote in the forthcoming elections: not the *shadow* of a chance. Intimidation would be used remorselessly to frighten the negroes from the polls. The whole aspect of the situation would say to the black man: "Try to vote, and the guns will speak!" Negro registration had been "messed up." Jim Jones, colored, when he went to vote (if he did go), would find "Sam" Jones on the register but no "Jim." A white registrar had seen to that, and Jim was shut out.

And the white men were prepared to play hide-and-seek with the ballot-boxes, of which under the law there were eight, bearing the names of the candidates. Most of these basic symbols of our "democracy" (concerning which, compared with other forms of government, we love to tuft ourselves with ostrich plumes) were old tobacco-boxes and easily could be shifted in such a way as to invalidate objectionable ballots. These boxes, moreover, "accidentally" could be knocked topsy-turvy and their contents scattered beyond the possibility of identification. One white man, a fellow-professional of mine, told me frankly he himself had voted three hundred ballots in a past election "in the cause of civilized government." And he continued:

"Our law requires a would-be voter to interpret a section of the United States Constitution. This great document of course has easy sections and hard ones. Need I say to you that whites get the easy ones and blacks the hard ones? Never yet have I seen a nigger able to interpret the Constitutional language we read to him." And this above-board journalist had not the slightest doubt that the white man's medicine was excellent for the black man's system: disinfected political society of "ignorance and shame."

Over all his doings affecting the negro the white man, quite honestly I am convinced, spread the soft garment of assumed benevolence. The negro was the political and economic ward of the white man. All the blessings of good government must descend from the whites to the blacks, and the whites must engineer and sustain all industrial and business activity which saved whites and blacks alike from starvation. The white man was right, God was on his side, and *one* on God's side was a majority.

That is how the Caucasian argument ran, and it ran (as we have seen) like a stream of fire.

I would obey Mr. Dennis's instructions; I would be impartial.

What had the colored men to say?

I heard of a negro by the name of J. E. Taylor. He was deputy customs collector of the port of Wilmington, and I was told he was a "high-class man and the smartest nigger in town." He received me at the customs office and listened half-incredulously to my statement of what I wanted: a full exposition of the negro's point of view respecting the racial trouble in Wilmington. I can see his round, smooth face smiling yet: a face attached to a large head set squarely on good shoulders above a portly body. I judged Mr. Taylor to be forty.

"We colored men," he began, "are not accustomed to sympathetic interest in our point of view. We generally meet the assumption that we have no point of view. You have heard the white man's case?"

"Yes," I said.

"Well then you can arrive at our case roughly by inference. That we do not agree entirely, or even approximately, with the white man is established by the fighting. The white man dismisses us as wholly unfit for any place in politics, says we pay no taxes, have no property, are ignorant and lazy, are exclusively a social liability. Should you mind going with me in my buggy for a ride about town? I can show you some things pertinent to this case."

We spent a whole day riding in Mr. Taylor's buggy from one place to another, stopping to look at stores, churches (Presbyterian, Episcopal, Baptist, Methodist), homes, and lodge property owned by the colored population. Only the Congregational Church had been built with Northern money. As to politics, Mr. Taylor said: "The white man does not offer us politics; he offers us war." Negro politics, so far as it had been applied in Wilmington, Mr. Taylor regarded as quite as good as the white man's. "That is not to claim perfection for negro politics here," he qualified jovially.

"The taxes we pay," he went on, "are of course far less than the taxes paid by the white man. We pay on $400,000.00, the white man on $5,500,000.00. But the negro is notoriously poor; he labors for little; the white man gets the wealth. As for the poll-tax of $6.65 a year, everybody white and black dodges it if possible. They say we are ignorant and lazy. Well, a lot of men of all colors, I suppose, are ignorant and lazy. Certainly the whites about here have their dolts and drones, and I question whether we are very much worse by fair comparison.

"Keep this fact steadily in mind," continued the calm but earnest Mr. Taylor. "At the bottom of all Southern prosperity and comfort, all Southern pride of possession and place, is the black man's labor in the forests and fields and along these shores. And black women do the overwhelming bulk of the work of the homes, some getting $1 a week for their toil, none getting more than $4. I will show you colored men and women slaving in the rice paddies, often above their knees in mud and water, for from twenty-five to forty cents a day, in order that some white folk may disport themselves splendidly.

"Our people also do the work of the pine forests. They get, make ready for shipment, and load on ships the tar, turpentine, pitch, and rosin, admittedly packing more pounds hold-for-hold than any other stevedores in the world. They clip and box the trees, dip the turpentine in the orchards, and operate the stills. For these pine-tree products Wilmington used to be the world's first market, and its loss of that rating was not due to the negro; it was due to the devastation of the forests by improvident white men. Now the market is in Georgia and South Carolina.

"Initiative in industry here is the white man's duty because of his better endowment and the wealth which has accrued to him because of that endowment. He has fallen short in this primary duty, and his failure has hurt the negro as well as himself. Not inborn laziness but lack of work is the black man's fundamental trouble. He will work if he can get work. You should go down to the river and see the colored stevedores sitting on the wharves waiting for ships which now never come in."

"What about the negro's morality?" I inquired.

"It is as good, I think," answered Mr. Taylor, "as that of any other people similarly educated and conditioned. One does not expect high morality from low education and living conditions. We are appealing to the same aids to morality as the white man: religion and education and organized methods of mutual help. We spend our poor earnings on these things, and we know that as they lift us up a higher morality will come to us as certainly as the sun comes first to the loftier heights. Mark this: never have I known or heard of an educated negro in this state who committed a crime or was accused of one. Our race here has no education worth mentioning, no high school and only six grades. Our children would be as well off without any book-learning at all."

"Much drinking among the negroes?" I asked.

"Very little. Not five per cent of our 14,000 people, despite their meager incomes, are without good clothes, and such clothes for families do not go along with high frequency in liquor saloons."

"Are the Wilmington negroes emotional in their religion?" I queried.

"Some are," was the reply. "Our illiterate people must see golden streets, milk and honey, and angels with their wings outspread. They hear divine music inaudible to less unlettered folk. They are emotional. But our educated black people—women and men from such institutions as are provided by the American Missionary Association—are rational in religion. They understand the vital difference between emotionalism and moral principle. One hears of white laughter over our practice of having our church-goers walk up and place their contributions openly on a table. We have this usage of course because those who pay wish to be seen paying. But do not white people, if they pay, wish the fact to be generally known? Exceptions there are, as I well know, but these are not confined to one race."

"I am told," I said, "that even a little white blood in a man makes him superior to the pure-bred negro."

"Yes; one hears that story all the time," replied Mr. Taylor, "but it wants examination. I think the fact is pretty well known that mixed-bloods, whether in the lower or in the higher animals, are not preferred to pure-bloods. Mixed-bloods, I have heard, are likely to inherit the bad strains rather than the good from their divergent ancestors. In the Southern states of America the persons of white admixture historically have been privileged over their black fellows. Prior to the War between the States, the mixed-bloods were put in trades and the pure-blacks put out to grub and ditch. As a result, the end of the war saw the mixed-bloods well in the lead as artisans. They could read and write. Their children were privileged. No pure-black could read or write, and his children were doomed to the same drudgery as himself. Is it surprising then that more mixed-bloods than pure Africans forged to the front in American life?"

It was enough.

I had the two sides of the bitter debate.

Nightly since I arrived in Wilmington (the time was November, 1898), I had been wiring long stories to the *Chicago Record* disclosing the irreconcilability of the contending points of view and the conclusion that white superiority of moral, mental, and military strength inevitably would carry the day. On leaving Mr. Taylor, I went to my hotel for dinner, far from happy over a situation in which both sides had so much to say for themselves and only one could prevail: an imbroglio so often encountered in human affairs great and small.

Eating alone at a small table in the main dining-room, scores of other guests about me, I suddenly heard terrific firing in the street, accompanied by the rush and sould of galloping horses. Jostling with other diners, I gained a window and saw a column of mounted men in red shirts, two abreast, riding past at top speed and firing pistols into the air as they flew. I asked a man at my side who they were and what the firing meant. He said they were "the Red Shirts from the hills" and had poured into the town "to put the fear of God into the blacks." I realized it was a maneuver addressed to election day. Returning to my table, I observed a red-headed man of giant stature coming toward me. His short hair stood straight up, and his face was a mass of freckles. Without ceremony he sat down by my side and gazed at me.

"You," he said very quietly, "are what we call a 'white nigger.' You've ridden around this town with a nigger. You're a friend of niggers. I just stepped over to tell you to leave Wilmington and stay away. Take the first train."

Before I could muster words to answer, the man had risen and walked off. I knew his warning must be taken absolutely at face value. Besides, my work in Wilmington really was finished. I had the arguments; anything else I could leave to the Associated Press. I left Wilmington on an early train the next morning, witnessing a terrible scene at the railway station, where a vast, milling mob sought to string up a negro to a cross-beam. Just as the hemp tightened about his neck, I saw a white man spring forward and cut the rope. I saw no more. And with great difficulty forged a way through the crowd to the train.

11. Dug It Out of Barrel Houses

Unflagging devotion to one's job always seemed to me good policy, no matter how slim might be the appreciation or the pay: it was something intrinsically due to the individual. Not all my colleagues on the *Chicago Record* shared my opinion in this respect.

"Do your assignment as well as you can and let it go at that. Don't mooch about looking for trouble. Come over to the Whitechapel Club[1] and drink wine with us out of human skulls."

That was their advice.

Capital fellows they were, but I could not convince myself of their prescience.

On a day off I was standing on the southeast corner of Madison and Wells Streets when I saw a short, heavy, shrewd-visaged man step inside the tall office building there and get into the elevator. I knew him. I had seen him at the Criminal Court building on the North Side quietly counseling State Attorney Charles S. Deneen (later United States Senator Deneen) in a murder case. He was Judge Wing, aged about 50, and was noted for the astonishing keenness of his facial expression.

I was interested in him. Everyone who saw him, I think, was interested in him. He was by no means a lime-lighter, however; anything but that. A lawyer

---

1. The Whitechapel Club was a professional club founded by Chicago newspapermen in 1889. Known for its literary members and bizarre decor (including a coffin-like table and several Indian skulls hung on the walls), the club folded after only five years due to debt. One scholar has argued that although the club was short lived, it was influential in professionalizing journalism in Chicago in the 1890s. See Lorenz, "The Whitechapel Club: Defining Chicago's Newspapermen in the 1890s."

esteemed especially by lawyers, and known to every member of the Chicago bar, he kept out of the papers and never appeared to have a case of his own in court. Civic idealists and reformers—men like the remarkable George E. Cole of the Municipal Voters' League[2]—admired Judge Wing immensely and profited much by his "serpentine sagacity." Yet his name never seemed to see the light in the arduous struggle to redeem Chicago from political blackguardism and rascality.

What sort of chap really was this Judge Wing?

I was on the mooch, as my colleagues would have said, "looking for trouble." Entering the hall of the office building, I examined the tenants' bulletinboard and learned that Judge Wing's rooms were on the sixth floor. I went up and sent my card in to him. He received me at once and desired to know if Mr. Lawson (publisher and editor-in-chief of the *Chicago Record*) had directed me to call upon him.

"No," I said, "I never have seen Mr. Lawson."

"Never have seen your boss?"

"No, sir; not yet. I've not been on the *Record* very long. I hope to see Mr. Lawson some day."

"Who sent you to me?"

"I just came."

"What do you want?"

"I'm a reporter, and reporters of course always are looking for good stories. I thought you might be able to give me one."

Deeply curious, and distinctly beguiled, was the look of that lawyer. He wished to know whence I had come, what my experience had been, and whither I was bound. I told him I was a Hoosier from the Raccoon Valley, had become somewhat of a newspaper veteran, and hoped I was on the way to heaven, though I was "not in a hurry." Thereupon Judge Wing got a ringing laugh out of something. I did not ask him what it was but surmised he felt Chicago, for a heaven-bound traveler, was a rum place to visit. Anyway he inquired:

---

2. When Chicago reformers chartered the Municipal Voters' League, they elected George Cole its leader. Cole, who owned a printing and stationery shop, had been involved in reform politics at the local level. His reform methods at the league were unconventional, including blackmail and publication of information that brought the league 987 libel suits (none went to trial). Cole's effective methods earned him the nickname "Buzz-saw" Cole. Lawson supported Cole, assigning several of his employees to work for the league while being paid by the *Daily News*. Lawson also personally gave more than $4,500 to the league. See Roberts, "The Municipal Voters' League and Chicago's Boodlers."

"Like Chicago?"

"Oh, yes," I said. "I think it's a great town."

Judge Wing became earnest.

"It *is* a great town," he declared. "It has all the essential elements of a great town. Its physical position is unmatched. Its people, the people who make it, have no superiors in the world. But our politics is filthier than the Augean stables ever were. Those stables, I believe, had not been cleaned for thirty years. Our Chicago and Illinois political stables *never* have been cleaned. It took Hercules and a river to tidy up for Augeas. I wish we had half-a-dozen boys like Hercules. If we had, we'd lend them the lake."

"Is the case as bad as that?" I asked.

"Worse!" snapped the Judge.

Before him lay a pile of foolscap paper with things written on it.

"Do you want a really big job?" he questioned, his sharp eyes raised to mine.

"I'd love it," I replied.

"Then I'll tell you what you do. Go over to the *Record* office and say to your editors that Judge Wing has a big story for the paper. Get that to Mr. Lawson preferably. Say I want you released from routine work to undertake an investigation requiring an indefinite time, possibly weeks or even months. Come back tomorrow and let me know what the *Record* heads say."

Was I excited!

It seemed as if "mooching about looking for trouble" really might be a better pastime for a reporter than drinking wine out of human skulls at the Whitechapel Club!

"Go to it!" ordered city editor Chamberlin, after a conference with managing editor Dennis.

Judge Wing thumped into his office the next morning to find me waiting for him "in full field-kit," so to speak. I was free. I was Judge Wing's man, heart and soul for that investigation, which I assumed was to be along the line of Hercules's service to Augeas. The foolscap paper was still on the Judge's desk as he sat down and motioned me to a chair near him.

"What did Mr. Lawson say?" he asked.

I explained that I had gone to my city editor, that he had conferred with Mr. Dennis, and that my instructions were to do whatever Judge Wing wished me to do. I said I did not know whether Mr. Lawson had been consulted or not.

"If not," remarked the Judge, "he doubtless will be. Now let us get on with this."

On the foolscap paper, as I immediately learned, was a long list of personal-injury damage suits against Charles T. Yerkes's[3] street railway lines.

"Look at them!" said the Judge. "Note anything peculiar about them?"

"Well," I replied, after some examination, "I note that Yerkes won all these suits. I note also that in every case the jury seems to have been hung."

"Precisely," said the Judge. "Yerkes wins every time, and every time the jury is hung by one or two men. Get what that means?"

"I don't know," I said.

"It means," asserted the Judge, with deliberation, "that Charles T. Yerkes's hirelings are bribing every jury in Cook County in the interests of his street railway lines."

A moment's silence, the Judge observing me narrowly.

"Do you believe it?" he demanded.

And before I could formulate a reply he went on:

"Of the correctness of my inference there can't be the faintest doubt. You know quite well that juries don't love street-car barons or barons of any other kind. Left to itself, any jury will find for the plaintiff, if at all possible, in such cases as these: cases of killed and mangled men, women, and children not spry enough to escape the wheels of street-cars. Wholesale bribery. That's what it is, and that's the strongest weapon in Yerkes's armory, whether he be dealing with juries or state legislators. He must be driven out of this city and this state, and *you* can do it."

"*I?*"

"Yes."

"Tell me how," I pleaded.

"I will tell you how. Take this list of cases to the courthouse and get the names of all these jurors, particularly the names of the men who stood out against their fellows for the street-car companies. Having the names, hunt up the pro-plaintiff jurors and question them carefully about the behavior of the men who hung the juries. Ask them for their opinion of the jury-hangers' motives. Caution them to treat your inquiries in strict confidence. When you have completed your investigation, so far as the pro-plaintiff jurors are con-

3. Charles T. Yerkes, a businessman in Chicago in the late 1800s, modernized the city's horsecar lines and made a considerable fortune for himself. He bribed state and local officials in an attempt to monopolize line operation. With the help of politicians, he acquired the public land he needed to make more money to build new lines. The politicians Yerkes bribed were voted out of office in 1899, and Yerkes himself left Chicago in 1901 for London. See Howard, *Illinois*.

cerned, try to find out where the most flagrant of the jury-hangers now are to be found and what they are doing. Then come back to me, and we'll lose no time in taking effective steps."

As I was leaving the Judge, he suddenly said:

"You know George Cole, don't you?"

"I've heard of him and seen him but do not know him," was my answer.

"Go over to his stationery store and see him. He knows all about my suspicions and has not a doubt of their validity. He's a great fellow, that ex-drummer-boy [Cole was a drummer-boy in the Civil War], and he's going to make a lot of people sick. He's the new chief of the Municipal Voters' League and the reformers' last-resort. Yerkes, Billy Lorimer, Hinky Dink Kenna, Johnny Powers, Little Mike Ryan, Foxy Ed Cullerton, and Bath-House John Coughlin[4] are amused highly over the choice of five-foot, black-goateed, chunky Cole as the spearhead of Chicago reform. All are whetting their knives for him. They think he's cheese. They'll find him granite. See him and say I want him to help you if he can."

Mr. Cole gave me a friendly, thoughtful reception.

"You're on a big job," he said. "I think you can make a success of it, but you will be compelled to work very hard and to go into many places no sensitive man would wish to visit. You can trust Chief of Police Schuettler (he's with us for a finish fight against the crooks), and he'll advise you about persons and conditions in the barrel-houses and other low-down joints of Chicago. Ask him for officers to go with you if you need them. He has six plain-clothes detectives whom he calls his 'night-flying squad.' They know Chicago from cover to cover, and they're not afraid of the devil."

"You think Judge Wing is right in his belief that Yerkes's men are bribing the juries in personal-injury cases?" I asked.

"Certainly he is. The hung juries establish the fact beyond reasonable doubt. The moral certainty is conclusive. But moral certainty is not proof. We want proof. One great advantage you will have in your investigation: the crooks, in office and out, the blackguards and the 'gentlemen' alike, have utter contempt for reformers, for 'church people,' as they dub us. Even the anti-graft newspapers only make them smile. Take our governor, John Tanner, for instance: he's been mocking at the 'power of the Press' all his political life.

4. All were players in corrupt Illinois politics. William Lorimer was particularly infamous for paying off Illinois state senators to elect him to the U.S. Congress. For more on corruption in Illinois, see Howard, *Illinois*.

He'd take you into his office, admit that he was a rascal, and ask you what the *Record* intended to do about it. As for Yerkes, he dines with the gods, shines in 'society,' lets his understrappers do his dirty work, and treats the newspapers with mute disdain. The dominion of scoundrelism and depravity in Chicago and Illinois politics is virtually absolute."

"By 'great advantage' on the side of the proposed inquiry," I remarked, "you mean that no one among the criminals will take any notice of us."

"Exactly. Even if you went straight to them, and announced your purpose to 'get' them, they'd rock with laughter, ask you to have a drink, and pass on."

"It's a challenge surely," I said.

Mr. Cole pulled his goatee.

"Now," I had to say by way of caveat, "I'm keen to do all I can in this matter. I don't mind brothels or opium-dens or barrel-houses. I can be a rat with the worst of them, and I don't think anyone will hurt me. I've done a heap of police work and seen plenty of bad men. But after all I'm a reporter and forced to think about myself some. I must ask that no one be told of what I'm trying to do and that in the end I shall have my beat if I get one."

Mr. Cole chuckled.

"Trust us, my boy," he said.

And I was off.

Musty and dusty and of all-round ill-suggestion were the court records through which I had to mole my way in search of jurors' names. Occasionally a clerk or bailiff or other officer stopped to look at me and show in his face that he wondered just what form of dementia possessed me. Once a fat greaser in a slouch-hat and stinking with bad cigars rubbed against me and smirked.

"Reporter, ain't y'?" he muttered.

I asked him what my business had to do with him.

"Nothin'," he answered. "But you're a reporter all right. I can tell 'em a block away."

And he shuffled.

"Great Scott!" I said to myself. "How I'd like to put a few bastards like him in jail!"

At the close of three weeks of the dreariest and the grubbiest work I ever had done in my life, I had all the names I wanted, the names of jurors who had argued and stuck it for verdicts against Yerkes and the names of the men who had been adamant for the magnate. Then I began fine-combing Chicago for the ex-jurors I desired to see. I found nearly all of them. I found the graves in which some of them were buried: just to be sure they were dead. Day and

night for weeks I was in and out of infamous places and places of respectability, dens of all sorts, little stores far-scattered in the city and in the suburbs.

And the tale from every man I saw was the same in substance: the jury-
hangers were silent, indifferent, sullen, obstinate, suspicious men. Nothing
whatever could be done with them. Refusing to talk, they would curl up and
go to sleep in their chairs or on the floor. Pro-plaintiff jurors (and they often
were as much as eleven to one) might reason and plead for damages through
days and nights without other result than their own fatigue and disgust and
the final call of the judge for the jury's dismissal.

"Do you think the hangers were bribed?"

That was my ever-reiterated question.

Many times the answer was a shrug and a laugh. Now and again it was
something like this:

"Looks like it, doesn't it?"

Several times during those wearisome weeks I had reported progress to
Judge Wing, and he had said:

"Keep at it! Fine! Keep at it!"

I also regularly had reported to city editor Chamberlin and received equal
encouragement from him.

Only a few times had I gone to Chief of Police Schuettler for the assistance of his "night-flying squad," six daredevils of stocky build and exhaustive
knowledge of Chicago-land submerged. We did the slummy underworld, the
"Red Light" district, "The Row" (a train of systematized and graduated deprav-
ities on show for a price), the opium-smoking "parlors," and gambling-dens
of every grade, our objective in it all the discovery of some ex-juror whom
I wished to interview or to locate for the information of Judge Wing at the
proper time. These redolent journeys were always at night, and I went home
at daybreak, dead-beat but sufficiently myself to be grateful to Schuettler and
his "night-flying squad."

How much decent Chicago owed to those sleepless, unresting, danger-
scorning men it never can know! Without fail ever after, when I saw dark,
silent homes, their occupants safely sleeping abed, I also saw my friends of
the squad probing here, there, and everywhere in the nests of crime actual and
potential. Not very long after all this was over, and my wife and I lived in a flat
in Bedford Court Mansions, Bloomsbury, London, we had the happiness of
entertaining Chief Schuettler at dinner and of seeing the mammoth man eat
nearly two whole chickens while he talked of Chicago and praised his "night-
flying squad."

"Unique men," he said. "Absolutely unique. Did the finest police work in America."

And we believed him.

The day came when I was ready for my final report to Judge Wing. Everything was typed out in orderly fashion for him, names, addresses, descriptions, conversations, impressions. The Judge buried himself in that voluminous report for the best part of an hour before saying a word or looking at me. Concentration, reflection, the patient weighing of this and that, anger on the point of bursting into flame, they were that lawyer. At last he said to me, his eyes half joy and half fire:

"You've done it."

"Done what, Judge Wing?"

"You've driven Yerkes out of this city and this state."

I waited for light.

"All the rest is detail," said the Judge. "Yerkes may be, will be, with us for some time yet, but this document writes 'Finis' to his career here. Leave it with me. I'll go at once with it to Charlie Deneen [state attorney], and you'll hear from us shortly. Please tell your editors what I have said."

"I will," I replied. "But—"

"But what?" asked the Judge.

"There are eight morning newspapers in Chicago," I said, "and seven of them are our competitors. This story (if it be a story) is mine. Mr. Cole assured me my reportorial rights in the matter would be respected. Will you kindly make sure of that with Deneen?"

Judge Wing shook my hand firmly.

"Don't worry," he said.

Several days passed, I reporting regularly to my city editor and impatiently marking time. One afternoon, as I made my usual appearance in Mr. Chamberlin's office, he handed me a note from the telephone operator. It was a message from Judge Wing asking me to call upon him as soon as I could. In less than ten minutes' time (the Judge's rooms were just across Madison Street from the *Record* office) I was there. He said:

"The fun's due tonight. I assume your full story of your inquiries and observations is in the hands of your editors."

"That's right," I answered.

"Good. All you'll have to write tonight will be the account of the arrests and what happens."

"The arrests?"

"Yes. Deneen's detectives go out at nightfall to arrest nine of the most impudent of the jury-hangers. They'll be taken to the cells in the Criminal Court
building. You be there early, say by 9 o'clock."

One by one those suspected men were brought in and locked up in the
dungeon-like bowels of that sinister old structure where the state attorney
(sometimes honestly, I believe) engaged his energies in support of his oath of
office. One of Deneen's assistants permitted me to see the prisoners as they
were led to their cells in different parts of the building, the jailers contriving to
make an ungodly din with their clashing keys and clanging doors, a proceed-
ing designed to terrify and confuse the supposed bribe-takers.

In Deneen's large office was enacted a scene charged with the essence of
great drama. I sat in an obscure corner and witnessed it all. Deneen occupied a high-backed chair at his desk on a platform at the upper end of the
room opposite the entrance. On his right, crouching low in a seat, was Judge
Wing, uncannily serpentine in mien. Hard below them were two male stenographers with notebooks and pencils at a table. Not far from me sat the
sawed-off, chunky man with the black goatee, Mr. Cole of the Municipal Voters' League. Here and there about the room were ranged a number of young
lawyers attached to the state attorney's office. Wall and overhead lights bathed
the setting in a mellow flood.

Such were the circumstances in which Charles T. Yerkes met his Waterloo
as a jury-fixer-by-proxy on behalf of the revenues of his street railway companies in Chicago and Cook County, Illinois. The technique of the lawyers
was that of bunk and bullying. Each suspect was put on the spot in that stagy
room and commanded to *confess everything as his fellow-criminals had done.*
Of course, in the case of the first man put on the rack, there had been no confession, but so overwhelming were the facts as poured out to him—the facts
attending the briberies—that he collapsed and revealed all the particulars of
the way in which the crimes were accomplished.

The rest was easy. Confession followed confession as the prisoners came
and went. No conceivable defense could have a dog's chance. All the culprits
back in their cells, Deneen, Wing, Cole, and I repaired to the state attorney's
private office. Wing and Cole shook hands with us and said "Good night,"
leaving Deneen and me alone. I telephoned to the *Record,* and Mr. Dennis
chanced to answer. It was nearly midnight. The managing editor knew big
things were moving. I asked him if he please would send a man for my copy.

"Whom do you want?" he inquired.

"You might send Freddie Wile if he's there," I replied. (Frederic William Wile, who then was a cub reporter but who subsequently won distinction as a foreign correspondent and later settled down in Washington as chief of a syndicate of his own.) Freddie limped. One always could tell his walk. The big lumberly elevator in the Criminal Court building long since had ceased to run. My lead finished, I waited and watched at the top of the shaft in a half-light. I heard Freddie's limp on the stone steps far below. Then I caught sight of him winding his toilsome way up.

"Freddie," I said, "take this stuff to Mr. Dennis. Mum's the word. Rather than give it up, *die!*"

Freddie guffawed and turned back down the steps.

Returning to Deneen (whom I had no intention of leaving prematurely), I found what I rather had feared: he was increasingly on pins and needles. The politician in him was fermenting. I took a chair between him and the telephone. I knew he was thinking of what probably would happen to him if he allowed the *Record* to administer a horrible news-drubbing to the other morning papers, especially the *Tribune,* in a matter in which the state attorney was the chief official actor.

"Bell," he said eventually, "this thing's going to hurt me badly, this scoop of yours. I ought to tip the other papers."

"No!" I said. "It's my story. Or the *Record*'s. We've spent months and money and taken risks to get the dope. The state attorney's office had all the facts brought to it on a gold platter. You can say that to our competitors, and they'll know they haven't a leg to stand on in badgering you. Both Judge Wing and Mr. Cole promised me that if I got the facts I should have the beat."

Deneen was glum.

If I ever was desperate in my life, I was desperate that night. And I must have looked it. Constantly apprehensive that the attorney would try to reach the telephone, I was determined he should not succeed. *I could not afford such a calamity.* Just what I should do I did not know, but I knew I should do every-thing in my power. And Deneen undoubtedly saw that. The night wore on, the hours spoke to us out of a steeple, and the presses began to rumble throughout Chicago.

"You're right, Bell," acknowledged Deneen. "I'll say nothing. We'll go home."

I kept awake long enough to tell my wife. As she roused me from sleep in mid-morning, she laid the *Tribune* and the *Record* in front of me. First-page banners across the *Record*'s strange-looking face (it was a quiet paper) told the

12. I See "Democracy" in Action

It was a smelly little hole, that negro lawyer's office, but the well-set-up black man who sat at the only desk in the room (a faded and rickety piece of furniture) was an uncommonly prepossessing fellow, strong, youthful, serious, and visibly intelligent. Johnson was his name, and he was a representative in the state legislature at Springfield, Illinois, where he had got himself disliked by the boodlers.

Johnson was refractory. He did not know his way about at Springfield. He entertained absurd notions about the reality and the sacredness of democracy; he habitually talked of its costliness as a measure of its worth to humanity; the flag, the Stars and Stripes, was dirt to Johnson unless it meant liberty and the Kingdom of God. And it meant nothing of the sort, Johnson claimed, at Springfield.

Accidentally one night, mooching about again for anything which might interest an enterprising and fearless newspaper, I came upon a mass meeting of colored men off Milwaukee Avenue, Chicago, and stopped at the sound of the name "Yerkes." It fell from the lips of the black man who was addressing the assemblage, and the man was Johnson. I had heard of him and knew something of his reputation.

The next day I called at his office.

"A *Record* man," he said on looking at my card. "What can I do for you?"

"I heard some of your speech last night," I said.

"*Did* you?"

He paused inquiringly.

"Yes. You were making some startling statements. You put it flatly that we have no such thing as representative government in Illinois. You declared that politically our citizens are 'humbugged incessantly' and that we are 'helpless in the grip of bosses, ringsters, and boodlers.' Was there some rhetorical license in your bolder flights?"

"None whatever," he averred. "Candidly, I'm a little surprised at your question. I should've thought a *Record* man would've been wise to what is going on. Did your paper learn nothing about Yerkes except that he was bribing the juries of Cook County? What is your Springfield man doing? Does he leave you in ignorance of the 'gaieties' of the capital? Take my advice: don't depend on me; send a man to size up Springfield and spread his inquiries over the state."

Later that day I was talking to Mr. Chamberlin. I reported to him on Johnson and said I felt in my bones the legislator was both well-informed and right. I suggested that I be commissioned to go into the matter thoroughly, as Johnson had recommended. Mr. Chamberlin, in view of what we had achieved, was inclined to endorse my suggestion. He would take the question up at once with Mr. Dennis and Mr. Lawson.

He did.

Within twenty-four hours I had packed for a considerable absence and journey and was on my way to Springfield. Our Chicago Caesar of Traction was in my mind of course: the ruddy, plump, white-mustached, magisterial, urbane, loftily-contemptuous Yerkes, who could "smile and smile and be a villain," though not one without an apology (as we shall see in time).

Down-state looked good to Yerkes. He wanted to "buy up" down there, and he had the skillful and energetic benevolence of Governor John R. Tanner on his side. All Yerkes had to do to get what he wanted at Springfield was to give Tanner what *he* wanted. Springfield had become easier than Chicago. Yerkes would march to his goal of franchise-monopoly through the state legislature.

My job here is to tell how Yerkes did it.

Summarily, he did it with cold cash and moral terrorism running concurrently. The facts I unearthed by unremitting importunity and labor extending through several months, and the entire story was published in the *Chicago Record*, with confirmatory names and documents. So air-tight in a legal sense was the detailed and lengthy exposé that no libel suit ever was instituted against the paper nor so much as threatened. We had the gigantic boodling enterprise spiked down and clinched, and Governor Tanner survived the crushing disclosures only a few days, dying in the Governor's Mansion with the knowledge that his long career of immunity, and of mockery at reform, was closed.

All sorts and conditions of men I saw during that investigation: lawyers, doctors, clergymen, merchants, farmers, industrial laborers. I pitched my tent in city and in country. I pressed my questions upon legislators and ex-legislators, good men and bad, wide-awake women, waiting sometimes for days on days and continually returning to the attack. Not a few persons in the know I found frozen like rock. They could not be thawed. But scores of men and women of unimpeachable trustworthiness, suffering a kind of moral nausea from what had been done, fell in with my urgency that patriotism and even public safety were crying for the truth.

"Did it with cold cash." That was simple, that part of the scheme of purchase; it was just like buying bullocks at the Chicago Stock Yards, only the required votes—the votes looking to a fifty-year exclusive possession of the streets of the lake-side metropolis—cost more than bullocks: they fetched anything from $300.00 to $25,000.00. But the "moral terrorism" feature of the business was a more complicated, and a more picturesque, performance.

A member of the House or the Senate would receive a charmingly-worded note inviting him to call "to meet some friends" at a stated hour in a hotel room. He would go and find that the "friends" consisted of two men and that they wished him to vote for a particular measure. He would say "No" or "Yes" according to his disposition concerning the proposition, the clear intimation being that there was "money in it." If he said "No," and became angry and menacing, he would be reminded that he was one against two and might be butting his way toward trouble.

"We might be forced," one of the proponents would say, "to expose you as a bribe-seeker who turned rough because you could not get the figure you demanded."

That settled it. The member woke up. He saw he was caught in the cogs of the "system" and would better at least bide his time. His day *might* come; it manifestly was not now.

This snaky and bullying device was used on members whose possible reaction to bribery proposals was uncertain: men who were not seemingly "fanatically scrupulous" and yet who conjecturably would have no ears when Ali Baba cried, *"Open, sesame!"* With law-makers who were unmistakably scrupulous, and even dangerously hostile, in relation to the whole scandal of bribery in public life, another procedure, vastly more artful and insidious, was employed. Here entered pretty and appealing coquettes. They diligently flirted with the men whose votes were needed by the street railway interests. They went about it slowly. They gave themselves time to "fall in love." They gave their attractions time to take effect on their victims, generally married men with families.

And finally a resolute agent of the "system" came upon the scene. He imparted the news that he knew everything. The case was bad from the point of view of the men who had "skidded." Their reputation for respectability was an asset they could not play with, could not afford to have clouded in the slightest way. Their families must not be forgotten. Constituencies in America were almost morbidly resentful of illicit love-making on the part of their public men. Such was the agent's argument, and the erring solons wilted under it.

What could be done?

Not much trouble about that.

The "system" was powerful. The agent knew his stuff. The amorous girls could go just so far, no farther. The agent knew them, and they knew him. All he had to do was to pipe his tune, and they would dance. All the trapped statesmen had to do was to vote for the bills the "interests" wanted. And they did.

Johnson had asserted that representative government in Illinois was dead. It was no exaggeration. Indubitably, government both in Chicago and in the state had been filched from the people. It was in the hands of a few men, financiers and corrupt politicians, a government by men of money and men to whom money made an all-powerful appeal. Such was "democracy" in Illinois in those days. At its apex when my investigations were made (1899) were the highly-perfumed trio, Charles Yerkes, Billy Lorimer, and Governor Tanner.

Some of my professional brethren I found on the payroll of the paymasters. Is it any wonder blindness fell upon them and its black-out on the Press?

The *Chicago Record* gave the facts to the world in clear language and clear type, leaving the "slandered" to take such action against a highly-responsible newspaper as might sit smiling to their souls. They took no action whatever.

Secretary of State Rose (a man as able and brave as he was clean) told me a lot and put many incriminating papers before me. He himself had been caught in the thieving vortex, but only by operation of law. The legislators had the privilege under the law of requisitioning the secretary of state for "supplies" presumably necessary in their official work: letter-heads and envelopes, paper of various kinds, fountain-pens, lead-pencils, typewriters. Mr. Rose found the requisitions colossal. They appalled him. Members, for example, were sending to their political friends back home *thousands of fountain-pens costing $8 apiece.*

These thefts crept up on Mr. Rose by degrees.

They grew until he revolted and cut them to the bone on penalty of resignation and remorseless divulgement.

Governor Tanner was no paper-shell pecan when it came to cracking him. He was hard. He was slippery. His evasive dexterity was the product of long and alert practice. He had gone scot-free for such a time that he had no fear of his enemies. He hated newspapers. They were after him perpetually so far as their publishers and editors were concerned. (Some of these chiefs had correspondents in Springfield, as I have said, who were among the grafters, but they did not know it.)

When I first arrived in Tanner's town, I was tired in body and in mind; sordidness, indifference to every sentiment of honor, unblushing and successful scoundrelism honeycombing public life had got into me. So my first act on arriving was to get some tackle and bait and go fishing in the blithe and tuneful stream. I met a man on its shore. He too was fishing, and we had a talk. He once had been in the State Senate. His honesty seemed to me self-evident. I told him what I was doing, and he said simply:

"See that tallest building yonder?"

I saw it.

"You will find a doctor at the top of it. He's the only doctor there. Lay your cards before him."

I did it the next morning, and the doctor instantly—with strangely keen and perceptible curiosity—admitted me to his consultation room. He was thin and sharp-cornered and almost wild-eyed. His blond hair was long and hung in disorder. I never before had seen an expression so brightly and nervously eager. The fisherman had told me the doctor was a mental specialist and used to be chief consultant at one of the state asylums. He himself struck me as not far from the border-line of insanity, though his mastery of his thinking apparatus was apparently perfect.

I did as the fisherman had instructed: laid my cards before him. He listened with deepening gravity, never taking his eyes off me. When I had finished, he hesitated a few moments and then spoke in an oddly brittle voice.

"This is confidential?"

"Strictly," I answered.

The doctor swung in his chair and pointed to a filing-case against the wall behind him.

"If you had in your possession the papers there," he said, "you could ruin the most sinister man in Illinois. He is the well-head of corruption in this state. He has enriched, and still is enriching, himself and his friends; and he has re-

duced representative government among us to an infamous sham. Hanging is
what he deserves."

"Then," I remarked, "let us hang him!"

"How long shall you be here?" asked the doctor.

I replied that I was "in the war for the duration," and he asked me to call
upon him again at the same hour the following day. Meanwhile, I looked up
my friend of the trout stream and learned a good deal about the doctor. He
was an ex–Tanner man and had resigned his public job after a severe set-to
with the Governor. Ever since, the doctor had been "like a smouldering fire,"
dropping many hints to his confidants but saying nothing categoric. Almost
on the moment of seeing him the next day, I said:

"May I ask if your papers relate to Tanner?"

"Yes," he came back like a shot, as if to inquire, "What of it?"

I took the floor, as it were, for the cause in which my feelings no less than
my material interests were enlisted. I argued for a grand political house-cleaning in Illinois. I declared that no citizen of the state, knowing half the facts,
could be silent and inactive and yet hold up his head. To the last mother's son
and daughter of us, we were bogged in a stinking mire of dishonor, and life on
such terms was intolerable. At last, noting that I had made a real impression
on my highly-sensitive auditor, I made bold to end on this peak:

"Frankly, Doctor, if I had such papers as you say you have, I could not keep
them hidden and sleep with my conscience. I should deem myself recreant to
every duty individual and social. Will you not put the papers in our hands—
the hands of *The Record*—and help us to strike a blow for the good name and
the whole welfare of Illinois?"

A slight quiver affected that none-too-robust frame, and the doctor pressed
his hands hard against his eyes. At last he sighed, got up, and walked to a window. For some time he stood looking out upon the winding trout stream.
Then he turned back to me and said:

"Can you come again tomorrow?"

I returned the next day. The doctor was calm in manner. He shook hands
with me without speaking. Then he opened the filing-case and drew forth four
letters on large letter-heads. He handed them to me.

"Use them as you like," he said. "They tell their own story. I've had them long
enough. They're coals of fire to me. My wife and I shall be much happier now."

Deeply touched, I thanked the doctor as well as I could and left him with
a hard hand-clasp, never to see or hear from him again. I felt my work down-
state was done and hiked bag and baggage for Chicago and home, my trunk

half-bursting with notes and documents. Only a few days later the *Record* published one of the most consequential stories of its life. It was the story revealing Governor John R. Tanner's use of his office to make the institutions of Illinois, even insane asylums, conduits of the people's money into the coffers of the men who were prostituting the democracy of the state and polluting its public morals unforgivably. As the doctor said, those four letters, bearing the familiar signature of Tanner, told "their own story," and we published them *in facsimile* on the first page of the paper.

How they come back to me now!

Four whitish islands in a flood of black type, the doom of Tanner in script against the white!

It was a great day in the *Record* office, as all great scoop-days are to modern newspapers. Wires crackled with messages from the Chicago editors to their Springfield correspondents. "See Tanner! Tell him the *Record* has an awful story about him! Brands him as a crook!" Such were the editorial yells from the lakeside as dawn broke. Tanner was hauled out of bed and faced by such a semi-circle of newshawks as suggested presidential press conferences in Washington. The Governor was all nonchalance and good humor.

"Ah?" he ejaculated. "The *Record* says I'm a crook? How novel! Has the *Record* and has the Press in general not been calling me a crook for years? That's what it all has meant. When was Victor Lawson not trying to hound me into the penitentiary? It's the bunk, boys. Go back to bed!"

But in the course of a few hours the *Record* was spread before the Governor. He stared at those damning letters and grew white. He needed no one to tell him what they signified for the lordly "John R." When he next left the Governor's Mansion (very shortly afterward), he was veritably negative to earthly influences whether of enticement or of trouble. Illinois lay behind him. One cannot say, I presume, that the state's heritage from his peculiar genius was wholly bad. His rascalities, let us hope, had defined a milestone on the road of the community's progress out of the dark jungle of Boodledom.

13. An Epochal Idea Oddly Born

There he stood, the man I wanted to see; I did not know him, but I had no doubt of his identity. He was dressed in white, stocky, pale-yellow, self-absorbed, busy with parcels. His eyes and hair were very black, and he had a pigtail. I was standing outside his window in South State Street, Chicago, and the mid-afternoon traffic of the great thoroughfare was at full-tide. My man was Chinese: that type which transudes satisfied introspection. He was doing a laundryman's job but looked as if he belonged in the regalia of a mandarin with a ruby at the apex of his hat.

I went in and said, "Good afternoon."

He looked at me.

"You are Mr. Sam Moy?" I suggested.

"Yep."

"Have you time to talk with me a moment?"

"What about?"

I told him I was a *Record* reporter on the track of a story.

"A story?" echoed Mr. Moy. "I have no story."

And he bent his mind and fingers on the parcels.

"May I tell you a little more about myself?" I asked.

He raised his sharp eyes.

"I work on crime," I explained. "You have heard of the Public Health Service of Illinois?"

"Yep."

"*Know* anything about it?"

"Nope."

"We've heard that you've had certain relations with this service and learned something of its methods. You'll be safe in talking to us."

"Now, listen," said Mr. Moy somewhat tartly, "you're on a false scent. I know nothing about what you're after. I'm Chinese and let American matters alone. Take that as final and let's save time."

Surely this fellow did deserve that ruby. How did it happen that such a man was a shirt-juggler?

"Have you always been in this business?" I asked.

"Nope."

"What were you before?"

"Diplomat. Represented my government at the World's Fair. Fair came to an end, and I'd made bad mistakes. I'd become a liberal in politics and said so. My government was waiting for me."

Mr. Moy and I joined in laughter.

"Then you're a Democrat?" I remarked.

"Yep. And I'll tell you something else."

Mr. Moy led the way to the back of his place, and we sat on white stools.

"*All* Chinese except the 'squeezers' are Democrats," he asserted.

Mr. Moy was warming up. In his black Oriental eyes slumbered a strange light. His talk began to break over me in a flood. I was spellbound. He was speaking like Mazzini[1] or Lincoln. Public Health Service? I had forgotten it. At last I plunged into State Street to find dusk gathering and the lights popping out all over the city. I knew I had a big story, but who would look at it? No news. Only views, and at that the views of a Chinese laundryman! How could any reporter have the crust to walk up to a city editor's desk with stuff like that?

When my shameless mass of copy dropped on Mr. Chamberlin's desk, his eyes bulged. He gave me a queer glance.

"What the hell's this?" he demanded.

"Read it," I said. "It's an interview with a Chinese laundryman who used to be a diplomat. He talks about the destiny of a quarter of the human race. I know we say here that any man who gets half a column on the *Record* owns the paper, and I know I'm asking for three-quarters. But read the stuff."

Irritated, nervous, Chamberlin read and went on reading. He drew a deep breath and settled into his chair. I think he forgot I was there. Reaching the

1. Giuseppe Mazzini was a nineteenth-century Genoese revolutionary who was a strong supporter of Italian unity and republicanism.

end, he looked at me, smiled peculiarly, sprang up, and went quickly out through a swinging-door. I knew Sam Moy and I were to stand before Caesar. I waited an eon for the in-swing of that city editor's door. When Chamberlin bustled back, bright-eyed and almost gleeful, he pointed to pencil-marks on the top of the first page of my copy: "Must. C.H.D." "Must" meant "This goes," and "C.H.D." meant Caesar. I was to "own" the paper that night and have a quarter of a column besides.

But wait a minute. Super-Caesar had spoken, but soon would arrive Sub-Caesar, Bob Holden, punchy, husky, capable chief of the copy desk. What would occur inside Bob when he saw Sam Moy? And what outside? Plumping down at his desk under a strong shaded light, he saw Sam staring at him. Chamberlin and I were peeping at Bob through the copy-window from the city editor's room. He ran rapidly through the copy, grabbed it up, and roared into our presence.

"Chamberlin," he said metallically, "what does this really mean?"

"It's a new sort of story, Bob. Look at it. It's great stuff."

"Great stuff? I call it tripe. We've no room for it. Where's the news in it? Not a line. The *Record*'s not a magazine. I've never before seen in this office such belly-wash. I'm going to kill it."

"Notice the hieroglyphics, Bob?" asked Chamberlin.

For the first time the czar of the copy-desk saw the penciled fiat of Caesar: "Must. C.H.D."

I was afraid to buy the *Record* the next morning and yet of course wild to see it. Nearly everyone on the car as I rode into the Loop from my home was reading it. I craned my neck to catch sight of my story but failed. Due at the *Record* office at 1:30 p.m., I was there an hour earlier and found Chamberlin's room vacant. Approaching his desk, I saw a copy of the paper spread out there and Sam Moy played at full length under a display head in the last column of the foreign page.

It was glorious!

But what was that vigorous script in blue pencil streaming from top to bottom of the white margin next to the story? Fearfully I leaned over it and read:

"*This is good journalism. Lawson.*"

I tip-toed from the room.

It was the first time I had seen the Chief's hand-writing. I wondered if I ever should see *him*. I never even had caught a glimpse of him. He lived in a pigeonhole somewhere up against the roof of our drab building. In one way or another he came and went. Many saw him; I never so much as spied him in our elevator. Time and again, noticing an important-looking stranger in the office, I whispered to someone, "Is that Mr. Lawson?" Always the answer was "No" or "I don't know." All I knew about the matter was that inexorable authority flowed down to the staff from the pigeonhole next to the rafters.

Yet I felt now he was not alien to me, the remote Mr. Lawson. He was no spot-news slave. The indispensability of spot-news he knew well; his career proved that; but there was more to be said. What a world of cruciality lay behind the spot-news! It wanted interpreting. Alone, it was skeletonic. "Put flesh on the bones!" I could imagine Mr. Lawson directing. In the light of Sam Moy, Mr. Lawson was revealed to me as having faith in the general intelligence of the people, their capacity to rise a little above spot-news.

"Is Mr. Bell here?"

I was in the company of colleagues about Mr. Chamberlin's desk. I stood up and looked at a large, dark, comely lady of apparently late middle age. Instantly Chamberlin was on his feet and saying:

"Yes, Miss Wehrner. This is Mr. Bell."

Miss Wehrner! I knew that name. Mr. Lawson's private secretary. She smiled sweetly and said:

"Mr. Bell, Mr. Lawson would like to see you. Will you come with me?"

At last!

The Chief was sitting at a moderate-sized flat-topped desk in a dinky room as high up as the old building would let him go. Of medium height, heavy and reddish-whiskered, he was in formal morning dress and wore a look of culture and of courteous command. His gray eyes glinted so merrily that I wondered how he had got his reputation for inaccessibility and sternness. I found him witty and full of pat stories and with a laugh which rang in that small room like a melody. I was warmed all over by the sun of his personality.

"Mr. Bell," he said suddenly, "how old are you?"

"Almost thirty-one, Mr. Lawson."

"Just the right age. I liked your interview with the gentleman of the shirts and collars, Mr. Sam Moy. It was sensationally unusual. It confirmed in my mind an idea I've been considering for some time. I mean the idea of enlarging the scope of my papers. We are too narrow. We are missing a large part, and I think the better part, of what we ought to supply to our readers. We are failing to present to them with any system or adequacy the feelings and conceptions and hopes which are crystallized in the news and decisive in human affairs. I wish to found a Special Foreign News Service to realize my idea. Do you understand me?"

I said I thought I did.

"We want more Sam Moy matter on our foreign page," declared the publisher. "We're buying all the spot-news now. The Associated Press serves us excellently in that respect. The bedrock principle of our Special Service will be, 'Don't duplicate the Associated Press.' Your Chinese friend told us more of what is truly significant in China than any number of spot-news stories could have done. He showed us *spiritual* China. And China spiritual today will be China political tomorrow. Moy's words clarify the social unrest in his country and reveal the Manchu dynasty[2] as tottering. *That is big news.* Your interview illustrates my idea perfectly. It is the idea of an absolutely exclusive service on the emotional and intellectual side of news. My mind is made up. Our head office will be in London. Should you like to take charge of it, Mr. Bell?"

I hesitated.

"It's yours if you want it."

"Any man would be proud to have it," I said. "If you haven't a better man for it, I'll be happy indeed to go to London for you and do the best I can."

Mr. Lawson swung in his swivel-chair and looked at a calendar on the wall.

"This is Saturday," he reflected. "Could you sail next Wednesday?"

"I'm afraid I couldn't arrange to leave so soon," I answered. "I doubtless could sail next Saturday."

"Good enough. Please see Mr. Dennis for a detailed discussion. Good-by and *bon voyage!*"

It was a thunderbolt, and no mistake, in that humble apartment in Groveland Park. It was precisely the time when my wife and I should have wished to defer so revolutionary a change in our domestic life. She could not sail with me. A separation more or less prolonged was inescapable. But there was no wavering. She kept saying, "Of course you must go."

A fortnight later (on the evening of February 17, 1900) I was huddling over a coal fire in a tiny grate in a London hotel. Lord, how dark it was! And I was cold. The colossal city, wet and frigid, roared about me. I was borne low by the outlook. I was homesick. I wished Sam Moy had died in China before the World's Fair!

Twenty-five years later I had changed my mind. I was saying to myself: "One day, God agreeable, I'll go back into South State Street and see my Oriental friend."

---

2. The Manchu dynasty (also, the Ch'ing dynasty) was China's last imperial dynasty. It lasted from 1644 until 1912.

We had done it. We had made that "absolutely exclusive service on the emotional and intellectual side of news." We had traveled far and created a new school of thought and practice in journalism. Money Mr. Lawson had poured out like water to drive his enterprise to acknowledged success. And neither the profession nor the public in America or abroad questioned that success.

I salute Sam Moy!

III
The Foreign Period, 1900–1922

14. Life Opens for Me in London

My first office in the world's greatest city was meek enough. It was just the requisite size for my roll-top desk (typewriter-swallowing), myself, and two or three visitors if they should come. But it delighted me. It was a little world where I could be alone and look out upon a big world. Hiding in the very top of the northeast curve of Trafalgar Buildings, it gave one through its single window a comprehensive view of Trafalgar Square, called by Sir Robert Peel "the finest site in Europe."[1]

For only a trifle less than a quarter of a century my professional home was in those buildings but not in that petty room under the eaves. Mr. Lawson wished his head office abroad to be comparable to his expansive idea about news. He wanted travelers to visit it and be charmed by it. He wanted them to imbibe its significance and to spread its fame far and near, particularly where that fame might affect the minds of lavish advertisers.

Victor Fremont Lawson's competitors never understood him, and he took no pains to set them right. Everlastingly they were judging him, and everlastingly they were going wrong. Two words served them in their vain efforts to resolve the great publisher-editor: "religious" and "visionary." He was a parson and a dreamer in journalism. He went to church too much, and was too self-communing, to be a newspaper promoter of any consequence. Brass tacks he did not know when he saw them. What he needed to do was to come out of

1. Sir Robert Peel was prime minister of the United Kingdom for several months in late 1834 and early 1835 and then again from 1841 to 1846. Peel was on the committee that in 1839 reviewed designs for Trafalgar Square, a site originally conceived to honor Admiral Horatio Nelson (who commanded and died in the British naval battle of Trafalgar), as well as the British monarchy and military. See Mace, *Trafalgar Square.*

his pigeonhole high above Madison and Wells Streets and mix with the real fellows of the great game.[2]

And yet this fanatic went right on making a million dollars a year *net* for fifty years!

It was funny to listen to some of Mr. Lawson's ablest competitors. One of these was Robert Wilson Patterson of the *Chicago Tribune*.[3] He came to London after I had moved down from the sky in Trafalgar Buildings and was arrayed in Solomon-like glory on the second floor with a magnificent sweep of the Square from the Strand to Admiralty Arch. Huge and beautiful rooms, lovely furniture, newspapers and magazines, rich carpets, a gigantic register for visitors' names, and the information above the book that all names daily were cabled to the *Chicago Daily News*!

I called upon Mr. Patterson at Brown's Hotel in Dover Street. He was comfortable, at leisure, and pleasantly talkative. He remarked that he had been sorry to miss me when he "looked in to see Lawson's London office." I said I also was sorry and added that I had not noticed his name in our register.

"No, no," he replied. "I did not register. I merely asked if you were there."

"What did you think of our office?" I asked, really curious.

"Oh, it's a marvelous place, very beautiful," he answered. "Lawson is doing something peculiar most of the time. He listens a great deal and says much less than many of us. Indeed I never have heard him say anything which threw light on his newspaper philosophy. He's a fine companion (if you can get at him). One always is refreshed by his acute, amusing, and sometimes enigmatical remarks. But he is silent about how he makes the *Daily News*. He lets us

2. This was not an uncommon interpretation of Lawson. Even Lawson's own reporters noted that he rarely, as Bell puts it, "mixed with the real fellows." *Daily News* Paris correspondent Paul Scott Mowrer wrote in his memoir that Lawson was "aloof" (Mowrer, *The House of Europe,* 120, 129, 525). Frederic William Wile, *Daily News* correspondent in London and later in Berlin, similarly commented that Lawson was "an invisible but omnipotent entity" (Wile, *News Is Where You Find It,* 70).

3. Robert Wilson Patterson was managing editor of the *Chicago Tribune* from 1874 until 1899 and editor-in-chief from 1899 until 1910, when he died. The *Tribune* was the *Daily News*'s chief rival. Patterson was the son-in-law of Joseph Medill, who was an early investor in the paper and eventually acquired it. Medill was known for his "personal journalism" and for his conservatism. Patterson was a Republican, but less political than Medill, who had been Chicago's mayor for a short time and spouted his conservative ideas through tactics like writing "Dictator" before labor leader Eugene Debs's name when it appeared in his paper. Under Patterson, the *Tribune* moved toward straight news reporting. See Kinsley, *The Chicago Tribune* (vol. 3); and Tebbel, *An American Dynasty.*

guess on that subject. He has us guessing concerning his big and expensive London office. It's the newspaper show-place of the world."

"And what is *your* guess?" I asked.

Mr. Patterson screwed up his face thoughtfully.

"Well," he said, "I think it's a rich man's whim. It strikes me distinctly as an eccentric fancy.[4] It certainly isn't *business*. Rich men do such things. Some have castles, some ranches, some racing-stables, some yachts. Lawson has an imposing office in the most prominent place in the biggest city in the world. It diverts him and gratifies his *amour propre*."

Contrast this surmise with the facts. Not in all his life, either private or public, did Mr. Lawson care a fig for idle show. Beautiful things he loved, but they must be substantial and to the purpose. His London office, with all which it symbolized in the way of an exclusive foreign news service, was characteristic of him. It satisfied not his personal vanity but his moral sentiments and his intellectual point of view: it would have its influence educationally upon his readers and also augment the prestige whose practical name was dollars and cents.

It stood alone, after its fashion, that pioneering London office and foreign headquarters of an American newspaper. That was true not only of Chicago but of New York. Even the *Chicago Tribune* at that time had no London office at all. Harry Chamberlain of the *New York Sun* was lost in a side-street off the east end of the Strand, Milton V. Snyder of the *New York Herald* worked in an attic-like dump above Fleet Street, and I. N. Ford of the *New York Tribune* wrote his cables and letters either at home or in the smoking-room of the National Club off Whitehall. Visiting me after our splendid London quarters had received its finishing touches, and already was becoming the Mecca of London-visiting Americans, Mr. Lawson said:

"Bell, you mustn't imagine this office is for you. *Your* office is under your hat!"

"On that point, Mr. Lawson," I replied, "I have no illusions!"

In Paris, as time went on, we opened an office similar to that in London

---

4. Others—not least Lawson's own correspondents—shared the view that Lawson's lavish foreign offices were an eccentricity, not a reflection of a keen interest in foreign news. After meeting with Lawson in Europe in 1906, Berlin correspondent Frederic William Wile wrote to Bell that Lawson emphasized "in great detail . . . the great advantage to the Daily News of this 'bureau' game in Europe. And I have the firm impression that it is *the* reason, of all reasons, for his continuing to keep the service up. I have the feeling that news is only an incidental feature of the enterprise" (Wile to Bell, January 31, 1906, Bell Papers).

and similarly conspicuous.[5] Like offices, if somewhat less sumptuous, we opened in Rome and Berlin. But London never lost its supremacy as the newspaper resort of Uncle Sam's peripatetics abroad whether they sought business or pleasure. Nor were Americans by any means our only visitors. We came to have callers from all over the world, notably the British dominions, colonies, and protectorates. As for distinguished Londoners, they took to us avidly. Possibly they liked us. I know they liked the gorgeous shows which frequently were unfolded in full efflorescence before our great windows.

Past those windows moved nearly every remarkable procession (the British never say "parade" in such a connection) London knew for the better part of a generation. Queen Victoria's funeral *cortège* stretched its sorrowful length below us in 1901. We saw the coronation processions of Edward VII and George V. We saw London's wonderful outpouring in honor of "dear old Bobs" (Field Marshal Lord Roberts)[6] on the occasion of his funeral service in St. Paul's Cathedral November 19, 1914, shortly after his ears had ceased resounding to the guns on the West Front in the Great War. Kaiser Wilhelm II[7] rode under our windows on his way to the Lord Mayor's luncheon for him at the Mansion House, where I sat fifty feet from him and heard him declare God had put him on the Throne of the Fatherland "to save the peace of Europe"!

It was in our windows that I learned how profound is London's love for the

5. Paul Scott Mowrer, *Daily News* correspondent in Paris, described the Paris office as "luxuriously fitted, like a club, with palms and Oriental rugs and leather armchairs." Of the large *Daily News* sign that adorned the building, he wrote, "No tourist could come into Paris without seeing [it]" (Mowrer, *The House of Europe*, 135).

6. Frederick Sleigh Roberts (Field Marshal Lord Roberts) was a British military leader during the late Victorian era. He commanded military forces in Afghanistan, India, and South Africa, and was commander in chief of the British army from 1901 to 1905. Roberts was one of the first advocates of mandatory military service. See Roberts's autobiography, *Forty-One Years in India*.

7. Friedrich Wilhelm Viktor Albrecht was German emperor and king of Prussia from 1888 until the last year of World War I, 1918. The grandson of Queen Victoria, Wilhelm maintained throughout his reign that he sought friendship with the United Kingdom. His actions, however, precipitated the First World War. The Kaiser feared that the Entente Cordiale between the United Kingdom and France (the series of agreements that established a permanent peace between the two countries) and the later similar Anglo-Russian Entente were meant to encircle Germany and strangle her political aspirations. Wilhelm allied with Austria-Hungary after the Serbian assassination of that country's leader—the event that eventually led to World War I. Hence, Bell ironically notes Wilhelm's declaration that he would "save the peace of Europe." See Ludwig, *Wilhelm Hohenzollern*; and MacDonogh, *The Last Kaiser*.

annual Lord Mayor's show.[8] The day of this show is different from every other day of the year in the British capital. It is the day when London has no adults, only children; the day when the most august become simple and frivolous. Our office on these days welcomed lords and ladies, knights and ladies, Cabinet ministers, diplomats, famous writers, ordinary folk, a charwoman or two, all as self-forgetful and excited as youngsters at a Punch and Judy show. A true democracy!

But the frivolity went when night came. London then was staid again. World politics took over. The new Lord Mayor entertained the Premier and his Cabinet in the Guildhall, and the nations heard an exposition of Britain's reading of international questions and especially her own attitude respecting them. It was the night when British eloquence reached high levels and quantities of costly food and wines contributed their delectation to a superbly brilliant company.

One of our most notable visitors in Trafalgar Buildings was the aged Lord Strathcona, the Scot of Labrador.[9] He was the most striking figure in polite London, attracting every eye at great public dinners and other functions, which seemed to give him immense enjoyment, though he was known to all his friends as rigidly abstemious. My wife and I once crossed Canada from Ottawa to Vancouver in mid-winter, and I wrote an article on the trip entitled *Three Thousand Miles of Snow*. I never saw Lord Strathcona, nearing his ninety-fourth year, without thinking of that journey. Not that he was cold; only that he was so white of hair and eyebrows and beard and face, and (with all his Highland accent) so like Canada.

Daily he worked in his office in Victoria Street.

8. The Lord Mayor is the mayor of the City of London (one of the earliest settlements of modern-day London; today London's central financial district, also called the Square Mile). He is a member of London's governing body, the Corporation of London, but his role is more ceremonial than political. The Lord Mayor serves for one year only. Every year, on the day after he is sworn in, the Lord Mayor processes to the City of Westminster—the section of London where most government buildings are located, including the Houses of Parliament and the Royal Courts of Justice. At the Royal Courts, the Lord Mayor swears allegiance to the Crown.

9. Born in Scotland, Donald Alexander Smith (Lord Strathcona) was a businessman and political leader in Canada and, later, England. As a businessman, he was involved in railroads, the fur trade, fishing, and newspapers. He also served in the Canadian Parliament. Smith was immensely wealthy, a supporter of British imperialism, and a Conservative, although he sometimes supported Liberal policies and also served in both Liberal and Conservative administrations. Smith was high commissioner in London from 1896 to 1911. See Wilson, *The Life of Lord Strathcona*.

"How do you do it?" I asked him.

"Do what?" he inquired, lifting those bushy, snowy brows.

"Work so hard and keep so fit," I said.

"Diet," he replied. "I never eat any lunch if I can avoid it. And I eat and drink sparingly at dinner. As for work, I do it and be done with it."

Sir Gilbert Parker,[10] another man of Canada, came to us on fête-days and others. Great romanticist, turner of stirring and picturesque Canadian history into novels which captured London, Sir Gilbert was also an ardent British imperialist and stanch for English-speaking solidarity. This, he argued, was the world's strongest stay of liberty and peace; and these were mankind's only hope of escape from a ruin which would be as ignominious as it would be complete. Sir Gilbert praised Mr. Lawson for establishing his luxurious London office. Other American publishers would follow suit, and we should have "a tremendous force for a free and stable civilization."

Shrewd, caustic, intrepid, amusing John Burns[11] often came to see us before he made the Cabinet in the Asquith government. That was in the days when he was working with Ben Tillett to organize the East End dockers and intermittently fighting with the police and getting into jail.[12] Tillett told me one night when we were eating pickled herring in the Three Feathers public house in Aldgate that Burns "lost his zest for life when he no longer could take punches at cops." Certainly the noted labor-leader wished very much to be there when the fun was on.

One day Burns and I were discussing politics in a tea-shop just below our office.

"Truth to tell," he stated, "*all* government is in the hands of the criminal classes."

10. Gilbert Parker was a novelist and political leader. He was a Conservative member of Parliament in the House of Commons.

11. John Burns was a British political activist who supported Socialist, pro-labor, and anti-racist causes. He was elected to Parliament in 1892, representing Labour, but he eventually allied with the more mainstream Liberal Party. Burns served in a cabinet position from 1906 to 1914. Contrary to what Bell writes here, Burns was actually appointed to the cabinet during Henry Campbell-Bannerman's administration. Campbell-Bannerman was a Liberal Party leader and British prime minister from 1906 to 1908. Herbert Henry Asquith, to whom Bell refers, succeeded Campbell-Bannerman in 1908. See Kent, *John Burns*.

12. Ben Tillett was a dockworker and union organizer in London. Burns and Tillett helped organize the London Dock Strike of 1889, when dockworkers fought for an increase in wages. In the process, Tillett's union—the Dock, Wharf, Riverside and General Labourers' Union—as well as Tillet and Burns themselves, grew in prominence.

Not long afterward Premier Asquith made Burns president of the Local Government Board.[13] I chanced to meet the fighting radical in Cockspur Street, where he was setting his watch by Dent's chronometer.

"Congratulations, Mr. Burns," I said.

He looked at me in silence.

"Congratulations on your appointment as a member of the new Liberal government," I elaborated. And I added:

"Is *all* government still in the hands of the criminal classes?"

Mr. Burns made off into Spring Gardens without replying, laughing over his shoulder as he went.

Two invaluable friends I had in my earliest days in London, where Gordon Selfridge[14] discovered (as he told me) that "good fellows" were "a mile deep." One of these friends was the great Zollvereinest, Joseph Chamberlain, father of the late Sir Austen, Foreign Minister, and of the present illustrious Premier, Arthur Neville.[15] Mr. Chamberlain had become the chief personal dynamic of the British Empire. He was approachable, practical, efficient. I asked for an appointment, informed him of my wish to be a good London correspondent, and received his assurance of "every assistance" he could give. Within a few days the statesman invited me to lunch with him at the House of Commons

13. Herbert Henry Asquith was a Liberal Party leader and British prime minister from 1908 until 1916. Burns was appointed president of the Local Government Board in December 1905, when soon-to-be prime minister Henry Campbell-Bannerman was forming his government. Asquith was chancellor of the exchequer then.

14. Harry Gordon Selfridge worked in Chicago's Marshall Fields department store, where his keen advertising sense gained him quick promotion. Selfridge opened his own department store, Selfridges, in London in 1909. Selfridge was an inventive owner and advertiser, selling his store on the idea that customers should buy what they wanted—rather than only what they needed. For more on this change in advertising in department stores, see Leach, *Land of Desire* (pp. 20, 27, 68–69, 86–87 for Selfridge). See also Pound, *Selfridge;* and Selfridge's own *The Romance of Commerce.*

15. Joseph Chamberlain was a British political leader. A more radical Liberal in his early political career, Chamberlain eventually allied with Conservatives and became a strong supporter of British imperialism. Joseph Austen Chamberlain, his son, was also a British statesman and leader of the Conservative Party. He held the positions of chancellor of the exchequer (1903–1905; 1919–1921), secretary of state for India (1915–1917), and foreign secretary (1924–1929). Neville, Chamberlain's younger son, also was leader of the Conservative Party. He was prime minister from 1937 to 1940 and is remembered for his role in the Munich Agreement of 1938, which Bell will discuss later. For Joseph Chamberlain, see Marsh, *Joseph Chamberlain.* For Austen, see Hughes, *British Foreign Secretaries.* For Neville, see Rock, *Chamberlain and Roosevelt.* See also Petrie, *The Chamberlain Tradition.*

and introduced me to a score of the leading men of London. It was a leg-up which helped me incalculably through all my years in Europe.

How very unlike his father was Sir Austen, the eldest son, and how very like the father was Arthur Neville, the former by the first wife, English, and the latter by the second wife, American! Sir Austen was one of the most cultivated and delightful men in the Empire, and a great diplomat, but he was passionately ideologic. Apriority was his master. He dreamed dangerous political dreams in the international sphere. He was among the politicians who believed Japan could be restrained by a firm Occidental front in East Asia, and Italy and Germany needs must listen when Britain and France cried, "Stop!"[16]

Separation from realities Sir Austen never got from his father. Joseph Chamberlain was as realistic as the screws he made in Birmingham, and Arthur Neville seems to possess the father's temperament and talent in full measure. Thankful, in my opinion, should be the British peoples and the whole world for this outstanding historical fact. Disraeli's "Oriental Imperialism," the great Jew's soaring and glamourous foreign policy, evoked Joseph Chamberlain's scorn.[17] He saw Disraeli, with regard to the world, as prone to excessive imagination, to unreality; as thinking more of the periphery than of the center of British power. Proud imperialist though he was, Joseph Chamberlain did

16. At least one recent scholar has come to a different conclusion than Bell here. Michael Hughes, joining British foreign policy scholar Richard Grayson, argues that Austen Chamberlain was, in fact, open to German proposals about how to secure peace between Germany and France. Hughes characterizes Chamberlain's ideas about how to solve the problem as "fluid and uncertain" (Hughes, *British Foreign Secretaries*, 65). Likewise, contrary to Bell's statement that "apriority was his master," Hughes argues that Chamberlain "shared the characteristic British skepticism about the wisdom of basing foreign policy on a grand framework of values and objectives" (ibid., 59). He calls him a "mixture of pragmatism and optimism," echoing Sir Charles Petrie, one of Chamberlain's early biographers (ibid., 60).

17. Benjamin Disraeli was prime minister of the United Kingdom in 1868, and again from 1874 to 1880. Disraeli was a staunch British imperialist. Although it is indeed true that Chamberlain opposed Disraeli's imperialist policies during the latter's tenure as prime minister, Chamberlain himself took a sharp turn toward "new imperialism" in 1886, emphasizing strong British rule in its colonies. This policy of imperialism he "pursued to the end of his life, becoming the most influential British Imperial statesman," according to one of his biographers (Strauss, *Joseph Chamberlain*, 12). Bell characterizes Chamberlain as an imperialist, but also a Liberal, who cared more for domestic affairs than foreign. Chamberlain's biographers seem not to support this conclusion. For Chamberlain's imperialism, see Strauss, *Joseph Chamberlain*; and Marsh, *Joseph Chamberlain*. For Disraeli's foreign policy, see Swartz, *The Politics of British Foreign Policy*.

not wince at the epithet, "parish pumpist." Birmingham looked better to him than Cyprus and the Transvaal and "the invasion of Afghanistan."[18]

"If you want your Empire to be great," he declared, "be very sure you are great first at home."

In that vein the father of Sir Austen and Arthur Neville often talked to me as his influence grew greater and greater with his fellow-countrymen. Disraeli was gone. Gladstone had swept him out of power in the great Midlothian Campaign.[19] Britain was dwelling not so much on Oriental magnificence as on poverty, ill health, over-crowding, slums, crime. I never could hear "the voice of voiceless England" (that of Joseph Chamberlain) in the accents of Sir Austen, but I hear them in those of Arthur Neville.

Sir Austen talked to me at the Foreign Office in 1929 (he was Secretary of State for Foreign Affairs then) when I was in London to try to induce Premier MacDonald to visit President Hoover.[20] He did not seem to me to grasp at all the hard facts of our world, the new Japan, the new Italy, the Germany of the Nazi renaissance. He was living in the past and in his personal aprioristic paradise. He thought Britain and France, particularly if America would help, could restrain Japan, Italy, and Germany imperialistically.[21] I told him I almost would wager my right eye that America would do nothing concrete to support any such policy. And I said further that it struck me as an extremely wrong and dangerous policy. Sir Austen of course held to his point of view.

18. Cyprus, Turkey; the Transvaal, South Africa; and Afghanistan were all centers of British imperialism during the Disraeli administration and around the turn of the nineteenth century.

19. William Ewert Gladstone was Liberal Party leader and British prime minister from 1868 until 1874. Gladstone was the longtime political rival of Disraeli, leader of the Conservative Party. Disraeli's tenure as prime minister ended in 1880 when Gladstone's Midlothian campaign brought the Liberals back into power. The campaign was a series of speeches Gladstone delivered around the country targeting Disraeli's policy of supporting the Ottoman Empire, which at the time was committing atrocities against Bulgarians. On Gladstone and Disraeli, see Swartz, *The Politics of British Foreign Policy* (pp. 112–8, 120–2 for the Midlothian campaign).

20. Austen was foreign secretary at the time. Ramsey MacDonald was the first prime minister to come from Britain's Labour Party (although he was expelled from that party in 1931 after forming a coalition with Conservatives). He was prime minister in 1924 and again from 1929 to 1935. Herbert Hoover was U.S. president from 1929 to 1933. As Bell recounts later in this memoir, he worked for a meeting between the two men in the wake of World War I to smooth Anglo-American relations.

21. It is clear from this passage and those that follow throughout the remainder of this memoir that it was Bell who did not fully understand the realities of Nazi Germany, Fascist Italy, and imperial Japan. For Chamberlain's tenure as foreign secretary, see Petrie, *The Chamberlain Tradition;* Hughes, *British Foreign Secretaries;* and Thorpe, *The Uncrowned Prime Ministers.*

How unenforceable was that point of view is now history: Japan has advanced, Italy has advanced, Germany has advanced and is advancing. And their aspirations and acts so far have provoked nothing more formidable or effective than protests. Japan follows her destiny in East Asia, Italy's conquest of Ethiopia has been recognized by both Britain and France, and the Anglo-French Alliance (for Alliance it is) prudently and properly substitutes conciliation and negotiation for the diplomatic stonewall in its relations with Nazi Germany. Munich! Name of splendid augury for Europe! I submit most sincerely that Joseph Chamberlain, as I knew him, would have done at Munich what Arthur Neville did there.[22]

Returning to our London office in those opening years of its story in Trafalgar Square, I recall with especial vividness a man as individual in his looks and in his mind as Lord Strathcona. I refer to Prince Kropotkin.[23] His lifelong friend, confidant, and political aid, Prince Tcherkesoff of Georgia, became a friend of mine immediately after I settled to my work in London. One day Prince Tcherkesoff came into my private room, walking ahead of a man small in stature like himself but with a beard, face, and head which one had only to see never to forget.

"My friend Kropotkin," said Tcherkesoff, smiling in happy pride.

Those comrades-in-revolution took me to the Horseshoe Restaurant, Tottenham Court Road, where the surroundings were plain but the cooking excellent and the wines sagaciously selected. (Come to think of it, I never have known a revolutionary without a keen palate for good wines!) I have seen a good number of famous men eat with lively, not to say voracious, enjoyment: I never saw a man consume an English mutton chop with more joy and fervor than Prince Kropotkin consumed his that day. Prince Tcherkesoff also ate eupeptically. And the three of us did very well by ourselves in respect of the velvety Bordeaux. We discussed grievous social matters, but the party was merry!

22. At Munich, Germany, in 1938 Britain, France, Italy, and Germany made a formal agreement that Germany should have territorial rights to the Sudetenland in Czechoslovakia. Neville Chamberlain and Adolf Hitler also signed an agreement that Germany and Britain would solve all future disputes between the two countries through peaceful means. Although some saw this appeasement as a success, it proved short lived. Hitler soon seized the remainder of Czechoslovakia, and World War II began. See Wheeler-Bennett, *Munich*.

23. Prince Pyotr Alexeyevich Kropotkin was a Russian anarchist who advocated a communal, but anarchical, society. He was a contemporary of Enrico Malatesta, the Italian anarchist Communist (see note 26). Kropotkin first went to England in 1876 after escaping from prison. He later moved to Switzerland, was expelled from that country, immigrated to France, was imprisoned there, and finally settled again in London. See Cahm, *Kropotkin*.

Kropotkin's ideas and ideals, his perils and escapes, his exploits against despotism, his sufferings in prison and in exile, are known to all who read.[24] Here I record only an impression of him. His head was mountainous. It seemed to me just that, and the more he talked the bigger his head looked. It spread like the expanse of his adventures and his labors. It was nearly bald, only thinly fringed with hair curling over his ears, but his beard made up for the hirsute shortage on the crown: it fell low and spread fanlike almost to the edge of his shoulders.

His nose was large, his cheeks chubby, and his eyes set far apart, so strangely far apart that one examined them separately. Intelligence and benevolence, if they ever owned a countenance, owned Kropotkin's. His smile, which rarely left his face even when his conversation was the most serious, seemed less a smile than basic geniality of character in visible translation. All he said was morally and intellectually on the highest plane, no slang, flippancy, artificiality, triviality, all refined gold. What I remember on the moral side of Kropotkin that day was his abhorrence of physical force and his faith in the perfectibility and the final liberation of man. So insistent were these suggestions that one fell inevitably under their inspiring and soothing spell.

I was grateful to Tcherkesoff for bringing within the circle of my acquaintances the Ajax or Prometheus of the slow and painful Russian Revolution. I was less grateful to the Georgian for letting himself go one night at my dinner table (where he was drinking his share of champagne) and denouncing me (as if it in any case were worthwhile) as "the friend not of the downtrodden but of Kings and Queens"![25] What malady of brain seized the Prince that night I never knew, nor could guess, but the detonation sundered our association for good and all.

This gentleman of the Near East, so gifted, so highly educated, so ingratiating with children, yet so eccentric (to forgo a stronger term), introduced another well-known man to my family and myself: Enrico Malatesta, the Italian anarchist, with whom (believe it or not) was linked no less a person than Benito Mussolini, then editor of *Avanti*.[26] Do you recollect anything of the

24. Kropotkin was jailed in 1861 in Russia for participating in a student protest; again in 1864 in Russia for circulating revolutionary material; and again in 1882 in France for his work with Socialist activists. See Woodcock and Avakumovic, *The Anarchist Prince;* and Cahm, *Kropotkin.*

25. Tcherkesoff, of course, was correct. Bell socialized with some of Great Britain's most important and well-known political leaders—and took considerable pride in that fact—as, indeed, he did in meeting Tcherkesoff.

26. Like Kropotkin, Enrico (or Errico) Malatesta was an anarchist and a Communist. Malatesta had been involved in anti-government movements from an early age and was forced to leave Italy in 1878. He spent much of his 35 years of exile in London. Benito Mussolini was leader of the Italian

widespread riots in Italy in 1914? They broke out at Ancona and were revolutionary in nature, the occasion being the government's action in forbidding an antimilitarist meeting.[27] And Malatesta and Mussolini marched shoulder to shoulder against the militarists!

Or did they? Malatesta did; all his life he marched against government in whatever form; he was an anarchist. But Mussolini, adorer of soldiers and arms and imperialism (when he regards them as the servants of justice and civilization); Mussolini the Fascist; did he march against militarists?[28] Was he fundamentally different in 1914 from what he is now? I think not. Men's attitudes change because circumstances change; men do not change; as they are born, so are they. Mussolini, in his heart of hearts, was Fascist in 1914. He did not march against the soldier *qua* soldier; he marched against the military in those riots because, as he believed, it shielded a régime of corruption and incompetence irreconcilable with either the glory or the safety of Italy.

Malatesta was likable and clever but always inscrutable and equivocal. One of his keenest delights was to outwit the police as he did in Italy when he escaped in a piano-box from a house surrounded by officers on the watch day and night. The piano-box was carried into the house through the police-cordon with a piano in it. It was carried out in a short while with Malatesta in it. And

Socialists during this time and would soon become leader of the Italian Fascists. Mussolini was prime minister of Italy from 1922 to 1943. *Avanti!* (*Forward!*), the Italian daily he edited, was the official voice of the Socialist Party. When Mussolini dissented from the Socialist position of neutrality in World War I and became more militarist, he was ousted from the party and the paper. For Malatesta, see Nomad, *Rebels and Renegades*, 1–47. For Mussolini, see Gallo, *Mussolini's Italy.*

27. In June of 1914, Socialists and anarchists launched an anti-militarist demonstration in Ancona, Italy, that led to others like it across the country. During "Red Week," as it was dubbed soon after, independent republics were declared, red flags were raised over cities, taxes abolished, and churches and homes ransacked. In a couple of cities where demonstrations were particularly active, government authority "virtually collapsed" (Seton-Watson, *Italy from Liberalism to Fascism*, 394). See Gallo, *Mussolini's Italy*, 29–31; Miller, *From Elite to Mass Politics*, 193–5; and Seton-Watson, *Italy from Liberalism to Fascism*, 393–5.

28. Accounts of the riots record that Mussolini did indeed participate. Max Gallo's account of Red Week puts Mussolini "in the front rank" of at least one demonstration (*Mussolini's Italy*, 30). But Malatesta and Socialist leader Pietro Nenni—not Mussolini—were responsible for inciting the 1914 riots. Their outbreak "owed nothing to [Mussolini] initially"—although he did support them and feed their fire with his rousing editorials in *Avanti!* that called for a general strike to continue (ibid.). A little over a month later, when World War I was beginning to sweep across Europe, the anti-militarist Mussolini used the pages of *Avanti!* to insist that Italy must remain neutral. Later in that year, however, Mussolini's position began to change. In October 1915, he renounced pacifist neutrality. See Gallo, *Mussolini's Italy*, 30, 33–6.

the police went right on guarding the house until the fugitive anarchist was well beyond the Italian frontier!

At Dymchurch (on the Kentish coast) one morning my wife and I were observing our children (we had three, Alice, Edward, and John) intent upon the construction of a fortress of sand on that broad and beautiful beach. It was a glorious morning, warm and tremulous with the sparkle of a white-capped Channel. Prince Tcherkesoff was with us; had motored down with us from our home in Sidcup, Kent. By and by who should come along but Malatesta? He had walked over from Hithe at the foot of Folkestone. Our children interested him. He waded in the surf and carried them on his shoulders and told them stories. At last he stopped by the fortress and stood frowning at it. Then, cataleptically, he leaped into the air, dug his bare heels into the center of the sand-structure on which the children had worked with such skill and patience, and effaced it to the last trace. Consternation is hardly too strong a word for the sensation which came upon all but Malatesta. He was smiling. He had demolished a symbol of what he hated. The children sobbed. I suspect they loathe that man yet.

As Joseph Chamberlain was my first invaluable friend in politics in London, so W. T. Stead[29] was my first invaluable friend in journalism there. His office was at the bottom of Norfolk Street, Strand, overlooking the Thames, where I talked with the bushy-bearded genius again and again and never ceased to marvel at his animation, fresh vision, and brilliance. Quite unmatched in their way were the character and the mind which went out when the *Titanic* sank, April 15, 1912. Stead introduced me to John Morley, T. P. O'Connor, Moberly Bell of *The Times*, and many other journalists of note, starting me on the way to friendship with virtually every great British editor of my time, first among them the incomparable Northcliffe.[30]

29. William Thomas Stead was an English journalist who wrote for and was an editor of the *Pall Mall Gazette*, a Liberal evening daily. His recent biographer, Raymond Schults, argues that Stead was ultimately responsible for "new journalism"—a style of writing and newspapering that aimed to produce a more readable newspaper, one meant for an expanding British reading public. Men like Lord Northcliffe, editor of several "new journalism" papers, today receive much of the credit for the new style Stead pioneered. (Bell will have more to say on Northcliffe in chap. 18.) See Schults, *Crusader in Babylon*.

30. John Morley, a Liberal British statesman, also edited the *Pall Mall Gazette*. T. P. O'Connor was an Irish nationalist political leader. He wrote for the *Daily Telegraph* and the *New York Herald*, and founded several newspapers and journals himself. Moberly Bell was editor of *The Times* of London for eighteen years. Lord Northcliffe (Alfred Harmsworth) was a successful newspaper owner and editor in London, who owned the London *Daily Mail*, the *Evening News*, and *The Times*.

15. More of Life's "Little Gleam" Abroad

Powder's smell has been in my nostrils at intervals most of my life. This pungent scent, according to Longfellow, is sweet if the powder be burnt in a righteous cause. Well, from one angle or other, has it ever been burnt in an unrighteous cause? In the Spanish-American War I found our powder sweet-smelling to us and Spain's sweet-smelling to her. We liked the smell of our powder in the Indian wars; the Indians did not. Reporting the Boer War[1] from London, I ran upon the same phenomenon: sweet-smelling powder on both sides. Again in the East Asian wars, the Balkan wars, the Great War, the Italo-Ethiopian War.

All British noses, however, did not react agreeably to burning British powder in the Boer War. Sir Henry Campbell-Bannerman, for example, raked British policy with a terrific fire of criticism, asserting that the war had been utterly unnecessary and was prosecuted against the Boers not as a war but as "a thing carried out in South Africa by methods of barbarism," the reference being particularly to farm-burning and the sweeping of Boer women and children into

---

1. The Boer War (also, the Second Boer War, the South African War, or the Anglo-Boer War) was fought between Great Britain and the independent Boer republics of the Transvaal and the Orange Free State. The Transvaal held great reserves of gold, and British citizens began to flock to the area to profit from them. But the Boers (South African settlers of European, primarily Dutch, descent) denied the Britons political rights and heavily taxed the gold industry. Foreign Secretary Joseph Chamberlain and High Commissioner Alfred Milner responded aggressively, and war began after a series of unanswered ultimatums between Britain and Boer leaders. Although British forces faced long months of guerrilla warfare, they eventually won the war, and the two independent republics became part of the British Empire. See Farwell, *The Great Anglo-Boer War;* and Pakenham, *The Boer War.*

concentration camps.[2] Lloyd George[3] "limehoused" against the war, and such men as Ramsay MacDonald[4] and John Burns[5] fought it with such boldness that they barely escaped with their lives from the super-patriotic mobocrats.

Moreover, the British leaders to whom British powder smelt otherwise than sweet in the Boer War rode into power on the tide of their spirit and point of view.[6] Joseph Chamberlain was eclipsed as the popular hero. Arthur

2. Henry Campbell-Bannerman was leader of the British Liberal Party during the Boer War, when Conservatives ran the government. He became prime minister in 1906 after the Conservatives lost power—the first Liberal prime minister since William Gladstone had left office in 1894. Campbell-Bannerman was skeptical of the war from its beginning. He complained to fellow Liberals in a speech early in the conflict that no one seemed able to answer the question, "What is it that we are going to war about?" But the Liberal Party was divided over the war, and Campbell-Bannerman walked a thin—and sometimes ambiguous—line to hold it together. On the right were the imperialist Liberals, led by Sir Edward Grey (see Preface, note 1), Lord Haldane (see Preface, note 1) and Herbert Henry Asquith (see chap. 14, n. 13). On the left was Lloyd George (see note 3 below) and the "pro-Boers" who opposed the war from its onset. Campbell-Bannerman and the majority of the party, the center-Liberals, first cautiously supported the war and later opposed the way it was being fought. During the war, the British burned Boer farms and constructed common camps for those whose homes were destroyed. They also began forcing Boer women and children to move into the camps, which quickly became overcrowded, short on food and drinking water, and ridden with disease. After Campbell-Bannerman met with British activist Emily Hobhouse, who had seen the conditions in the camps and returned to raise awareness and protest in England, he began to denounce the war. He called the British practice "methods of barbarism"—a phrase he would use frequently in public discussions of the war. For Campbell-Bannerman and concentration camps, see Farwell, *The Great Anglo-Boer War*, 392–419; and Pakenham, *The Boer War*, 533–49. For the Liberal Party and the war, see Cross, *The Liberals in Power*, 11, 18–9.

3. David Lloyd George was a Liberal British statesman who was prime minister from 1916 to 1922. During the Boer War, he was an outspoken representative of the left-Liberal faction of the Liberal Party, known as the "pro-Boers." Lloyd George was a fervent critic of the war, the Conservative Party, and its leaders. See Farwell, *The Great Anglo-Boer War*, 314–7; George, *Lloyd George*, 288–352; and Gilbert, *David Lloyd George*, 149–214.

4. Ramsay MacDonald was the United Kingdom's first Labour prime minister—although he was later expelled from the Labour Party for forming a coalition with Conservatives. During the Boer War, MacDonald was secretary of the Labour Representation Committee, whose purpose was to see Labour Party candidates elected to Parliament. Many Labour statesmen allied with the pro-Boers in the war. MacDonald himself was resolutely opposed to the war. See Marquand, *Ramsay MacDonald*, 64–6, 76–8.

5. John Burns (see chap. 14, n. 11) was in the left-Liberal, "pro-Boer" camp along with Lloyd George. See Kent, *John Burns*, 97–116; and Cross, *The Liberals in Power*, 17.

6. When Conservative prime minister Lord Balfour resigned in December 1905, Campbell-Bannerman led the Liberal Party to form a new government. In the parliamentary election that followed shortly after, the Liberals won decisively, partly owing to Conservative blunders in South

James (later Lord) Balfour stepped out of the premiership, and Campbell-Bannerman stepped into it to win deathless fame for himself and his Cabinet by bestowing full British citizenship on the Africanders. Oh, the wisdom of magnanimity! Ten years afterward, the free Boers were making their powerful contribution to the salvation of the British Empire![7]

They used to say Campbell-Bannerman's name sounded like a man falling downstairs.

It always has sounded to me rather more like a man falling upstairs!

One of my deeply-imprinted memories of the Boer War throws what I regard as a most interesting light on British character. The British never liked the Boers until these hard-riding and straight-shooting warriors gave an awful hiding to the British Army! Why, one night when I went as usual to the War Office (in May, 1900) I was told that British officers were in Pretoria dictating terms of surrender to Kruger and that the war was "practically over."[8] In June, 1900, Lord Roberts himself entered Pretoria, and everyone supposed that was the end. But it was not. The Boer guerrillas still were going strong, and they were not conquered until well into 1902, more than a year after Queen Victoria died!

"Great boys, those!" cried the British public. "Give them anything they want!"

And Campbell-Bannerman gave them the Union!

St. James's Hall, Piccadilly, was renowned for its concerts and political rallies from 1858 to 1905 (when it was leveled to make room for a modern hotel). In that hall I had my ineffaceable view of Campbell-Bannerman. It was at night in

---

Africa. After the Boer War, Balfour's government allowed 46,000 Chinese to work in the gold mines in the Transvaal as indentured servants. The conditions of this system resembled slavery—the men were forced to live in compounds that they could not leave; they worked 60 hours a week and were beaten if they violated the rules. As information about these conditions spread in England, public opinion was outraged. The Liberals capitalized on the issue. See Cross, *The Liberals in Power*, 18–9; Packenham, *The Boer War*, 607–613; and Farwell, *The Great Anglo-Boer War*, 443–54.

7. Under the leadership of Jan Christian Smuts (who had fought against England in the Boer War), the Boers supported Great Britain in the First World War. In that war, Boer forces successfully battled against German South-West Africa and sent 20,000 troops to fight against German forces in East Africa in 1916. Smuts himself, who was twice prime minister of the Union of South Africa and one of the engineers of that union, eventually took command of forces in East Africa. See Ingham, *Jan Christian Smuts*, 62–88.

8. British military and government leaders prematurely thought the Boer War was over. While commanders like Field Marshal Lord Roberts (see chap. 14, n. 6) assured British leaders that Boer resistance was finished, the Boers were preparing for almost another two years of guerrilla warfare. Paul Kruger was president of the Transvaal Republic during the Boer War. Pretoria was the capital of the Transvaal. See Pakenham, *The Boer War*, 478–510.

the very year of the hall's demolition. Liberal rank-and-filers thronged the auditorium, their greatest leaders packed the platform, and the spirit of Liberalism never ran higher. Psychologically the situation was tremendous, so charged with feeling that no one, however disinterested partisanly, could remain unmoved.

In the shadow of 70, the bulky Scottish Liberal wheel-horse, risen clean from vile abuse due to his damning of the Boer War and the way it was conducted by the British, at last was Prime Minister, and his supporters were assembled to do him honor. Broad and ruddy and bald, he rose, and the house went wild. That was it. We were eye-deep in bedlam. Then all sat. Silence. Why did not the big man speak? He stood motionless and rigid, staring at us with tight-shut teeth. Then the tears streamed like water down his cheeks. Not a dry eye in the hall. Both his big hands Sir Henry used to wipe away his tears. And in less time than it takes to tell it the old oratory was rolling, the old wit was flashing, and the house was yelling its plaudits and rocking with laughter.

What magic in the so-called "harlot of the arts"![9]

Of Lord Balfour (or rather Mr. Balfour) many pictures abide in my mind, especially before his earldom (1922). He loved to walk alone round and round the lovely lagoon in St. James's Park, where the flowers and the water-fowl were so varied and fascinating, rhododendrons, hydrangeas, pansies, petunias, geese and ducks of almost numberless genera and species. Impudently I used to break in upon his meditations there, and he did not garrote me because (I suspect) I was from America, where our tradition is one of impudence! More than once, in the midst of children's laughter, and while we gloated upon the bloom and smiled at the antics of the aquatics, the statesman and philosopher put me right on great and obscure matters of the moment.

I used to catch him too as he was walking, shoulders drooped, eyes on the ground, across the Horse Guards Parade from Downing Street to Carlton House Terrace to lunch in his home. That was when big things were on, and I wanted to know. And the charming Balfour told me. He was always the perfection of tolerance and kindness toward me, and I naturally remember him with affection.

The Germans were bombing London from the air, Zeppelins and Gothas, sometimes by day, more frequently by night.[10] One morning I counted forty German bombing planes from my office window in Trafalgar Buildings, Tra-

9. The "harlot of the arts" is rhetoric.

10. The Zeppelin was a large, rigid, balloon-shaped airship, which Germany used to bomb England during World War I. The Zeppelin carried many more guns and bombs than a typical aircraft and, at a flying altitude of above 10,000 feet, was out of range of British anti-aircraft

falgar Square, all dropping bombs, the great city intermittently and dully roaring with the explosions. Instantly I flashed the *Daily News:* "Our office safe." That meant to our editors: "The heart of London is under bombardment from the air." The censorship was in full rigor, but our paper leaped into the streets of Chicago with a clean beat on the first day-time air-raid over London.

At noon I was on the Horse Guards Parade. Shortly afterward Balfour issued from the narrow west mouth of Downing Street and came slowly in my direction. He smiled as he saw me, and said, "Well, they're at us." We walked on toward his home, and I asked him to let me fly in a British airship over London at night. "Why?" he asked, stopping and looking curiously at me. I explained that I desired to see for myself whether the Germans told the truth when they claimed (as they did persistently) that their night-bombers could distinguish military targets.

"If their statements are untrue," I said, "I can say so in my cables to America." Balfour resumed the walk, thinking.

"No good," he muttered. "Our ships fly low, the German bombers high. Military targets distinguishable from our ships would not be so from the enemy planes. Your observations, if reported to America, might do us more harm than good through no fault of either yours or ours. However, I'll take your suggestion up with my advisers."

Within a day or two I received a letter from Mr. Balfour confirming his attitude as orally stated, and I did not get my flight over London as proposed, though I flew over the metropolis many times subsequently in aeroplanes and convinced myself that military targets, however honest might be the airmen who tried to aim at them, were apt generally, over great cities, to be hit (if at all) by accident only. Balfour kept me out of the air, but as First Lord of the Admiralty he gave me numerous journalistic opportunities, particularly with Jellicoe and Beatty, on the North Sea.[11]

---

guns. The Gotha was an airplane used for bombing England. Germany raided England from the air frequently in 1915 and 1916, and less often in 1917 and 1918, as British fighter planes became more efficient at defense. England was the first country in history to be attacked from the air. See Castle, *Fire over England.*

11. Arthur Balfour was First Lord of the Admiralty during World War I from 1915 to 1916 in Herbert Henry Asquith's government. John Rushworth Jellicoe was an admiral in the British navy, and in 1914 became commander of the British Grand Fleet, which defended British territory. David Beatty also was a naval admiral. He became commander of the Grand Fleet in 1916, after Jellicoe was promoted. Both men fought naval battles in World War I, including the Battle of Jutland—the largest naval battle of that war, in which the British lost more ships than the Germans and both sides claimed victory. See Massie, *Castles of Steel,* 56–71, 83–96, 578–634.

I sat by his side on one lively occasion in the Guildhall, that noble unit among London's historical shrines. How it happened that our seats were adjoining I never knew, but I was glad of the fact, for a remarkable American was the principal figure of the evening, was to address the distinguished audience, and it would be most interesting to see at close quarters how the visitor and his speech affected the great British politician and thinker. How would the subtle author of *Defense of Philosophic Doubt* behave under the impact of the great Rough Rider?

"Teddy" already had captured England, arriving (1910) after a triumphal procession from Africa (whither he had gone on a scientific expedition for the Smithsonian Institution) during which he spoke stirring words at Khartum, almost got himself assassinated over a pro-British speech at the University of Cairo, acted somewhat snippety toward the Pope, spoke at the Sorbonne in Paris, spoke at the University of Berlin, and by the Kaiser's side reviewed the Imperial Guard, so winning the distinction of being the first civilian ever to review German troops.[12]

Glory, in fine, was all over the fellow as he stood up to speak on the red-carpeted dais of the Guildhall. His audience was bewitched before he uttered a word. Rugged (if one rejects the word savage) he certainly looked. And yet in his ruggedness, in the storminess of his concentrated expression, there was a strange gentleness which went straight to those British hearts. They could see the naturalist, the bird-lover, in their friend of Khartum and Cairo. His speech at the Guildhall went much farther than anything he had said previously. He more than approved of British imperialism. He said its only fault was that it was "too timid"!

"Tickled to death" may not be either fresh or classic English, but it fits Balfour's condition that night under the spur of Roosevelt. His imperialist fervor was hardly that of some of his contemporaries (Chamberlain, for example), but he *was* an imperialist, and "Teddy's" judgment and audacity filled him with delight. It seemed to lift a sort of load from his conscience; a great man of an-

---

12. Theodore Roosevelt (U.S. president from 1901 to 1909) spent the year after his presidency hunting in Africa for the Smithsonian Institution and making a European tour. Roosevelt believed developed nations—such as the United States and Great Britain—shared a duty to extend civilization. He often compared America's post–Spanish-American War occupation of the Philippines to Great Britain's possession of India. Roosevelt thought America should echo Great Britain, not in colonization, but in building a stronger presence in the world, especially in its own hemisphere. See Tilchin, *Roosevelt and the British Empire*; Tilchin, *Artists of Power*, 45–65; and Collin, *Roosevelt*, 154–98.

other country was not traducing but praising British imperialism! Balfour sat the whole time bent almost double, a not uncommon posture with him. Not once did he look at me or speak to me, never taking his eyes off the speaker. He smiled and smiled and cried a hundred times, "Hear, hear!" and "Bravo!"

In 1922 Balfour published the "Balfour Note" on the War Debts, addressing it to the French Ambassador in London and to other European powers, stating in brief that Britain could not pay America unless her European Allies paid her.[13] It was a note containing all the Balfourian qualities of dialectical craft and delicate irony. It shocked a great many Englishmen and roused the ire of Americans. At that time (under Northcliffe's persuasion) I had become almost a public nuisance as a writer of letters to *The Times* on topics of Anglo-American importance. I at once, by that medium, took as hard a fall out of Balfour as I could manage, declaring that his "Note" was not really a diplomatic paper at all but "a sort of argumentative magic-lantern constructed to throw Uncle Sam on the international screen as a Shylock."

Northcliffe backed me up. So did the great Strachey of *The Spectator*[14] and the dazzling Garvin of *The Observer*[15] and many other British editors in the first rank of their trade. All agreed entirely with Balfour's thesis, but all regarded his manner as exquisitely calculated to elevate America's blood-

13. As Bell writes here, Balfour's note was not well received in America. According to one of Balfour's biographers, "Americans immediately perceived an attempt by Britain to evade its obligations and fix the whole odium of international debt-collection on the USA" (Tomes, *Balfour and Foreign Policy,* 190).

14. John St. Loe Strachey was editor of *The Spectator,* a British weekly magazine, from 1887 to 1925. Strachey, one of England's finest newspaper editors, was known for his love of America and his support of Anglo-American friendship. He held weekly tea parties at his home for the American correspondents in London, to which he also invited British leaders of note. In the preface to the American edition of his autobiography, Strachey wrote, "I have always loved America and Americans" (Strachey, *The Adventure of Living,* v). In the same work, he acknowledges "Mr. Edward Price Bell of the *Chicago Daily News,* known throughout the world of London as the doyen of American correspondents. He is a man for whom respect is felt in this country in proportion to the great number of years which he had devoted not only to the service of his newspaper but to improving the relations between this country and his own" (ibid., 333).

15. James L. Garvin was editor of *The Observer* from 1908 to 1942. When popular newspaper proprietor Lord Northcliffe bought *The Observer* in 1905, the paper was a model of respectable, opinion journalism. Northcliffe wanted to keep it that way—despite the many failing newspapers he had turned into successful "new journalism" ventures (see chap. 17, n. 2). Northcliffe hired Garvin, whom he thought the best journalist in England, to maintain the Sunday paper's high reputation while turning around its lulling finances. Garvin supported the Conservative Party, although not always Balfour as its leader. See Ayerst, *Garvin of "The Observer";* and Gollin, *"The Observer" and J. L. Garvin.*

pressure: something no prudent person in either Britain or America wished to see done. I received a flood of congratulatory letters from both sides of the Atlantic, more especially from America. Colonel Edward Mandell House,[16] for one, wrote me autographically from his home in New York City (I quote his exact words): "Your *Times* letter will please all men of sense. I wish there were more like you, for then the world would be a better place in which to live."

When George Harvey[17] came to London as American Ambassador (1921), I met the most astute realist I have known in any diplomatic service. For cold deliberation, Prince Metternich had nothing on him. And he said just what he thought if he spoke at all. In his very first public utterance as Ambassador (at a Pilgrims dinner in the Edward VII room of the Hotel Victoria), he swept away the current illusion that America entered the war "to save Europe." "We fought," he proclaimed drily, "to save ourselves."[18] It was a chilling blast to many listeners: realism frequently works in that way.

Harvey was on holiday in Scotland when my *Times* letter on the "Balfour Note" appeared. He scribbled a note to me: "When I read your letter, I threw up my hat as high as it would go." He added that he would see me soon in London, and he did. "Balfour likes you," he said. "And I'm going to make him

16. Edward M. House was President Woodrow Wilson's most trusted foreign policy adviser during World War I and the peace process.

17. George Harvey was American ambassador to England from 1921 to 1923. As Bell mentions later in this memoir, Harvey once worked on the *Chicago Daily News* staff. He also was a reporter in New York and later editor of Joseph Pulitzer's *New York World*. Before he was sent to London as ambassador, Harvey edited a weekly journal in Washington, D.C., *Harvey's Journal*. The weekly carried Harvey's fiery criticism of then-president Woodrow Wilson, his war policy, and the League of Nations. See Willson, *America's Ambassadors to England*, 469–78; and Johnson, *George Harvey*.

18. When Harvey arrived in London, he gave his first public address to the Pilgrims' Society, an organization devoted to maintaining peace and friendship between England and America. Harvey said: "Nothing could be more futile, more delusive or more mischievous than to pretend that, however deep and true may be our affection for the Mother Country, our proffer of a help-ing hand is attributable primarily to a tender susceptibility. It is not. My country stands ready to work with yours, first because it is to her own interest to do so, and secondly because it is to the advantage of both . . . Prevalent until recently was the impression—and this was and still is, in a measure, sincere—that we went into the war to rescue humanity from all kinds of menacing per-ils. That is not the fact. We sent our young soldiers across the sea solely to save the United States of America, and most reluctantly and laggardly at that . . . We were afraid not to fight. That is the real truth of the matter" (quoted in Johnson, *George Harvey*, 297). The speech was well received by the British press, whose leaders praised its honesty. It was not well received, however, by the American press. See Johnson, *George Harvey*, 295–305 (298–9 for press reaction); and Willson, *America's Ambassadors to England*, 469–78.

like me, for I'll be square with him. He's accepted a bid to dine with me at the Carlton, and I want you to be with us. Just the three of us." I felt a little qualmish after my letter, but I went to the dinner and had one of the loveliest evenings of my life. Balfour and the Ambassador were in great form, and the friendly clash of those keen intellects was enchanting.

History comes to me here.

Balfour was on record with his declaration for a National Home for the Jews in Palestine.

This matter came up somehow just as we rose from the dinner table, and I was struck by the look of deep seriousness which crossed Harvey's face. Looking into the British statesman's eyes, and pointing his right forefinger firmly at those eyes, the American diplomat said:

"Balfour, you're in bad in Palestine!"

Three years later (1925) Balfour visited Palestine. The Jews warmly welcomed him. The Arabs were grimly silent. He extended his journey into Syria. There Arab wrath flamed forth so menacingly that the French authorities hurried the visitor out of the country. Today I read in the newspapers that Great Britain has in Palestine 20,000 picked troops, with tanks, artillery, and bombing planes, to shield the Jews from Arab attacks. And I read two other things: That Britain has given up her partition idea in Palestine and is taking her whole policy respecting that country "under advisement."

Is it any wonder I see and hear Harvey again as I saw and heard him that night?

"Balfour, you're in bad in Palestine!"

Wonderful all through his life, this great man of British blood was yet more wonderful at the end. His amazing powers of body and of mind were intact. In his 80th year he still was playing tennis and golf and was at the top of his magical gifts as a parliamentarian. He died universally revered as philosopher, scientist (he was president of the British Association in 1904), orator, debater, writer, musician, aesthetician, one of the last survivors of distinguished aristocracy in public life, Nestor of British statesmanship. The last truly great speech I heard him deliver he uttered in the Guildhall four years after I had sat with him there to listen to Theodore Roosevelt. He was the embodiment of solemnity; from the first to the last word not a smile on his face. The Great War was on. He declared it was "for civilization, for man's most sacred right: freedom." The war might be short or long; in any case freedom would win. That night Balfour was in his sixty-seventh year. It was November 11, 1914. On November 11, 1918, the Armistice.

Had freedom conclusively won?

Ah, before that victory, smiths long will be hammering iron!

Bonar Law, Balfour's successor in the leadership of the House of Commons and finally (1922–1923) Premier, could get hotter under the collar, and be ruder, than any other man I knew in the upper air of British politics. He was a Canadian of course but esteemed himself a dyed-in-the-wool son of the homeland and played the role to the life. Coming immediately after the debonair Balfour in the Commons, he displayed his rudeness to full advantage. One night I was listening to Asquith speaking in the Commons when he said something about his principles.

"You haven't got any principles!" yelled Bonar Law.

Asquith's shoulders rose slightly.

"We are getting on with the *new style,*" he said and proceeded, pausing only when the uproar of laughter and applause drowned him out.

The House, I think, had heard nothing just like that since Joseph Chamberlain (who could be as raw as most men) said to Campbell-Bannerman: "If you can't be a statesman, you at least might try to be a gentleman!"

But it was not in the House that Bonar Law usually worked up the most personal heat and attained to the last height of candor. One day Harry Brittain[19] (later Sir Harry) had the American correspondents in London to tea with him and his delightful wife in their nice home in Cowley Street back of Westminster Abbey. We were invited to meet Bonar Law, who (Mr. and Mrs. Brittain hoped) would make a good impression upon us and do something to affect American opinion favorably to British sea policy, which just then was threatening to enrage the Americans to the point of throwing the Republic, effectively, into the Great War on the side of the Central Powers.[20]

---

19. Harry (Henry) Brittain was a newspaperman, businessman, and Conservative member of Parliament. Brittain, who worked for the *Standard* and later the *Evening Standard,* was interested throughout his life in strengthening the Anglo-American relationship. He was the founder and leader of the American Officers Club in London—whose purpose, as Brittain tells in his memoir, was "to look after American Army and Navy officers who found their way to and through Great Britain" (Brittain, *Pilgrims,* 128). Brittain was also the originator of the idea for the American Correspondents' Association in London. (Bell was that group's first president.) See Brittain, *Pilgrims.*

20. Bonar Law was a Conservative British statesman. He was Conservative leader in the House of Commons in the years leading up to the First World War—years when the Conservatives were the opposition party. In 1915, when Henry Asquith (see chap. 14, n. 13) formed a coalition government, Law served in the cabinet as colonial secretary. He remained in the cabinet when Asquith left and Lloyd George (see n. 3 of this chapter) took his place. Law was prime minister for a brief period in late 1922 and early 1923. Bell refers here to American frustration over Great Britain's naval blockade of Germany. British ships began to intercept American cargo en route to neutral

Well, the very able Canadian Britisher (and he *was* very able) made a good impression upon us but not in the way Brittain expected. He did not talk about our "great country" nor indulge in flapdoodle of any kind. Standing in the midst of us, and occasionally gulping his tea, he walloped America right and left, actually sometimes frothing at the mouth. We were narrow and sordid, hypnotized by the parish pump and profits, had no conception of what the war was about, and must not imagine Britain would flinch in enforcing her "absolutely legitimate sea policy" however much Washington might "splutter."

At last we felt we had had a breath of pure ozone.

To a man we left the Brittain party delighted with Bonar Law (an honest and outspoken man in politics), and we often thereafter went to the House of Commons just on the off-chance of hearing him razz somebody.

Asquith (Earl of Oxford, 1925) was anything but a horn of plenty to journalists. He simply could not understand or trust them. He did not call them names, said nothing harsh to or about them; he merely eyed them askance and sealed his lips so tight they looked it. St. Loe Strachey, the great editor of *The Spectator,* and a fair-and-foul-weather friend of America, was fond of Asquith personally and wanted to "break the ice" between him and the American correspondents. We all were invited to lunch with the statesman (then Premier) at Strachey's house in Queen Anne's Gate, St. James's Park. The war was in its second year, and the Asquith Ministry was under a withering fire of criticism for alleged lack of alertness, energy, and competence. Strachey laid himself out to bring the Liberal leader and the correspondents into relations of intimacy, but his failure was complete. We left Mr. Asquith with an enormous respect for his reserve and kindliness and his capacity for dry champagne!

Mr. F. E. Smith I knew quite well before and after he became Lord Birkenhead and Lord Chancellor under Lloyd George, a gifted lawyer, "the deadliest cross-examiner in England," and a politician after Joseph Chamberlain's own heart. They gave Smith the job of controlling the Press Bureau.[21] I made a

---

countries (Great Britain feared these countries could funnel American goods to Germany). The United States protested that the blockade was a violation of neutral maritime rights. Great Britain continued the practice in spite of the protest. See Traxel, *Crusader Nation,* 155–75. For Law, see Adams, *Bonar Law.*

21. F. E. Smith was a statesman and lawyer, known for his quick wit, powerful debate, and conservatism. He was appointed inaugural director of the Press Bureau in August 1914—a post he held for little more than a month. As his biographer tells it, Smith was thrown into the office with conflicting instructions as to its aim. Lord Kitchener, secretary of state for war, intended the office to function as a censorship bureau. Winston Churchill, who was first lord of the admiralty at the time, intended the office to function as a publicity center for the War Office and Admiralty.

speech before the American Luncheon Club (H. Gordon Selfridge, the celebrated American merchant, in the chair) asserting that the Press Bureau was "stupidly censorious" and was "helping Germany to win the war by hiding Britain's magnificent efforts at home and in the field."

"Galloping" Smith (the name he acquired from his all-over-the-place activity in support of Sir Edward Carson on the Ulster question)[22] received me in his improvised office in the thick of scaffolding, building timber, and brick-and-mortar on the west side of Whitehall next to the Admiralty. It was the first time I had met him personally, and he wanted to know if I were the Price Bell who had been "slating" the Press Bureau. I confessed, and he said:

"Perhaps you're right. What do you wish of me?"

I told him I should like an exclusive interview on the war "unveiling Britain as a fighting government and people."

"Right," he replied. "I'll do it."

"Now?"

"Not now. I'll do it myself and let you have it."

Do it himself! That took me back twenty-five years, to Evansville, Indiana, when Colonel Ingersoll wrote my first great "interview" in its entirety and shed upon me so much undeserved luster. Was I to have another triumph like that? Scarcely. Though I did very well. And was amused more than I can say. Smith stepped clean out of his barristerial and parliamentary clothes and slipped into the humble raiment of the reporter. He described himself in detail, pictured his "rubbish-heap of an office," asked himself questions, and poured out his witty and sardonic replies. He took a slap at Winston Churchill[23] and the

---

In fact, the Press Bureau did mostly censorship, and many of its decisions appeared inconsistent and aimless. At the same time, the bureau issued almost no official information—resulting in a frustrated press. See Campbell, *F. E. Smith*, 372–7; and Sanders and Taylor, *British Propaganda during the First World War*.

22. While much of Catholic Ireland fought for parliamentary independence from the United Kingdom (known as Home Rule), Protestants in the province of Ulster wished to remain part of Great Britain. Their cause, known as Unionism, became a decisive issue between Liberals and Conservatives (the latter party's title grew to Conservative and Unionist Party). Conservatives used Ulster to oppose Home Rule generally—while Smith supported both Ulster's determination to remain a part of England and the rest of Ireland's determination to break from it. Edward Carson was leader of the Irish Unionist Party in Parliament and a leader of Ulster opposition to Home Rule. See Campbell, *F. E. Smith*, 323–47.

23. Winston Churchill was Great Britain's prime minister during World War II. Before this, he was a member of Parliament—first as a Conservative, then as a Liberal, than again as a Conservative. In the years leading up to World War I, Churchill was first lord of the admiralty and later, under Lloyd George's coalition government, minister of munitions. See Gilbert, *Churchill*.

Socialists, declaring that nothing kept "Winnie" from stealing the dress of the Socialists while they were in bathing except the fact that they never went in bathing!

Lacking the beauty, eloquence, and power of the Ingersoll production, Smith's "interview" yet made a hit in America and was cabled back to London for a splash in the British Press. Despite his dearly-held turn for mockery and vulgarity, one hardly could refrain from a relish for Smith. *I was fond of him.* One night he and I spoke to a large gathering of journalists at a dinner at the House of Commons. Smith sat across the table from me. As I resumed my seat after speaking, he drew a card from his case, wrote on it, and pitched it over to me. I have it yet. On it in pencil are the words:

"Damned fine speech!"

That sort of thing makes one like a fellow!

"Little Winnie" or "Dear Winnie," as the suffragettes called Winston Churchill, is one very eminent British public man whom I never was able to regard as much more than a politician with a prodigious displacement as a national and international diversion. Balfour said of him that he carried "heavy but not very mobile guns." His ideals among great men are said to be Napoleon and his own dad, the radiant Lord Randolph Churchill. I know he liked to throw artillery and troops about as in Sidney Street and the railway strike, and I know when he went to the Admiralty under Asquith (1911) his notion of naval needs in view of a possible German attack caused him, as was stated at the time, to "knock over the admirals like ninepins."[24]

24. Churchill's 1911 tenure in cabinet was not without controversy. He was home secretary for most of that year, during the "Siege of Sidney Street" and the national railway strike. In the "siege," members of a group of Latvian anarchists who had several days prior killed three policemen were cornered in a building on Sidney Street. Local police asked Churchill to send reinforcements, and Churchill sent the Scots Guards, a regiment of the British army. Churchill himself went as well to witness the showdown. When the building in which the men were hiding caught on fire, Churchill did not allow firemen to stop the blaze. Two of the Latvian anarchists died inside. Churchill was criticized for calling in troops and for stopping the firemen—both from Conservatives and his own Liberal Party. Later that year, railroad workers declared a national strike. British troops were not supposed to intervene in domestic disputes unless at the request of local authorities, but Churchill sent them anyway, declaring: "The Army Regulation which requires a requisition for troops from civil authority is suspended." The event likewise provoked criticism from both parties. When Henry Asquith appointed Churchill lord of the admiralty in 1911, Churchill reorganized the department by forming a naval war staff and removing First Sea Lord Admiral Arthur Wilson, who opposed the reorganization. For the railroad strikes, see Manchester, *The Last Lion*, 422–3; for the Sidney Street Siege, see 418–21; for the Admiralty, see 431–43.

Once as Admiralty Chief (there had been a brush between British and German naval units) Churchill told the public of "a certain liveliness on the North Sea." Liveliness surely has been a prominent and permanent quality in his life. As soldier, war correspondent, parliamentarian, administrator, simple social companion, he never has been dull, always daring, vivacious, picturesque, epigrammatic. His mother begged the militant women to vote for "Dear Winnie" in a by-election. Instead they strafed him, and he is said to have done a strange thing for him: broke down and cried in a Liverpool street.

Britons know how to use their political "talents." A neighbor of ours in Kent said to my wife: "Lloyd George? Oh, we'll use him, and when we're finished with him we'll hang him." Another plain British citizen, believing Lloyd George's public usefulness to be over, voiced the hope that when the Welshman went to the Naval Review he would "ship aboard a nice leaky submarine." Still another citizen wanted him to "jump off the deep-end of a Channel pier some rough night and forget how to swim." The Welsh Wizard himself tells the story of a swimmer who went to the rescue of a drowning man and reported on the incident thus: "I turned the chap over, saw he was not Lloyd George, and pulled him out."

British wisdom of race has known how to profit by the genius and the impetuosity of Winston Churchill without allowing him to ruin the Empire.

16. Our Fight for Side-Light News

Has it ever occurred to you that one commissioned to realize the ideal of "an absolutely exclusive service on the emotional and intellectual side of news" confronts a difficult task? We found it such. Not seldom, for a good many months, it got us down; Mr. Lawson or Mr. Dennis fired at us cables like this: "You're duplicating the news agencies. Quit it." Or this: "We've lots of stuff besides yours. When in doubt, don't." These cables hurt, but they refreshed our sense of what we were there for and put us on our toes.

I had a wonderfully fine principal aid in getting our work under way in London. Often, probably, you have heard this man broadcasting political news and views from Washington, where he has been a well-known correspondent for many years. I refer to the long-ago "cub reporter" who toiled up the stone steps of the Criminal Court building, Chicago, at midnight to get my "lead" on the jury-bribing beat which made Chicago's journalistic teeth rattle.

Frederic William Wile.

Let me pause to say here that Freddie, in my opinion, never has had a superior as a reporter. And what man of intelligence does not take his hat off to a *good* reporter? You may recall that when Mr. Dennis, on that big night long ago, asked me over the telephone whom I wished him to send for my copy, I said: "Freddie Wile." Having made my first hasty size-up of the London situation from our point of view, I cabled Mr. Dennis for an assistant from the home office. He wired back: "Whom do you want?" And again I said: "Freddie Wile." I always was friendly with myself over my choice. Freddie's loyalty was of the same high quality as his newspaper ability, and he went far. Co-worker with me on the Boer War for a year in London, he went to Berlin for us and in four years' time did so well that Lord Northcliffe took him away from us at a salary which would have made La Porte, Indiana, his home town, gasp for breath.

"Lord Northcliffe," I said to the world's peerless journalist at *The Times* office one day, "how do you like your Hoosier-Chicago boy in Berlin?"

Northcliffe gave me one of his quick looks and said:

"Wile's the best news man in Europe."

And he was!

If news comes out with a bang, there you are: the agencies have it; the exclusive man is outside the breastworks and must *run for it*. We perpetually were *running for it*. We loved the dear old Associated Press but loved more to beat it, as the records prove we often did. How often it beat us I leave to the filial piety of the sons of that great news-gathering organization. Billy Goode was one of its London men, its star London news man indeed, in 1900. He is Sir William Goode now; got that way on his merits during the Great War. He and I used to drink Scotch and soda in Victoria Street near the old American Embassy and talk shop.

"Ed," said Billy, all smiles and cigarette smoke (we were at our pub one morning waiting for Whitelaw Reid,[1] then ringmaster of the "Gilded Circus," as his ambassadorship to the Court of St. James's was called), "Ed, you fellows up there in Trafalgar Buildings are a bunch of egregious asses," with strong accent on the English "a." I wanted to know why, and Billy explained:

"You're too enterprising. You shake down your persimmons before they're ripe. You pick a green story today. I get that persimmon when it's ripe and beat you on your own yarn."

And the smiles became hearty chuckles.

Quite a bit of truth in it. But the truth was not due to any fault of ours; it was due to our imperative need to get the puckery fruit before it was ripe or not get it at all. There were those pesky cables from Chicago never to be forgotten: "You're duplicating the news agencies. Quit it." We many times were compelled to be "too enterprising," to be anticipatory, or let good stories go

1. Whitelaw Reid was an American journalist and politician. Reid covered the Civil War before stumbling onto a job at Horace Greeley's *New York Tribune*. He became proprietor and editor of that paper in 1872. Reid was a strong supporter of the Republican Party. Benjamin Harrison (U.S. president 1889–1893) rewarded him with the ambassadorship to France in 1889, one of the most prestigious posts in the Foreign Service. In 1905, Theodore Roosevelt gave Reid the most coveted post, ambassador to the United Kingdom (also known as ambassador to the Court of St. James). Reid held that position until 1912, when he died in England. See Duncan, *Whitelaw Reid.*

hang. When the Associated Press "beat" us on a yarn we had had, our recourse was to the venerable wheeze, "As foretold in these dispatches"!

Modesty must not keep me from telling that we gave Billy and his pals plenty to look after. Our opening in London found the hotels there "uncovered," though the hotels in America had been a regular source of news for years. We jumped at this opportunity. At first the hotel people were decidedly glacial. Strangers wanting to see their registers! Must be a new variety of American crook! Nothing doing! I brought some "pull" to bear, saw the managers, expounded the business, showed them where *they* would "get off," and soon we were whanging the old "AP" with one hotel beat after another.

"I say, Ed," exclaimed Billy as we met in the pub, "this hotel game of yours is rotten. New York is raising hell with us. We've got to drive you out of the hotels."

And they did.

As a fact, they drove us from pillar to post. We blazed the way for them in perhaps a dozen directions. No sooner had we taken up a position where we could do exclusive work than the "AP" was on top of us, horse, foot, and dragoons, and we were forced to scurry for cover. To us there was only one cheerful feature of this aspect of our duties: the "AP" *could not beat us.* No matter how important the story might be, if our "routine" competitors had it we were assumed by the home office to have known that fact and to have lain off the story deliberately. Of course this assumption was not invariably correct, but we were discreetly mum on that subject!

It never pays to let the home office in on *everything!*

Hard put to it for a field of inquiry neglected by both our "AP" and special rivals, I thought of the organized idealism and endeavor of London. In every great city restless folk join up for innumerable purposes. They form committees and societies and leagues and associations and that sort of thing and push their points of view. They may be political or social or economic or artistic or religious or humanitarian or doggy or horsy or anything. But they are always emotional, idealistic, on the job, sometimes probably pestiferous. And again and again, frequently in the most surprising ways, there is *news* in them.

How to find them?

Well, I opened the colossal London directory, and there before me, unfolding in black and white page upon page, lay the whole of this broad field of hidden possibilities in news, and especially that kind of news which inheres as much, if not more, in sentiment, opinion, and purpose as in passing action. Signal was the service of that field to us, and not the "AP" nor any "special," so far as I am aware, ever followed us into it. It was the *side-light* correspondent's region of gold. Times without number it panned for us excellent stories on the verge of popping and so passing out of our hands into those of the Associated Press.

Eventually a balance accrued between the news agencies and ourselves. We attained to what had been in Mr. Lawson's mind from the first: a settled status complementary to that of the spot-news correspondents. The Associated Press learned something. It learned the futility of attempting to drive the "exclusives" into the wilderness and thus hog for itself the wide and rich domain of news. Strong as it was, able as it was to break us in certain circumstances, it found out that we always bobbed up in a fresh and unexpected quarter. It found out too that no facilities are adequate to the proper handling of spot-news and also of the vital side-lights bearing upon that news.

Why, the dear "AP" became nice to us! It got so it would call us up now and then and tell us what it was sending just to protect us from those stinging "Quit it" cables from Mr. Lawson or Mr. Dennis, who never seemed to sleep!

Ideas, we discovered (not without righteous ire), are precious things hard to safeguard. And ideas capable of development into appealers for the headlines were our stock-in-trade. I will give an illustration. Leader of the Irish Parliamentary party in the House of Commons at that time was John Edward Redmond,[2] a good and brilliant man. I went to him with an idea of what struck me as promising a big Irish story. He saw it; there was very little he did *not* see. He would prepare the stuff I wanted. He did. And he did the job superlatively well. But I never got the story. He gave it to the Associated Press. I sought him out at the House of Commons and expressed my astonishment.

"I am deeply sorry," he said. "I really had to do it. The story was of importance to Ireland, and my duty to my country comes first. The Associated Press was able to give me a public in America far wider than your service reaches. I think you will understand."

I understood all right. But I never forgot the lesson that no politician or diplomat in the world ever breaks his heart to be just, let alone chivalrous, to a newspaper man. This is true of presidents and premiers as of ambassadors and

2. John Redmond led the Irish Parliamentary Party from 1900 until his death in 1918. Redmond supported Home Rule for Ireland—an arrangement by which Ireland would have limited self-government while remaining part of the United Kingdom. Redmond's cooperation with British Liberals and his policy of urging Irish to fight with England during the First World War soon became unpopular. Increasingly after Redmond's death, Irish leaders in Parliament sought not Home Rule but an independent Irish republic. See Finnan, *John Redmond and Irish Unity*.

ministers and the dimmer lights of politics and diplomacy. That unique genius among reporters, the marvelous De Blowitz,[3] knew it, found it out long before me. He says in his *Memoirs*: "An Ambassador never will hesitate to throw a journalist quite overboard and sacrifice him body and soul . . . to further that Ambassador's own designs." Perfectly true. And I hope to cite some examples before I write "Finis" to this volume.

Our position in London as "exclusives" made secure, my duties were enlarged. I was given the title and the work of general manager of the Special Foreign News Service of the *Chicago Daily News*. My shocking experience with Mr. Redmond, like similar experiences generally, did me some good. It gave me, if not sweetness and light, stiffness and light. I had ascertained for myself, and could tell our men, a little about politicians in their relations with correspondents dependent upon original and substantial ideas for their excuse to exist. *Real life was helping us to get on.* I shouldered my knapsack and went on a great hike. I visited Paris, Rome, Vienna, Berlin, and a score of lesser cities from Scandinavia and the Baltic to the Black Sea. I hiked throughout Europe, and Frederic William Wile functioned for me in-chief on the Thames.

Everywhere I carried my evangel of the larger and (as I believed) the greater journalism, the journalism which was alert and objective and honest and went deep into the hearts and the minds and the latent acts of governments and peoples, the journalism which was a clean mirror not of what we *wished* to see but of what we *saw*. "Be *historians,* not *partisans*. Be *reporters,* not *advocates*." That is the preachment I put to our men, and back there in Chicago (thank God!) were the great editors to cry, "Amen!"

If there is such a thing as treason to one's own people and to humanity, it lurks in the reporter who colors or lies!

Education of our foreign staff in the conception and the methods of our side-light journalism was a toilsome and slow business. We needed newspaper men. In the great capitals, Paris, Rome, Berlin, we placed writers from our own office, and they progressed rapidly in the theory and the practice of exclusive news reporting and of side-light stories composed of expository matter, principally in the form of interviews with women and men of authority,

---

3. Henri Georges Stefan Adolphe Opper de Blowitz was a Bohemian journalist who immigrated to France in his early twenties. De Blowitz spent much of his career there, eventually working as Paris correspondent for *The Times* of London, a post he held for twenty-eight years. De Blowitz scored several beats in his tenure at *The Times*. The most famous was securing an advance text of the Treaty of Berlin in 1878. He was also known for his eccentricity in appearance, dress, and personality, as well as his tendency to make things up. See Giles, *A Prince of Journalists.*

but partly as our own specified interpretations of interesting and important persons, situations, outlooks, and events. One of our most reliable men from the home staff was an Englishman, Robert Atter, Chicago-trained, long resident for us in the beautiful old capital of Austria-Hungary, music-loving Vienna. Such correspondents, comparatively, found their way about in our new journalistic world with ease.

But our idea of a foreign news service spread far beyond the capitals. In each of the greater countries we set up a news-gathering system, centralized in the capital and reporting to it. This required specially-educated writers in many important towns, and we could not staff the whole service from the Chicago editorial department. That was neither possible nor desirable for the reasons (1) that the home office could not spare the men and (2) that the minor posts furnished for the correspondents only part-time work. Our constituent systems were unified in a big one, and the whole stream of European news flowed through London and was modified and reduced as we thought fit there. Thus, while much money was wasted on European telegraph tolls, we saved a fortune every year on useless Atlantic cable tolls.

In Germany, for example, I trained correspondents for our Special Service in such places as Stuttgart, Munich, Halle, Nuremberg (happy hunting-ground of the Nazis), Frankfort, Cologne, and Bremen. I trained men also in the Scandinavian countries, which were of great significance to us with our tens of thousands of Swedish, Norwegian, and Danish readers. I picked out newspaper men, some mature, some immature, all with at least a little knowledge of English. This knowledge sometimes was emphatically and humorously small. In Christiania (Oslo since 1925), for instance, we had one man who represented himself as speaking English "perfectly." We discovered, however, that all he could say in our tongue was "Well." He *understood* everything. Say to him: "I should like you to show me some of your fine streets, museums, and galleries." "Well," he would answer, and do it.

"Now," you would say, "perhaps we could have a look in on your Parliament?"

"Well."

And we did that.

So it ran until one was limp with suppressed mirth.

But our permanent correspondent in Christiania was one of the best journalists in Europe, both understanding and writing English good enough for anyone. Mons Monsen Mjelde was his name, and *Tidens Teyn* was his paper, a journal which he represented nobly at a later time as its London correspondent. Mjelde was a splendid Norwegian, a naval officer as well as a journalist, strong, upright, brave, sincere, and with an instinctive grasp of what side-light correspondence meant. One of my great treasures is a large silver urn, of Norwegian design, with the inscription on its base: "From *Tidens Teyn* and its London Correspondent."

With Mjelde no labor was needed to show him what we sought. But with the majority, stereotyped as spot-news men and nothing else, it was a case of *de*-education first and *re*-education afterward. I stayed from one to two weeks in each town and practically did the tyro's job for him as he listened and looked on, precept working itself out in performance before his eyes. Linguists I met often, men who spoke from two to half-a-dozen Continental languages, however ill-equipped they might be to handle English. Of their adeptness in languages they were uniformly proud. They thought it meant nearly every-thing. What did the task of a little reporting amount to if one could sling most of the lingoes from the Volga to the Seine? All these self-preening gentlemen I found haughtily disdainful of the one-tongue man.

But (the world would be relatively empty but for its buts) experience taught me a good deal in this relation. I learned, for one thing, that a multiplicity of languages supplies several media for hot-air emission. I learned so much more on this head that I coined a saying for our service: "A man's ability to do first-class newspaper work is generally in inverse ratio to the number of languages he speaks." It is all right, it is fine, to know one or two languages other than one's own (French and German say), but I found that a brain crowded with linguistic forms of countless varieties has scant room in it for the clear and practical stuff of newspaper competence.

One of the moral vitalities we strove to instill into our men lay in the idea that they were neither canine nor leonine, neither flunkies nor almighty men. Journalists in those days were not held in very high esteem in Europe; doubt-less did not deserve to be: roughly, I fancy, a man usually mushes through to the goal of his real deserts. We dreamed of workers in our profession (and pro-fession we purposed it should be) worthy of and demanding respect; taught that unimpeachable *self*-respect insured the ultimate respect of others, how-ever high-riding. Of egotism, however (a quality implanted quite commonly in men), we desired as little as might be. "Don't be so modest," we laid upon each correspondent, "as to walk always the last man in the procession. And yet don't assault your keyboard under the illusion that your real name is Buddha."

Egotism. It came out persistently in dogmatism. Correspondents tended to over-positivity in the assertion of opinion. They did not *think* things; they *knew* them. That vice, with its revelation of insufficiency of both knowledge and thought, we cried down. I told our men of an interchange I had heard long before in Chicago between an airy young reporter and old Dr. Andrews, superintendent of the city schools. "Dr. Andrews," said the reporter, "we know that *absolutely*." "Your knowledge is *absolute?*" queried the old scholar. "I had supposed that all knowledge was *relative*." It is the peculiar fault of egocentricity in a correspondent that he loses sight of realities, material and immaterial, and so is no longer a reportorial journalist.

Words. Words holding within themselves broad suggestion. Words wrapping up in their meaning the whole range of human interest and activity. I used them to stimulate and guide our searchers for emotion and ideas and acts of international appeal and importance. *Political, Social, Economic, Religious, Moral, Intellectual,* these were my key-words. What fresh things were going in the correspondent's country in politics; in education, temperance, housing, philanthropy; in manufacture, trade, finance; in religion and morality; in art, literature, science, philosophy, fashion? What were the emperors, kings, queens, *élite* doing? What the government? Who were the outstanding personalities and what did they come to? What were the *people* feeling, thinking, doing? What was the national *story* from the peak to the pit of the country's life?

Prophecy, I found, comes easily to eager journalists in the bud. We discouraged it as the thing Goethe thought it was, "pernicious superstition." I recommended to our correspondents the advice of Josh Billings, "Don't prophesy unless you know." Speculation, however, was permissible. Inventive sprightliness was entertaining and harmless. But it must not take the form of definite prophecy. We might deal in the probable, in the possible even, but for only what they actually were, not as things revealed to us in a crystal ball.

"Dig deep for your stuff" was one of our battle-cries. We learned the deceptiveness of the *superficies* of human life, the treacherousness of gossip, the essential falsity of rumor, the frailty of much thinking in even high quarters, the ubiquity and often abominable rascality of organized propaganda. Radicalism of inquiry, delving to the roots of things, was our ideal and our practice. "Try your utmost," I said to our men, "to grasp *governing fundamentals* and then hold to them as a skipper holds to his compass in a storm."

Pretty well it worked, this dope. It consolidated a capable and zealous body of people, mostly men but partly wonderful women, in the foreign service of an American newspaper strictly, imaginatively, incorruptibly dedicated by its great founder to the proposition that the *public* was its *only client:* that special interests of whatever sort or power had neither welcome nor influence within its doors, and that the *world* was the theater of its duty to those who bought it. Our European model, sprung from the germ of that interview with a Chinese laundryman in Chicago, hurdled religious, ethnic, national, and geographic boundaries until it was yielding results in every continent and in many islands of the seas. Writing, I rejoice that I worked for and with Victor Fremont Lawson and Charles Henry Dennis upward of forty years without ever once feeling the weight of thistledown from headquarters to deflect me from the line of conscience.

Let those who can rise today and say:

"Ditto!"

Summarily is the only way I can speak of my splendid colleagues in the far-extending work. Many of them are well known, famous, now. Harry Hansen worked with us, notably in Belgium during the Great War. Edmond Percy Noel and Louis Edgar Browne and Negley Farson and John Gunther worked for us throughout Europe. Two of my most noted associates in Europe were Paul Scott Mowrer and his brother, Edgar Ansel, both still with the *Chicago Daily News,* Paul as chief editorial writer and Edgar as Paris correspondent. That sound journalist and prince of good fellows, Hal O'Flaherty, now managing editor of the *Chicago Daily News,* served us honestly and ably overseas. On great assignments I have chummed with him.

Hiram Kelly Motherwell, now a critic of the drama in New York, did graceful and most intelligent work for us in Rome. He was interpreter when Signor Mussolini talked with me at such length at Palazzo Chigi in 1924, our first interview, and his mastery of Italian was illustrated happily that day. I barely can wave to Bill Hard (always Bill and always brilliant), Constantin Brown of Washington, Raymond Swing of early Berlin days, John Russell Kennedy of Tokyo, Jimmy Butts of Peking, the sturdy Walter Robb of Manila (still productive in his fascinating West Pacific post), and numerous others. Henry Justin Smith,[4] most gifted, I think, of them all, moved into our orbit only occasionally but long enough to let us see something of why he wrote with such insight and felicity of newspaper men.

A word now about those "wonderful women." Only three or four will I speak of here. Miss Harriet Dewey, "Mother Dewey," autocrat of the Chicago office and the foreign service, worked to the end and died in her 90's. She was

---

4. Henry Justin Smith was an editor at the *Daily News* when Bell, Mowrer, and other eventual foreign correspondents were city reporters. He became a legend among the staff. He wrote two novels about journalism: *Deadlines* and *Josslyn: The Story of an Incorrigible Dreamer.*

cashier, and her money talked, but her character and sympathy talked more. We loved her. Miss Judith Waller too we loved. When we came home from the cities and the wilds of the world, from scenes of lovely peace and scenes of mud and blood, Judith let us talk to millions over her *Chicago Daily News* radio. Sweet and pretty as a slip of a girl, extraordinary as a woman, she blazed the trees in radio management.

And she is radio's bright particular star today.

Autocrat of the London office was Miss Alice M. Archer, and her like in Paris was Miss Theresa Murphy, both vital supports in our foreign scheme. Miss Murphy was light and language for many a groping and tongue-tied visitor to the French capital. Her place in thousands of hearts is secure. Miss Archer, "the best-known secretary in the world," kept our records, tabbed our correspondents, edited cables, wrote some, killed some, reenforced our battery of professional counsel, welcomed our visitors from London, the British Isles, America, the circuit of the globe. Tranquil now in her retirement in St. John's Wood, London, Miss Archer can brighten her contemplative moods with the reflection that persons unnumbered and in far-sundered lands remember her with a sentiment compact about equally of admiration and affection.

17. Luminaries of the British Press

Joy and profit virtually unalloyed came to me at the hands of the luminaries of the British Press. Stead's friendship, and how I prized it, I already have tried to make clear. I owe a debt of gratitude to many others, notably Northcliffe, Scott of the *Manchester Guardian,* Garvin, Strachey, Sir Robert Donald, Lord Burnham, Beaverbrook, Wickham Steed, Geoffrey Dawson, John Morley, William Hill, Spender, Greenwood, Massingham, Gardiner, Blatchford, Marlowe, and Blumenfeld, remarkable journalists all, embodying as a group practically every distinguished quality in our profession.[1]

1. Alfred Charles Harmsworth (Viscount Northcliffe) was England's greatest newspaper magnate. His newspapers—the *Daily Mail, The Observer,* the *Evening News,* and *The Times* among them—ushered in the era of British "new journalism." Charles Prestwich Scott was proprietor and 57-year editor of the *Manchester Guardian,* a Liberal weekly that was the forerunner of today's *Guardian.* J. L. Garvin was editor of *The Observer,* a Sunday paper. John St. Loe Strachey was editor and proprietor of *The Spectator,* an influential Conservative weekly. Sir Robert Donald was editor of the *Daily Chronicle* for fifteen years. Sir Harry Lawson Webster Levy (Viscount Burnham) was proprietor of the *Daily Telegraph,* London's first penny daily paper. Aitken Maxwell (Baron Beaverbrook) owned several British newspapers, including the *Daily Express,* the *Sunday Express,* and the *Evening Standard.* Wickham Steed was editor of Northcliffe's *Times* of London for three years and exercised editorial control over several other of Northcliffe's papers, including the *Daily Mail,* the *Evening News,* and the *Weekly Dispatch.* Geoffrey Dawson was editor of *The Times* before Steed, until 1919, and again after Northcliffe's death and Steed's dismissal in 1922. John Morley was a Liberal member of Parliament who had been editor of the *Pall Mall Gazette,* a Liberal evening journal, in the 1880s. William Hill was inaugural editor of the *Tribune,* a Liberal weekly, and later editor of the *Weekly Dispatch.* John Alfred Spender is probably Bell's reference here (as opposed to his brother, Hugh F. Spender, who was diplomatic correspondent for the *Westminster Gazette*). John Alfred Spender was editor of that paper. Frederick Greenwood was the founder and editor of the *Pall Mall Gazette.* Henry William Massingham was editor of the

Superb newspaper management, statesmanship, high culture, new eminences of journalistic imagination, the loftiest sense of journalistic responsibility, independence which would not compromise, writing power never surpassed in newspaper history, every one of these could be found here or there in that amazing cluster of genius and talent. Sensationalists among them? Yes. But sensationalism is not inevitably exaggeration or untruth. Sometimes it is merely fresh vision and unprecedented vigor creating a noise among dry bones.

I saw and heard a lot of that sort of thing in my time in England![2]

Reviewing journalism as it passed into history before my eyes in Great Britain and Ireland for more than a generation (approximately the first thirty-five years of this century), I should say its improvement on the whole has been prodigious. Presumption, smugness, negation, apathy have been swept from Fleet Street[3] and the whole British newspaper world. Those public prints which incarnated reaction in its broad sense are gone. Open-mindedness, imagination, enterprise, the spirit and the will of eternal challenge have superseded the *credo* of death among the makers of the British Press, whether publishers or editors and writers.

Star and the *Daily Chronicle.* Alfred George Gardiner was editor of the *Daily News,* a Liberal daily founded by novelist Charles Dickens. Robert Peel Glanville Blatchford is probably Bell's reference here (as opposed to his brother Montagu John Blatchford, also a newspaperman). Robert Peel Glanville Blatchford was instrumental in the success of the novel British Socialist weekly the *Clarion.* Thomas Marlowe was editor of Northcliffe's *Daily Mail.* Ralph David Blumenfeld was editor of the *Daily Express,* founded as a competitor to the *Daily Mail.* See Griffiths, ed., *The Encyclopedia of the British Press.*

2. Bell's time in London coincided with the rise of "new journalism" in England. New journalism in many ways resembled the rise of the popular press in the United States during the late nineteenth and early twentieth centuries. Newspaper proprietors and editors like W. T. Stead and Lord Northcliffe turned mainly political highbrow newssheets into cheap papers written to inform and entertain a wider, less-educated audience. New journalism innovators introduced large headlines, illustrations, gossip columns, and "sensational" human-interest stories. Mathew Arnold, poet and literary critic, coined the phrase *new journalism,* which he described as "full of ability, novelty, variety, sensation, sympathy, generous instincts, its one great fault . . . that it is feather-brained. It throws out assertions at a venture because it wishes them true; does not correct either them or itself, if they are false; and to get at the seat of things as they truly are seems to feel no concern whatever." See Koss, *The Rise and Fall of the Political Press in Britain;* Wiener, *Papers for the Millions;* and Lee, *The Origins of the Popular Press.*

3. "Fleet Street" is both a term used to describe the London national press and the location of many London newspaper offices. Although most London newspapers moved elsewhere during the 1980s, Fleet Street was home to almost every major national newspaper during Bell's tenure in London. See Wintour, *The Rise and Fall of Fleet Street.*

One mind gave primary leadership in all this. That mind belonged to an Irish-born boy, son of an English father (a barrister) and an Ulster mother, a lady of beauty and of the rarest attributes of character and of intellect, worshiped by her brilliantly-endowed son as few worship anybody. That boy was Alfred Harmsworth, finally Viscount Northcliffe, in many overmastering respects, I think, the greatest journalist who ever lived. *He* was the human typhoon which left the Old Fleet Street, with its prejudices and fatuities, in irreparable ruin. Loud and piercing were the cries amid the wreckage, but progress did not listen.

Northcliffe knew a lot of things about journalism unsuspected by his overweening contemporaries. The most basic thing he knew concerning it was that magazines and newspapers which live and grow must look outward rather than inward, must think enormously more of the masses and of public opinion than of themselves, must realize what a very big and wonderful force is *news,* how immeasurably more important it is than *views,* even those views held by great and proud editors. Northcliffe believed, and overwhelmingly demonstrated, that the life of the people is journalism's life if it have any life.

How he loved to spend money to exemplify and vindicate his ideals! Poor as a dog at 20, he was rich at 22, and then his wealth began to flow like a river in parched Fleet Street. Salaries jumped up astoundingly. Ordinary reporters began to eat decent food and wear decent clothes. The melancholy crows disappeared from the War Office at midnight. I used to see them there unfailingly when I went for the latest official news from the British-Boer war. They were reporters. They snacked and drank bitter. They wore black felt hats and shabby frock coats and looked as if all life were a funeral. Their pay was a guinea ($5) a week. Northcliffe waved his wand, and they vanished. Ralph Blumenfeld (Beaverbrook's editor-in-chief) told me the last time I saw him that the poorest-paid reporter in Fleet Street today gets eight pounds ($40) a week.

"You can't do anything without money," said Northcliffe. And his idea was that a liberal use of money is required especially in successful magazine and newspaper production and circulation. "Magazines and newspapers," ran his doctrine, "can carry on only if they be thoroughly alive and surpassingly intelligent. In order that they may be so, the moral and mental powers at their command must be at the highest level the country affords. You want men and women who will stand up for what they believe. You want men and women sufficiently intelligent to understand, and so be able accurately to interpret, the people. And will someone tell me how such persons are to be had for a pittance?"

Wide open was swung the door of Fleet Street for the wisdom, the brilliance, the conviction, the versatility of Great Britain and the world. For Northcliffe had no smallness about him. Races and religions and frontiers meant no more to him than they mean (or ought to mean) to mathematics or astronomy. He was just as quick to welcome a French or Italian or German or American writer as one of his own land. All he asked for in ideas or in articles was excellence, the power to amuse, inspire, inform. Nearly everyone of passion or knowledge began to write for him, novelists and poets, playwrights, artists, scientists, experts in many lines, humorists, politicians. Fleet Street knew an unheard-of moral and intellectual blooming!

I will not say that journalistic transformation in London and elsewhere in Britain has been *all* to the good: the tide of human advance seems to submerge as well as to bear on good men and good things. I saw more than one fine journalist go down in what might be called the "Northcliffe Flood." I saw historic newspapers sink. I heard wails which reminded me of those which rose into the night when the *Titanic* struck an iceberg in the mid-Atlantic. I saw proprietorial predominance floating in triumph while editorial independence perished. Many a familiar hand was raised which I fain would have seized. But nothing could help. The "deep and dark-blue ocean" rolled on!

Proprietorial predominance, however, did not send all editorial independence to the bottom. Scott of the *Manchester Guardian,* for instance, remained to the end of his life an editor first and a publisher afterward.[4] I remember his white hair and his magnificent head so well. He used to come to London once in a while, and I had the treat of talking with him repeatedly in the lobby of the House of Commons, where he took pleasure in sauntering about and exchanging views with politicians high and low and of every shade of opinion. There he met also callers of diversified pursuits from all over the United Kingdom and indeed all over the Empire. One day I found him there talking with Premier Poincaré of France,[5] who had come to England on a political mission,

4. Charles Prestwich Scott edited the *Manchester Guardian* for almost six decades. He bought the paper in 1905. Scott supported Prime Minister William Gladstone's policy of Home Rule, opposed the Boer War, and supported women's suffrage. These stands were not always popular or profitable for the paper. See Hammond, *C. P. Scott*, 60–91; and Ayerst, *The Manchester Guardian*, 165–477.

5. Raymond Poincaré was five-time prime minister of France. Noted for his strong anti-German bent, Poincaré was instrumental in France's foreign policy throughout the First World War and the peace settlement. His first term as prime minister was during Bell's tenure in London, from January 1912 to January 1913. See Keiger, *Raymond Poincaré*.

had discussed public questions freely with journalists, and was having a look at the Commons "from without," informally.

"Perhaps this is the most interesting spot in our country, at all events sometimes," said Scott to me on a gloomy winter afternoon when the lobby was crowded and babbling like a fountain. "It is a mirror," he went on, his gray eyes wandering over the pre-occupied throng. "I come to the lobby to inspect the country. I can see it all here, heart and head. It helps me vitally in keeping the horizon of my journalism wide enough to take in our citizenship as a whole."

"As you think journalism should?" I said.

"Unquestionably. Rich, poor, educated, uneducated. We all sink or swim together. I don't think much of a newspaper man who doesn't know that. An editor has his opinions. They're a part of him. He is maimed unto death without them. But his paper is much bigger than he. It must comprehend and reflect not a man, not a circle, but society. A newspaper belongs to humanity."

I understood then why Scott, in that great psychologically multi-colored lobby, seemed (with all the strength and inexorableness of his individuality) to have only friends, all vying with one another to catch his eye or grasp his hand. In May, 1921, the *Guardian* celebrated Scott's fiftieth year of association with it. Everyone appeared to have a sense of the greatness of the occasion. King George V did. He wired his congratulations to Scott and the paper which "under your courageous and high-minded guidance has secured for itself a position of such eminence and esteem in the world of journalism." Never, I venture to think, did that wise and lovable monarch send a message with more of his heart in it than his wire to Scott contained.

Frederick Greenwood, successor of Thackeray at *The Cornhill*, editor of the *Pall Mall Gazette*, editor of *St. James's Gazette*, friend of Gladstone, supporter of Disraeli, first a philosophic Liberal, then a Conservative, then a Liberal again (his views changing as circumstances and his conscience changed), Frederick Greenwood will live always as an exemplar of the ideal editor, every other consideration yielding to his editorial feeling and point of view. Up against a proprietorial stonewall he did not like, he resigned: left his job and kept his fidelity to right as he saw it.[6] He exercised an immense influence on public affairs.

6. Frederick Greenwood and his political writers tended to support the Conservative Party, although they were not above criticizing it as well. When the paper's proprietor sold it to Henry Yates Thompson, a Liberal Party man, Greenwood quit. He wrote to William Gladstone, prime minister at the time: "My paper . . . [has] been sold into the hands of a thorough going party-man of Liberal views & is henceforth to be no erratic independent but to be printed as a supporter of

So honorable was Greenwood that he would forego a tremendous score for his newspaper, a crashing world beat, for what he deemed the larger interest. He got on to the fact that the Suez Canal shares of Khedive Ismail were for sale (1875) and that France purposed to buy them. (France was the enemy then!) The government was ignorant of these facts (as governments often are ignorant of momentous things), and Greenwood informed it. The beat of course was his. But he said not a word till the government had bagged the crucial shares and announced the purchase to the world. That, I suggest, is journalism rising to the full height of its inherent responsibility.

I knew Greenwood from 1900 to 1909, when he quit the London scene for the ultimate Home of Great Editors. I used now and again to lunch with him at the Garrick Club.[7] His moral lineaments as a journalist and publicist were those of Scott. Personally he was stolid, grave, circumspect, gentle, always a center of interest to his professional and artistic friends of the Garrick. I drew great inspiration from the depth and the purity of his spirit and the sagacity of his mind. He was a student of Napoleon, had written a book about Napoleon III. He considered the first Emperor's true greatness to consist in a realization of the inalienable sovereignty of the people. No general could fight successfully unless grounded in the confidence of the people.

"That," said Greenwood, "is the principle of principles in politics, war, and *journalism*. Moral greatness and lasting material success are denied to the journalist and the journal without knowledge of the real seat of social power: the people. Governments may come, and governments may go; governmental systems may wear one nominal tag or another; newspaper editors and newspapers may be what they like. But the people will carry on as arbiters, in their nature supreme. Bell, I'm glad to have been a journalist and to have accepted no brief except from the true democracy: the people."

Branded upon my memory to the last day of my life are Frederick Greenwood's philosophy, his faith in it, and his glorious loyalty to it. Pure abstraction though it was, it meant infinitely more to him than anything concrete. Commercialism more and more taking charge of the London newspaper world,

---

your government." Greenwood left the editorship a few days after he penned that letter. Taking most of his political writers with him, he began the *St. James Gazette*. Similar problems with the proprietor followed him there, and Greenwood quit again. See Scott, *The Story of the Pall Mall Gazette*, esp. 235–42.

7. The Garrick Club is an exclusive gentlemen's club in London named for David Garrick, the English actor and writer. The club is devoted to the support and patronage of literature and drama.

this journalist and man of letters packed up his philosophy in his old kit-bag and carried it with him into semi-retirement. For retire totally he never did. At intervals to the end of his days he reappeared in newspapers, magazines, and reviews, and every time his spiritual and mental features were the same. I dwell upon him a little because he typifies with such perfection the editorial personalities who went down with their ships as the big London journalistic storm of this century raged with ever increasing violence.

Surviving at the moment is one editor and editorial writer, and one only, of the illustrious school of which I speak. His name is Garvin, the famous "J.L.G." of *The Observer*, the most powerful Sunday newspaper in the world, and a journal which bears Garvin's personal imprint from the first page to the last and in practically every paragraph and sentence, truly a one-man baby.[8] Garvin is *independent.* He is as brilliant as he is independent, and his audacity and courage equal both. His hand falls upon a man or a thing he hates with pile-driver force. If American money ever has done any good abroad, it did good when it presented *The Observer* (Lord Astor owns the paper) to J. L. Garvin as the unreserved medium of his unmatched journalistic enlightenment and power.[9]

Of course he has ruffled the Zoo. He has stirred up the animals journalistic and political. Some people have poked fun at his "weekly Niagara of words." One day I spoke to Stanley Baldwin[10] about Garvin, referring to the journalist as a "glowing genius." Baldwin was Prime Minister then and was smoking his pipe and smiling in his private room at the House of Commons. He broke out laughingly: "Oh, yes. But I wish he more frequently would glow in the right place!" Possibly light on this crypticism may be found in the words of that other dashing editorial (as opposed to industrial) journalist, Alfred Gardiner: "In ten thrilling years, Garvin knocked British Toryism into a cocked hat."

8. Bell is not alone in his opinion of J. L. Garvin. British press scholar Stephen Koss writes: "In some cases, [the influence of journalists] transcended the influence of their papers. Garvin was the last of the breed, a political editor who held his chair through the ensuing age of great proprietors" (Koss, *The Rise and Fall of the Political Press in Britain*, 11).

9. Waldorf Astor, a member of the American-British family that also owned the *Pall Mall Gazette,* bought *The Observer* from Northcliffe in 1911. Although neither Northcliffe nor Astor gave Garvin "unreserved" independence, both recognized Garvin as one of the brightest stars of British journalism and allowed him considerable freedom as editor.

10. Stanley Baldwin was a Conservative British statesman and three-time prime minister. During Bell's tenure in London, Baldwin was a Conservative member of Parliament and during the First World War served as secretary to the chancellor of the exchequer. See Middlemas and Barnes, *Baldwin.*

Gardiner described this achievement as a "triumph of sheer rhetoric." No! Garvin's stuff may have in it (does have in it) the rainbows of Niagara, but it has also the weight of the Falls!

Later in these pages I hope to show Garvin in action.

England had no journalist of loftier character or more precise and cutting mind than Strachey of *The Spectator.* He died in the Great War like a front-line soldier, not in Flanders or France but in his country home at Newland's Corner, near Guildford, Surrey, where he housed and waited on ill and wounded men, Tommys, and contracted their maladies. All through the war he stood four-square for British-American friendship, "no matter what the price," and he went to bat for the American correspondents in London as did no other editor. His teas for us, weekly affairs, were an effective *liaison* between British authority and the American Press. We loved him for his goodness to us. Our most impelling memory of him, however, is that of the firmness of his will and the soundness of his judgment. Very great seemed the darkness to me when Strachey's light failed!

Lord Burnham, a man of the most pleasing manners, I saw at many times and in widely divergent situations. One day in the middle of the war he and I were taking cover in Tincourt Wood, near St. Quentin, France, under the aegis of General Monash's redoubtable Australians.[11] With us in the timber-sheltered huddle were Billie Hughes, Australian Premier, Robert Blatchford, soldier as well as journalist, and Ralph Blumenfeld. Great preparations were going on quietly but incessantly for the British-French-American push which brought St. Quentin permanently within the Allied ring of steel. Monash and his army were growing ever more taut for the fight. The sleepless Germans were nervous. We were there to see, had crouched and crawled into Tincourt Wood. It was so still in the cool and bright morning light that every leaf-rustle was a whisper one could hear.

And then hell belched.

A strange crescendo. At first I thought it a ringing sound such as one has sometimes in one's ears without external cause. Then it was a deafening shriek. Then a terrific bang and roar, and our little party was thatched with leaves, twigs, and splintered tree-trunks. Lord Burnham was closest to me, and I smiled at him through the *débris.*

11. Lieutenant General John Monash led Australian troops during the First World War. St. Quentin, France, was a town on the front line of fighting in the spring and summer of 1918. It was the site of the great German offensive of 1918 (called the Battle of St. Quentin or the Second Battle of the Somme), in which German forces pushed Allied troops back almost 40 miles.

"Hurt?" I asked.

"No, thank you. And yourself?"

None of us was hurt.

Another crescendo and crash. The earth shook. I thought the whole forest was shivered. We clearly were in for burial alive unless something were done. By a common impulse we got upon our feet and did what even the bravest troops wisely do in some cases: *ran.* Lord Burnham was heavy, and his legs were short. I stayed with him, thinking I *might* be able to help as my own avoirdupois was relatively slight and my strength considerable. He made a wonderful job of his running, eyeing the ground closely, minding his step, a look of intense concentration in his face. Billy Hughes ran well too. And the Michigan boy, "Blumy." And Blatchford, though he then was nearly 70 (one forgets age when the Germans get after one!). As for myself, I was not behind the party when we emerged into safety with that tornado of dust and flying timber well to our rear. And how happy we were that night in Monash's tiny cottage-headquarters, listening to the General's hearty laughter and sharing his excellent food and wine!

Even war is not *all* hell!

Wondrously different was the conjuncture in which I next found myself by the side of Burnham. He sat on my right. On my left, rather tired-looking but very handsome, sat Garvin, chairman. It was a round table covered with gleaming linen and sumptuous with beautiful china, glass, and silver, wine glasses in clusters. At the table were a dozen men whose names all the world knew, men of the British government, of science and industry, of letters, of art, of journalism. Sir Alfred Mond (Viscount Melchett, 1928) represented the Cabinet. Sir Robert Hadfield, great metallurgist, and H. Gordon Selfridge, merchant prince, sat opposite me. James Keeley, noted Chicago editor, and my *confrère* Frederic William Wile were in adjoining chairs.[12]

It was a big room. And crowded to the doors with rose-adorned tables and happy-faced guests in full evening-dress. Two ladies, and two only, were present: Mrs. Wile and my wife. And they were in hiding behind tall screens at the remote end of the hall.

12. Sir Alfred Mond was a Liberal member of Parliament. Robert Hadfield was a British metallurgist who developed manganese steel. For Selfridge, see chap. 14, n. 14. James Keeley was the colorful and enterprising editor of the *Chicago Tribune,* for which he coined the famous slogan "the world's greatest newspaper." He later left the *Tribune* and was part owner of the *Chicago Herald.* The reader will remember that Wile was Bell's fellow reporter in Chicago and later joined him in London.

A splendid public dinner was what it was, the largest ever held at the famous Carlton Hotel. The hotel management was not pleased. It had stated that only a certain number of diners would be let in. Too many would spoil the spectacle. The hotel rule was adamant. The management had not reckoned with D. Campbell Lee, celebrated American barrister in London, who had organized the dinner. He publicly had invited everybody to come, and seemingly nearly everybody did. And as the guests came he demanded and got places for them until the room would hold no more. Journalists had preference, for it was a journalist's night. Britain's star newspaper men from both London and the Provinces were there.

To honor whom?

Pluck is necessary to answer, but truth compels:

Me!

I sometimes think I am dreaming about it all, but there is the record: *examine* it. My biographer of course ought to tell the story. Unfortunately I have no biographer. And, recurring once more to Poincaré in his interview with me in Paris when he was Premier, *"Somebody must stand up for history!"* Northcliffe was kept away from the dinner by illness, but he did a thing perfectly characteristic of him. He sent a verbatim reporter to the dinner with these instructions:

"This is Bell's night, the only one he ever has had in London. Report his speech *only.* Merely say the others spoke, *even if the Prime Minister is there.* Hear me?"

The reporter heard him, and I really was sorry, for some capital speeches were made that night, by Garvin, by Mond, by Burnham, by Selfridge, and Keeley, and Wile. So numerous were these speeches that I was not introduced until a few minutes past midnight. I spoke rapidly off-hand on "Let Us Build the Great Peace Bridge," and when I got my *Times* the next morning I had a column of solid nonpareil, and my far more eloquent friends, official and unofficial, had nothing but mention. I am bound to confess that from my point of view it was *delicious.*

That was in May, 1919, and I was leaving for a vacation at home, the first I had had since the initial gun spoke at Liège.[13] My friends, British and American, apparently thought I had done some good in the war, which I had reported both as a war correspondent and as a political and diplomatic interpreter. They called me "America's Unofficial Ambassador." I was not. I was

13. German forces occupied Liège, Belgium, on August 5, 1914, on their way into France.

merely what God seems to have intended me to be, a journalist. Wile in his speech said he hoped I would return to London as American Ambassador. Lord Burnham in *his* speech said: "No. Price Bell undoubtedly has every fitness for ambassadorial work, but let us ask him to come back to us as what he is, a journalist, free from any official gag. He can do more for his fellowmen in that quality."

For the most part Burnham was in light vein. He gave an amusing account of that unexpected bombardment and wild stampede in Tincourt Wood. And he said:

"If Price Bell's exterior spoke truly that day, he was the calmest man of us all."

It was then I got the full measure of the lying possibilities of one's exterior!

Two ladies at the dinner, and they hidden. But their triumph was at the end. When the screens were removed and the diners discovered them, they threw all competition into the shade and became small mountains of moving roses.

18. Northcliffe in My Own Finder

Give historians fifty years to a century more, and they may visualize Lord Northcliffe in his true and full proportions.[1] At present their view of him (in any event as I knew and understood him) is astonishingly shallow, fragmentary, contradictory, erroneous: altogether an inadequate and pretty bad picture. However rash I may seem, I purpose to try broadly to reveal the "true and full proportions" of Northcliffe in this chapter.

Since one must be trusted by a man before one can learn much about him, I think it pertinent and pardonable for me to give some indication of Northcliffe's feeling toward me. First, very early in our acquaintance (shortly after I went to London to live), he offered me the post of New York correspondent of the *Daily Mail,* his opening venture in daily journalism. When he bought *The Times* of London in March 1908, he asked me to become "American Correspondent-at-Large" for his great paper.

Need I say I was tempted? Even then I was aware of his unrivaled journalistic genius (as I saw it) on both the publishing and the editorial side. I felt sure his pioneering, his path-finding, in his profession would be the newspaper miracle of his time. It all seemed to me crystalline in his personality if one were permitted to look directly and closely (as I was) into that personality. I was tempted, and tempted deeply, to go with Northcliffe; "American Correspondent-at-Large" of *The Times* was a new and striking idea, signifying the

1. Although Northcliffe was—and remains—a figure of some controversy, history by and large remembers him as a positive and powerful force in the development of British journalism. One historian has called him "the most powerful and inventive newspaper genius of the century" (Wintour, *The Rise and Fall of Fleet Street,* 1); another, "the greatest newspaper man" (Griffiths, ed., *The Encyclopedia of the British Press,* 292).

biggest job ever offered to a correspondent (one never offered before or since). But I decided to stay with the *Chicago Daily News* and my tested supporters and keep unmixed my sense of patriotic homage.

"Can we not, nevertheless," I said to Northcliffe, "work as comrades so long as I shall be here?"

"Yes!" he said.

A smaller man might have been miffed. Not Northcliffe. I had done what I never have doubted *he,* had the situation been reversed, would have done. I knew him from 1896 (the year he established the *Daily Mail*) until the day of his death, August 14, 1922.[2] He treated me precisely as one of his staff and welcomed my family in friendship with his own. He often asked me to write for his papers and published my letters to *The Times* even when he himself "could not believe them," as he said, and when he had to override his editor to do it.

Let me give a few illustrations of Northcliffe's attitude to the writer who presumes to submit an estimate of him here. Louis Blériot's flying of the Channel in 1909 (thirty-two miles in thirty-seven minutes) was a thumping, thundering event.[3] Northcliffe gave a choice luncheon for him at the Savoy Hotel and had me at the head table. He honored me similarly when he entertained Ferdinand Foch.[4] I sat not rarely at his own table with his nearest and dearest in his home, "Elmwood," and in London.

One summer day he gave a luncheon to 7,000 of his employees at Olympia in London. It was the most rousing scene of the sort I ever looked at, row upon row, tier upon tier, of women and men, old and young, their countenances shining with loyalty to "the Chief" and with semi-hysterical enthusiasm. Lady Northcliffe sat on her husband's left, his handsome, stately, white-haired, wrinkled mother on his right. With them sat my wife, my daughter Alice (a very small girl to whom Northcliffe was markedly kind), and myself. Stretching away on either side of us were the principal associates of the great publisher in his multiform undertakings. The climax of the function came when Northcliffe suddenly rose and without speaking held aloft a bit of bunting.

It was a little flag, the Union Jack and the Stars and Stripes woven in one.

2. Bell apparently met Northcliffe during his first trip abroad in 1896.

3. Northcliffe's *Daily Mail* sponsored an aviation competition—1,000 pounds to the first man to fly across the English Channel. Louis Blériot, a French engineer who had been experimenting with and building flying machines for a decade, accomplished the feat in about 30 minutes. See Pound and Harmsworth, *Northcliffe,* 374–5.

4. Ferdinand Foch was a French military officer and commander of Allied forces in the later years of World War I. See Aston, *The Biography of the Late Marshal Foch.*

From end to end of that immense throng, instantly, the mates of that flag broke forth. Everyone was standing. Cheers and cries beat upon the rafters. The waving dual colors shimmered like a sea. That was all. Not a word. Nothing said about "the two great branches of the English-speaking race." The dramatist in Northcliffe let the flags and the cries and the ensuing silence speak. My family and I, so far as I know, were the only Americans, certainly the only non-staff persons, present. Yet no one, least of all the Northcliffe group, looked particularly at us. The implication was, I took it, that we merely belonged to the big family!

Gloom almost palpable, a kind of invisible fog, hung over London, especially the West End in the region of Carlton House Terrace and Carlton Gardens, the latter the street of Northcliffe's London home. Northcliffe had become very ill, and gradually the news had spread throughout the metropolis. Someone had said the disease was endocarditis and incurable.[5] Lady Northcliffe telephoned me one afternoon and said, "Northcliffe would like so much to see you. Will you kindly come?" He lay far back in a roomy leather armchair in his library and did not attempt to rise. He did, however, grasp my hand firmly and smile brightly if feebly. I sat near him, and he talked slowly for nearly an hour, mostly about the "ignorance" of statesmen, "fellows," he said, "entrusted with our destiny." Lady Northcliffe came in, chatted for a moment, and then excused herself, saying she must go out for a time. Northcliffe got up, put his arms round her, and kissed her lips.

"Bell," he said, looking after her as she left the room, "there's the most efficient woman in England."

And he stared some time at the door when she was gone.

"By the way," he said, turning quickly to me, "I hear your editor, Mr. Dennis, is in town."

"Yes," I replied.

"Know where he is now?"

I said I thought I could find him.

"Do, please. I've never seen him. My departmental heads are dining here with me tonight. I'd like Dennis to come. My men would like to talk with him. I'll reserve a plate for him. If he can come, well and good. If not, all right."

Scurrying about London for some time, I finally found Mr. Dennis in a barber's chair pretty well snowed under with lather. He was delighted to have Northcliffe's invitation, though greatly surprised that a man reputedly so ill

---

5. Northcliffe died in 1922 of endocarditis, an inflammation of the heart.

could be having guests to dinner. I told Mr. Dennis that Northcliffe had not mentioned his illness to me and seemed to have lost none of his interest in either his own affairs or those of the world. Mr. Dennis went to that dinner and assured me the next day he had had "a most interesting and profitable night" and had been "amazed at Northcliffe's buoyancy and brilliance." Mr. Dennis had been a student of Northcliffe's journalism for many years and found the wonderful man he expected to find.

Primarily of course he was a man and a very great man; neither great journalists nor great persons of any calling are makable from little men. His sensitivity to truth was so wide that it embraced the world. The heart-beat of humanity he felt as a boy when he was penniless, rejected by editors (who naturally are repelled by genius), burdened with a father too ill to work, a mother without money, some younger brothers and sisters, and delicate health of his own. I have in my study the British "Who's Who" (an oddly modest volume) for 1902. Northcliffe gives in this book as his recreations "automobilism, angling, cycling, travel." He adored motoring, fishing, and riding a wheel, doing so much of the last-named (he was always surpassingly keen on machinery and its social significance) that he all but killed himself. But above everything else he esteemed travel.

"Listen, Bell," he said to me one day as he reclined in his favorite chair at *The Times* office, Printing House Square, "while I tell you something important. No man attains to maximum stature without travel. No man, in other words, can benefit fully by his psychological inheritance without travel. He cannot do himself justice, he cannot do his fellows justice, without travel. Fools, I well know, travel and learn nothing. But wise men *never*. The word, I tell you, is *never*."

He was very earnest.

"Think of it!" he exclaimed. "How many men in the British Cabinet know anything *first-hand* about the world? Yet our racial and national responsibilities are *all over the world*. Our presumption is stupendous! We have gigantic imperialist ideas, and a gigantic imperial position, and know next to nothing beyond the parish pump. Nine-tenths of our statesmen don't know their own constituencies well. They don't travel radically even there. They know only the polite surface of things. Yet they rule us and hold in their hands the fate of our Empire. Can you conceive anything more incongruous or ridiculous or *dangerous*?"

I said I did not think I could.

"Nor can anyone," he affirmed. "At times I wish we had an absolutist at the head of this country; I should wish it all the time if we had the right man and could keep him, both of which conditions unhappily are contrary to fact. If we had such a ruler, my papers would say to him: 'Have as many world-travelers among your counselors as you can. If you have what you call a Cabinet, lay down this minimum principle: *No man in this Cabinet unless he, at the very least, has had personal contact with the United States of America and the British Empire from end to end.*'"

Silent a moment, he added:

"Even so, our boss would have considerably less than a half-size Cabinet."

"But, Lord Northcliffe," I ventured, "if Britain had an absolute boss, would not your papers say only what he wanted them to say?"

"If we had the boss I'm thinking of," was the reply, "he would *want* my papers to say that."

Unfaltering confidence in the people, their eager readiness to follow great leadership, appears to have belonged to Northcliffe pre-natally. At all events he is found speaking and writing of that confidence from the earliest days of his known articulation. This point of view I have shown as held firmly also by some of Northcliffe's great editorial contemporaries, Scott, Greenwood, Garvin, Gardiner. But the maker of modern British journalism differed fundamentally from them all. He stands out like a lighthouse on a lonely beach.

Granted that the people (not the kings, the princes of the blood, the dukes, but the Toms, Dicks, and Harrys) were ultimately all-important, the question was, "How are these basically vital elements in the community to be reached and helped to become worthy of their supreme obligation?" It was precisely at this point that Northcliffe and all his fellow-journalists parted company. Inelegantly, as the common view ran, it was highbrow against lowbrow, and the boy down-from-Dublin was lowbrow. His *confrères* trusted to their learning, their intellectuality, their high taste, their sound logic, their beautiful language, their passionate sincerity. Northcliffe trusted to wholesome substance finding vigorous and vivid expression in a language the people could understand.

And so were born *Answers, Comic Cuts, Forget-me-not!*[6]

Up in Great Britain, under the very nose of Fleet Street, had grown a country, a democracy, of which self-satisfied Fleet Street knew nothing. Popular education had been at work among a previously illiterate people: such states-

---

6. Northcliffe launched his first newspaper, *Answers,* in 1888. *Comic Cuts*—a paper comprised of short jokes and bits of humor—came two years later. In 1891, *Forget-me-not!,* a penny weekly for female readers, was released. These first few of Northcliffe's "new journalism" papers were successful and helped build his early fortune. See Pound and Harmsworth, *Northcliffe,* 72–89, 114–7, 128–9.

men as Gladstone and Joseph Chamberlain had seen to that. Great Britain suddenly had become a new and fresh land, able to read, anxious to read, but not able to read and understand the immemorial and infinitely dull ponderosities of Fleet Street. It could not manage even the lucid, stirring, and brilliant rhetoric of Garvin. It came wide-awake at the cry of Northcliffe.

With the thirsty soul of the British people (after he had fought a mighty fight against stupidity, self-admiration, intellectual reaction) ready for what he had to offer, Northcliffe became, I verily believe, the most heart-searching young man in Europe. And he did and did not look it. I saw him at least two or three times a week, frequently oftener, in those testing days, usually in his private office at the *Daily Mail* in Carmelite House. Nearly always he received me as he lay at full length on a divan, several cushions under his head; he told me he thought more easily and clearly in that position, remarking one day, "You'll pardon me, Bell; occasionally I get dizzy." His non-robustness of constitution was in evidence then. Strange indeed was the contrast one saw: the spiritual cast of an old man, the face of a fair-haired boy.

In this respect Northcliffe differed from any other great man I have known. Aside from him, every such man of my experience, Occidental or Oriental, has shown in his appearance and behavior, as one watched and studied him, unmistakable tokens of his life-achievements. The work, so to speak, was a portrait of the man, the man a portrait of the work. And the two were inseparable. But quite the contrary with Northcliffe. He was the most boyish-looking man I ever saw. I could see him riding the footboard of an express locomotive at night and getting an unutterable thrill out of it. I could see him pedaling his safety[7] from Bristol to London in a cold rain and dreaming of the unimaginable mechanical marvels to come. I could see him in his humble home on Hampstead Heath playing joyously with his first box of type.[8]

But I could not see that handsome, diffident, gentle boy demolishing the Old Fleet Street, laying the foundations of what we see there now, and giving us a British democracy reborn! Still less could I see him performing the prodigies of discernment and of daring which signalized his entire Great War career. Looking back at him in those thick hours of unparalleled stress

7. The "safety" was a type of sturdy bicycle frame new in the late nineteenth century. Northcliffe loved bicycles and cycling all his life. In fact, one of his first newspaper jobs was as editor of *Bicycling News*. See Pound and Harmsworth, *Northcliffe*, 34–5, 218.

8. George Jealous—a neighbor of Northcliffe's family at Hampstead, England, and printer of the local paper—gave Northcliffe a toy printing set when he was thirteen. See Pound and Harmsworth, *Northcliffe*, 26.

for everybody, and chiefly for men staggering under the load of public duty, he strikes me as about the only non-dodger I knew. Premiers were dodging. Cabinet men high and low were dodging. Admirals and general were dodging. Britain's military god, Herbert Kitchener, was dodging![9] All afraid to face the truth! "Keep it dark!" That was their panacea. And they had no other. What did that fair-haired, strangely boyish, modest, kindly man in Carmelite House and Printing House Square[10] say and do? He said:

"What this country needs is the *news*. It is not afraid."

And he told the censorship to "go to hell."[11] In all its blackness (and it was quite black enough at that time), Northcliffe published the news. His own men got it. The country was thrown into an uproar. It had not realized for a moment that it was losing the war; that the rosy face painted for it by authority was a lie.[12] At first, in its convulsive sense of disillusionment and outrage, it was ready to tear Northcliffe limb from limb. He must be a maniac, a ghastly *traitor*. One almost could hear the feet of millions rumbling upon London to exact a terrible revenge.[13]

9. Herbert Kitchener was a distinguished British military leader who led forces in Egypt, the Sudan, and South Africa. He was secretary of state for war during the First World War and one of the few to predict that the war would last for three or four years instead of months. His military successes made him a popular hero. But he was criticized from some quarters, notably by Lloyd George and Northcliffe. They claimed he sent the wrong type and too little ammunition to the Western Front, a blunder that cost many lives. See Warner, *Kitchener*. For Lloyd George and Northcliffe's criticism, see Cassar, *Kitchener's War*, 180; and Pound and Harmsworth, *Northcliffe*, 476–8.

10. Carmelite House was the office of Northcliffe's *Daily Mail;* Printing House Square, the office of his *Times*.

11. Northcliffe's papers largely abided by the Press Bureau's censorship rules. But Northcliffe's attitude toward the consequences of printing critical commentary was characteristically cavalier. As Northcliffe became more convinced that British suppression of information was damaging the war effort, he became more adamant in his refusal to keep quiet. He began to attack Kitchener, who directed the war effort as secretary of state for war. He told one of his war correspondents, "This war can't be run in the dark. They can shoot me if I put anything in my newspapers that I shouldn't" (Pound and Harmsworth, *Northcliffe*, 469).

12. Under Kitchener's direction, British censorship "operated on the assumption that British nerves could not stand bad news" (Pound and Harmsworth, *Northcliffe*, 470). British officials first operated under a traditional supposition that foreign affairs were not a matter for public opinion. What few officially sanctioned news reports and Press Bureau communiqués there were painted a picture of unrealistic success. "The authorities," Northcliffe said, "suppress everything except optimistic twaddle" (Pound and Harmsworth, *Northcliffe*, 470). See Sanders and Taylor, *British Propaganda during the First World War*.

13. The day the *Daily Mail* published Northcliffe's "Kitchener's Tragic Blunder," criticizing the military hero's war policies, clubs banished the *Daily Mail—and* the Northcliffe-owned

I found Northcliffe in his room at *The Times*.

He was perfectly natural and quiet.

I felt it might be the last time I ever should see him alive.

"The ball is rolling," he said.

"You will remain here?" I inquired.

He regarded me with sharp surprise.

"Bell," he said, "only *news* can win this war. I can get the news; I've the organization to do it. I can give the news to the people; I've the machinery to do that. Trust the people to do the rest. Our ostriches are far worse than no good in this crisis. They must go. Kitchener must go."

"Kitchener!" I gasped.

"Yes, *first of all,* Kitchener. To keep him at the War Office is to present victory to the Germans with our compliments. The politicians have him bluffed. He's no longer a general; he's a politician, caught and helpless in their peculiar net. He's a brave man, but the situation, the political side of it, has bested him. He never was a brilliant soldier anyway, no such military man as French. I'm going to call for his immediate removal. The people say, 'Leave it to Kitchener.' They believe him infallible; that's the danger. He's sending the wrong shells to the front, shrapnel. What use is shrapnel against barbed wire, behind which the Germans are slaughtering our army? High explosives are the need. I'll tell the people the truth, and you watch what happens."

I watched.

And the storm launched was the most violent I ever have seen in politics. Northcliffe told the truth about the national idol, the Man of Khartum, the maker of "Kitchener's Army," volunteers attracted to the colors before the politicians had the nerve to do their obvious duty and institute conscription in the spring of 1916. Consternation, indignation, maniacal wrath swept the nation to the uttermost water's edge. *The Times*, the *Daily Mail,* the *Evening News,* every Northcliffe publication went up in smoke amid the execrations of the people. Dignified men trampled and spat upon the papers on the stone floor of the London Stock Exchange. The papers were shut out of every library in the land. On every hand rose the cry, "To the tower with the arch-traitor and have his head!"

But Northcliffe kept his head and held it high. He went every day to his

---

Times. Fifteen hundred men in the London Stock Exchange burned copies of the paper. (Pieces of the burnt paper were sent to Northcliffe by post.) Subscribers canceled subscriptions. The paper's 1,386,000 circulation dropped by 238,000. See Pound and Harmsworth, *Northcliffe,* 478–9.

offices, and every day he published the news. He had his way. There were more shells, and the right shells, for the hard-pressed British troops on that awful West Front.[14] Kitchener left the War Office. Conscription came, long overdue and above price in its value to the Allied cause. The Anzacs were pulled out of the death-trap at Gallipoli,[15] Northcliffe's work with the aid of Bonar Law. The Northcliffe papers resumed their place in the libraries and were read with something nearer reverence than rabies on the London Stock Exchange. As for the Germans, they frankly declared: "The triumph of England's greatest rascal, Northcliffe, is complete." The British people now acclaimed Northcliffe, not Kitchener, as the savior of the Empire.

What was the solid rock of this man's philosophy?

"People, if they are to be great, require two kinds of excellent food; food for the body and food for the brain, 'brain' meaning the whole non-corporeal man."

That is what he said.

And at once he set about to attain a position which would enable him and the forces he commanded to feed the British people in this comprehensive sense. First he must get to them; must sit with them at their firesides, Henry Martyn's[16] "earliest and most influential of schools." Traditional British journalism gave him no chance to do that. He tried his more "popular" journalism. Alone it would not work; failed to magnetize the public mind; the people were fixed in the idea that newspapers were for the *intelligentsia* and not for them. Balked but not dispirited, Northcliffe called to his aid a born business man, his younger brother Harold (now Lord Rothermere and master of the Northcliffe Press). Then, aware of the gambling ardor of his compatriots, Northcliffe determined to use it: offered a pound ($5) a week for life to the person of either sex or any age who guessed nearest to the amount of bullion in the Bank of England at a stated time.

Britishers rose to that offer almost as a man.

14. Facing internal pressure, Prime Minister Asquith appointed Lloyd George head of the newly organized ministry of munitions. Under Lloyd George's direction, there were more and better munitions. This turnaround in the War Office is controversial among historians. Some see Kitchener as an inept handler of the war, while others argue that his work made later success in the war possible. See Cassar, *Kitchener's War*, 179–81.

15. In a plan engineered by Winston Churchill and Kitchener, the Anzacs (the Australian and New Zealand Army Corps) planned to strike at the Central Powers through an amphibious landing on Turkey's Gallipoli peninsula. The effort turned out to be a military disaster.

16. Henry Martyn was a British Christian missionary in India in the early 1800s.

And Northcliffe found himself sitting at the firesides of the people.

True, his "lottery" scheme was banned officially, but he had gained his end. His name was on all lips. His papers mounted into circulations of millions, a thing unheard of and beyond belief. Old Fleet Street was flat on its back and gasping for breath.

And then?

Then Northcliffe started his feeding operations. He cried day after day for the universal eating of "Standard Bread" as verily the staff of life. And it was eaten from John O'Broat's to Land's End. He published simple menus and recipes and lessons in cooking. He displayed in all his papers clearly-written articles by the greatest dieticians in Great Britain telling everybody what and how to eat and drink if he wished to join "the healthy, happy, peace-loving, unfearing host" which was "marching to Britain's New Day."

That on the bodily side.

On the side of the brain, Northcliffe fed the people purity, honesty, facts, beauty, the best ideas, and the most brilliant expression he could buy, come who would. No sexual effluvia for his press. No show for bad morals in any sphere. No colored or lying news if he could stop it, and his scent for it was preternatural. No pressure from the county in-room. No sacrifice of journalistic honor for money. No making people drunk and poor in order that he might be rich. And then beauty, beauty in and about the home, roses for the humblest, window-gardening, an unsullied country-side, an England people must rejoice in and love!

How one wishes every ear round the globe might listen to Northcliffe's flaming words against all who "soil the souls of children"! The thought of this crime was the only thing I ever knew to make him violently angry. It made him more than angry; it cloyed him with moral horror. At his Thanet home one Sunday afternoon, speaking to Keith Murdoch (then a London correspondent, now Sir Keith Arthur, multiple newspaper owner in Australia) and myself, Northcliffe said: "I see a girl or boy, a young woman or man, reading a diseased book or watching a diseased picture or play, and I'm a *murderer* at heart. It's the only time homicide looks really good to me. I yearn to punish the producer and circulator of the stuff. I don't want to assassinate him; I want to stand up to him face to face and *cut him down*."

I think he made Murdoch and me quake a little.

And he went on:

"For what is the wretch doing? Poisoning the wells! Bringing feebleness, misery, decay, death to the individual and to the race! Let these basest of the enemies of mankind beware! I tell them, whoever they may be, they are en-gendering an appalling Nemesis!"

We all were silent for a moment. Then Murdoch said:

"But, Lord Northcliffe, the writers and publishers of 'diseased' matter argue they only are giving the public what it wants."

Northcliffe's scorn was a thunder-cloud.

"I know!" he cried. "As the Americans say, the scoundrels 'pass the buck'! Even if what they say were true—and I say it is *not*—is one to give a baby arsenic because the baby cries for it?"

The great editor rose abruptly and composed himself by standing for some time silently gazing at the splendid elms about his house. He had been moved more deeply than I ever had seen him moved before, and I am sure neither Murdoch nor I ever shall forget that cauterizing outburst. Later in the day, I said:

"Lord Northcliffe, will you allow me to tell you what I think your culminating ambition is?"

"Yes, Bell," he answered quickly. "I'd like very much to know what's in your mind."

"You're a great champion of imperial unity," I observed.

"Right!"

"I think you wish to federate the British Empire and be the first federal premier."

"Bell," he retorted seriously, "you've shown yourself a shrewd judge of our politics. I'm astounded that you could misapprehend me so completely. Whatever else I may be, I'm not a party man, and we're a party Empire, a democracy. No premier such as you suggest (if there could be one) could be without party ties, more or less bound. I'm a journalist and will not be bound. I want to keep my freedom to serve the Empire by attacking any party of men who seems to me to imperil its greatness and safety. Bell, did you ever attend a party dinner and find me there?"

"No, I think not," I said, reflecting.

"Well, I attended one a long time ago. It was a Conservative party. At dinner a great party secret was discussed. I went straight home shortly after midnight and turned in without a word with my office. The next morning I was horrified to find that 'secret' blazoned in the *Daily Mail*. I knew I should be called a cad. I *was*. And all my protestations did no good. My men had got the story of course absolutely on their own. I quit party politics then, and I'm out of it for good."

One of my few colloquies with Northcliffe over the telephone chanced between 1 and 2 in the morning of a blustery winter night in 1916. I was in my home, "Silverbirch," Sidcup, twelve miles out in Kent, and Northcliffe was in *The Times* office in London. I was sound asleep and barely heard the telephone bell ring and my wife getting out of bed to answer. Then I was asleep again. My wife pulled at me and said: "Lord Northcliffe wants you." I jumped out, stumbled downstairs, and cried, "Hello!"

"Bell," came Northcliffe's quiet tones, "I've just got some bad news. I hear Wilson is going to take America into the war on the side of Germany."

"Who tells you that?"

"I have it from the *New York Sun* people in Effingham House. They say it comes direct from their Washington Bureau through their foreign editor in New York."

Thinking a moment, I replied:

"Lord Northcliffe, if you haven't anything but that to worry about, I'd advise that you go to bed and dream sweetly."

"Ah!" he murmured. "Thanks so much, Bell."

However rough my drawing may be, I feel I have projected after a fashion the world's greatest journalist in his "true and full proportions." Contemporary misapprehension and caricature I have set aside for what I think them worth: nothing. I have drawn the man as I think he will be found in the dispassionate record of after days.

19. I Go to Tea with Royalty

One of the many remarkable social phenomena of the Great War was that of the rise of the journalist in general esteem. His social position was not a great one when I first knew Europe (at the turn of this century). I am afraid it was not a great one anywhere. Journalism was not an educated profession comparable to the learned professions, law, medicine, and theology. Its output Carlyle dubbed "ditchwater."[1] A favorite saying of Balfour's was, "I never read the newspapers."

Admittedly we journalists came in for a good deal of cajolery at the hands of our superiors, particularly in America and among politicians and business men. We were "the boys." We were patted on the back and given cigars (sometimes cigars one could smoke and still live). If we would have it, once in a while we landed a free drink or mounted to even the height of a first-rate complimentary meal. But we were cynics about it all. We knew quite well what we should find when we searched the wood-pile.

Towering personalities of course already had come forth in our profession. We had our Greeley, our Dana, our Bennett, our Pulitzer, our Victor Fremont Lawson, the last-named I think (regarding him from all angles) the greatest of the galaxy.[2] We had abroad the glittering names of such masters as Walter

1. Thomas Carlyle was a Scottish essayist and historian. He was known for his satire, his religious doubt, and his admiration for German literature and history. Carlyle once wrote that rapid writing in some men flowed on "forever, a mighty tide of ditchwater . . . But indeed the most unaccountable ready-writer of all is, probably, the common Editor of a Daily Newspaper."

2. Horace Greeley was the founder and editor of the *New York Tribune*. Both Greeley and the *Tribune* were instrumental in the formation and success of the American Republican Party. Charles Dana, who worked for Greeley's *Tribune* in his early career, was the famous editor and

and Delane of *The Times* of London,[3] with Northcliffe and his like (if he can be said to have had any like) just beginning to blaze above the horizon. But we rank-and-filers of the trade were tiny twinklers, what the English would call "ha'-penny dips." So far as we were valued at all, it was not for our own light but for the light we could train upon our betters. As late as 1914 (the year Armageddon crashed), I went to report a big Anglo-American society event in Mayfair. A doorman in the plumage of an Ecuadorean macaw, learning I was a correspondent, waved me toward the basement. Above a doorway, I saw this sign:

"Food downstairs."

With my colleagues, I found myself waiting for the news handout in the servants' quarters. Now, let me interpose definitely, I have nothing against servants. A good servant is in my eyes precisely as admirable as a good king or duke or anybody else. Humanly, I would not toss a copper between a good servant and Caesar or Charlemagne. I mention this incident of the servants' quarters in fashionable Mayfair merely to indicate the high-hat view of rank-and-file journalists until very recently. I will not say that view is gone entirely yet. It is not. But our profession in its fulness had an undeniable re-birth in the Great War.

And why was that?

Rather a fine tang of irony one gets just here.

Anciently (among rude nations) the only profession honored was that of arms. Prognostics in every direction today suggest that we may be returning to that outlook. Even we Americans, we Americans relatively so far from external danger; we Americans who see ourselves as loving peace and righteousness in general more than most others; even we are going in for fighting machines and fighting men at a rate which appears to point to the elevation once

part owner of the *New York Sun*. James Gordon Bennett—a leader of the popular press revolution in the United States—was the founder and editor of the *New York Herald*. Joseph Pulitzer owned and edited the *New York World* and the *St. Louis Post-Dispatch* in the late 1800s. Pulitzer is remembered for his papers' "yellow journalism"—a sensational method of gathering and presenting news. Lawson, of course, was owner and editor of the *Chicago Daily News*.

3. John Walter founded *The Times* in 1785. Walter established *The Times*'s reputation for independence quickly: after criticizing King George III's sons in 1789, he was fined and imprisoned for 16 months for libel. John Thadeus Delane was editor of *The Times* of London from 1841 to 1877. Delane was well known in the highest circles of London politics. An adviser once spoke of him to Queen Victoria: "The degree of information possessed by *The Times* with regard to the most secret affairs of State is mortifying, humiliating and incomprehensible" (Griffiths, ed., *The Encyclopedia of the British Press*, 197).

more of the profession of arms to the social apex. Well, that may be all right
(so long as we do not go crazy about it). We certainly do not want to present
to the world (it is a fairly coarse one) the spectacle of American weakness in
the things men *respect*. What I wish to note is that journalism climbed to new
altitudes of evaluation and honor in 1914–1918 not because it was recognized
to be a powerful promoter of peace but because it was recognized to be *a tremendous engine of war.*

Slowly, and not without distress, came that appreciation to England. The
Press? What man of authority, what man of light and leading, cared anything about the Press? Was the Crown, was the aristocracy, were the high and
mighty of politics, was the government to take serious notice of the Press in a
life-and-death grapple of the nations? Away with it! Sponge journalism from
the slate! There was nothing but deadly mischief in it! As Northcliffe wrote:
"Our most vicious criminals we smile at today. Our journalists are lepers." I
appeared before Kitchener at the War Office and asked him to let me go to the
West Front, to the Ypres Salient.[4] He said: *"This is a time for you newspaper
men to be careful!"*

Public opinion as a force in the war had no meaning to aristocratic and
official England. Trained statesmen and strategists, politicians and military
and naval commanders, they would do it all. The place for the journalist, and
especially the nosey correspondent, was out of the country or in jail. And
several over-inquisitive correspondents came into more or less violent collision with the authorities. Many a one was marched into camp by the military
and had to fight for his freedom if not his life. I myself was in tight pinches in
both Great Britain (where I went about much studying the life of the people in
war) and on the West Front between the Channel and Nesle after the anti-cor-
respondent embargo had been broken down. With a blindness never exceeded
in history, British authority, with war going overwhelmingly against the Allies,
forced the flaming sword of public opinion to rust in its scabbard!

Till.

Till the persistent howling of correspondents, and the thunder of Northcliffe's guns, woke it up! Its dull eyes gradually perceived that sword flashing
elsewhere than in Great Britain and the Empire, flashing for the Central Powers. It saw the British peoples, at home and overseas, in the dark while others
were in the light. It came at last wide-eyed to the fact that populations could

---

4. The Ypres Salient was the principal arena of battle on the British West Front during the war.
Ypres is a town in West Flanders, Belgium.

not *fight* unless they *knew*, and to the correlative fact that they could not know unless the despised men and mechanism of the Press told them. Then I re-appeared before Kitchener, not yet gone from the War Office, and renewed my request to go to the Ypres Salient.

"Your credentials," said the man of Khartum, "will reach you by hand today."

Nothing any longer about that being a time for newspaper men to be care-ful! Indeed Kitchener said:

"Personally, Mr. Bell, I admire the good correspondent, the man with the right sense of his responsibility in the critical business of war. I mean a man of conscience and understanding, a fellow who will not betray wittingly or unwit-tingly the army to which he is accredited. Might I suggest to you a model?"

"Thank you," I replied.

"I suggest Steevens. George Warrington Steevens.[5] Great war correspon-dent. Have you read his books, *With Kitchener to Khartum* and *From Cape-town to Ladysmith*?"

"Yes," I answered. "I long have been a worshiper at the shrine of Steevens."

There was real warmth in the soldier's smile, and he stood up to shake my hand and wish me well at the front. The next time I saw him, and the last time, he was striding down the main aisle of St. Paul's Cathedral, a tall, gloomy, grim giant, heavily mustached, in field marshal's uniform, his sword clanking as he walked. He was the object of all eyes, the eyes of an assemblage packing the magnificent cathedral to its doors. Like the rest, he had come to lay the wreath of his reverence upon the bier of Field Marshal Lord Roberts of Kandahar, Pretoria, and Waterford. When that mine struck the British cruiser *Hampshire* off the coast of Orkney, and Kitchener sank with the ship, I felt almost as if the mine had hit me!

Public opinion informed and aroused (and it could not be aroused without being informed), fresh spirit and power, and immeasurably augmented effi-ciency flowed into the whole British war effort, flowed from the far-scattered lands of British allegiance and from the British Isles. It was, from the British point of view, *a new war*. It was a war no longer of the *upper* stratum only but of *all* strata of society. Britain with every part and the totality of her strength was in it heart and soul and to the death. It was a war by *peoples* esteeming themselves free against a system, a puissance, and a leadership which they

---

5. George Warrington Steevens was a journalist who wrote for the *Pall Mall Gazette* and the *Daily Mail*. Steevens covered the Boer War in South Africa. His *With Kitchener to Khartum* helped form Kitchener's public reputation.

though despotic, impudent, arrogant, criminal. And such a war (as Bismarck so well knew) needs must be *pugnis et calcibus*.[6] *And this new war on Britain's part was made by journalism.*

Yes.

"The boys," the rattling linotypes, the ink, the news-print, the rumbling presses, the rushing mechanics of distribution had turned the trick.

Royalty saw it. One of the best kings of history saw it: George V. As for myself, I had been among the correspondents who reported the coronation of King George and Queen Mary in Westminster Abbey (June 22, 1911), and I had observed his public acts and followed his public utterances long before he ascended the throne (May 6, 1910). U.S. Ambassador George Harvey had a great opinion of the King, used to walk over from Grosvenor Gardens to Buckingham Palace frequently after dinner and have a chat with his Majesty over coffee and Courvoisier, "the Brandy of Napoleon."

"The world's best judge of European politics, that man," said Harvey to me. "I think I might enlarge that observation and call him the best judge of world politics. I certainly never have found him wrong about Dominion or American politics. He's supposed to be a political frontispiece. The fact is that his reasoned judgment is pretty nearly all-powerful in the British Cabinet today. Of his splendor of *character* no one has any doubt. But hardly anyone outside his immediate circle does justice to his *mind*. On difficult problems I'd rather talk with him than with any other man in the country."

"By gracious," said an American politician to me in Washington one day when I spoke of Harvey's remark, "the Courvoisier must have been good!"

But nobody who knew George Harvey need be told that *any* brandy was ever good enough to deteriorate the realism, not to say cynicism, of his judgment.

To me one day came an invitation from the Lord Chamberlain (Chief Officer of the Royal Household) to come to tea with their Majesties King George and Queen Mary on a stated afternoon at Buckingham Palace. It was explained that the Royal Family desired "to have the pleasure of meeting members of the American Press." I put on my top-hat and the other appropriate articles of adornment and went. Six of us went, five representing New York or other Eastern papers, I carrying the load of standing for the backward journals of the Wild and Woolly States, the "West."

Our hosts, and the simplest of hosts they were, included besides the King and Queen their most charming children Edward and Mary (to be respectively

6. That is, with might and main, with all one's might.

King Edward VIII and the wife of Viscount Lascelles). To speak of the children first, Edward was the modest, good-looking, flexible, polite, fluent-spoken, intelligent boy whom the world came to know and to like so well. Princess Mary (the only daughter of the family) was rosy-complexioned, pretty, dignified, friendly, sweet, quick in response, a darling of a school girl with a lively temperament and intellect. The "American Press" went solidly for her; at least I know the backward "West" did!

Queen Mary was *herself* in the full English sense of that word as applied to *materfamilias*. She was *herself* also as queen, reserved, formally erect, some might have said prim, but the soul of queenly dignity and kindliness. She spoke to us indeed in a strangely motherly way. Her humanness was so pronounced that none of us, I believe, ever thought of her again as we had thought of her before: as stiff and cold. I noticed several times her attentiveness and tenderness toward the King. She seemed to have a maternal feeling relative to him too. Ever since, I have had the notion that he *never* was a hale man, and that this fact abode in the Queen's consciousness all the time.

George V was exactly what Harvey said he was: deep, thoughtful, wise, steeped in the humanities, a grand idealist, and yet above all a man acutely aware of the very great perils hidden reef-like in golden mists. He told us of his sense of the high importance of words; they might be blessings, they might be curses, to humanity. He himself, he said, made it a rule of his life to use in private and in public such words as he felt might enlighten, and certainly would not embitter, human relations national and international. To arouse anger and animosity among nations, he emphasized, was "probably the world's least forgivable sin."

Not a lecture, and yet a lecture, it was. It did not at the time strike me as a lecture; it struck me as merely a pleasingly persuasive *causerie*. But I realized afterward that his Majesty had been on the infinitely fine job of doing what he could when he could for the cause of good-will among men. That cause was eternally his. And he was very commanding in it, had not a peer in that role, I am satisfied, among the ruling personages of mankind. People said the King did not write his speeches and messages; the work was done for him. After talking with him, I knew the people did not know. He was the only man alive who could have written those speeches and messages. King George, and King George only, was in them: his special sweep and sincerity of fellow-feeling, the truth and weight of what he said, his naturalness and propriety of form. I conceive it to be incontrovertible that this monarch, from the start to the end of his life, never uttered a word which did any harm.

And who can count his words which did good?

I commend his example to certain gentlemen in high public places today!

Journalism's power in war raised it, symbolically speaking, from the servants' quarters in Mayfair to the drawing-room of Buckingham Palace. Journalism's power in war put top-hats and morning-coats and striped trousers and spats and patent-leather shoes on correspondents. And it did it not only in England but in every great seat of fighting force on earth. Correspondents no longer had to go cap in hand to big-wigs, however big, however wiggy. They were *invited*. Sometimes they were *begged* to come. This was true not only of thrones and cabinets but of the lords of armies and navies encircling the globe.

My tea with British Royalty revealed to me of course the King's understanding of the place of the Press in modern warfare, the warfare of whole nation against whole nation, of men, women, and children against men, women, and children, of last personal and social ounce against last personal and social ounce. But I knew the King's thoughts were running beyond the Armistice, whenever it might come. He was thinking of the peace, near or far. And he was seizing an opportunity to do his bit to influence the Press to serve peace, in its time, as effectually as it had shown itself able to serve war. That was in the being of the man.

But what surprised me was the subsequent discovery of the same sentiment, the identical attitude, in the great British admirals and generals whom I met intimately. I found John Jellicoe, commander of the Grand Fleet, talking in the same vein in the cabin of his flagship on the North Sea. Ditto the jaunty David Beatty on his flagship after Jutland. Ditto the American admiral William Sowden Sims as we talked together on the deck of his flagship, watching the slow steaming of the beaten German armada into the Firth of Forth on its way to early doom in Scapa Flow, the only High Seas Fleet ever to commit suicide.[7] Sims said all his British brethren-in-arms had said in this sentence:

"The Press has been decisive in war; now let it be decisive in peace."

I was with Field Marshal Lord French when, almost naked of artillery, he was holding the Teutonic legions at Ypres, saving (at an awful cost of precious blood) the Channel ports and so nailing down once and for all the Allies' only

7. William Sowden Sims was a U.S. naval admiral. He led the U.S. fleet that fought with the British Royal Navy during World War I. Scapa Flow—in the Orkney Islands to the northeast of Scotland—has traditionally been an anchorage for the British navy. When the British fleet held the defeated German armada there in 1918, German crews cut holes in the hulls of their ships and sunk them.

chance of victory.[8] It was then he was calling almost piteously to Kitchener for the right kind of shells (high-explosive, no shrapnel) and for more heavy guns. He was calling too for the lifting of "the fatal hand of the censorship." His slogan was that of Lord Northcliffe: "Let in the light!" He said to me (in an interview published duly throughout the world): "I want the British peoples to see with my eyes. I want them to see this the most vital of all our salients. I want them to see our sons dying here by tens of thousands, largely because the government is failing them."

The Press, beginning with Northcliffe's *Times*, tore the veil from that picture in its every line. I interviewed Lord French again. He was back in London, and Field Marshal Lord Haig had taken his place as commander-in-chief of the British troops in Flanders and France. This second interview (also published throughout the world) took place in French's cabin-like office above the black-and-gray stone arches overlooking the Horse Guards Parade.

> The Press of all countries has been fundamentally important in this war. For a time Britain fought without its aid, and the loss of the war stared us in the face. We were pitted against armies, navies, air forces, *and* the Press, the latter manufacturing and sustaining the national *morale* without which no fighting arm could prevail. When the Press of the Allies came unrestrainedly into action, our fortunes ceased to wane and began steadily to wax. We had, I think, the better story to tell. I consider it the very greatest story *ever* told. At bottom, it was the pen and not the sword which changed the course of history: another way of saying that *morale* rather than *steel* is winning this war.

So spoke the sad-faced, gray, brilliant hero of Ypres.

And then he said:

"Peace, dear Bell, after all, is what matters in the end. War can't save civilization. Peace can. When we shall have peace again, let the Press save it."

"And how, Lord French," I entreated, "can the Press save it?"

"Well," he replied, "by knowing the world better than statesmen know it and by being fairer than statesmen are."

I thought I was listening to Northcliffe again!

8. John French was a field marshal who led British forces in the Western Front from the outbreak of the war until late 1915, when he was replaced by Douglas Haig. Although French had been a successful cavalry officer in the Boer War, some in the British government thought him an ineffective commander in the First World War. More than 110,000 British soldiers died under his command in the first two battles of Ypres. Also, French had trouble cooperating with other Allied commanders during the war, and with Kitchener, then head of the War Office. Bell, however, praises French, both here and later in his memoir. See Cassar, *The Tragedy of Sir John French.*

20. Historic Pageantry of the News

Love of pageantry was born in me. I think I loved it more than I loved stories, though these also laid hold of me with a strange power. Pageantry first hit me hard in the Indiana forests in fall, the astoundingly gorgeous coloring of the rounded and undulating leaves stretching away until they kissed the horizon. I have stood on the hills bordering the Raccoon Valley when Nature's autumnal glory seemed to chain my feet to the ground. There were moments, I verily believe, when I *could* not have moved.

And then a tawdry pageantry, with thrilling accompaniments, raced through my system. I was sitting in a window commanding a long view of Wabash Avenue in Terre Haute, Indiana. I felt ineffably important. I was a boy reporter on the *Terre Haute Gazette,* and I was in an observation post which seemed to me as essential then as any similar place ever seemed to me in the Great War.

Behind and on either side of me (all round me except in front) were people, all excited, all babbling, none of them presuming to obstruct my view: *I* was a reporter; I had business in that window; *they* were there for pleasure. It was Circus Day. My job was to paint the parade as it should be seen in my section of the main thoroughfare of the town. I was what the reporters nowadays call *tense,* no Field Marshal ever more so. And why not? It was no ordinary circus. It was *Barnum's.* Half-a-dozen counties had poured nearly their whole populations into the burg. Wabash Avenue was a seething mass of urbans, suburbans, and rurals out-tinting the rainbow, and every window and roof was chock-a-block.

Moreover, it was only my second circus, and it was my first as a reporter. Still further, I never had seen *Barnum's,* and the very name in those days was enough to rattle a youngster to his toes.

Glare and heat from the great round sun. Chit-chat, quips, laughter, odd cries from thousands of throats. Then a silence like thunder. Drums were beating. Cops were clearing the middle of the street. The parade was coming! *Barnum* was here! Flags, banners, calliopes, brass. Plumed horses: how magnificent! Tinseled showmen: how straight, muscular, and grave! Shapely women in bedizened tights: a reporter *must* look at them! And, God, the animals: elephants, kangaroos, camels, water buffalo, ravening lions, tigers, hyenas in huge gilding cages drawn by four horses and driven by men who looked like kings!

Wish I had my story of that spectacle. If it did the show half justice, it was a daisy!

> What pageantry, what feats, what shows,
> What minstrelsy, and pretty din,
> The regent made. . .
> To greet the King!

Whosoever loved a show as Shakespeare?

Reporting in America led me into many sordid scenes but set before me few spectacles worth remembering. As a roving correspondent in Europe, however, I witnessed pageantry, and historic pageantry, the pageantry of the news, in opulent exuberance. Earliest of all the great historic scenes of my experience came in the red flush of this century, that of the marriage of Queen Wilhelmina of Holland, then a plump, rosy, pretty girl, rapturous with enthusiasm, a queen as well as a Queen, to the Duke of Mecklenburg-Schwerin, four years her senior. My wife and I traveled over to The Hague from London, with us such well-known correspondents as Julian Ralph of the *Daily Mail,* I. N. Ford of the *New York Tribune,* Harry Chamberlin of the *New York Sun,* and Robert M. Collins of the Associated Press.

Gorgeous was my luck on that assignment. It did not come from my ability; it came from my disability. I represented a "provincial," not a "metropolitan," newspaper; Chicago was a jay town somewhere out in the sticks. New York and the East voted me out of an opportunity to see the grand ceremonial in the church at The Hague, the climax of the nuptial festival. So many seats for the American Press. None for the West when the East got through voting. I was troubled, but all is fair in love, war, and the "Great Game"; I would do the best I could. Anyhow there would be a mammoth show outside, a great royal procession, cavalry, artillery, infantry, the august of Europe in scintillating equipage. And the royalty-adoring multitude!

Enough, I thought.

"So sorry you've been excluded from the church," said dear old Ford of the *Tribune,* always kind-hearted and square. "I tried to get you in, but I was helpless."

"My great thanks, Ford," I said. "I'll manage in one way or another. It's not my first assignment, you know. I'll dream the damned wedding scene if I *must.*"

Ford haw-hawed.

"Do it!" he said.

August Kiehl (afterward Count Kiehl) was our correspondent at The Hague, a polite, clever man with two brilliant sisters, a family commended to me by the famous W. T. Stead of London. (August finally left our service, and one of his sisters assumed his duties, he marrying a lady of the Dutch aristocracy and moving to Buenos Aires, where I met him more than a quarter of a century later in picturesque circumstances to be described in a subsequent chapter.) August appeared to know everyone in The Hague. When we walked down the street at all events he bowed and tipped his hat right and left every few steps. I never previously had seen the like.

"I'm amazed!" he avowed.

He was "amazed" that I was to have no place in the church.

"Even *I* have a ticket," he said.

"That will serve quite well," I assured him. "Let us have a look at the church, and I want to learn the adjacent streets, especially the streets leading by the quickest way to the telegraph office. You're going to have an awful jam?"

"Heavens, yes!" he said. "All Holland, all Europe, will crowd into this little town!"

We examined the church, so still, so beautifully set off for the great day, waiting. It had a portico with columns rising above the street. I asked Kiehl if he thought he could make his escape from his seat in the church to this porch on the instant of the conclusion of the main ceremony.

"Yes," he affirmed decidedly. "I can do *anything* in The Hague."

I was compelled to laugh. I knew the gentleman meant exactly what he said, and I was plucking up confidence. We made our investigation of the narrow and tangled streets, and I learned just how to get to the telegraph office in a jiffy from a particular spot off the processional route where I constantly would be in sight of the church and its portico.

"Now, Kiehl," I said as we stood on that spot looking at the portico, "the moment it is clear to you that everything has gone off according to the official program, that there has been no hitch or untoward happening, you get to that porch like a shot and stand in the corner next to the building with your hat held steadily in the air. I'll be watching here."

"It'll be done," he said.

Gathered the crowds ocean-like on the wedding morning. My rivals, happy in their possession of the requisite cards, entered the church well ahead of time, Kiehl with them, I in the streets collecting material and laying up impressions for my descriptive cable, Mrs. Bell with me and using her miss-not-a-thing eyes. Ocean-like. So the crowds were. My wife and I stood at first close to the street along which the procession would pass, but we continually moved back to make sure of not losing touch with access to what after all was the place of places for a correspondent on that day: the room where the telegraphic sounders were singing.

Glitter answering to glitter, the well-up sun pouring its unclouded rays lavishly upon a show of immense beauty and splendor, the procession passed to the church, the lovely Queen bowing from her carriage to her enraptured subjects and to strangers in almost equally wild acclaim from all over the world. My wife and I had been pushed far from the line of march, but we still could see the fateful portico. Just as the Queen was opposite us, a tall, strong, old Dutchman, his seamed features melting with patriotic pride and emotion, suddenly seized my wife round the legs below the knees and lifted her high above the floor of heads.

"Look, lady!" he said.

And she looked as if a Hollander herself!

My competition, the boys who had relegated me to the "provincial" *status* where I belonged, were in the church all right. They were well in it. How were they going to get out? There was the rub. They were frozen in that church like so many frogs in ice or so many fossils in rock. The solid mass of the multitude had them fast and how long it would hold them no one knew. Meanwhile I was disinherited but free. And I knew my way to the wires overland and undersea to the jay town somewhere out in the sticks.

I stared at that portico, on my toes for the sprint.

Up rose a hat.

It remained steady in the air.

What became of my wife I do not know. I know only that in about three shakes of a sheep's tail I was in the telegraph office and writing like mad my story of the marriage of Queen Wilhelmina of Holland. The official program, detailing the procedure minutely and exhaustively, lay before me as I wrote. And the rest was in my notes and in my head. The scene in the church I dreamed (as I told Ford I might), but I dreamed it partly out of what I actually had seen and partly out of the authentic pre-projection. The ethics of it? Well, they looked good enough to me then, and they look good enough to me now.

In any event, Kiehl and I whammed the world, not only our competition but the world, just as in like case, I fancy (having the chance), we should wham it again. Our paper was an afternoon paper, and it was the only afternoon paper to publish the story of that great historic event that day. All other stories for afternoon papers perished in that telegraph-office avalanche of copy. Indeed, by the time the afternoon men got through the crowds, gained the wire, and wrote their stories, the afternoon presses throughout the world were still. More than that. Bob Collins of the Associated Press did not reach even the next-morning papers! Kiehl and I handed to our dear old AP friend (and he *was* and *is* a dear friend) an uncommonly juicy twenty-four-hour beat!

My wife I found at our quaint little hotel, where the gentlemen at luncheon or dinner always rose and saluted when a lady entered. They did it at breakfast even, a time when not everyone yet has been able to get on his best manners. We had a good meal with a spot of dry sparkling wine. The "provincials" were feeling pretty well. My wife was a shade uneasy about the scene in the church, but I told her not to worry; I thought it would be all right.

Two days later, just as we were checking out to return to London, Kiehl rushed into our hotel with a cable for me. It was from Chicago. It congratulated Kiehl and me on our "great work" and wound up with: "Description church scene especially fine." We all of course were tickled nearly to death and celebrated becomingly. When I saw Kiehl half a lifetime later in the lovely capital of the Argentine Republic, he still was laughing!

Britain's passion for the pageantry of testimony, for testimonial pageantry, flowered in sustained splendor when George V and Queen Mary took the throne. It said in a language no one could misunderstand: "The throne, the monarchy, apex of British democracy, is here to stay! We love our king and queen, and we know why!"

That same old fight I had over again. My loving friends of the American "metropolitan" Press, perpetually in good appetite for big news privileges, were out to hog every available seat in Westminster Abbey for the coronation of the new king and queen. Our Trafalgar Buildings office, I have said heretofore, was the only decently sized and furnished American newspaper office in London. With a palate for ironic flavor, I presume, the American correspondents gathered in my office, sat in my easy chairs, and voted me off the coronation map. There would be no ticket for "provincials," just sufficient tickets for the news agencies (which represented all the papers) and the "metropolitan" specials. I was like the long-antlered elk amid the thick trees; getting through was *my* business. Mind you, I was not sore. My colleagues merely were looking after their papers and themselves, and a chap from the corn-belt was out of bounds in London anyway!

Dear old Ford was grieved again.

Before me as I write lies an autograph card from him, dated May 30, 1911, written from his home, 115 Oakwood Court, Kensington, in which he deplores that I "had been singled out for attack on the ridiculous plea that Chicago lacks metropolitan prestige." My knightly comrade proposed: "If you do not obtain a seat, I shall be very glad to furnish you on Coronation Day any notes or copy you may require on any particular lines you may specify. These notes I shall put in your hands, if you want them, as soon as I can reach your office after Coronation."

To get all the chivalry of that proposal from the most dignified and the ablest American correspondent in London at that time one must know that my *Chicago Daily News* was an afternoon paper and Ford's *New York Tribune* a morning paper and that the coronation, taking place before noon, with a six-hour time differential in favor of Chicago, was an afternoon-paper story primarily. Ford, in other words, was proposing out of the bigness of his heart to work for me ahead of his own paper. Greater magnanimity than that, surely, hath no man!

Of course one could not dream the coronation, as I dreamed the acme-scene at The Hague: even journalistic dreams have their limits! *I must crash the Abbey gate!* And that was far more easily said than done. I thought of Lord Grey. He was foreign minister then. I had been worrying him for an interview ever since he went to Downing Street in 1905, and he had executed six years of graceful side-stepping. I felt he was a little sorry for me. I told him what had happened and asked him if he could not help. He was interested deeply. The "sectionalism" of the matter did not please him. *All* American specials, he thought, should have equal treatment, and "especially the West should not be forgotten."

That was the way *I* looked at it!

Grey made good, and more. In ample time I received from Earl Marshal Norfolk, the Premier Duke, a ticket, "not transferable," admitting me by the "North Door" to the "North Triforium" of the Abbey, whence I had a perfect view not only of the coronation itself but of its immediate and most magnificent setting. And the Earl Marshal, stimulated by the Big Chief at the Foreign

Office, was still more considerate. There was to be a resplendent royal procession. It would enter the Mall, St. James's Park, through Admiralty Arch from Trafalgar Square. Just within the Arch were vast blocks of choice seats for the show. The Duke of Norfolk gave me one of those, and I was the sole correspondent of any breed or geographical part to be there!

Long and complex, infinitely disciplined, very wonderful was the coronation ceremony in the Abbey, central object in a bewilderingly beautiful scene. Sitting here in my study nearly a generation later, what do I remember of it? I see the grave face of the King and the proud face of the Queen as they play their exacting rôles. How poised and patient they are! I see the stately processions up and down the blue-carpeted nave of the great cruciform church. I see her Majesty on her knees before the altar, that immense train spread out behind her, the diamonds blazing on her neck, four handsome women holding a canopy of gold over her bowed head.

Rich, soft, glowing Persian carpets against a background of blue: I see them again. I see the crowns, priceless things. I see the ampulla, the spoon, the holy oil falling upon the heads of the King and Queen. Archbishops and bishops come and go, come and go. Peers and peeresses sit silent, entranced, in their robes and coronets. I see fair ladies more than I can count, garbed in close-fitting *décolleté* gowns of silk and satin, white, cream, pink, yellow, snowy feathers in their hair and jewels at their throats.

My reflections are crammed with uniforms of every cut and hue. I hear the chant of ecclesiastics. I hear the shrill of trumpets. I hear staccato cries from the Westminster Cadets. I hear the mellow sighing of organ-thunder and high sweet voices in the choir. About me, and as far as I can see, are rank upon rank of people rising dizzily in steep slopes, motionless. And then the grand climax: music swelling to overpowering volume, the melody-bells of St. Margaret's crashing, and from afar the muffled roar of cannon in St. James's Park and at the tower. So let the curtain fall on the greatest civil spectacle of my journalistic life.

21. Two World-Rousing Interviews

Pre-war England was anything but a happy hunting-ground for the newspaper interviewer. This fellow, in truth, was classed as a nuisance, over-inquisitive, vulgar, flagrantly un-British. His form of journalism was one of those rather numerous American novelties which were really barbarities. Let the British look to it! There must be no transplantation of this iniquity from America to England!

That was hard on me.

For newspaper interviewing was my lifelong professional darling. I had believed in it, seen great possibilities of public good in it, ever since Bob Ingersoll had taken pity on a frightened young reporter in Evansville, Indiana, in 1890 and written for that reporter one of the most brilliant and moving interviews ever published. Newspaper men, I felt, spoke the language of the people. Why should not great women and men speak to the people through them and the vast machinery of dissemination they commanded?

Why not indeed?

I was highly resentful of what seemed to me gross stupidity. I grew in firmness to make a fight against that stupidity. No one, so far as I knew, ever had regarded me as a fighting man, a walloper, of any kind. Adorable Dr. Burroughs, President of Wabash, once had astonished me by declaring in public: "Edward Price Bell is the most modest man in this college." To be entirely frank, amazed though I was by the President's statement, I secretly suspected there was much truth in what he said! And yet I forever was getting into situations demanding audacity, colliding with circumstances calling for the push and the fight which I should have been delighted to leave to those better suited for that sort of thing.

And now I was up against another, and a very difficult, problem wholly unresolvable by reserve, modesty, or any other variety of decorous abstention. I had to *do* something. My reportorial skin, as I thought, depended upon it. It was a case of make good in London, and make good in no commonplace way, or assemble my wife and my unpaid-for household goods and go home. How could I "jar 'em"? I certainly could "jar 'em" if I could smash the immemorial and unbroken tradition of no newspaper interview with a British statesman.

How about an interview with, say, the Secretary of State for Foreign Affairs? I went cold at the very thought!

I had fixed upon the first portfolio under the Premier himself. Surely that was going some in a country where no man of official responsibility, and assuredly no member of the Cabinet of any grade, ever had been interviewed for publication in the long history of the Empire. Still the idea stuck in my head, and I immediately set about trying to translate it into reality. I worked five years on the job without making a perceptible dent. And for some reason or other I was not fired; my usual work must have been somewhat better than I had dared hope.

In 1905 a uniquely charming man came to the Foreign Office, a Liberal, a Roseberyite.[1] And he had as much brains as he had charm. He was a nature-lover, a bird-lover, a duck-lover; and he loved fishing as Isaak Walton[2] loved it two or three hundred years before him. Tennis also, and sports in general, gave him pleasure; he was amateur tennis champion of England. Politics came as natural to him as sports. And he had one of the keenest and soundest judgments in the political history of his country. I went after him bald-headed for an interview, and did not get it.

You will have guessed his name: Grey, country gentleman of Northumberland, Sir Edward Grey, Grey of Fallodon.[3] His exquisite and sincere courtesy salved my disappointment but did not cure it. Bluntly there could be no such interview as I wanted, an exclusive interview on high politics for publication.

1. Archibald Primrose, Earl of Rosebery, was a Liberal British statesman with an imperialist and sometimes Conservative bent. Rosebery was foreign secretary under William Gladstone and prime minister from 1894 to 1895. In the early 1900s, when the Liberal Party split over the Boer War, Rosebery was a strong Liberal imperialist, as was Lord Edward Grey—to whom Bell refers as a "Roseberyite."

2. Izaak Walton was an Englishman who wrote several biographies and, most famously, *The Complete Angler*.

3. Edward Grey was a Liberal statesman who was foreign secretary during the buildup to and beginning of the First World War, from 1905 to 1916.

The Foreign Secretary's responsibilities were much too ramifying and too grave for that. At such a hint, Prime Minister Asquith would curl up in agony, and the House of Commons stand aghast. I must remember I was in England, not America!

Rather desolate, I pondered. The British Foreign Office undoubtedly, as I reasoned, was turning down a fine chance to talk frankly to the world. Would it ever see? Time wore on. European politics became progressively confused and threatening. Concurrently, Grey became nationally and internationally more important. I met him at public dinners. I followed his speeches to his constituents and to the Commons. And right along I esteemed him increasingly and more and more desired, and believed in, that proposed interview.

Ten years passed, and I still was waiting. Grey had stood up in the Commons and made his declaration that the Central Powers were attacking and Britain must fight,[4] so shocking London that gold sovereigns ran like frightened quail: ran and are not back yet! I jumped for my interview, begging Grey to tell mankind why Britain was bound to fight. But the old tradition held, held in spite of the urgency of Eric Drummond (Sir Eric of the League of Nations and later of Britain's ambassadorial post in Rome), who was then Grey's private secretary and had enthusiastic faith in my proposal. More of my friends, and friends of Grey, plugged hard for me, but nothing happened.

Then I turned to another great man, Haldane, Viscount Haldane, Lord Chancellor of England, lately War Minister, a bosom friend of Grey and Asquith. On a Sunday afternoon (March 7, 1915) I found myself along with Haldane among his books and engravings in his most pleasing study in Queen Anne's Gate overlooking St. James's Park. On a desk before him was a red dispatch box. Lord Haldane unlocked and opened it and took out one paper after another, reading each to me in low, deliberate tones, pausing to explain the documents and to make comments upon them.

What were they?

They were Haldane's original dispatches to his government on what he saw, heard, felt, and thought throughout his world-famed visit to Kaiser Wilhelm and Chancellor Bethmann-Hollweg in 1912: a visit conceived and carried out by England's greatest student and admirer of Germany and Germany's culture

---

4. Bell is referencing Grey's famous August 3, 1914, speech before the House of Commons, declaring Great Britain must intervene in the war to protect Belgium's neutrality. See Grey, *Speeches*, 297–315, for the speech.

(Haldane) to bring about, if possible, an everlasting Anglo-German peace.[5] It was the first time, as the Lord Chancellor said to me then and subsequently repeated in a letter in his own hand-writing, any public disclosure had been sanctioned of "what passed at Berlin in 1912" (Haldane's written words). And as the disclosure progressed on that Sunday afternoon in the Lord Chancellor's study, Haldane gave me the world-reverberant interview which was one of the real and lasting sensations of the Great War. It crashed over America, rebounded to London, and was caught up in every language of the world.

From 28 Queen Anne's Gate, Westminster, exactly ten days later than the date of the interview (March 17), Lord Haldane wrote me autographically: "I have delayed returning to you the revised copy of our interview until I could go over it with Sir Edward Grey. He has now seen it, and you may tell Mr. Bonham Carter (private secretary to Premier Asquith) that the Foreign Office approves it as slightly altered in pencil. I think your words, written without a note taken at the time, are a marvellously skilful reproduction of the substance of our talk. It is wonderful what you have made of this. . . . I hope your work may result in much good in America."

And, from Cloan, Auchterarder, Perthshire, on April 3, 1915, Haldane wrote me: "Thank you for your letter. I think you have done a very valuable piece of work. I should like to see any Press comments that reach you, for they will guide us here. The importance of the article is that it discloses for the first time what passed in Berlin in 1912, and that what I have said has been approved both by Sir E. Grey and the Prime Minister."

Official Germany reacted indignantly to the interview: denied the truth of one allegation of fact. Writing me again from Queen Anne's Gate (on April 8, immediately on his return to London from Scotland), Haldane stated: "With all deference to whoever in the German Wireless *démenti* asserted that Belgium was not mentioned in the conversations in Berlin in 1912, he is wholly inaccurate. As you heard from what I read to you of the record (made immediately and on the spot) of the conversations at Berlin, Belgium, along with Japan and Portugal, was assigned as one of the reasons why we could not pledge ourselves to Germany to be neutral under all circumstances. The wireless message admits that France was quoted. But the treaties with the coun-

5. Haldane—secretary of state for war at the time—went to Germany in 1912 to negotiate a decrease in German naval expenditures with Chancellor Theobald von Bethmann-Hollweg. See Maurice, *Haldane*, 291–319.

tries, including Belgium, which we had undertaken to protect were assigned as at least equally cogent reasons for the refusal I was instructed to give. We were always ready to agree not to be parties to any aggressive attack on Germany, but that was not enough for them."

Journalism throughout the world (except in that part of it which was at war with the Allies) did me the honor not only to reproduce the interview *in extenso* but to pay high tribute to it both as a journalistic achievement and as an historical pronouncement. Dearest to me of all the praise was that of my editorial chiefs and my colleagues in the field. Two emotions glowed in my chiefs' cables: astonishment and glee. Paul Scott Mowrer, my principal aid in Europe, wired of our "great triumph." That gifted *Daily News* international correspondent and writer, Edmond Percy Noel, wrote me from Paris: "Have just read your really wonderful interview with Lord Haldane. I take on myself the honor to congratulate you. Certainly this is the biggest story any newspaper man has sent to America since the war began. I hope it will have a far-reaching effect in America, as it should, for it is powerfully convincing."

Chief editor of the *Shipping World* (London) at that time was an ardent Welsh-American, Evan R. Jones, "silver-haired cherub of the Savage Club," a most serious man in spite of that somewhat humorous appellative. In his vigorous and highly-respected journal he opened a long editorial with these words: "The great State paper produced through the interview with Lord Haldane by Mr. E. Price Bell, the correspondent of the *Chicago Daily News,* is perhaps the most masterful document of its class known to our language."

Many another editorial, far and wide and in many languages, was scarcely less panegyric, a fact established beyond debate by quantities of clippings in the library of the *Chicago Daily News* and in my own files. Major Jones (he was a major in the American Civil War) had chosen the right descriptive phrase: "Great State paper." That is incontrovertibly what it was. It came from a great statesman in high office. It bears his *imprimatur.* And it was passed upon and approved formally by two other great statesmen, no less men than the Prime Minister and the Foreign Minister of Great Britain.

So the title of the interview to an historical place of its own is twofold: first, it is the "ice-breaker," the original example, of all interviews with British public men of primary responsibility, notably Cabinet members; and, secondly, it is the first (I think the *only,* bar one, to be told of later) newspaper interview which ever has attained the distinction of a great state paper released with all formality for universal publication by one of the foremost governments of the world. If this belief be a mistaken one, I should welcome information of the fact. Not all, however, was rejoicing, in Great Britain even, over the interview. Chauvinistic passion assailed Lord Haldane and drove him from public life. He had said to me that he came away from Berlin "uneasy." He had *not* said that to Britain when he came home. And the jingo struck at him with blind ferocity.[6] But the blow left him unembittered; left him *great*.

"Now," I said to myself, "I'll resume my pestering of Grey."

And I did.

And again Drummond and a number of others, men of weight, took up the cudgels for me.

But Grey was obdurate. He thought to do more in the interview line would be violative of dignity and probably prejudicial rather than helpful to the Allied cause. Months went by, and never did I miss what seemed a reasonable chance to reenforce previous arguments. Nothing, no idea, no fresh turn of events, altered the opinion of the Foreign Secretary. Hope gradually faded out of both my advocates and myself. And anyway, the echoes of the Haldane victory persistently were coming to me.

One evening about 7 o'clock, my dinner waiting for me twelve miles away in a little wood in Kent (somehow I was not there), I was sitting at my desk in Trafalgar Buildings, the office very still, everyone but me gone for the day, the rumble from the Great Square indistinct. Suddenly the telephone bell shrilled startlingly in the silence. It must be my home calling.

"Hello!" I answered.

"Mr. Price Bell?" came a quiet voice over the wire.

"Yes."

"Grey speaking. I wonder if you conveniently could come across to the Foreign Office to see me for a few moments *now*."

"Yes, Sir Edward, I certainly can."

"Please come straight to my office. I'm alone. The doorman will let you in."

Not unlike one in a dream, yet moving pretty rapidly for a dreamer, I passed down Whitehall, entered Downing Street, climbed a flight of stone stairs, traversed a long, broad, high-ceilinged, gloomy corridor, and was admitted to the Foreign Office, the secretary's room.

"Mr. Price Bell," said Grey, meeting me halfway between his desk and the door, "it's awfully good of you to come. Your dinner hour, isn't it?"

I told him a correspondent never had a dinner hour if there were anything else to interest him. Grey said, with one of his fine smiles, that "apparently

---

6. Haldane was suspected of pro-German sympathies and, in 1915, resigned as lord chancellor.

correspondents and some politicians" were "not wholly unlike." And he went on without circumlocution:

"That interview which you have been seeking for: how long is it?"

"Well," I laughed, "I've been hounding *you* for more than ten years. I was at you in 1905, and this is 1916. And I tackled Lord Lansdowne in 1900.[7] About sixteen years is the record, Sir Edward."

"Extraordinary!" he exclaimed. "Of course you know Drummond. He's for you very strongly, and so are many others whose opinion I respect. But it's a formidably delicate matter. I'm dubious. The thing has incalculable contingencies. It *might* wreck a government. Could you lunch with Drummond and me at Winston Churchill's house in Eaton Square tomorrow at 1?"

"Delighted," I said.

"I must tell you I feel slightly uneasy about this matter," Grey remarked, appearing to study the blotter on his desk. "Your work probably will go for nothing. Asquith and Haldane (Premier and Lord Chancellor) would have to approve anything I said. They might or might not do so."

I reminded Sir Edward of the acknowledged success of the Haldane interview the year before, and of his own and Asquith's approval of it.

"I know," he said. "But even that interview caused a storm and brought abuse upon Haldane. Besides, you must not forget that his position is different from mine in degree. I'm Foreign Minister. My international responsibility is primary in the Cabinet. This must be my proposition: If you wish to do the work and risk complete failure, well and good; come."

"I'll come," I said.

And I went.

Grey, Drummond, and I sat down to the meal at 1, and the conversation lasted till 5, Grey talking slowly in a low voice nearly the whole time, reviewing European political and diplomatic history for many years, especially the decade of his tenure in Downing Street, and making out what struck one as an unanswerable case against the Central Powers as the aggressors in the Great War. He wore his dark glasses, removing them occasionally and wiping them. At such times one was saddened by the strange look of his eyes: obviously darkness was not far from him. He seldom so much as glanced at Drummond or me; looked either at his plate or the white cloth before him. He was grave beyond words.

---

7. Henry Petty Fitzmaurice (Lord Lansdowne) was foreign secretary before Grey. Bell had tried (unsuccessfully) to convince him to grant Bell an interview.

"Mr. Price Bell," said Sir Edward as I rose to leave, "we've covered much ground, and you've taken no notes."

"Notes confuse me," I replied. "I'll try to remember. It will take me perhaps a week to recall your remarks and prepare them for cabling."

"You'll cable all that?" he inquired.

"If you approve it, yes," I said.

Sir Edward had the manuscript within a week. What would he do with it, to it? I felt fatalistic. For a week I waited expectantly, thinking the manuscript might come back at any moment, or I might hear something. An utter blank. No matter. To hell with it! I had waited sixteen years, I could wait sixteen more.

Why, I do not know, but I stayed late again at the office, having no thought of the interview, then more than a month overdue, with not a whisper about it. Precisely as previously, the telephone bell shrilled startlingly in the silence, and Grey was at the other end of the wire in his office alone. He was "so glad" to find me in, and would I "kindly come over?"

As the door to the Minister's office opened, I was shocked terribly. He did not come to meet me, as formerly, but stood at a small table covered with green baize and lit brightly by a shaded electric light. In the focus of that light lay my manuscript, but my eyes were not on it; they were on the dark glasses and the almost haggard face of the statesman. As I drew near him, he smiled as was his wont and shook my hand, the smile and the act of a man to whom the journey manifestly had been long and the burden sore.

"Mr. Price Bell," he said, "your interview, practically in its integrity, has met our approval. I like it, and both the Prime Minister and the Lord Chancellor (Asquith and Haldane) have O.K.'d it. You're, therefore, at liberty to publish it. A few words I've ventured to change, to soften a little (the Minister turned the pages and indicated the changes) and at the end I've added a few lines of my own. (These lines were in his own handwriting.) I'll read them to you."

Holding the pages very close to his eyes, he read slowly, asking at the end (in his consummately courteous way), "Do you think my additions worthwhile?" He slipped the manuscript into a large envelope, handed it to me and said:

"This war is heavy with the fate of freedom. Your interview may clarify some vital matters and help democracy."

He extended his hand.

"We're grateful to you," he said. "I particularly am so. Good night. I look forward to seeing you again soon."

Precious to me was that sentiment. It was expressed again in a letter by Grey to me (the letter I find reproduced in Trevelyan's rarely excellent *Grey of Fallodon,* page 375),[8] but to my inexpressible regret I saw the great foreign secretary that night for the last time. Shortly after the interview, he left the Foreign Office and also public life except for infrequent appearances on the platform and in letters to *The Times,* living serenely if by no means happily (he had many deep personal sorrows) until September 7, 1933, in his wood-and-water-girt Northumbrian home, loving to the last his birds and ducks, though he could not see them, only sense their movements and listen to their voices. Profoundly as post-war politics disappointed him in many ways, he never lost the great happiness which came to him because of his success in averting a fatal quarrel between Britain and America in the Great War.

And he always said the interview he gave me "helped materially" in that direction. He said so to Lord Bryce and to historian Trevelyan,[9] among others, as he personally told me. I have a letter from Grey speaking with unwonted feeling and emphasis (for a man of his habitual moderation) of the "fine effect of the interview." And from Drummond I have the following, written from the Foreign Office under date of May 17, 1916: "Sir Edward specially desires me to send you a line of congratulation on the interview. He very much appreciated the way in which it was done and considers the greatest credit is due to you for having made such effective use of what was really rather rough material. The effect produced seems to have been admirable."

Well, the truth is that the Grey interview swept the world in a manner never equaled before or since, so far as I know, with the single exception of the Haldane interview. And Grey's words differed from those of Haldane in that they gave rise to no *contretemps* of any kind, even the Berlin government making no effort to discount them.

The British Press Department, observing how public opinion everywhere was responding to Grey's exposition of pre-war history and diplomacy, issued the interview in brochure form in all the major languages of the earth and sowed it broadcast over the continents and among the chief islands of the seas, calling the booklet, *A Free Europe.* When, twelve years later (1928), as one of the Press party with Hoover on his Good Will Tour to Latin America, I visited

8. George Macaulay Trevelyan, *Grey of Fallodon* (Boston: Houghton Mifflin, 1937).

9. James Bryce was a Liberal British statesman. He served in various Liberal cabinets and was ambassador to the United States from 1907 to 1913—influential largely because of his sympathy and admiration for America. During the war, Bryce investigated German atrocities in Belgium. G. M. Trevelyan was a British historian and, as Bell mentions above, Grey's biographer.

the Central and South American capitals from Amapala to Rio, I found myself pictured in the local Press as "the correspondent who interviewed Grey and Haldane during the Great War."

One uncommonly curious incident belongs to the story of the Grey and Haldane interviews (two of the five I had with members of the British Cabinet). Following the war, I came home for a vacation, the first since 1913. Lunching with a friend in Chicago, he said to me that he had "enjoyed greatly" my book on the war.

"My book!" I exclaimed. "I've written no book."

"Haven't you?"

And he produced a good-sized volume, *The War of Democracy: The Allies' Statement.* It bore the imprint of Doubleday, Page & Company, 1917, and my friend told me it had been sold for $2.50 a volume. The Introduction was written by the Right Hon. Viscount Bryce, O.M., and he was the author also of one of the leading chapters of the book. Other world-known contributors were Balfour, Lloyd George, Asquith, Paul Hymans, Maurice Barrès, Trevelyan, Gilbert Murray.[10] But the foremost, and the featured, articles of the work were the two interviews which had cost me so many years of scheming and waiting, those with Grey and Haldane.

Was I angered by the liberty which seemed to have been taken with my copyrighted stuff?

Not angered but amazed.

I went directly to Mr. Lawson and asked him if he had authorized Doubleday, Page & Company to lift our interviews and publish them for sale.

"Never heard a word from them," he said.

Both of us, on reflection, decided not to say anything to the publishers. Indeed we felt they had done a good job in giving yet wider publicity to what they termed on their title-page "the fundamental significance of the struggle for a New Europe."

---

10. Paul Hymans was Belgium's minister for foreign affairs in the last two years of the war and during the peace process. Maurice Barrès was a French nationalist statesman and writer, whose essays explained the French cause for war. Gilbert Murray was a British classical scholar.

22. When My Hair Grayed a Bit

I was one of those who with their own eyes saw Walter Hines Page[1] spiritually and bodily crucified by the Great War. Our ambassador to Great Britain gave his life to what he believed to be the cause of human freedom. He gave that life in its fulness, especially the last five years of its high development (1913–1918), and he gave it with a brilliance and a good humor matching its devotion. During the whole period of his ambassadorship to the Court of St. James's, the war period, he had no equal among Americans in respect of the admiration and affection which were his.

It was very hard to see such a man killing himself, but one could do nothing about it. To beg him to spare himself a little, to be careful, to rest, was merely to get from him a smiling urgency of something further to do. He seemed to be forever at the Embassy and busy. I never went thither day or night, and I went often, without finding him in conference or at his desk alone. Sometimes he was as bright as the morning. Sometimes he was so deep in anxiety and discouragement that he only could look at one with his steady, gentle eyes.

But I never once left him looking sad. His natural vivacity, the wonderful courage which was the man, could not be borne low for long. His parting

1. Walter Hines Page was U.S. ambassador to Great Britain during World War I. Page had been a journalist before the war, editing the *Atlantic Monthly* and founding the Doubleday publishing company (originally called Doubleday, Page and Company). Like Bell, Page was an Anglophile. Although he publicly supported Wilson's policy of neutrality, in private letters to the president he advocated early U.S. Allied involvement in the war. As Bell tells here, Page became very ill during the war. He asked to resign in 1918, returned to his home in America that year, and died there of heart failure. See Hendrick, *Walter H. Page;* and Cooper, *Walter Hines Page.*

salutation was invariably cheerful, and one felt the amazing tenacity of his will. On one occasion, when the danger of war between Britain and America over the sea question was very great, I was with the Ambassador at night in his office. His fear and distress finally overmastered him. I had risen to go, and we were standing near each other. He took my hand, lowered his head upon my shoulder, and wept. For a moment only. He dried his eyes and cheerily said: "Good night, Bell. We'll have better news soon, possibly tomorrow."

"I feel sure we shall, Mr. Ambassador," I said, pressing his hand.

"Yes," he replied. "The threat which now hangs over us, and darkens the world, will pass. Such a mistake as is, we must admit, all too near us cannot happen. Civilization will not go under in this war, nor in any war. Mankind will go right on marching toward not a lesser but a larger freedom."

Transcendently fine looked that man in the glow of his unquestioning faith. And he looked an American of Americans, not an alien touch about him in feature, manner, or dress. All his hair was on the back of his head. His forehead and face, with that strikingly wide and flat nose, filled the view. His eyes were shining behind his glasses. He was tall-slender, a well-articulated figure in a neat-fitting double-breasted tweed. I have exquisite pleasure in that memory.

People said Page got solace and strength in his trials from his association with me, and particularly from what I wrote for my own papers and for the British Press, notably *The Times* of London and *The Observer*. Scotland's great journal, *The Scotsman,* gave in one issue the place of honor to a long report of a speech in the House of Commons by Sir Samuel Chapman in which the well-known Scottish member used these words: "I do not believe our great friend, Walter Page, would have lived to witness the victory he did so much to win if he had not had the constant and powerful support of his journalistic fellow-countryman, Edward Price Bell." However that may have been, my letter-files hold dozens of autograph notes from Page expressing in terms of the liveliest approval my war cables and articles, scores of which were reproduced in Britain and throughout the Allied world.

It was incredible that any man so buried in preoccupations as Page should find time and energy to write so many notes and letters and telegrams with his own hand. The typewriter vexed him. He loved warmth and felicity of expression; said they proceeded from "almost a divine talent." I have seen his nose turn up at the thought of the typewriter. "Bell," he exclaimed to me one day, "*nobody* can be warm or flexible or naturally fluent on the typewriter. Even hand-written stuff takes on a certain stiffness and coldness when machined."

When Burton J. Hendrick came to write Page's biography, he found it a great task to collect the Ambassador's uncopied hand-written letters.

Returning to London from the West Front one night, I went direct to 4 Grosvenor Gardens to see Page. He listened intently for a good while to my story of conditions in the Ypres salient. Then he said abruptly: "Do you know, Bell, that no American ever has addressed the boys at an English public school, Eton, Rugby, Winchester, Christ's Hospital, Haileybury, Repton, Malvern, Dulwich, Marlborough?" I said I knew nothing about it.

"Well, it's a fact," affirmed the Ambassador. "Our history is unknown here or practically so. Even historical experts know next to nothing about us. We passed out of English historical cognizance with the 'Rebellion of the Colonies.' We became a bunch of barbarians scattered over the wilds and historically negligible. Any honest English historian will tell you that."

"Ah," I replied. "And what of it?"

"I'll tell you what I want you to do if you can get Victor Lawson's consent. I've been talking the matter over with some of the leaders of British politics and scholarship. We want you to deliver a series of lectures to the English public schools on America as an experienced journalist knows it. We are agreed in the opinion that the boys will be more interested in a practical than in an academic man, and especially in the newspaper writer who has gained such renown as yourself in this war. We think the boys will be wild to hear you."

That, as I saw it, was what one might call a poser. It caused me to go slightly weak-kneed, I am afraid. I had a disquieting flash of bumptious boyhood much keener on a whale of a good time, perhaps a rough time, than on anything the tongues of ten angels could say about America. Page, eyeing me earnestly, anticipated any reply I had ready.

"I know what you think," he said. "You think the boys cannot be held down, will not listen, may embarrass you greatly. Nothing to it. I tell you they'll hang on your words. They want to *know*. They'll give you an ovation. All my friends say that. Cable Lawson and fix it up. We're already in communication with the headmasters, and they're for the thing to a man."

"Mr. Ambassador," I said finally, "I'll think it over and let you know."

"Fine!" he answered. "Tell Lawson I particularly ask him to let you do this."

My wife and I had a chat about it. I talked of the idea to some of my closest and most discreet friends, British and American. All were for it, my wife especially. She bucked me up by saying repeatedly, "Of course you can do it; you *know* you can do it." I did not know I could do it. I was by no means sure I could do it. But the call was there. I thought it should be answered. My conscience said so. I cabled Lawson in some detail, and he replied within a few hours:

"Feel you should attempt what Page proposes."

And thus it came about that I lectured from time to time (on occasions when home from the Fleet or the Army) to the English public school boys from end to end of the country during the winter of 1914–1915. They *were* attentive. They *were* generous. They *did* give me ovations. Upon platform after platform they swarmed after my lectures with their autograph albums, strong, friendly, glorious boys, who said a thousand times, "*You*'re the first American who ever spoke to us!" And yet my theme was highly abstract: *American Moral Dynamics.* I showed them as well as I could the principles which had moved us as a people from our earliest days, and they understood. The kindly letters of the headmasters are deposited among the things I prize.

Page's overpowering agony of apprehension and suspense dragged through the fall and the winter of 1915–1916. That was when he was crucified in *morale* and in health. And that was when my hair grayed a bit, Page's suffering affecting me, as it affected many others, particularly. His ever-present terror was that the Central Powers (meaning to him the doom of popular liberty) would march over a catastrophic American blunder to world victory. He feared, as Grey and Haldane and countless others feared, that Washington would pursue its conception of neutral maritime rights to the extreme of a British-American war, as happened during Britain's struggle with Napoleon a century earlier.[2]

Grey and Haldane, in language of the deepest solemnity, had signalized the danger in the great interviews they had given me. In effect they had begged America to put the hopes of free men above a unilateral view of neutral rights in a life-and-death conflict between autocracy and democracy. We could not beat Napoleon without stopping American supplies to him; we cannot beat the Kaiser without stopping American supplies to *him.* That is what Grey and Haldane said. That is what Page believed. And who will say it was not true?

Personally, as my friends knew all the time, and as the world learned from my writings in 1916–1917, I never was alarmed so profoundly as were Grey, Haldane, and Page, doubtless because their crucial responsibility was not mine. On the very morning following Britain's declaration of war on the Central Powers (August 5, 1914), Aeneas O'Neill, one of the great correspondents of *The Times* (a man ranking with De Blowitz), was in my London office with

2. Around the turn of the nineteenth century, Great Britain's blockade of European ports during its conflict with France incited American opinion and led to the War of 1812.

me in Trafalgar Buildings, Trafalgar Square. My wife and several other persons were there. O'Neill was in a state of almost mute awe.

"This war will crack the world," he said. "I know the great Continental empires well. Their armed strength, and their perfect psychological preparation for war, are quite unequaled. No one else is prepared really, not France and certainly not Great Britain. Italy may go as she likes, with or against the Central Powers, it will make little difference. I consider we are on the threshold of the supreme crisis of civilization. I do not see how any vestige of political and social freedom can survive."

Just why, I do not know.

But that black pessimism angered me.

"O'Neill," I said, "park the hearse."

Silently gazing at me for a moment, he remarked:

"You clearly think I am wrong."

"I do. At least I think it's a little early for us to admit we're licked. O'Neill, I'm going to tell you something."

He waited with raised brows.

"I myself," I said, "know something of the preparedness of the Central Powers for war. It undoubtedly is all you say it is. Just two years ago, I spent several months in Germany and wrote for my papers a series of articles expounding the thesis that Germany intended to attack France and to do it through Belgium. Her entire strategic posture seemed to me to prove that. Our good Germans in Chicago, some of them men of unusual brains and weight, stormed the *Chicago Daily News* office and demanded my recall from Europe. Germany was resolutely peaceful. I was a 'liar,' a 'fool,' a 'dangerous alarmist,' and 'Anglo-Franco maniac,' and I was 'ruining business.' Victor Lawson gave them the deaf ear. He was a *newspaper man* and ran his business with *newspaper men.* Only his professional invincibility saved my job!"

"Yes?" interjected O'Neill.

"Now," I said. "What you regard as proof that the autocracies will win this war I regard as evidence that they will lose it. Their preparation is so thorough and their strength so great, their threat to human liberty is so wholly without parallel, that before the war is over the entire free world will be fighting them. Self-preservation will see to that."

"You mean," cried O'Neill, "that *America* will be forced into the war on the side of the Allies?"

"I mean precisely that. I can foresee no other issue."

Events hit Page their most cruel blow in the third week of December, 1916. It was then that he was compelled to communicate to his Majesty's government President Wilson's almost stupefying Peace Note in which the President seemed to state that both combatants in the Great War were fighting for "virtually the same thing" and in which he called for a specific and complete declaration of war aims from the Central Powers and from the Allies.[3] Page realized instantly that this note would be misapprehended and would convulse the Allies with astonishment and rage. He confessed to me some weeks afterward:

"I thought it was the end. I went to bed."

The note appeared textually in the British Press on the morning of December 22. It dazed me like a terrific thunderclap. I read it again and again. At first I could not see through the fog of it. What under Heaven did it mean? What was the President getting at? I did not like him any too well at that time. He had called me and Americans like me, for our war activities, "expatriates engaged in thoroughly mischievous work from the standpoint of their country's interests." We would not "think neutrally." We refused, at the President's bidding, to commit moral and convictional hara-kiri.

At last the fog of the note yielded to my puzzled scrutiny. I saw the President's strategy. I saw his subtlety. I saw his meaning. Thrilled to the center, I hurried to the Foreign Office. I wanted to explain the note. Balfour would not receive me. No one would talk with me. I sought my old friends in Fleet Street. They stared at me dully. They did not speak. They snarled. It was beyond all question a sickening situation. What could *anyone* do? What, particularly, could *I* do? I did not go to see Page. I returned to my private office and spent the morning cudgeling what brain I had. I lunched alone at the Devonshire Club, not a soul taking the slightest notice of me. By the time my lunch was finished, I knew what I should do.

That afternoon I wrote a letter to *The Times* in which I said: "I hope you will permit me to say that in my judgment President Wilson's Peace Paper has been thoroughly and deplorably misunderstood by the Allies. First they have

---

3. Wilson sent his infamous "Peace Note" in December 1916. The premise of the note, argues a biographer, was that the conflict was not an epic struggle of might versus right, but a European civil war solvable through mediation. In the note, Wilson called "attention to the fact that the objects which the statesmen of the belligerents on both sides have in mind in this war are virtually the same, as stated in general terms to their own people and to the world" (quoted in Heckscher, *Woodrow Wilson*, 422). Great Britain and France "received the note as if it were deliberately hostile" (ibid.).

understood him to say that the combatants are fighting for 'virtually the same thing.' What he meant to say, I am sure, is that *according to the general affirmations of the statesmen of the combatants* they are fighting for virtually the same thing: a very different statement."

And I went on:

I think the President's purpose is absolutely friendly, and wisely friendly, to the Allies. I think he honestly is seeking to discover the exact present aims of the belligerents in order that America may know into which scale to throw her strength if she must throw it into either. The Allies have perfect confidence in the moral unimpeachability of their case. Then why should they not enlighten America and other neutrals as to their precise aims? Stated generally, their purposes are unexceptionable; why should they not be so when stated specifically? Germany's aims, as President Wilson says, also seem irreproachable in their general terms: why not require Germany to reduce these general particular terms and see if they remain irreproachable?

Then I shot my real bolt in these concluding paragraphs:

I have not a doubt that President Wilson would be inexpressibly happy to see America fighting with the Allies against the Central Powers in this war. I believe if he could induce Germany, formally and officially, to state that she was fighting to subjugate Belgium, to take a slice of territory away from France, to extinguish Serbia, in a word to realize any of the aims of her scheme of world conquest: if he could do this, I believe he would appeal to the American people to join the Allies in defeating this monstrous project. In other words, I believe President Wilson wants to go to war; I believe he wants to fight Germany; and I believe he wants Germany to commit herself to a programme that would warrant him in asking the American people to enter the conflict.

There is another reason why President Wilson and every other person who understands the situation in America would like to see Germany forced to "put up or shut up." At present through her gigantic American megaphone she is shouting to the American people that she is fighting for the freedom of the world.[4] This is splendid propagandist business for her. If she can be led into a confession that she

4. German propaganda began in the United States early in the war. Germany organized the German Information Service as its propaganda agency in New York in August of 1914. That office produced daily news bulletins for the press, funneled funds to German-American newspapers, and published propaganda pamphlets and books. Its members also delivered speeches around the country and wrote articles and editorials for the press. Although these techniques changed after conflicts over submarine warfare began to heat up in 1915, propaganda efforts did not stop. See Link, *Wilson*, 31–6, 40–3.

is fighting not for the freedom of the world but to force her detestable domination upon at least a part of the world, what will become of this great propagandist cry? Why prevent President Wilson, if he be able, from trapping pan-Germanism into revealing by words, as it has revealed by acts, its brigand soul?

That was the letter. Darkness had fallen when I typed the last word. As quickly as I could, I wrote autographically a covering letter to Lord Northcliffe personally and hastened the two to Printing House Square by a district messenger boy in a cab. Then I took a copy of the letter to *The Times,* jumped into a taxi, and in a quarter of an hour's time was alone with Page at the American Embassy. He sat in a crouched position in a big red-leather chair before a grate-fire and studiously read the letter.

"Now, Mr. Ambassador," I said as he finished reading and looked at me, "I've sent that letter to Northcliffe with a strong appeal to him to use it prominently in *The Times* in the morning. I said to him: 'I know you'll not believe a word of it. But publish it anyhow. Put the responsibility squarely on my shoulders.' Mr. Ambassador, I'll admit I'm troubled. If you think I've gone off my chump, or think the letter will do more harm than good, say so, and I'll telephone Northcliffe not to publish it."

Page was smiling.

"Go home," he said. "I've reached the same conclusion as yourself. Let the letter be published. I think it will do good."

"You note," I cautioned, "that I say the President wants to go to war against Germany?"

"Yes."

"That statement, Mr. Ambassador, will raise hell."

"Probably," replied Page. "Let it!"

I thought real happiness was discernible in the Ambassador's worn and drawn face, and I traveled to my home in the country with a deep gladness of my own. This sure sense that I had done the right thing was fortified as I watched my wife read the letter and received her assurances that it was in full harmony with her own intuition and belief. At daybreak the next morning (December 23), *The Times* was laid before me. Northcliffe had made good. The letter was given prominence under the head, "Mr. Wilson's Note," and the long leading article of the famous newspaper was devoted to it.

Vigorously endorsing the King's speech from the throne reaffirming emphatically the purpose of Britain, homeland and Dominions, to prosecute the war to a "victorious consummation," the leading article went on:

That this is our purpose is proved once again by the pain and resentment aroused in all quarters by Mr. Wilson's unhappy Note. These feelings may be due to misapprehension, and we are disposed to believe that they are due to it, at least in part. . . . The London correspondent of a well-known Chicago journal contends in a letter we publish this morning that the object of the President is to discover the exact aims of the belligerents "in order that America may know into which scale to throw her strength, if she must throw it into either." His purpose, Mr. Price Bell thinks is "absolutely friendly to the Allies," and "he wants Germany to commit herself to a programme which would warrant him in asking the American people to enter the conflict." The theory is ingenious, and it may, perhaps, be thought to receive some color from the curiously discrepant statements which Mr. Lansing, Mr. Wilson's Secretary of State, is reported to have made to representatives of the American Press.[5] We heartily wish that we could accept it, and there is certainly a great deal that is obscure about the origin of the Note.

Shortly after reaching my office that morning, I had a telephone call from Northcliffe. He sounded very earnest and subdued, yet by no means unhappy. "Bell," he said, "you've loosed a typhoon. We're stemming a tide of messages from everywhere wanting to know what the letter means. Germany is making the air crackle with code inquiries to Washington. The whole world is excited. I do *hope* you have the President right, and I *believe* you have. All my papers will back you up. One thing is final: you've damped the powder of an awful potential explosion. You've caused *a universal suspension of judgment.* Thank God for that!"

I found myself as popular on December 23 as I was unpopular on December 22, although most people, especially Americans, hardly could conceal their suspicion that I was a lunatic. Their behavior seemed to say, "We're interested in you; your audacity is magnificent; but we're afraid you're mad." Even Balfour had relented and wanted to see me for "a few words about your most interesting interpretation of President Wilson." My secretary, Miss Alice

5. Robert Lansing, Wilson's secretary of state from 1915 to 1920, was an ardent defender of U.S. neutral maritime rights. But he also firmly believed that U.S. interests were tied in with Allied interests and that the Central Powers could not be allowed to win the war, even if that meant eventual U.S. involvement. When Wilson released his Peace Note, Lansing issued a statement to the press that was "so subversive . . . as to make it nothing less than an act of betrayal" (Heckscher, *Woodrow Wilson*, 422). He said: "we are drawing nearer the verge of war ourselves . . . The sending of this note will indicate the possibility of our being forced into the war . . . Neither the President nor myself regard this note as a peace note" (quoted ibid.). Wilson was furious; he had Lansing release a second statement, essentially negating the claims of the first. See Smith, *Robert Lansing;* and Hackscher, *Woodrow Wilson*.

Archer, was busy all morning acknowledging luncheon invitations I could not accept. I lunched with Page at the Embassy, and he was more deeply amused, and looked infinitely brighter, than I had seen him in many a weary month.

"Bell," he said, "that letter is going to make great history. A ghastly danger has been deferred, to say the least; no one today, unlike yesterday, is talking of a British-American war about neutral sea rights or anything else. I believe that danger is gone for good. I've cabled the President full particulars, and I think you'll hear from him."

Then the Ambassador burst out laughing.

"What's the joke?" I asked.

"Why weren't you with your colleagues in my office early today? You'd've seen the sight of your life. The place was packed with wild-eyed correspondents of every tongue and color, every man seeming to have it furtively in for me. What had I told Bell? Had the Embassy any responsibility for that letter? Was there authority of any sort, in Washington or in London, for the letter? Or was Bell merely crazy?"

After we had had a good laugh together, I asked the Ambassador what answer he had given the agitated news-hounds.

"Well," replied Page, "it was short and sweet. These are about the words I used: 'Gentlemen, Mr. Bell's opinions are his own. In writing his remarkable letter to *The Times,* he was inspired neither by Washington nor by this Embassy. We may not all see eye-to-eye with him, but he is trying to avert a world calamity, and *I* for one am with him!'"

I did hear directly from President Wilson over his own signature.

He wrote from the White House:

"You may rest assured I greatly appreciate the efforts you have been making rightly to interpret to the English people my real attitude and sentiments. Sincerely and cordially yours, WOODROW WILSON."

23. The Six Letters to *The Times*

On December 26, 1916, four days after my first letter to *The Times* of London, I wrote the second of my six letters to the great journal in Printing House Square. This second letter was published the next morning (December 27) with even more prominence than the first, which set going such a tumult in the world. The head-lines were arresting, and the letter was preceded by this editorial note:

"We publish today, among other letters on the peace suggestions, an interpretation of Mr. Wilson's Note by Mr. Edward Price Bell, who sees in it a preliminary to possible American participation in the war."

Why did I write the second letter?

Because the effect of the first was tending to wear off! Fog was gathering again. Apparitions were about. German propaganda was working at tremendous pressure. Those who had seen some hope in my first letter began to doubt and to speculate gloomily. This is how I plunged into the business for the second time:

> Do the Allies want America in the war on their side? If they do, now is the time to exercise vigor inspired by sagacity.
>
> You know our history. You know we fought first to free ourselves; then we took a stand to fortify freedom in the Western Hemisphere; then we fought to free our negroes; then we fought to break the Spanish yoke in Cuba. Yokes we do not like. Peace we love, but *not* peace with a yoke.
>
> To your statesmen I would appeal to listen understandingly to President Wilson's words. I would say to them: "Give President Wilson a great programme, a flaming programme, such a programme as will enable him to attract practically every drop of non-Germanic blood in America to the banner of freedom." Real

Americans are struggling to guide the flood; put no shackles upon their limbs. Among such shackles are mistaken and unfriendly interpretations of President Wilson's obscure language, language made obscure of deliberate purpose. Here, it seems to me, is a job for Mr. Lloyd George with his magic gift of popular appeal.

All President Wilson has asked for is a precise statement of aims. The Allies need not hesitate to make such a statement. But how about Germany? Honest men can afford to state their intentions; criminals cannot. We know Germany's criminal acts in the past; we want her to confess her criminal intentions for the future. We want her to be convicted before the American Congress and the American people not only by her deeds, which are unmistakable, but by her words at this moment. There are times when words are more important than deeds, and this is one of them. When we have both the evidence and the confession, we can act.

President Wilson knows, as every other sane man in the world knows, what the Allies are fighting for. You have told him in what you have said, and you have told him much more eloquently in what you have done. All he now requires is a reaffirmation, a definite reaffirmation, a powerful reaffirmation, of these purposes.

America cannot keep out of this war unless Germany gives way. The time may come very soon when President Wilson will be under the necessity of making his appeal to the American nation. The Allies have done things that have been very painful to us. They have committed acts that we regard as forcible invasions of our sovereignty. But the Germans have done worse. They not only have invaded our sovereign rights but have slaughtered and drowned our citizens in outrage of all law and of the first rudiments of humanity.[1] The Allies have done us *some* harm, but they are fighting for what we cherish; the Germans have done us infinitely *more* harm, and they are fighting for what we execrate. For whom, then, will we be likely to fight, when we must fight?

Now, of all times in their history, is the moment for the representatives of the English-speaking peoples to exercise all the penetration and all the prudence they can command.

This letter, though less sensational in its visible effects, deepened the impression of the first and was dispatched by wire and wireless to every capital in the world. The entire British Press gave it both news and editorial space, and there was clear evidence of a general yielding of official and public opinion to its point of view and argument. Nevertheless, the case, as I thought, would be the better for further support; and I wrote four more letters in an endeavor to supply that support. This epistolary sextuplet became known as *The Six Letters to The Times Definitely Foretelling America's Entry into the Great War.*

1. A German submarine attacked the British ocean liner *Lusitania* in May 1915, killing almost 2,000 passengers—128 of whom were American.

One of the most effective of these letters, the fourth, was written on Washington's birthday, February 22, 1917, and appeared in *The Times* the next morning. In this communication, a matter of 300 words, I burned my bridges: we were "on the edge of great things in America, things worthy of the country of Washington and Lincoln." America was "about to fructify internationally, about to make her real contribution to humanity and history." I asked: "Why has not President Wilson acted sooner for the glory of his country and for the good of his kind?" And the answer was: "Well, perhaps the tide was out; perhaps Wilson only could have scrambled in the shallows. Quite possibly the tide now is in, and Wilson can take the country with him on the flood."

At this, Northcliffe and his conservative advisers at *The Times* waived all their dubieties and precautions: came down explicitly on my side of the fence. Their leading article of February 23 opened thus:

> The sagacious and racy letter upon American opinion which Mr. Edward Price Bell, of the *Chicago Daily News,* sends us today deserves careful consideration by all who are trying to understand the situation in Washington. Mr. Bell hopes and believes that his country is "on the edge of great things," and that presently she will "make her real contribution to humanity and history." He expects and wishes her to take part in the Great War on the side of justice and of right, and he thinks she will enter into it more readily on the broad ground of her responsibility to civilization than upon the specific issue of American interests. We have very little doubt that he is right upon the second point; we think that in all probability he is right upon the first. But the most interesting point of his letter is his interpretation of the seeming changes in the attitude of the President. Mr. Wilson, he suggests, is an apt pupil of events. "Perhaps the tide was out; perhaps Wilson only could have scrambled in the shallows." Perhaps now the tide is in, or at any rate is rising fast, and the President "can take the country with him on the flood." The view is ingenious, and it appears to fit the facts, so far as foreigners can know and judge them. It would explain a great deal, particularly if we might also suppose that Mr. Wilson possesses the wonderful instinct by which certain organisms, when the sea is at its lowest ebb, know that it will surely flow before long.

I saw Page at the Embassy shortly after he had read the above article.

He shook hands with me jovially and said:

"Bell, it was a close fight, but you've won."

Among Page's closest British friends in London, and the man whose astuteness as an intelligence officer struck the Ambassador as "absolutely unmatched," was Rear-Admiral Sir William Reginald Hall, chief of the Intelligence Division of the Admiralty War Staff from 1914 to 1918. So enthusiastic was Page over Hall's "wizardry" that he wrote President Wilson about the matter and declared it explicable only on the theory of "a clear case of genius." I too could think of Hall as only a genius in his line. His eyes and face, always full of a strangely tantalizing light, were the most alert and penetrating any of us knew. He befriended me as a correspondent in many ways, and long before the war was over I regarded him as a comrade.

But one night, when I was working late at my office, he gave me a bad turn. He called on the telephone from the Admiralty and blurted out in his sharp way:

"Price Bell, you're in bad. A big man is out for your hide. I've just picked him out of the air. You'll have the dope shortly."

And he rang off.

I knew there was a certain prankishness in Hall. He loved to startle people and to worry them in a mild fashion. But my nerves were somewhat on edge anyway (we were living in pretty trying times), and I must confess I was on the hellishly hot side of Uneasy Street. I paced my room and waited for the knock I was sure would not be delayed many minutes: Hall was as quick as he was smart. The knock came, an Admiralty messenger placed an envelope in my hand, and vanished without speaking. There was a bit of typed flimsy in the envelope, and these words in Hall's handwriting.

"Just a little joke, Price Bell. We caught this as it was riding the air to Washington."

It was Herr Zimmermann's apology for the German government's attempt to bring off a war on the United States by Mexico and Japan if the United States went to war on the side of the Allies.[2] Herr Zimmermann, it will be remembered, was State Secretary of the German Foreign Office and had handled Germany's plot against the peace of the United States from the beginning. But where did *I* come in? Why had the Admiralty's "wizard" rushed the Zimmermann message to me?

Because the German State Secretary asserted that I was responsible, or at least partly responsible, for the plot. My letters to *The Times* had been read in Berlin, according to Zimmermann, "with a full sense of their apparent reality." He continued:

2. Arthur Zimmermann was Germany's foreign secretary during World War I, from 1916 to 1917, and the author of the infamous "Zimmermann telegram." In that telegram, he authorized the German ambassador in Mexico to propose an alliance with that country against the United States, in the event that the United States should decide to enter the Allied side of the war. Zimmermann planned the conflict hoping to weaken U.S. power in Europe. The telegraph was one of the major factors of U.S. entrance into the war. See Tuchman, *Zimmermann Telegram,* 107–83.

"We could not dismiss these letters as of no concern to us. This was so not only because of the character of the letters themselves but because they were confirmatory of other evidence in our possession. We already had, for example, the Argentine newspaper *Prensa*'s revelation of the plot of the United States to win the Latin-American Republics to her side for common action against Germany and her Allies. We regarded *Prensa*'s story as trustworthy. It also had numerous facts to give it the aspect of truth. We do not know whether Edward Price Bell wrote from authoritative information. But we do know he wrote convincingly. And what he said went with other things we could not overlook to justify us in doing anything in our power in anticipation of an American attack."

So I was co-author of Germany's move toward a Japanese-Mexican war on the United States!

Within a few hours after Sleuth Hall's communication reached me, it was in every newspaper office in London and in the British Isles and on its way overseas, credited to "Admiralty, per Wireless Press." Ambassador Page of course had been fully aware of Germany's diplomatic maneuver for some time. The immortal "Zimmermann Telegram" had been nipped from the ether by Hall and delivered to Foreign Minister Balfour, who lost no time in handing it to Page. The telegram had been de-coded from German into English, and Edward Bell of Page's Embassy staff had turned it back into German in order that President Wilson might have the document in the language of its origin.

Zimmermann's reported effort to bring Japan (one of the Allies in the Great War) across the Pacific Ocean to join Mexico in war upon the United States was published in the most respected newspapers of the world only to be laughed at. It was an "obvious hoax." Japan's ambassador to London, told of the Zimmermann Telegram by Page, cried out with loud laughter: "Fantastic! A canard!" President Wilson wanted some convincing, and our Anti-Entanglement Diehards in Congress wanted more. Zimmermann gave it them. He honestly *confessed*. Mexico, our neighbor Republic, let us remember, was more than willing to have a try at us with Japan's support; victorious, she was to have back what we took away from her in 1846, Texas, New Mexico, and Arizona.

But our presumed militarist enemies in the Far East did not choose to fight us. Baron Shidehara, Vice Foreign Minister of Japan, promptly repudiated Zimmermann and proclaimed Japan's "inflexible loyalty" to the Allies and her "unalterable friendship" for America. Naturally mirthful, Tsuneo Matsudaira, Secretary of the Japanese Embassy in London (later Ambassador), became very nearly paroxysmal. He gleefully pointed out to me the deadly weakness in Zimmermann's pious reminder, in the wirelessed confession from Berlin, that the German-Mexican-Japanese alliance was to come to birth only if and when the United States declared war on Germany.

"Ha! ha! ha!" chuckled Matsudaira. "The Secretary of State in Berlin *is* amusing. What does he do? He starts out in his telegram by saying, 'We intend to begin on the first of February unrestricted submarine warfare. We shall endeavor in spite of this to keep the United States of America neutral.' That's what he says. It's the funniest thing I ever have seen in a diplomatic document of any kind. Herr Zimmermann announces categorically that Germany intends to make war, and war unprecedented for its ruthlessness and inhumanity, upon *all* maritime Powers not allied with the Central Empires. That is a bald, a perfectly frank, declaration of war on the United States. Germany, in other words, will make war on the United States and still endeavor to keep the United States neutral!"

Ambassador Page began with the discovery of Zimmermann's telegram to be genuinely cheerful over the international outlook. It was the *first time* he had been so during the whole war. There is no use in pretending anything else. Loyal as he was to President Wilson, and faithfully as he tried to represent the President with almost ultra-fidelity in every situation, *Wilson's way was not his.* He thought Wilson myopic with reference to the great realities of the war, its implications for mankind. *I know this.* I saw it as clear as noonday again and again. Occasionally it got into the Ambassador's words; it was always in his bearing, in his suffering, things he could not hide from those in near and almost daily intercourse with him.

True, he stood by me when I entered upon my series of studies of Wilson in the six letters to *The Times.* He did not give actual *public* encouragement to me further than to say what he said to the correspondents in his office on the morning of the publication of the first letter: "Mr. Bell is trying to avert a world calamity, and *I* for one am with him." Ambassadorial duty restrained him from encouraging me publicly. He said to me both orally and by letter that he deplored that fact. "I wish I had your freedom" was one of his statements. He *hoped* Wilson would turn out favorably to what he considered the interests of humanity. I think he prayed in that *sense.* But he could not *believe.* Until Wilson actually asked the Congress to reply with war to Germany's *de facto* war upon us, the President was to Page a Great Big Ambiguity.

Now, did I get my idea of Wilson's perspicuous insight, and of his stability against Germanic pretensions and acts, from an examination of the *man*? No. I thought him a great man, the greatest American after Lincoln. His *New*

Freedom[3] I had read with deep rejoicing that we had a man who could write that book. I thought I perceived in it the *light* we must have if we were to live as a democracy. But no single man however great bred in me my faith in the issue of the war. *Circumstances* were my guide. The irreducible world factors were against any possible frailty, any possible failure, on Wilson's or any one person's part presenting victory to the Central Powers. Their battalions were moving against *History,* and no battalions are heavy enough for that job.

Southern-born both, boyhood companions academically and in work and play, long in sympathetic association as respectively author and editor, Woodrow Wilson and Walter Page yet seem to me to have lived and died essential strangers.

Perhaps *all* men do.

Perhaps it is the very characteristic, the ultimate fact, of individuality to be unknowable!

My letters to *The Times* brought to me, speaking very moderately, a tempest of Press praise. I was called "famous," "extraordinarily able," "far-sighted to the point of clairvoyance," a "prophet," a "seer," all of which terminology bewildered one who fancied he merely had been screaming for recognition of conditions, facts, governing fundamentals as conspicuous as the side of a house. John St. Loe Strachey declared in his *Spectator:* "Edward Price Bell has established himself as Chief Liaison Officer of the English-speaking world." On the day (not long after America's declaration of war on Germany) of the moving and magnificent Thanksgiving Service in St. Paul's Cathedral, Lord Northcliffe had Frederic William Wile write for the *Daily Mail* an editorial-page feature, *Bell of Chicago,* in which the story of the letters was told with a vigor and brilliance matching its generosity.

But not the *whole* Press had been with me. I was criticized and ridiculed by a few editors and writers. I was "Edward Price Bell Johnny-on-the-spot." When they said, "Look out for the Jack-in-the-Box," they meant me. I was "insuppressible." I was "poor Wilson's poor London mouthpiece." I was a "nuisance." "We've had too many Peace Notes and other Notes from Washington. We've had too much of this fellow Price Bell. There's just one thing for our Government and our Allies to do: *skid the Wilsons and the Price Bells and get on with the war!*" So ran the adverse criticism, and it was stocked with intrinsic evidence of its sincerity.

If my own profession, with the exceptions noted, gave full weight to the letters and their influence upon the critical events of the moment, I am not aware

3. Wilson's *New Freedom* is a collection of his 1912 campaign speeches.

that historians did, or ever have. Politicians likewise permitted the letters to pass without much, if any, public notice. Acknowledgments handsome enough were made by political leaders to me privately. First-rank diplomats behaved similarly. I have no record of one of them publicly designating the letters as belonging in the slightest way to the stream of influences which made the turning-point in history in 1916–17. I make no complaint; I merely mention the truth in passing.

Much more serious criticism than I have indicated overtook me, and gave me plenty to think of, as a result of my journalistic activities in Great Britain during the war and the years immediately following. Sinn Féiners, Ireland's energetic and determined Nationalists, did not like me; they said I was "in the pay" of England; I was an enemy of Nationalist Ireland. The letters to *The Times* gave great offense to these warriors for a Free Ireland. They sent two of their strongmen to see me in my London office. These envoys did not tell me their names, and I never learned their names. They remarked to me:

"England and Ireland are at war; they have been at war for centuries. *You* are fighting on the side of England. We hardly need to tell you, we think, what that means."

Language could not have been plainer, I thought: it was a frank threat of assassination. I surveyed my visitors carefully. They were short, heavy men, brown-haired and brown-eyed, watchful, fairly well-dressed but rather brutal-looking, not at all the typical Sinn Féin intellectual. I observed that the door between my office and that of my secretary, Miss Archer, adjoining, was ajar. I suspected what was true: she had left it so deliberately. She did not take to my visitors. They had declined to give her their names when they asked to see me; had said lightly that they were "friends" of mine. Miss Archer was suspicious. She listened. She took notes.

My reply to the threat was this:

"I have nothing against Sinn Féin as a political creed. It is none of my business. I have written much in attempted objective explanation of it. But I have been opposed, and am opposed, to the effort of Sinn Féiners to disturb the peace of the English-speaking world. That, in my settled view, is too much to pay, and will continue to be too much to pay, for the realization of Sinn Féin ideals or any other political purpose I can see. If the peace of the English-speaking world went, *I* think Sinn Féin would go with it. It would be an all-embracing world catastrophe. Let me say to you men, with all respect, that it is not the habit of the *Chicago Daily News* to yield to any form of external pressure affecting what it shall and shall not publish."

My visitors rose abruptly and left without returning a word. Their action seemed to say:

"You have heard us."

That was in the summer of 1921. My wife and daughter were on a visit to America, my two sons were in school in Switzerland, and I was living alone in my home, twelve miles southeast of Trafalgar Square. The home was looked after by Mary Burton the cook, Ethel Burden the house parlor maid, and Jordan the gardener. One night I went home rather late and found Jordan and the maids waiting for me in a state of ill-concealed excitement. Strange men had been about in the fields and in the wood. Hay-ricks had been fired close to my home; and the telephone wire had been cut. I reassured the servants.

"Never mind," I said. "That's probably as far as it will go."

My opinion was that Sinn Féiners were behind the demonstration.

On entering my office the next morning, Miss Archer was told by the junior secretary (who arrived earlier) that I was "wanted as soon as possible at Scotland Yard." Turning up a few minutes later, I found Miss Archer calm enough but somewhat white. She gave me the message without comment. The chief of Scotland Yard then was Sir Basil Thomson, a friend of mine. I got him at once on the wire, and he said:

"Come over."

He sat at his desk in his tiny private room, a room just big enough for the desk, his chair, two or three other chairs, and a book-case. The moment I was seated he said:

"Price Bell, one of these mornings there's going to be a dead man in Kent."

"Oh," I replied. "And who will the dead man be?"

"*You.*"

"Who's going to kill me?"

"The Sinn Féiners."

"I'll bet they don't," I said. "They're threatening me; sent two men to warn me; have burned hay-ricks near my house and cut my telephone wire. That doesn't look to me like murder; it looks like staged intimidation. When the Sinn Féiners want to kill anyone, they don't play about over it; they do it. I think it'll be a long time before they regard the murder of Americans as likely to profit their cause."

Sir Basil pulled out a drawer of his desk and showed me quotation after quotation from the Sinn Féin Press, Irish and American, in which I was abused with almost hysterical vehemence. Many sentences had been underlined by Sir Basil's secretaries in blue pencil. These sentences Sir Basil pronounced "brazen incitements to assassination." I told him nevertheless that my opinion was unchanged.

"Whatever your point of view," he retorted, "I'm going to place a guard of two ex-service men, crack shots, on your house. They go on duty tonight. They will remain on duty till the danger is past. Sinn Féiner gunmen are going to turn up at your house sooner or later, and it is our duty to look after them."

"Of course you must do as you please, Sir Basil," I answered, "but you probably will get me killed. Sinn Féin, I fear, will react decisively to your challenge."

Followed two weeks of such uneasiness for me as I have not gone through at any other period of my life. My only satisfaction was that my whole family was away. One of those ex-service men met me at every train and saw me to every train from and to London. All night long they tramped round and round my house. I left the garage open for their shelter. Ethel and Mary gave them sandwiches and stout. I sometimes had a glass of port with them. They were nice men, keen and grave, eager for anything. Reaching home one night about 10 o'clock, I missed the guard and found Ethel rather sad. She told me the men had been "called off." They did not know why.

Sir Basil Thomson summoned me to his office the next morning and said: "Well, I called off the guard last night."

I told him I knew it and was glad of it.

"Know why?" he inquired with lifted brows. "We raided a Sinn Féin nest in Dublin and seized the minutes of a meeting recording a vote that you were less harmful to Sinn Féin alive than you would be to it if dead at its hands. And I may tell you confidentially that at the same meeting the vote on Field Marshal Sir Henry Hughes Wilson[4] was the contrary of the one on you."

The next year (June 22, 1922) as Sir Henry, former chief of staff of the British Army and head of Ulster's defenses, was in the act of entering his home in Eaton Place, London, two men shot him to death with their big army revolvers. He was in full uniform and fought his assailants with his dress sword. The murderers were caught by citizens and police, and in less than two months' time were hanged. They gave their names as James Connelly and James O'Brien. I am not certain but always have suspected (if the names given were bonafide) that the men who brought Sinn Féin's message to me in Trafalgar Buildings were James Connelly and James O'Brien.

4. Henry Hughes Wilson was a British field marshal who served in the War Office and as military adviser to David Lloyd George during late World War I. Wilson was a Conservative, whose support of union between Ireland and Great Britain led Lloyd George to deny him a post in his government in 1922. Wilson represented Ulster in the House of Commons. See Collier, *Brasshat*.

IV
The Great War, 1914–1919

24. Flying in the Great War

Life in the air, fighting in the air, caught and held my especial interest in combative operations from the beginning to the end of the Great War. Louis Blériot had been rather a mesmerizer to me as I watched him, and pondered on what he had done, as he sat enjoying his food and wine at Lord Northcliffe's luncheon in his honor immediately after he flew the Channel in his monoplane in July, 1909. I thought he was a great man. And even before that those marvelous American boys, Orville and Wilbur Wright, had filled me with admiration and pride: made me vainer than a peacock that I had been born under the Stars and Stripes.

So, when the Great War broke, me for the air!

Flying privileges, like all other opportunities with the British fighting forces, were at first denied to all correspondents, British and foreign. But that stupidity, as I have shown in earlier pages, finally succumbed to militant journalistic intelligence (mainly Northcliffe's), and we men of the Press went practically whither we pleased. My great desire to fly over London at night for purposes of military observation was defeated by Balfour as I have said, but other privileges innumerable were granted to me and to other correspondents with every arm of the services.

What probably was my narrowest escape from death in the air did not occur in the war at all but some three years after "Cease fire!" Remember the R-38? She was a big rigid airship built by the British Air Ministry for the American Navy. I saw her building at Bedford, England, and wrote minutely of her bewildering construction, the most gigantic and intricate maze of girders and wires and gas-bags I ever had seen. Duralumin, stronger and lighter than aluminum, was her body. She would *stand any strain*. And she would *fly*.

Never have I met engineers and workmen keener on, or prouder of, what was growing up under their minds and hands than the engineers and workmen were keen on, and proud of, the R-38. Patterned as were all British-built airships on the Zeppelin (one of which had been brought down in good condition at Colchester in 1916), the R-38 embodied new features believed to be improvements.

Here was a great chance for a correspondent. This big ship, costing $2,500,000, must be flown across the Atlantic for delivery to the American government. The story of that flight would be historic. I went to the Admiralty (where my standing had got to be pretty good) and put in a request to be allowed to fly to America on the R-38. With only a short delay, the request was allowed but conditionally: the Admiralty would let me aboard only if I carried the *laissez-passer* of the American Navy. That meant I must have the consent of Josephus Daniels, then secretary of our Navy. The American Embassy in London sanctioned my request, but Josephus said "No!" Only technical men would be permitted to fly on the R-38. She rose above Hull, with forty-four officers and men, British and American, in control of her, broke in two and took fire a thousand feet up, and all were lost. The next time I was in Washington, I went to the Navy Department and thanked Josephus Daniels for saving my life.

We newspaper men were not supposed to fly over the German lines. If we did, and were brought to earth, we should be shot as spies. In that respect, when violating the etiquette of the front, we took more risk than the soldier, for the soldier's uniform gave him the protection of a prisoner of war. Notwithstanding either the supposition or the risk, we flew over the German lines quite regularly. Frequently we got into hot spots, and perhaps our pulses went up a bit, but usually the cruising was surprisingly tranquil. On many a bright morning, the sky as beautiful as ever it was on the Riviera, I have flown with British pilots while bursting German shrapnel made the blue about us look like a cotton field in blossom. Yet we had no more sense of risk than we should have had if our position had been on a liner on a quiet sea.

Curious, no doubt, but true: there are many curious things of the mind in war! But as the desperate struggle on the West Front proceeded, life in the air over the enemy lines grew steadily less comfortable. The liner on the quiet sea was much to be preferred! For one thing, the scouting planes and all others were endowed with the quality of instability. They must be able to jump like fleas, to shoot upward, to nose-dive, to list and dip great distances with appalling suddenness. The liner on *any* kind of a sea was much to be preferred! For another thing (and this explains the first), the Germans learned not to scatter but to concentrate their Archies, their anti-aircraft artillery. This concentration was deadly to any plane which kept to one position long. Stable planes were out.

How wearing, how very arduous, became above-the-enemy flying before the war ended I saw illustrated startlingly on a West-Front air field one summer day. To the field in the morning came an Army major with a yearning "to view our friends the enemy from the air." He never had been in a plane. He was a fine-looking, good-humored, gallant type of soldier, aged about 35, a man of the "For Valor" bronze, the Victoria Cross.[1] For three hours this major was in the air in a light scout-plane. When the plane returned to the field, the pilot sprang from his seat and cried to the major: "How'd you like it?" The major smiled but made no move to alight. His voice and motor nerves were out of action. It required an hour of rigorous treatment to restore the major to normal after he had been carried from the plane to a hangar-surgery.

Potting sausage balloons[2] came near, I think, to being the number one sport of the West Front on both sides of the long battle-line. "Sport" is what the soldiers called it, but the most terrifically exciting kind of air-warfare is what it was. I never took part personally in "a dive at a sausage," but I saw several of those death-be-damned acts, at least as much of them as the retina could record, for they go like lightning. The sausages of course were gas-bags anchored in the air at a height of a few hundred feet for observing the enemy lines. They were unsightly things, perhaps the ugliest implements of war used by any army; and the airmen loved to shoot them down.

Here is how it was done: A fast light plane, incendiarily armed, mounted to a great altitude, manned by a pilot and a gunner. Deemed out of sight and of hearing, the plane went at a high speed until an enemy sausage was sighted. Then, in the veriest twinkling, it dropped its nose and shot like a cannon-ball toward the balloon. Within range of the vulnerable objective, the gunner poured a hail of fire into it, while the pilot "scooped" his plane in a neck-breaking movement upward to escape the instant and fierce blaze of the gas. Again and again pilots and gunners engaged in these exploits regained their shelters with hair badly singed and eyebrows missing. Occasionally a man suffered serious if not fatal burns. Usually the balloon crew escaped to its own lines in parachutes, though there were cases in which stiff winds carried them into prison camps.

1. Great Britain's highest military decoration.

2. Slang for the large gas-filled balloons from which men observed the enemy lines in World War I.

Gordon Stiles, an American correspondent who tired of waiting for America to enter the war, joined the British Army, and was assigned to the Royal Air Corps. Eventually he found himself observing the German lines from the gondola of a lazy sausage in the Loos area.[3] It was a dull morning (dull weather and dull everything), and Stiles himself said he was "more than half asleep" when he heard "a mighty hissing noise" and saw the tip of his balloon "shooting tongues of flame fifty feet high." He already had his parachute attached and "instinctively jumped." The umbrella opened at once, and Gordon sailed placidly earthward "thanking God for a little excitement." Descending in the ruins of a village, his feet caught in a V-shaped shell-hole in a brick wall, and before he could draw his sheath-knife and cut himself free he almost was "pulled in two." Lying for months in a hospital, he was invalided out of the Army and became one of the most daring correspondents on the war staff of the *Chicago Daily News*. His zeal for the impetuous action was not exhausted in the war; he died at the wheel of an automobile in New England. His speed was (it is said) between sixty and seventy when the car left the road and hit a tree.

By far the most complicated and interesting air-battle I watched during the war was fought above that monstrous example of devastation, that incredible mass of artillery-made rubble, known as Ypres, the town in West Flanders where the British, Belgians, Canadians, and French checked the German advance in 1914–1915, and where that brilliant commander, Field Marshal Lord French, won his earldom. It was my third time in Ypres, and every time under bombardment. I was in company with a British Army intelligence officer, Colonel Roberts. We were in a basement. Above us was a shell-shattered floor and crumbling walls, and through the many apertures we had a good view of the blue sky, a view now and then obstructed by clouds of brick, mortar, and stone powdered by perpetually roaring German shells.

"Look!" suddenly cried Roberts, laying a hand on my shoulder and pointing to the sky.

Scores of planes had appeared; we could hear their motors between the artillery detonations.

"British and German planes!" said Roberts. "It's a full-dress air-battle!"

Ordinarily, when a German plane swam into sight over Ypres, every British anti-aircraft gun sprayed shrapnel. Not so today. No white puffs, no cotton-tails, of bursting shells from the ground against the blue. Why not? Why had the shrill whistles (warning of German air-raiders) not gone as customarily in

---

3. Loos, a town in northern France, was the site of a major British offensive in late 1915.

the ghostly streets? Because British planes were in the air and so tangled with German that no British gunner dared trust his marksmanship. Skimming, mounting, diving, side-slipping, swerving in graceful curves, banking all but vertically, they fought, the boom of opposing land-cannon interspersed with tearing bursts of machine-gun fire among the combatants overhead. One held one's breath!

Were men dying?

They were!

But it did not seem so. I felt as if I were watching not a battle but a game: a game so close and complex and brilliant that the spectator was transfixed. Now and again a plane fell plummet-like, often ablaze. Sometimes the victim was British, sometimes German. One's common human emotions were in abeyance. One was amazingly detached, impartial, scientific, soldierly. Who was maneuvering, who fighting, with the greater daring and skill? We were not looking at the righteous and the unrighteous, at the democrats and the autocrats, at Allies and "Huns," that day. We were looking at *men*.

"Forced down," "shot down," "down in flames," "forced to land," "severely injured," so came the news through a field telephone to our basement under the debris, telling without favor of disaster to British and to Germans. The Germans, in a wavy phalanx, drove the British back over the grassy slopes of Scherpenberg.[4] Rallying with a splendor of coordination to stop the heart, the British brought the whole German armada sweeping again over the white skeleton of Ypres. The battle was at meridian above us. And then, slowly, fitfully but surely, it moved eastward and was gone.

Flight Commander E. P. Graves took me on my first great cruise over the North Sea. He was a young, muscular, blue-eyed, care-free fellow to whom risk and warlike enterprise of every sort seemed a kind of elixir, what Keats called a "blithe wine." If I had been with him a little longer, I think he would have made a brave man out of me. After our cruise was over, and while we were refreshing ourselves at the naval station on Southampton Water, we fell to talking of the war as it was going in Flanders and France. By and by, remembering with such particularity (as I did) the air-battle over Ypres, I began to tell Graves about it. His interest was surprising; men like him as a rule were not very keen on such stuff. He asked a lot of questions. They were almost irritatingly searching, and a queer smile continually flitted across his fine features. At last I got sore.

4. Scherpenberg is a Belgian town northwest of Ypres.

"Graves," I broke out, "what's the matter with you? Do you think I'm faking this yarn, *lying*?"

"No," he said. "I know you're not."

"*Know* I'm not? How do you know it?"

"Well, I'd know it from the story itself. That's one thing. Another thing is that I happened to be fighting over Ypres that day myself."

What was a seaplane observational cruise like in those days, and what was the plane like? Ours (Graves's and mine by courtesy of the British Admiralty) was a 150 horse-power Short.[5] Closely hooded, heavily goggled, leather coated, girdled with life-belts instantly inflatable by thrusting plungers into tubes of compressed air inside the belts, we sailed forth at dusk above a gently-rolling North Sea. We were bound for the waters close to the German mine-fields and the Kaiser's blockaded Navy. The air was sharp but not too cold, and we were in great spirits, Graves avid for military information and I for all I could feel and see of possible interest to the millions who must know the war, if at all, through the printed word and such pictures as they could get.

Great was my confidence in our little wide-winged ship, as great as it was in the pilot, who sat tandem behind me, I hard in the prow. We were new and glossy, cream-colored. Our engine, just in front of me, was encased in polished metal; it would not roar at me and spew me with hot fumes as many a land plane had done at the front. Above the glistening engine-case, the tall, narrow radiator, and before all the huge, two-bladed, mahogany-hued propeller. What a pull it had in it! We indeed could mount up as on eagle-pinions; we sometimes did to scale a cloud-bank, the moon meeting us at its crest. And sometimes we dipped sharply and low. It seemed as if we should touch the waves. Graves fancied he had seen something, a stray boat perhaps, or possibly a periscope, on the water, and he was looking more closely.

Did these sudden dips frighten one?

No. The machine was firm and its handling firm. We were double-planed. Beneath each lower plane was a light rubber float to prevent undue listing of the craft when on the water. Underneath the fuselage or body of the ship were two large parallel wooden floats with watertight compartments like the webfeet of some great aquatic bird. Besides, we had our life-belts. The margin of chance in our favor struck one as quite sufficient.

Glancing round from time to time, I found Graves, so to speak, always

5. "Short" refers to planes manufactured by the Short Brothers company, which specialized in seaplanes throughout both world wars.

discussing matters with his instruments. The bubble in his white spirit level tells him when he is on a level keel. Red fluid in another spirit level says to him, "You are rising," "You are dipping," "You are moving straight ahead." He attends the compass on the floor. He works a pump for putting air-pressure on petrol. Levers are all about the busy man, but on this flight he will use relatively few of them. He does not need the bomb-releases. He does not need the cluster of electric lights for illuminating these devices. His feet push pedals for steering. His hands operate a wheel like that of a motor car. The wheel moves ailerons or fins on the upper planes to control listing to right or left, and it lifts or lowers a horizontal rudder by which we head upward or downward. And so we speed on into the night.

How merrily spun our propeller blades, refined from hardwood into thin flitting shadows! Husky-throated, the engine was not deafening. I found it much nicer to be in a seaplane than in a landplane. The sky was big. The horizon was soft. The sea, strangely bright, danced and sang. Moreover, it looked more yielding than mother earth, tree-tops, house-gables, church-steeples. Falling, I am told, one finds water as hard as a boulder. I have my own opinion! I will chance the water, please!

Following the coast for a time, the moon slowly coming up, we passed sheltered roadsteads and lively harbors. We saw steady-paced liners steaming into the Atlantic, smoke-pennons in their wake, flags at their masts, upward-gazing people lining their rails. We sailed over warships, trawlers, tramps, huge merchantmen. We looked upon valleys, red-blotched with cattle and white-blotched with sheep, here a lone cottage, yonder a close-clustered village. We viewed wooded hills, rounded and somber, imposing white residences occasionally standing out like castles in the beautiful night.

And then we went to sea really!

England faded and was lost. We were alone in a roomy world of sky and sea, not a sail, not a wing but our own. At last came dimly into view, far to the east, the extended outlines of the German High Seas Fleet behind its protecting mines. Graves swung his ship about, smiled at me, and drove hard into the West; he did not like the possibilities of a too-near approach. More than that, he had done his work; he had explored his sector of coast and sea; he was prepared to report to his station, "All's well on my beat!" No surface raiders abroad, no submarines observable, no Zeppelins in the air, no fresh mine-laying, the Kaiser's sea-might quietly at anchor.

We had been several hours (just how many I do not know) on that absorbing flight, and I was a glad voyager when I sighted our air station a mile ahead and 1,500 feet below. Graves dipped the good Short slightly and stopped her engine. We glided earthward silkily. It was just a spot of earth at the end of a long, slim tongue of land curving out from the main shore. We were running directly into groups of buildings. Or were they hurrying up to meet us? In either case, we just missed them. You have seen a gull drop from a great height, skim past a headland, plane evenly downward, and wings far-spread stretch its feet gracefully into the waves? Thus did our bird of cotton, wood, and steel slip sweetly into the sea.

Britain's air-patrol work in the war, and the oversea fighting of her naval airmen, make one of the greatest stories of the world conflict. It was vigilant, ceaseless, comprehensive, this big job, and it developed thousands of dramatic features and incidents which never can be known. Many enemy submarines were bombed as Bigsworth bombed one off a Nieuport in 1915,[6] and many more were located and put on the spot by wireless for the Navy. British planes became the terror of Zeppelins *en route* to England. These great gas-bags were set upon with high explosives from above, as the same Bigsworth showed off Ostend in May, 1915, and as Warneford showed over Belgium a few weeks later.[7] Enemy warships and mine-layers were destroyed. Enemy mine-fields were discovered and charted. Crews of trawlers and merchantmen sunk by hostile ships or mines were found in open boats at sea and reported to the nearest naval station for succor. And British airmen of course played their part in every naval battle fought.

Carrier-pigeons, those powerful-winged wonders with an unerring sense of home, were among the dearest and most important friends of the Navy as they were of the Army. A pair or more of them went with all British airmen at sea and were decisively serviceable on countless occasions. The story of the war carrier-pigeons on the North Sea, those waters of alternating storm and fog, is an ornithological saga. Here is the barest bit of it: Two flying men fell with their plane into a smooth sea utterly blotted out by fog. They were about thirty miles from shore and the nearest air station. So violently did they strike the water that their plane was damaged and they were inundated for a few moments.

6. A. W. Bigsworth was a flight lieutenant and later flight commander in Britain's Royal Navy. He flew during the First World War, primarily in anti-Zeppelin operations. "Nieuport" refers to planes manufactured by the French company of that name, which made fighter planes in World War I.

7. Reginald Warneford was a British naval officer who received the Victoria Cross for his successful attack on a German airship in midair over Belgium in June 1915.

And what more?

Their two pigeons were helpless, apparently drowned. Icy water had gone some way to freeze them stiff. No two brave men probably ever looked into each other's eyes with less hope. For not only were the pigeons out of action; the radio set was smashed. The sea was smooth, yes. But the fog was like wool. They might sit there for hours, even days. And the North Sea was not given to smoothness for long. The men looked at their poor carriers, and an idea struck them. They opened their shirts and snuggled the birds under cover against their warm breasts. The birds recovered. They became alert, eager-looking, as if they understood and wished to help. And by and by the men tagged their legs and gave them to the air. At first they seemed overwhelmed. They circled flutteringly about the men's heads. Then they flew straight upward out of sight. Only a little more than an hour later, the fog breaking into crevices, the airmen caught sight of a light destroyer steaming on a beeline toward them. The pigeons had reached their destination swiftly above the fog.

Graves had the story, he told me, direct from the lips of the men who were saved.

Of all the flying I did on the North Sea, whether in Jellicoe's time or Beatty's,[8] none led me into any narrow squeak to write about; it all was fascinating, picturesque, and informing but never sensationally dangerous. I had my great air scare not above the water but above the land. A flying friend of mine with some scent for novel reporting suggested that I go for a *record* flight from London to Paris and back. There had been no such attempt, and no one knew in just what time the fastest plane of that day could make the double journey. The proposition pleased me, and I set about pulling the necessary strings. Publicity, so tardy in its appeal to British military minds, finally had won them completely, and I had little trouble in getting a sympathetic official hearing. One delay followed another, however, and I did not get my great air scare until after the war was over, and the victors were making the "'Peace' of Versailles."

On the morning of September 26, 1919, the *Daily Mail* (London) published the following:

> In a De Haviland, or Airco 4a, aeroplane last Friday and Monday, Mr. Edward Price Bell, London correspondent of the *Chicago Daily News,* won three world's flying records:
>
> 1. The fastest flight ever made by a journalist from London to Paris, 1 hour and 50 minutes over a route of 270 miles, or more than 135 miles an hour.

8. For more on John Rushworth Jellicoe and David Beatty, see chap. 15, n. 11.

2. The fastest double flight ever made by a journalist between London and Paris, 3 hours and 58 minutes over a route of 520 miles, or more than two miles a minute.

3. The fastest double flight ever made by *any* passenger between London and Paris, 3 hours and 58 minutes.

And then the *Daily Mail* appended my description of these flights as cabled back to London from my paper. I did not fly alone either way. The War Office said the Rt. Hon. J. H. Lewis, P.C., M.P., Secretary of the Board of Education, would like to accompany me to Paris. He did, and he was a good fellow if ever one boarded a plane; lightning, crashing rain, clouds, air-pocket bumps to make the teeth rattle left the statesman sedate and smiling. Our engine was a proper bawler, deafening. Mr. Lewis had been assiduously peering, first on one side and then on the other, at the green landscape. He shouted at me. I shook my head. He wrote with a lead-pencil on a bit of paper and handed it to me. The words were: "I've seen England for the first time!"

My fellow-traveler on the return trip was another good fellow, a young Swiss journalist, Mr. Albert Heider, Paris correspondent of the *National Zeitung* of Basel. It was side by side with him that I got the wind up. My pilot going out was Lieut. A. C. Campbell-Orde and coming back Lieut. G. B. Powell, R.A.C., friendly, modest, nervy, skilful men "bent on the bacon"; determined, that is to say, to give me the records I was after. They took practically the crow-line from Le Bourget near Paris to Hounslow, 250 miles, doing the flight in 2 hours and 8 minutes. It would have been done in much quicker time but for rain-squalls, low-flying clouds, and a dense fog over the North Downs near Sevenoaks.

Those clouds and that fog are the things which gave my Swiss colleague and myself something to remember. As, flying in hazy sunshine, we neared the cliffs of Dover and Folkestone, huge clouds came piling down upon us from the land. It was a vapory avalanche absolutely blinding. Our altitude at the moment was 1,000 feet. The engine took on a deeper roar. Pilot Powell was climbing for dear life. We were an age (as it seemed to Heider and me) in reaching clear air and the sun. Dover, Folkestone, and the coast were blotted from view. Behind us the clouds were like mountain ranges hurled from their bases by some titanic earth-convulsion. Beneath and before us (we had risen to 3,000 feet) lay England's sylvan splendor in a brilliant sun. And Heider and I breathed again.

Earthward dropped our plane and drove at top speed toward London and Hounslow. We were joyous. It was all over but the shouting. How lovely was the valley south of the Downs by Sevenoaks! And then came tumultuous clouds again. They pelted down upon us from the hill-tops. We flew within 100 feet of the ground. No use. Once more Pilot Powell climbed for dear life, knowing the Downs at that point were at least 800 feet high. We straightened in the direction of Hounslow at the 1,500-foot level, no longer in cloud but in something worse: the thickest white fog I ever saw. Powell bore steadily on his course until he knew he was well over the Downs. He knew he was somewhere in the vicinity of Hounslow, but he knew little else; he was blind. And Heider and I were scared. There could be nothing but a desperate gamble in landing in such conditions, and our petrol was far from inexhaustible.

Powell, after an agony of just nothing, began very slowly to drop. I had my eyes glued on the fog over my side of the cockpit and Heidler over his. We saw tree-tops at the same instant and let out yells which Powell could not hear; we could not hear each other. Powell could not *hear,* but he *saw.* And that De Haviland, with her 360 horse-power Rolls-Royce engine, jumped skyward as if from a catapult. And we jumped into sunshine! We could *see!* There were London and the sinuous Thames. There were Hounslow aerodrome and the mechanics waiting. We landed almost as sweetly as Graves and I had landed in the sea. As Heidler and I gained the ground, he grasped my hand and spoke, Frenchily, just one word:

"For-mee-da-ble!"

25. What I Saw in the Ypres Salient

Tired of writing of war, and also inclined to have some actual part in it when America drew the sword, I went to Ambassador Page for a chat on the matter. I told him I was ready and anxious to do my bit, whatever it might be, in a struggle which had seemed to me from the first certain to involve the United States as one of the great exponents of liberty in the abstract, and as a defender of her own liberty in the concrete.

"I quite understand," said Page. "Do you wish to enlist as a soldier?"

"I wish to place myself unreservedly at the disposal of the American government," I replied.

"You're married and have a considerable family," Page remarked. "And just how old are you?"

"Forty-eight and a few weeks."

"I'm afraid," said Page, "they'll not want you as a soldier. But there should be many places in our service for which you would be suitable. I'll discuss the question with our military attache and perhaps write Washington."

There the matter ended so far as I ever heard. I received no encouragement to add my feeble resources in any capacity to the fighting strength of my country. Thus humbled, I returned to my interesting if unheroic preoccupation of political commentator and war correspondent. Along with these duties, I continued to act as general manager of the Special Foreign News Service of the *Chicago Daily News,* whose regular staff on the various far-separated fronts was regarded by experts as the most complete and brilliant in the world. Their enterprise, ingenuity, and courage not only gave the *Daily News* numberless beats but supplied it with an unremitting flow of great war articles. One is proud of the memory of a long association with such men.

My own experiences of land-warfare, and particularly of the enormities of modern battles, were confined almost wholly to the British end of the West Front, the line between the Channel and Nesle, where British and French uniforms met. I never have known a correspondent or a soldier who liked to talk of or think of the worst things he saw and heard and suffered. I have known some correspondents who closed their eyes to scenes of mutilation and slaughter and would not write a line about them. For my own part, I will write about them only what seems necessary to some conception of their reality. After all, men do other things, and more interesting things, than lose chins and jaws and eyes and heads and arms and legs and bowels in war. They do other things than die in war. Of these other things I will try to write.

Most varied of my war experiences were those in the Ypres Salient, that most doleful of all British military memories. I was there by courtesy of Field Marshal John French in 1914–1915 and by courtesy of Field Marshal Douglas Haig in 1917. I was there during the first German onslaught against the Canadians with mustard gas and asphyxiating shells. Gas-emission by the enemy, a new, unexpected, and overwhelming form of warfare, lasted at one time for four and one-half hours, and the wall of fumes was forty feet high. I was well back of the front trenches when the gas horror arrived but near enough to mingle with fleeing soldiers who gasped, swayed, stumbled, and fell as they ran. I saw men bury their noses and faces deep in grass and sand in a hopeless struggle to escape asphyxiation.

That was on April 22, 1915, some six months after the First Battle of Ypres and the close of the German "race to the sea." The first gas (chlorine from cylinders in the German trenches) rose in a yellowish cloud late in the afternoon of a quiet day and bore down upon the African troops and the French territorials. Simultaneously the whole of the German artillery opened with shrapnel and high-explosive shells, and the victory of the assailants was complete. On the second day following, at 4 in the morning, the Canadians were gassed and driven from their positions. Attacks and counter-attacks came in quick succession, and the battle raged, with heavy casualties on both sides, till May 25. The town of Ypres was held by the Allies, but the apex of their salient was pushed in more than three miles, and its base of eight miles was reduced to five and one-half miles.

With the end of the battle, except for continual heavy-artillery reminders that the opposing lines were intact and on the job, I raced by car over the famous road from the small Belgian town of Poperinghe into what was left of Ypres. This road, along which slept many scores of thousands of British soldiers, is nine miles long, with the Belgian village of Vlamertinghe midway between Poperinghe and Ypres. It pierced an avenue of elms. When I speeded over its cobblestones, holed by shells, many of the elms were cut in half, splintered, some destroyed entirely, by German high-explosives. The hop-fields on either side were scarred with shell-craters.

Why did we go so fast over the rough road?

Because speed, while in itself very dangerous among those holes, was the price of life. The German artillerists never tired of taking pot-shots at motor cars or moving detachments of soldiers on this vital line of communication. As we came close to the first broken walls of Ypres, our driver simply pressed the accelerator to the floor and let his high-geared car fly.

"Suicide Corner," said the officer by my side.

I smiled; it occurred to me that *every* corner thereabout was "Suicide Corner." Twigging me, the officer explained:

"No. This corner is especially deadly. It is commanded by enemy guns both north and south of Ypres. These guns are trained on the corner all the time."

We passed successfully, but I think my hair was on end. We were amid the ruins of what had been a prosperous and beautiful city of 36,000 people. It was uninhabited now except for riflemen and gunners. When the rain of heavy German shells started, some of the inhabitants sought shelter in their cellars, and hundreds perished there. Other thousands streamed out upon the road to Poperinghe, where they met British reserves rushing to support the thin Allied line. Surge and counter-surge of soldiers and panic-stricken refugees, the maelstrom constantly under German shellfire. The cobblestones were awash with human blood and strewn with human remains. People swarmed into the eastern end of Vlamertinghe. German gunners wiped them and it off the map.

I have had few sadder days in my life than that first day in Ypres. It is what I should describe as the City of Infinite Vicissitude. Ancient, renowned for hundreds of years for its lace-makers and cloth-makers, it was born to trouble; it had risings, sieges, fire, the ravages of the iconoclasts, plague, chaos. And yet it lived and was lovely. Then Armageddon roared out of the East. Military expediency would not be denied. The Spanish ravager Alva[1] became by comparison a nice Sunday-school boy. Ypres was no longer a city. It was a tomb.

---

1. Fernando Alvarez de Toledo, the third duke of Alba (or Alva), was a Spanish soldier and governor in the sixteenth century, known for his ruthless Machiavellian rule. Alba was governor of the Spanish Netherlands, where he abandoned local law and established a tribunal, known as the Council of Blood, which tried and executed some 6,000 Protestants. See Kamen, *Duke of Alba*.

And it was a tomb from which British howitzers[2] were screaming and into which German shells still were pouring.

East of the ruins, curving from a point due north to a point due south, ran parallel lines of trenches, Germans in the outer line, Britons in the inner. Surrounding these troops, equally tough and intrepid, were the gory reminiscences and the graves of three battles so prolonged that each was like a campaign. At the base-line of the salient stood what had been Ypres. For two hours I walked and crawled about its shattered buildings and littered streets, while howitzers split the ears and German shells blackened the air with earth and smoke. I felt all the time in the heart of a torn sepulcher, huge, white, crumbling, echoing with ghostly voices.

Snags of walls and of towers. Prodigious heaps of formless brick, mortar, and stone. Gutted dwellings, churches, schools, shops. In vacant living-rooms fragments of furniture, ripped pictures, shreds of carpets and rugs. I did not see one whole piece of furniture. I saw wrecked pianos and bedsteads and easy chairs. I saw a large divan with an unexploded shell stuck through the middle of it. One whole thing I did see; a delicate china vase, very beautiful, standing on two inches of the remnant of a marble mantelpiece. In a hillock of rubble I found a thesaurus of the Scriptures in Latin. The book was swollen from rain, and one side of the binding was torn loose; otherwise it was as it had been before a high-explosive shell demolished the house of its owner. I saw a sewing-machine with a piece of cloth in it, the thread in position. The seamstress or sewer was not there.

An officer pointed out to me what he designated as "the most tragic single spot in Ypres." It was in an open square. The first German "42" fell there,[3] and fifteen school children happened to be in the way. They were playing. The shell killed them all and splattered the powdered residue of abutting walls with their blood and tissue. That "42" was the shell which threw all Ypres into a horrible panic and precipitated the terrible scenes on the Ypres-Poperinghe road. Where the children were slain a priest appeared and was seen to lift his

2. The howitzer, a field artillery used by both the Allied and Central Powers, is distinguished from other cannons by its ability to fire at trajectories greater than 45 degrees, resulting in gunfire that falls from above, instead of at a sharp angle.

3. The "42" was a 42-centimeter, heavy-artillery howitzer, which the Germans used to bomb fortresses and towns. The 42, also called the Big Bertha, could fire shells weighing almost a ton up to nine miles. Contrary to what Bell says here, the first 42 did not fall at Ypres, but at Liège, Belgium.

eyes and hands to Heaven. That was his last act. A shell on the heels of the first blew him to pieces.

Most important of the structural ravages of that first rain of shells was to be seen in the great show-place of Ypres: the wide spaces about the vast Church of St. Martin and the celebrated and unique Cloth Hall. These were buildings known for their beauty throughout Europe and the world. But did they go to dust utterly? Happily, not. I stood long looking over what remained of them. Each lifted whittled and ragged shafts high in the air. White, delicate, appealing, these shafts seemed to say: "We are not dead; we shall live again!"

Melancholy as were these splendid ruins, they did not move one's feelings as did the devastated homes of the people. Mansions and cottages and hovels went down in a common havoc. Imposing buildings of the 13th and 14th centuries were damaged beyond hope of restoration. Picturesque gables, baroque facades, Gothic facades, turrets, towers, spires, paintings, statuary, brazen screens, alabaster statuettes of saints, exuberant carvings, infinite minutiae of an old and cultured civilization, all became one expansive and astounding desolation.

The whole of this immortal salient was a region of wonder. After the first wild and wholesale exodus of the people, hundreds returned and resumed life as best they could in the remnants of their homes. They lived and went about their work and play under an arch of whistling steel, for the opposing artilleries were always more or less active and sometimes fiercely so. The German shells were known first by a whining crescendo, then by a resounding crump and roar as they struck and exploded. The British gave off a sound like that of a violent thunderclap, then curved invisibly with a waning cadence toward the German lines. I saw children playing under the arch of fire, and prospecting amid ruins, wholly unmindful of the guns.

In the West Flanders village of Messines, well shot to pieces and subject to periodic gun-fire, I bought from an affable and unperturbed woman shopkeeper a small Valenciennes[4] handkerchief as a souvenir. Her shop and home had been wrecked, but she was doing business in her basement. French and German soldiers had fought steel-to-steel outside her door. When the Germans were driven from Messines, this woman ventured abroad to find the village almost totally destroyed. Her church, a few paces from her door, was a gaping skeleton, its walls holed, everything inside demolished, not a piece of glass an inch square in any of its windows. Her daughter, aged eight, I found

4. Valenciennes is a town in northern France once renowned for its lace.

searching the wreckage. She was slender, black-haired, bare-legged. I shouted to her:

"Bonjour, petite!"

Her dark eyes flashed a smile at me. I inquired what she expected to find in the brash.

"My ring," she replied.

And her mother explained:

"Every day she looks for her ring. It was emerald, an heirloom. She quite believes she will find it some day."

And the child went on diligently searching.

All over the Ypres Salient, behind the British lines, young folk and old folk were occupied similarly. I came upon an old man who had been looking for days for a walking-stick he had treasured. And he had the faith of the little girl.

"Ah, yes," he said, "I'll find it."

In and about the church one saw an incredible spectacle; pillars, shafts, statues peeled, gouged, splintered, riven. One monument covering a grave was rent from its base and broken in two; the coffin, half exposed, stood up-tilted in the air. Bodies and bones were disinterred, flung sometimes hundreds of feet. Men worked for days re-burying the dead. I saw priests pursuing their duties with bared heads in pelting rain with never a surcease of shrieking shells.

One entire week of watching from the British front-line trenches failed to yield me a glimpse of a German soldier. Like the British and the French, the Germans were in ditches and holes. I swept the trench-area for miles with powerful binoculars; it was a desert; not a gun, not a man, in sight. And yet war was raging, and men were dying, every moment of the round day. I listened to the gun-thunder. I spotted the white smoke of shrapnel. I observed the ragged blotches of black smoke from lyddite.[5] And not a man to be seen! Who can wonder that trench-warfare turned men into stone?

And I mean precisely that.

I saw hundreds, brigades, of British soldiers taken from the trenches and re-taught how to shoot. I mean riflemen. They had turned mentally to stone in the trenches. They had forgotten that a rifle had any other use than that of pushing a bayonet into a German when he came. They had forgotten that a rifle would *shoot*. Instances were known of soldiers in both the German and the Allied armies rushing from their trenches to bayonet men whom they

---

5. Lyddite was a British explosive made from picric acid, a chemical explosive developed in the eighteenth century.

could have shot easily and much more safely. With all his fortitude, all his resource (pedagogically imbued), the soldier is still a man.

From the standpoint of personality, I recall the Ypres Salient particularly for two men, John French and Herbert Plumer,[6] both of whom (with abundant merit, I thought) were made field marshals. French was delightful as a man, and so was Plumer. And I do not believe the war produced greater soldiers. Northcliffe, I gathered, regarded French as the soundest strategist Britain had; French knew that to lose the English Channel ports was to lose the war; and he defended those ports with an intelligence and a valor probably never excelled by a general.

And the full story of what he bore in doing it never can be told.

Plumer was surely a soldier worthy of French, his chief. And he was likewise worthy of Douglas Haig, a great general, his later chief. I ate luncheon with Plumer before Messines. At that time he was laying his plans (plans never surpassed for completeness) to attack the Hill.[7] It was a stubborn hill. I dare not say how many good men, Germans and British, had died there. And the Hill had not changed hands; it was neither German nor British; it was an objective for which both armies were contending with science and resolution. It meant just this: the British or the men from over the Rhine prevail on the vital south shore of the English Channel.

"Will you take the Hill?" I asked Plumer.

"I rather think so," he said. "I am weaving into my scheme of attack everything we have learned in the war and notably in this salient. Our deepest trouble has been that we were not prepared adequately to support the offensive. We hurled armies forward with insufficient thought of what was necessary to their support. This was not unnatural because of our relatively slight knowledge of war on a great scale: one must bear in mind the fact that prior to the lessons of this war, except for certain broad principles of military science, we did not know a very great deal about what has been called 'the sport of kings.' We could not feed our soldiers properly, nor bring up sufficient supplies of water quickly enough; supply organization was unequal to the great demands upon it; and soldiers in the terribly arduous labor of a fast advance over shell-cratered country get wolfishly hungry and perish of thirst.

6. Field Marshal Herbert Plumer was commander of British forces at Ypres, which he famously led to victory in the Battle of Messines in 1917. See Powell, *Plumer.* For John French, see chap. 19, n. 8.

7. "The Hill" is Messines Ridge, south of the Ypres Salient, which Plumer and Haig took in June 1917.

"Messines, you know, is a hard-fought hill; it has been battled for some three years; the Germans have fought for it with immense dash and tenacity; we have stood their onsets with great loss. You must have noted what preparations we are making for what we hope is to be the final attack. Have you seen our waterlines? They mean more than our guns. There is going to be a big explosion to the east of where we now sit. It will happen soon. You may see it if you like. And Messines Hill will be changed by that explosion. We're going to blow the biggest mine ever blown on this front. Our soldiers will be there to reap the whole advantage of the explosion. They will trench the German side of the hill, and ten minutes after our soldiers seize their positions they will have ammunition, food, and water."

It seemed to me the frankest language a general probably ever had used to a correspondent. But the English, I found, were like that, I mean the English of responsibility in the war; at first they did not trust one at all, and then (their confidence won) they trusted one in a way which I thought the very height of imprudence.

Plumer added suddenly:

"We are doing some interesting work, I think, under Messines. It has been going on patiently for some weeks; you know everything goes slowly in this war if it goes wisely; rashness has been very costly on both sides. I like your journalism; your work in *The Times* of London (which I read, sometimes with approval, sometimes not) has pleased me, if I may say so; I thought it was substantial and fair to the cause of the Allies, and I regarded the cause of the Allies as the right one for everyone in the long run, not excepting the Germans."

"Naturally, General," I said, "I am happy over what you say. Frankly, I'm proud you approve my stuff."

"Oh, I don't flatter," he said. "Soldiers (at least I like to think so) don't have much respect for flattery. I want you to go to Messines Hill. I'll send an officer with you. If you can stand the hardship, I should like you to go under the hill and see what we have done and hear why we have done it. I may be a little vain in this matter; I'm afraid most of us are so; who doesn't like to have his work appreciated? Anyway, I want you to go, and some day you can tell the story of what you yourself discovered. I'll say to you that no other journalist ever has been or will be under Messines Hill under British authority. About the Germans I do not know. I presume German journalists are following the work of their generals and of every feature of German life in the war."

I went under the Great Hill.

I will not say I liked it.

But for my knowledge of mining, gained when I was a boy in Indiana (my roughing it with the coal miners in the region where I published my little paper), I doubt if I could have borne what Messines Hill's diversified preparations required. It was a hill of countless galleries run by expert miners on both sides. The great object was to mine the hill preparatory to a tremendous blow-up to be followed by a decisive infantry onslaught. To prevent this stupendous piece of mine-laying, which was purposed for the center of the hill in order to destroy enemy trenches and soldiers, each side did its best to defeat the necessary gallery-running of the other. And why? For the reason that these galleries were the arteries through which explosives must flow to the prospective crater. Bent half-double I went through several of the galleries well toward the center of the hill to observe actual mining operations there.

It was back-breaking work for one unused to it, but it was worth all it cost to any mind at all alive to great human realities. Miners were at the end of the holes, not with torches on their caps (as were familiar in Indiana mines), but with small electric lights suspended from the woodwork of the ceilings. Those miners were lying down and driving their galleries forward with ordinary picks and shovels. They were cheerful men. I wondered how war could have affected them so little. They had a drink once in a while and smoked pipes and chatted like men on the most commonplace jobs and did not appear to care whether the war ever ended or not.

"Are you much afraid of the Germans?" I asked a swarthy chap with a big mustache.

"Do you mean the German soldier?" he inquired.

"I mean the Germans generally."

"Well," he replied, "they've shot hell out of Ypres and damned near won the war, haven't they? But that's one thing. Do you know what the truth is about the German? In some ways he's too clever. He knows too much. He knows too much under this hill."

"And how's that?" I asked.

"If you'll wait a few minutes," he answered with as captivating a smile as I ever saw, "I'll show you. You see these tools here, just old miner's tools such as you would find in any pit in Cornwall. The Germans would laugh at them. And they *are* a bit absurd in the light of modern engineering. But the point is *you can work with them silently.* And silence is often important in war. It's important under this hill."

Then he came straight out with it.

"The Germans run galleries with boring-machines which go like hell. They can travel underground at least ten feet while we're traveling two. But they make a *noise*. See this little instrument? I think it's called a geophone or something like that. We call it an earth-listener or German-spotter. A German gallery is being run toward us right now. The sounds are faint just yet. But we know where they are, and we're tunneling in their direction."

"And what shall you do about it?"

"We'll pack the end of our gallery with high-explosives, wire and charge, build a rock-like structure against back-fire, and when those blond boys are in exactly the right place we'll press the button. We'll hate to do it of course. But do you know anything about war which isn't hateful? This hill is too old. It's going one of these days soon. And when it goes we expect Plumer's Second Army to be on the east side of the big hole."

"And that will mean?"

"Now you're asking me questions a Cornish miner can't answer. But I'll tell you what a common chap thinks of it. He thinks if Plumer gains the ridge, French's long and bitter fight for the safety of the Channel ports is won. That has a great meaning for us in England. And remember. This great fight in the North, so strongly supported by Haig, was French's fight primarily. All Englishmen, the humblest of us, know that."

I made my hard way out of that gallery with a renewed tenderness toward the so-called common man and a deepened respect for the wisdom God so strangely has implanted in him.

Then I saw the great attack. I saw the fruition of Plumer's patient plans. I saw what the mining had done. I saw the mangled bodies of thousands of men almost (as Mussolini said of his aeroplanes) darkening the sun. And I saw the food and the water rushing up to Plumer's victorious troops in such abundance as epicures might have envied. I stood on the edge of the gigantic bowl-shaped depression which spelled the end of Messines as a battle-factor in the Great War. It was 200 feet wide, the greatest crater of the British Front, and put an end to the bloody campaigns in the North, with which we justly can name no other name but that of infinitely glorious Verdun.

26. A Lively Day on Vimy Ridge

My last talk with Field Marshal Plumer was on the day after the battle of Messines Hill. He seemed to me, having regard to the completeness of the Allied victory, to be extraordinarily sober, not to say depressed.

"Are you not satisfied with the result?" I asked.

"We have made progress," he replied. "Our plans worked out reasonably well. But the war is not won. The Germans are still very strong and hold good positions and are among the greatest fighting men in the world. Incidentally, I might remark that a great and determined nation is back of the fellows we are facing on this front. It is true, however, that Messines Hill was the key to the battle issue with reference to supply-conditions in the North. If the Germans could have taken the Hill, they could have swept away not only our line of communication by way of the Channel but the French line as well. That, one need not say, would have been a very great, if not irreparable, disaster to the Allies. The Germans are soldiers; they are intelligent men; does anyone suppose they have fought these battles of the Ypres Salient irrationally? Their sacrifices on these fields have been heavy; they did not make them for any light purpose. When they attacked Liège,[1] they were attacking *their* problem with unquestionable political and military wisdom. Happily, from our point of view, we have been able (though at a cost of manhood which we should prefer not to think of) to stand against their assault."

As I bade the General good-by (loving him as one was bound to do) he said:

"I'm a soldier, or a bit of one; at least I have a command. It's my profession; everyone, I presume, must have some kind of profession or business or trade or

1. The German army attacked Liège, in eastern Belgium, in August 1914.

some way of living. I don't know quite how it happened, but I got into the Army, and here I am. And I must do my task. But I'll tell you a secret of soldiers: *they all hate war.* It's not that they're cowards; men usually are not cowards. I sometimes wish they were not quite so brave and a little more intelligent. One can't sit at a soldiers' mess anywhere at any time and hear one warlike word. *Soldiers do not hate.* They no more hate than science hates. All of which I say merely to let you know how soldiers admire every journalist and every woman and man who do what they can to oppose the powerful war forces of the world."

And so I left the hero of Messines.

A bunch of correspondents were on our way to Vimy Ridge.[2] John Burke of the *New York Times* and Joe Grigg of the *New York World* were there with several others. We were going fast in a motor car over a rough military road, a bright young orderly driving. As we met the rim of German artillery fire, a shell crumped into a tree within twenty feet of us and scattered us deep in twigs.

John Burke, a big fellow, seized the orderly by the left shoulder and commanded:

"Stop this car!"

With quick military obedience, the car was stopped, and John got out. He spoke not a word but started back at a brisk pace on the road over which we had come. All of us were astonished and for a moment silent. Then Joe Grigg (always a lad of some virility of ego) bellowed after John:

"Burke! Where in the hell are you going?"

John glanced back at us long enough to say:

"To London, you bastards! I've a wife and six children there."

"For Christ's sake," roared Joe, "didn't you know that before you left London?"

Voiceless, a large moving speck on the road, John knew his own mind. And with loud laughter we proceeded on our way to Vimy.

It was on the west side of Vimy Ridge, which towers so loftily in Canadian and in world history,[3] that I met General Sir Henry Wilson,[4] finally slain by

2. The Battle of Vimy Ridge was fought at this sight in northern France in April 1917 and won by Allied forces.

3. It was the Canadian army that successfully took Vimy Ridge—believed to be an unassailable German stronghold—after failed attempts by British and French forces. See Swettenham, *To Seize the Victory,* 145–63.

4. For Henry Hughes Wilson, see chap. 23, n. 4. From the outset of the war, Wilson argued for a war strategy that the government eventually adopted, fighting alongside the French, as opposed to attacking the Germans from within Belgium, which several other British military leaders advised. See Callwell, *Field-Marshal Sir Henry Wilson.*

Sinn Féiners as told in a previous chapter. He occupied a commodious chateau with a few of his principal officers and had the appearance and demeanor of a monarch. He was rather cold and stern but very handsome and civil. I could not take to him whole-heartedly, for I had learned that with many rooms in the chateau to spare he required most of his officers to sleep in the open in extremely disagreeable weather. Presumably he did not believe in molly-coddling soldiers, at least those below the higher ranks.

General Wilson entertained me at dinner and put me up for the night together with my colleagues. He was good-humored and most interesting at dinner, talking a great deal in a pure English with much sparkle in it. I found him, like Plumer, a politician and a humanitarian, a thinker far beyond the limits of his fighting profession. He was a remarkable critic and debater, and I was not surprised either that he spent his last days in Parliament or that he finally so incensed his fellow-countrymen of the twenty-six counties of South Ireland that they voted for his assassination and carried out the vote. He made it clear at the dinner that he was a great believer in Ferdinand Foch and his principle of unity of command on the West Front.[5] Both his mastery of the French language and his temperament plainly showed why the French called the British Army Corps the *Corps d'Armée Wilson* and why he was made principal liaison officer with the French field headquarters. He has been called "the builder, though not the architect, of the *Entente Cordiale.*"[6]

Statesmanship gleamed in Wilson's talk that night, as it gleamed at Versailles and afterward in the British Parliament. This revelation of foresight and of high intelligence came to nothing in Allied post-war policy, but it is, I think, worthy of remembrance and of careful study. Certainly it remains with me in sharper outline than anything else about the man who then was on his way to the chiefship of the General Imperial Staff in London. As everyone at the table listened with all but breathless interest, General Wilson said:

5. Ferdinand Foch was a French military leader who commanded forces during the first three years of World War I. When he became adviser to the Allied forces in May 1917, he urged British and French leaders to consolidate command of their forces under one head, lest separate forces fall apart in the face of mounting German opposition after the close of the Eastern Front. Foch's predictions proved true, until British and French prime ministers Lloyd George and George Clemenceau made Foch commander of the Allied forces. Foch was largely credited with the Allied victory. See Aston, *Foch.*

6. The Entente Cordiale between the United Kingdom and France was an agreement made in April 1904 that settled a number of disputes between the two countries, preparing the way for a lasting peace and making possible their cooperation in World War I.

"Of course we shall take Vimy. That hill is a mass of wire and a maze of trenches, and the Germans both strategically and tactically are frightfully strong. But our attack cannot be resisted; it will spread too far and be pressed to the last extremity. We not only shall take Vimy but shall win the war; America's entry leaves no doubt of that. One easily can apprehend the most notable war-fact of the moment; it is the state of mind, the *morale,* of Germany from end to end of its army and from end to end of the nation behind the army. All hope of a German victory over the world safely may be said to have gone out of the hearts of the whole of Germany, military and nonmilitary. Hard fighting lies ahead still, but all the odds are now against our gifted and gallant adversaries; they will fight without hope, and he who fights without hope loses."

General Wilson swept the company with serious eyes, and continued:

"Let us assume that what we call Armageddon is over, the armies demobilizing, the men of politics assembling to determine the peace, humanity hugging the notion that 'the War to end war' had done it. I am thinking of those days quite a lot now. And I am apprehensive. Central Europe, despite its magnificent efforts, will be crushed, impotent. This condition, I fear, will work great evil at the Peace Conference. It will be an invitation to disastrous folly there. Germany's extremes in warfare have aroused violent hatreds outside Germany. I am fearful that there will be more passion than prudence, more revenge than enlightened political thinking, at the conference."

The General fell silent for a moment, and I ventured to ask if he would be somewhat specific relative to the folly he feared.

"Well," he replied, "Europe from time out of mind has been one great battlefield, war following war with tidal regularity. Statesmanship has piled failure upon failure. Words, and often very eloquent and percipient words, have been uttered to illuminate the indivisibility of Europe's common interests, of the fatal effect upon all of perpetual antagonism and war, but what good did those bursts of oratory and wisdom do? History moved on in the same old way. The tides of war came and went as if never a tongue or a pen had moved. It has been impossible to keep the peace of Europe in the past. Do you think it will be possible to keep it in the future? However much we all may hope so, I doubt it. My knowledge of statesmen and of public sentiment and opinion compels me to doubt it."

"General," said a tall, gray-mustached colonel, "what mistakes are the peacemakers likely to fall into?"

"I cannot guess what particular mistakes they will make," answered Wilson. "But I can foresee mistakes in plenty issuing from two things: bitter hatred of Germany and the conviction of the conquerors that their supremacy is unassailable and permanent. This feeling and this conviction almost inevitably will lead to politics of reprisal, varied and far-reaching, and to a prolonged endeavor to cast out Germany from civilized society and from equality of opportunity among the powerful nations whose eternal problem is the problem of living and living in some degree of prosperity and happiness."

A low murmur went round the table.

Was General Wilson pro-German, this British soldier so greatly admired and trusted by the French?

The General, with quick understanding, went on:

"Peace in Europe never can rest upon fixed discrimination against any great nation in Europe. Neither is the welfare of any European people to be promoted by such discrimination. We might as well face the fact tonight that if we are going to be friends to France we must not be implacable enemies of Germany. Franco-German reconciliation and mutuality of trust and justice are absolutely necessary to European tranquillity and well-being. We all must forget this war except for what it has taught us of the unqualified and universal disaster of war. We cannot carry hostility and unfairness and a yearning for revenge into the peace and have any peace. Such a course on the part of the conquerors would be not only abominable from the point of view of humanity but fraught with the certainty of a renaissance of enemy-power in one form or another and of one more bloody world conflict."

"General," said the tall colonel, "is it not likely that the point of view you express will be presented forcibly to the makers of the peace treaty?"

"It will be presented no doubt; how forcibly I do not know. But I have a strong feeling it cannot be presented successfully. Popular world emotion is blindly and probably overwhelmingly against it. What is more, objectivity, sanity, hardly can be expected to find voice among the most powerful and the most authoritative men at the Peace Conference; these men, if I do not misjudge them (and I know them nearly all intimately), are apt to be swept from the road of sagacity and reality alike by their own fiery impulses and by the passionate unreason of the international masses. If the principal representatives at the Peace Conference stood with all their talent and strength for a peace of common sense, the masses might cool off and support them. But I myself am quite unable to predict such leadership."

I could not sleep that night for thinking of Wilson's gloomy prognosis. It sank deeper and deeper into my mind as truly-conceived. And how very many times, for nearly a quarter of a century, and always with fresh admiration and wonder, I have reviewed contemplatively the philosophy, the prescience, of that soldier-seer speaking at dinner on the western slopes of Vimy Ridge! What a pity he spoke in vain not only then but again and again later! Even he could not picture imaginatively the specific follies of Versailles and after, but the great general fact of the impending international unwisdom he saw as plainly as I saw the vast bulk of Vimy at dawn the next day!

Tramp, tramp, tramp. For miles upon miles back of the Vimy sector. Sometimes in trench mud. Sometimes in green fields. Dog-tired, dead-beat, at night, almost too exhausted to speak or think. And what did we men of the Press see and hear? We saw the painstaking and proficient teaching of wild-animal savagery and hate. It was a commonplace part of the business of war. British officers, on a desert plain, were teaching British troops (many of them recently peaceful and kindly British citizens of London and elsewhere) to hate the Germans and to burn with a maniacal desire to thrust bayonets into them.

Art was helping. It painted revolting features upon straw-stuffed canvas human dummies strung on wires across the plain. These features were of such men as the Kaiser, Ludendorff, Hindenburg, and Tirpitz,[7] and they were made to look monstrously wicked and depraved. Confronting these caricatures, and under command to stare at them exclusively, were long lines of British soldiers with bayonets fixed. When the loathsome objects were assumed to have exercised their maximum effect upon the minds of the men observing them, "Charge!" rang out along the line, and the soldiers rushed forward like madmen to puncture and tear to shreds with their bayonets the symbols of the soldiers whom they were in preparation to fight.

Horrible?

Yes; but such is war. Never afterward had I the least trouble in appreciating the absurdity of the idea of attempting to make war humane. War has nothing to do with humaneness. War despises and violates the very conception of that quality. And so it should. In logic and in fact, war is the exact and absolute contradiction of peace. Let logic win! Let war go as war until men tire of it as

7. Kaiser Friedrich Wilhelm Viktor Albrecht was German emperor and king of Prussia from 1888 until the last year of World War I, 1918. Erich Ludendorff was a Prussian military commander and the mind behind Germany's military strategy in the latter years of World War I. Ludendorff was co-commander of German forces with Paul von Hindenburg, another field marshal, who eventually became president of the Weimar Republic. Alfred von Tirpitz was the chief architect of Germany's navy in the years leading up to the war.

the contrariety and abnegation of what every woman and man of sense and decency in the world is struggling for: peace! War will disappear the more quickly for being war and not an impossible hodge-podge of war and peace.

In the wastes behind Vimy we learned something of the ways of sharp-shooters in modern military theory and practice. We learned particularly how the British came to defend themselves against such riflemen. At that stage of the war, immediately before the taking of Vimy Ridge, the Allies on the West Front were composed of 3,900,000 men, British, Belgian, and French, Gallic and native. Two million five hundred thousand Germans held the opposing lines. Sharpshooting rose to deadly efficiency on the enemy side. Thousands of Allied soldiers were dying every month in testimony of the effectiveness of German camouflage and marksmanship.

I will tell of my own observation. With me, and talking to me as frankly as if I had been his other self, was a man said to be the tallest in the British Army. His name I never knew. I was surprised that he wore no uniform, merely a close-fitting civilian shirt and trousers of a neutral hue, his boots and puttees encased in yellow clay. He seldom stood erect. He crawled, and I crawled with him. I was told he was "the cleverest spotter of German sharpshooters in the British Army." He went from one sector to another, summoned to spots where concealed enemy-rifle fire from long-sighted weapons was taking especially heavy tolls of Allied soldiers. I could not help wondering why, for such a job, the British command had chosen the tallest man in their long line!

"Why?" he echoed. "I'll tell you one good reason why. A man like me learns quickly what we find so hard to beat into the brains of trench-fighters: that nothing else pleases a German special marksman so much as a British head above the parapet. Tall men like me are head-conscious in war, and we can work upon our indiscreet shorter comrades with peculiar doggedness and sincerity. 'Keep your damned head down!' is an expression I use so much every day that I wake myself at night (when I try to sleep at night) saying with angry disgust, 'Keep your damned head down.' I've heard that women are excessively curious. I don't believe any woman could be so curious as a soldier in a trench when bullets are flying from hidden sources on the other side. Every chap is not, I admit, just curious; he fancies he may be able to mark the hide-out or camouflage of the invisible rifleman. But he usually gets killed."

I found my companion an intense scrutinizer of bumps along the upper edge of enemy parapets and of similar irregularities on the enemy's side of No Man's Land.

"What do those bumps mean?" I asked.

"Something different from what they used to mean," was the smiling answer, and my face, I presume, was all perplexity and attention. "German sharpshooters used to be in those earth-seeming little protuberances. We finally got on to the ruse, and our machine-gunners enjoyed several interesting days killing Germans who had been killing us. After that we found the bumps were made not to hide Germans but to fool us. Then we knew too much to consume much more ammunition in firing upon features of the landscape not nature-made but man-made. We shifted our attention to the level spots and to bush-covered places, small leafy hillocks, where we suspected enemy sharpshooters might be watchful on the skirmish-line."

German crack shots, I learned, were fitted into the trunks of trees and painted to blend with the color of the bark about them. It was impossible to distinguish them; they were simply one with the tree-trunks. And the trick was not discovered until one day when my lengthy friend was scanning a wood with powerful glasses and suddenly saw what looked like a part of the base of a tree bend down for an instant to scratch its leg! Machine-gun bullets soon were peeling those tree-bases over the whole front of that wood, and instructions were flashing north and south for similar action over the entire Allied line. My friend marked one German rifleman in the skin of a dead horse in No Man's Land, and he spotted another in a shock of grain.

"How did you happen upon the right shock?" I asked.

"It was this way," he said. "I knew the shocks in a large field might be used more or less by our opponents, but we didn't care to spray precious ammunition all over the place. I set myself to watch the shocks. One morning I noted that a certain stack of grain which I previously had examined through my glasses was not just where it had been. It had ambled off several feet to slightly higher ground overlooking our trenches a little better. 'What ho,' I said to myself, 'there must be a Bosch cracker inside those sheaves.' And I ordered a volley through the shock. A great hole was torn in it, and I could see daylight on the other side. Nothing moved. I bore my glasses some time on the object and decided our volley had been misapplied. That night, however, we sent out a crawler with a luminous ribbon to guide him home, and he came back with the report that he found among the sheaves a dead German rifleman with his weapon, cartridges, and food in the straw by his side."

Most ingenious of my friend's devices for locating camouflaged enemy marksmen was a *papier-maché* human head painted to look like Tommy Atkins.[8]

---

8. "Tommy Atkins" was slang for a British soldier used commonly in World War I.

At a point where accurately aimed bullets from the enemy side were going home repeatedly, and with impunity so far as the firers were concerned, my friend slowly raised his *papier-maché* head above the breastwork. Ping! Bits of pulped paper about the trench. The head was lowered and inspected. It had in it a clean-cut rifle-ball hole from the center of the forehead to the back of the neck. Mr. Spot-'em-right, using his periscope, looked through that hole and determined both the direction and the arc of the enemy's fire. Upon this line he set a machine-gun and let her go. There were no more sharpshooters' bullets from the concealed riflemen at that point.

"In ten weeks' time," said my friend, "we whittled down the effectiveness of Germany's specially selected and carefully distributed rifle experts more than ninety percent. What we did, in other words, by methods greatly diversified and highly adapted to individual conditions, was to transform a deadly into a relatively negligible form of enemy warfare. Our own sharpshooters worked at a disadvantage for a long time. We were less inventive in this sphere than the enemy, and the enemy from the first raked every spot on our lines where a rifleman could hide. He took it that our stratagems and camouflages would be much like his. Yet in the long run we did deadlier special rifle-firing than the Germans. We managed this by sewing up our sharpshooters in gunny, stitching grass all over the cloth, and mingling them with the natural growth of No Man's Land. Not one in a score of these men was discovered and shot."

We correspondents were permitted to observe the taking of Vimy Ridge only from a distance. We witnessed the great and successful operations of the Canadians under Sir Arthur Currie[9] within fairly effective binocular-range, after an appalling tempest of high-explosive shells had strewn the ridge with flattened barbed wire and turned its trenches into uninhabitable holes. Laboriously a few hours later we trudged our way through wire and craters and mud till we stood on the eastern top of the ridge. All was still and serene there then. But abruptly broke on our ears, slowly increasing in loudness, the familiar scream of a German shell. It crumped fifty yards from us and spattered us with mud. The enemy on the plain had seen us. Another shell came, a third, a fourth, and the air was black with smoke and earth. We ran, we scrambled, we lay prone. We lost touch with one another. I neither could see nor hear any

---

9. Arthur Currie was a Canadian military leader who replaced an Englishman to become commander of Canadian Allied forces in 1917. He led the Canadians to victory in the Battle of Vimy Ridge. See Swettenham, *To Seize the Victory.*

one of my colleagues. Unrecognizable from mud, clothes torn by barbed wire, I finally reached a hollow near where our motor car was buried in leaves. Every one of my colleagues was already there. We sped away as fast as we could, our ears filled with the noisy guffaws of several hundred soldiers safely cuddling in caves under the big ridge.

27. In the Thick of It at Bapaume

Kindliness was mingled with austerity and severity in a remarkable way in Lt.-Gen. Sir John Monash, commander of the Australian Army Corps in France, the only Jew, I think, who held really high military rank on the West Front. Already something of his personality and of his hospitality has been told in these pages. He was an educated man of great versatility, particularly gifted as a civil engineer of originality and energy in his own country. Soldier he had not been in any professional sense at the outbreak of the Great War. But soldier he became thereafter almost overnight. Everywhere he was irrepressible and distinguished. He rose by sheer merit to the chiefship of the Australian command and to a place of first-rate importance in the swift and unbroken advance which led to the Armistice in 1918.

I treasure no memory of the leaders in the Great War more than that of this great Australian. I met him first when his preparations were going diligently forward for the attack upon Mont St. Quentin.[1] It was a position critically important to the proposed general advance to end the war. General Monash and I motored together pretty well all over his narrow but vital front. His men were working hard building roads and bridges and bringing up guns and large supplies of ammunition. I was astonished that they paid little or no attention to their commander unless he directly addressed them. Then they saluted with soldierly promptness and rigidity.

As we were moving at a snail's-pace over a bridge not yet finished, Aus-

1. Monash led Australian troops to take Mont St. Quentin, in northern France, in August 1918, in the Battle of Mont St. Quentin.

tralian officers and privates hard at their tasks on either side of us and taking notice of nothing else, General Monash turned to me and said:

"You have seen much of the war."

"Yes," I replied. "I have been much with the British forces on sea, land, and in the air. But that is nearly the whole of my experience of the war."

"You have taken account, I daresay, of the general punctiliousness of the salute," said the General.

I agreed.

"You have not observed a great deal of that punctiliousness on our journey today; you have noted that the Australians are not very formal in even the presence of their commander-in-chief."

Again I agreed.

"Informality, I suppose, is native to the Australian. He is courteous, he is cordial, but he is not formal," expounded the General. "Nicety of etiquette is not conspicuous in Australian life whether civil or military. I should be sad if I saw my men attempting to change their characters on this battlefield. For that they have no time, and they would be the worse if they had. I do not object to the punctilious salute, though I feel it is often overdone. But my men know what they are here for. They know they are not here so much to display fastidious military manners as to fight. They are all right for that highly-practical purpose."

General Monash pointed to the summit of Mont St. Quentin, a few miles to the east.

"Mark that bold eminence?" he queried.

I took a good look at it.

"My fighters are going to take that difficult and crucial position, now wonderfully trenched and wired and strongly held by the Germans. An awful lot will be doing all along this and adjoining sectors in a little while. We shall give the Germans more to look after in August than they gave us to look after last spring. Then they gunned and stormed us out of the whole area of the Somme battlefields on which we had fought so bitterly as far back as 1916.[2] The British Armies will retake that area, and St. Quentin and Péronne[3] are the key to such an operation. In our hands, they will turn the Somme line, and more than half

2. Monash is referring to the Second Battle of the Somme, Germany's spring 1918 offensive, which General Erich Ludendorff launched hoping to break apart British and French lines before American troops entered the war. The offensive was only partially successful: Germany did gain much of the Somme area, but its soldiers were unable to push British and French lines apart.

3. Péronne is a city in northern France, in the Somme region.

of what the Germans took away from us in the spring will return to us in the early fall. The Hindenburg line[4] will be naked. The war will be not very distant from a victorious close for the Allies. I speak with all confidence, for I know the decisive relatives of the case."

In barely a fortnight I stood with Monash on the top of St. Quentin, the village of the same name at our feet, and both were firmly held in his vise of steel, steel men as well as weapons of steel, and the whole of the re-conquest he had foretold was a fact. His brilliant operation to unlock the door for the general advance brought great honor upon him, fervid acknowledgments of his own genius and of the amazing fighting qualities of his men reaching him from all the greatest leaders on the West Front from sea to sea. He was pleased, very greatly pleased, but not observably agitated.

"Not a great while from now," he said to me, "my men and I shall see Australia again."

"Many of your men," I interjected, "will not."

"Right," he said. "A single Australian brigade went forward with 1,200 rifles, and when the flag of triumph was raised it saw in that brigade only 600 rifles. Our dead will not go back with our living to their beloved and bereaved Australian homes, but they should sleep peacefully here, for they did their duty as fate, destiny, laid it upon them. Men who die thus, I think, offer a profound mitigation to our grief."

I wrote a description (the best I could do) appreciative of Monash and his all-important contribution to the Allied cause at St. Quentin and Péronne. This description was reproduced from the *Chicago Daily News* by the British Press both in Great Britain and in Australia and the rest of the Dominions. It came to Monash's attention, and I have an autograph letter from him expressing in surprisingly warm terms his "grateful thanks." One of the sentences of his letter is this:

"It is the first time, to my knowledge, that any correspondent has said a good word for me, or even given evidence of my existence as a Commander in the Great War."

General Monash was the first and only military chief who allowed me to advance in the actual company of an attacking army. I asked him if I might

---

4. The Hindenburg line was a German system of defenses and fortifications along northwestern France. The line, the brainchild of Field Marshal Paul von Hindenburg, was created during the winter of 1916–1917 and withstood Allied attacks until late 1918.

go with the Australians into Bapaume.[5] He stated that the movement against Bapaume would be a more than commonly difficult and dangerous one for the reason that the advancing troops would be confined to a single road across treeless and crater-holed fields. These fields were boggy and holed to such an extent as to defy the passage of either guns or men. Every man and every unit of equipment, the advance and its support, would be bound to the graded road. It would be an awkward matter altogether, and "nasty mix ups" were certain, for even after the Germans were cleared out of Bapaume their artillery would play upon this road with all possible concentration and violence.

"However," concluded the General, "the question is up to you and your sense of what you ought to do."

"I should like to go with the troops into the historic old town," I replied.

And General Monash gave me the necessary *laissez-passer*.

But before the column-march on Bapaume along that aisle-treed bee-line road, I was to witness the most harrowing affair of war I saw at all from the outbreak to the Armistice. Field Marshal Douglas Haig's push to redeem the Somme region was on and in several sectors the fighting was close and bloody. I was under the reciprocal artillery-curve but not too close to the cockpits of two-sided mutilation and slaughter. It was night and very dark. All at once, as I stood in the open watching and listening to the sights and sounds of battle, the head of a stretcher-bearer column approached. I descried it in the flash of an anti-aircraft gun not far from me. I could see the white armlets with the Red Cross on them. Members of the Army Medical Corps were bringing back the wounded, plodding slowly through the dark.

My stomach seemed to tie itself in an aching knot.

Then came the series of horrors.

Only a short span from the mercy-carriers in the lead a German star-shell burst, lighting up whitely a considerable space of earth and throwing high into the air curious arched and circled threads of illumination, a startling spectacle, weird and beautiful. I glimpsed in that momentary glow a column of stretcher-bearers fading beyond vision toward the farthest front trenches. Burst another star-shell more distant from me in the direction of the fighting. Shells of this sort followed one another for a little time so rapidly that the darkness became intermittent daylight. Shrapnel followed. It cut a yawning gap in the advancing column, hurling helmets, arms and legs, fragments of stretchers, the shredded

5. Bapaume is a town in northern France, in the Pas-de-Calais region.

bodies of borne and bearers upward, to the right, to the left, a crimson scene of demolition ringing with the anguished cries of men hurt unto death. Another gap. More crimson, more cries, the sounds reminding one of the piteous shrieks of wild animals pierced by hunters' bullets.

How many shattered and bloody clefts thus were made in that unhappy column of wounded soldiers and their Red Cross helpers I cannot say. My eyes could not have seen if I had looked, and I did not look after the first explosions. I turned to the dark. What at this moment, more than twenty years having come and gone since that night, do I recollect as one of the night's principal impressions? It was that of the utter composure of the unwounded bearers. Every scathless man seemed to be saying, "It's all in the night's work." And the column neither slowed down nor quickened its march toward succor for the suffering. I saw several men, some doctors among them, I think, leave the column and search on either side of it for comrades not yet dead. Such comrades, so far as possible, were loaded on human backs and so brought in. But many were left to die where they fell amid the flash and whistle of enemy shells.

Did the Germans deliberately sight their guns on a long file of rescued and rescuers?

I cannot believe it.

I never found a British officer who believed it.

Why fire upon Red-Crossers and soldiers already out of action? "Well," one may say, "the wounded have a promise of recovery and may be returned to the front. Only a dead man is a safe man for an enemy in war. *Morale,* moreover, is the bedrock essential of successful war. To cut a column of stretcher-bearers and their burdens to pieces is not good for the *morale* of any army or any army's home-support." Such is a conceivable argument. I do not accept it. Military men always think of the wounded not only as sacredly exempt from attack but as substantially eliminated from hard-pressed war. And that *morale* thesis? I think it stands bottom side up. If I were an officer, and wished to stiffen my enemy's back unbreakably at the front and at home, I should do to him what the Germans did to the British that night in Haig's Army. I must conclude that the Germans mistook the rescuing column for a long line of moving British able-bodied fighting men.

I went about a great deal behind the front lines of Monash's Corps before the bombardment of Bapaume (a slashing and remorseless action) and the subsequent march along that tree-lined, mud-and-water-flanked road into the shell-riven town. I saw some great trench-architecture of earthwork and reenforcing sandbags, laughing, chaffering, kidding, singing antipodes lining the rather homelike ditches for many more miles than one cared to walk. I saw great, belching guns housed in roofs and walls of sandbags ten feet thick all round, their tanned and rugged companies as happy apparently as they were busy. I came upon groups of officers in council. I saw lonely sentries climbing rocky hills to their posts of night vigilance, steel-helmeted, caped, sturdily-booted, their rifles under their capes, the bayonets uptilted in front, the butts almost touching the rocks.

I saw the desolation of Mametz[6] after the bombardment. And I never could understand how any man could have survived in such wreckage. But many a man did. I saw hundreds of captured German guns and mortars. I saw thousands of German prisoners being searched by serene, friendly, and smiling Tommies. I met or passed by thousands of infantrymen entrenched in wooded hollows. I chatted with Red Cross men attending the wounded underground. I watched Australian pioneers, half-naked in the sun behind the trenches. I grinned over trench-sentries, their hats of steel strapped on with bands of leather beneath their chins, their rifles lashed to their left shoulders, their eyes gazing distressfully upward through improvised periscopes attached to the tops of sticks struck in the walls of breastworks. I marveled at surgeons and nurses in their swift ministrations to mutilated soldiers in subterranean hospitals. Platoons answering roll-call, platoons moving up for the attack, mules laden with baggage, horse, foot, and artillery, stretcher-bearers by the score, motor-cyclists screaming and rushing past all at fearful speeds, what a movie the whole was, and what a glut of frenzy, struggle, noise, smoke, mud, and blood it portended!

Studying the unloading of boxes of shells from transport wagons (a labor constant day and night), walking round vast stores of ammunition, seeing the deadly stuff arranged in limbers by the hundred to be hauled to the guns, I could understand Monash's confidence in Haig's proposed Great Push. Astounding were the congestion and the activity one mingled with at night. Camouflage, secrecy, the obscuration of corps (the British homelanders, the Canadians, the Australians, the contiguous French) were practiced best in the dark, and the British desired to spread all the mystification possible on the German side. No ammunition dump was formed in daylight. Artillery units moved from point to point after nightfall and before daybreak. The more important artillery concentrations were concealed by only little firing by day; the less important guns in relatively noncrucial positions flashed, banged, and

6. Mametz is in northeastern France, in the Alsace region.

recoiled from morning till night. Twenty miles east of Amiens,[7] at the foot of the lee side of a roundish hill, I stumbled upon an impressive naval cannon so mounted (on a hundred-foot base) as to seem to say, "No retreat here; we have come to stay." That mighty gun, with a barrel fifty feet long from base to tip, could be swung from right to left by touching a lever. It had been pouring desolation into Amiens. How it ever was brought to that spot I could not guess; the task struck one as fabulous. But the gun was torn from German hands, and British soldiers, officers and men, cut their names and their regimental marks in that long steel barrel so thickly I could not see room for any more.

Now for the march into Bapaume. Already the place was a mass of ruins, the Germans having shelled it rigorously in ousting the British a few months before. And now the British artillery laid upon it such a bombardment as it never dreamed of antecedently. Swarms of German soldiers streamed eastward to escape the hurricane, but some hundreds were left in sheltered caves and cellars to greet with rifle and grenade and machine-gun fire the Britishers whose return to Bapaume the German command knew to be certain.

Low, thin mist obscured the road to Bapaume. Just as I insinuated myself into the throng of General Bacon's troops for the crossing of Leech Lake to quell the Chippewa uprising in northern Minnesota two decades earlier, so I made myself a molecule in the columned body of armed Britishers marching, or rather struggling and stumbling, toward Bapaume. How we thanked God for that mist! It at least helped some, but the prior sighting and setting of German guns made it a very imperfect protection. I felt as if we were crossing an endless bridge instead of following a highway, for the flanking fields were potted thick with shell-holes, and the shell-holes were pools of muddy water. To leave the road was to sink to the hips in marsh.

I was shoulder-to-shoulder with infantrymen who either ignored me (it was not a situation favorable to needless civilities) or gave me an occasional inquiring and smiling glance. Shells tore our line here and there, and we made room for bearers bringing back the wounded. The dead were rolled off the road. Limbs and twigs rained upon us from the side-rows of trees smitten by enemy shrapnel, and many a man thus was injured, some fatally. We continually were climbing over trees which the Germans had felled across the road to hamper the advance. Continually also we were wading knee-deep or body-deep in transecting streams of liquified mud where bridges had gone skyward in answer to the retreaters' dynamite. Onerous indeed was that march and

7. Amiens is the capital city of the Somme region in northern France.

tormenting its scenes of blood and misery. We labored. We panted. We were shapeless cakes of mud. Streams of sweat ran from our bespattered faces till they made tiny rivulets in our vestments of black mire.

I had had enough. I was dizzy. I felt I must slip down the bank nearer me and fall asleep. And then, almost in a twinkling, came revival. The mist was gone. My part of the line was in full view of the city (they called it a city, though it was only a village of 3,000 souls in peace-time), and the well-risen sun was bathing us in warmth and light. I saw the head of the line break into a run and heard it raise an ear-piercing shout. I saw it debouching upon the objective and caught the snap and crackle of rifles and machine-guns. Then our section, the men about me, began to run and utter strange cries. An astonishing strength welled up in me. Dizzy no more. Tired no longer. I ran as easily and lightly, it seemed (with all my mail of mud), as I had run on our Indiana farm when I was nail-hard and forty years younger. Inexplicably, I was *crazy* to rush into Bapaume. I did not want to hurt anyone. I was unarmed. I simply wanted to be there. I wanted to see. I wanted to get the full flavor and reality of war.

And I think I did.

Those rear-guard or last-stand German riflemen and machine gunners amid Bapaume's unpicturable havoc knew at least two things well: how to shoot and how to stick it. For a time they were under dual shell-fire, the Germans strafing the village from the east and the British from the west. The German guns pounded the rubble till the British had swept the place clean and were pressing their march toward the enemy lines. Then there was artillery silence on the east. Allied forces were advancing to the south and to the north. It was time for a speedy and comprehensive German withdrawal from that newly-made British salient. Upon Bapaume had fallen a peace not to be broken again in the Great War.

Well, if I saw, what did I see? If I tasted the full flavor, if I grasped the reality, of modern conflicts between highly-efficient and abundantly-equipped armies, what were they like? I saw German marksmen aiming coolly through cracks in walls and shooting attacking Britishers down. I saw German machine-gunners meting out slaughter to their advancing foes as if death to them (the Germans) would be a trifle lighter than air. I saw Britishers rush upon riflemen and gunners alike as if bullets were bouquets. Soldiers fell firing, soldiers rushed on firing, the awful bayonet did its ensanguined work. The black mire no longer was visibly wet with sweat. The rivulets now were rivulets (one almost might say rivers) of blood.

Writhing, screaming men, bleeding, some rolling over and over, were all about me. But I was calm. I was no more confused or flurried or afraid than I am as I write these lines in the quiet and security of my study more than four thousand miles from Bapaume and upward of twenty years distant in time from those hours of risk and fury and unspeakable pain. We all were preternaturally wide-awake in some respects; we had the keenness and alertness of supermen. But in other respects we were desensitized by the hypnotic of enveloping savagery and violence. We had drunk the "drowsy syrup" of war. Segmentarily we were asleep. We were insulated from the perils and the abominations encompassing us. And but for that merciful insulation, I doubt if one man would have come out of it much short of a volitional derelict, not to say a madman.

After all the Germans in Bapaume were killed, wounded, or sent wildly fleeing to the east, I went about with an officer surveying the gore-stained chaos in which we walked as in an unearthly wilderness. I spied a German saw-bayonet on the rubble-strewn floor of a broken brick building and made for it.

"No!" cried the officer. "Don't touch that! Don't touch anything like that just yet. We must await the searching explorations of our mine-detectors before harvesting souvenirs in Bapaume."

"That bayonet may be connected to fire a mine?" I suggested.

"Oh, yes. We have found the Germans good at those pranks."

I marched eastward for two miles with the troops who were continuing the advance. As we booted it wearily along a dirt road with grassy fields on either side (so different from the miles of mud-holes west of Bapaume), I caught sight of the top of a German helmet in the roadside grass. Instinctively I reached for it only to be hauled not too gently back by a burly non-combatant, with a bandaged left arm.

"Leave it, boy!" he ordered. "Ever hear of mines?"

I dropped out and retraced my steps to the village. I happened upon my old friend, Colonel Roberts, of the Ypres Salient, and we prowled observantly about the ruins.

Surprised and delighted, I learned from Colonel Roberts that Sir C. Arthur Pearson,[8] one of the well-known newspaper publishers and editors of that time, was coming to the front and would be billeted in an officers' chateau

---

8. Sir C. Arthur Pearson entered newspaper publishing in 1890 with *Pearson's Weekly,* a North-cliffe-style, "new journalism" paper that was a quick financial success. He soon launched other papers of a similar ilk, including the famous *Daily Express* in 1900. He later acquired two other national papers, *The Standard* and the *Evening Standard,* as well as numerous local papers. He competed with Northcliffe for ownership of *The Times,* a battle Northcliffe won. See Griffiths, ed., *The Encyclopedia of the British Press.*

just north of the Australian front. Sir Arthur, in his letter to Roberts, had said he knew I was with the armies of Australia and New Zealand and hoped to see me. I went directly to that chateau and ran upon Sir Arthur himself in the entrance hall, where an orderly was looking after his light luggage. The next day Sir Arthur and I motored over a considerable area of stricken villages and followed the line of bursting German shells for some miles. Sir Arthur was blind then; he could not see his hand before his face. But one had to stare at him to know it. He discouraged assistance.

"Thank you, no," he would say. "I can make my way unaided."

Only once in a while, when we were walking, minding to keep clear of the spots where the enemy shells were crumping monotonously (I have known such shells to burst in one spot all day long), I would touch Sir Arthur's arm and warn him of rough ground.

"Ah," he would answer. "Thank you."

And he would get over that rough ground as if he could see as well as I.

At one point we were so near a bursting shell that its black smoke rolled over us chokingly, and our clothes and faces were besmeared with equally black earth.

"Well," he said, "that *was* close!"

Everything I could see I described to him as clearly as I could, and he gazed intently as I spoke. I could not avoid saying to myself again and again: "Surely this man is not blind!" He did his own listening, commenting upon the peculiar crump of the German shells and the distinct difference between the sound of those shells in the air and the sound of the British shells as they traveled toward the German lines. That night we dined with the officers at the chateau. Sir Arthur was taken to his room before dinner, first "having a look," as he said, at the dining-room and marking its location with reference to his bedroom. He asked the dinner hour and remarked that he had a watch which told him the time through the sense of touch.

"Please take no further notice of me now," requested the distinguished Londoner. "I shall be down to dinner on time."

He was, and dinner-jacket. He sat on the right of the principal officer at the table, I directly opposite him, our dinner companions (quiet, handsome men) numbering probably fifteen or more. Sir Arthur talked volubly through the whole meal, and the manner in which he related what he had "seen" and heard along the front fairly bowled me over. He was accurate. He was detailed. He appeared to have forgotten nothing. And he entertained that company hugely. I fancy he made the greatest hit of any civilian who ever visited the British front.

V
The Peace-Seeking Period, 1919–1941

28. From War Trail to Peace Trail

Early in October, 1918, I had a talk with Field Marshal Lord Haig. He was thin-faced, quiet-eyed, sad-looking, his rather heavy mustache, iron-gray, drooping till it almost hid his lower lip. His tall, slender, muscular body was straight and military in his smart uniform. All the heavy war seemed to be weighing upon him.

"It's about over," he said to me.

"The war?"

"We didn't get the boys out of the trenches by Christmas of 1914," he said with a sly smile, "but we'll have them out before Christmas in 1918. The German war-power, the home front and the fighting front, is broken morally and materially. The Allies, with the Americans rising like a great war-cloud on the German left (a war-cloud with plenty of lightning in it), and the rest of us driving irrepressibly against Ludendorff's center and right, have the situation as they so long have wanted it."

Within a day or two, after further inquiry and thought, I wrote for the *Chicago Daily News* a long cable in which I ventured (without quoting Haig) to state that the armies of the Central Powers, with mere shells of non-combatant strength behind them, might collapse at any moment. I explained that this view was held universally by the primary Allied commanders on the West Front and appeared to be buttressed impregnably by the battle-line *status quo* and everything related to it. That cable was published on October 7. Just then our most-experienced war correspondent, John Bass (who had been on the Russo-German Front and in every war for a quarter of a century), was studying the West Front situation. His conclusions led him to cable the *Daily News* in flat contradiction of my cable. Ludendorff, he thought, was not beaten but in orderly and wise retreat upon the vast and elaborate defenses of the Hindenburg line. Nor was that his only remaining bulwark against the Allies. Farther on he was preparing the Hermann line.[1] He would stick during the winter and renew his offensive on a grand scale in the spring. There would be unprecedentedly hard fighting in 1919. Less than a month later we had the Armistice.[2] John was wrong, and I was right not because I was his superior as a student of war (I certainly was not) but because I knew that West Front as he had had no chance to know it.

It is impossible for me to tell you how deflated, how inert, indifferent, ambitionless I was when the tremendous buoyant of the war dropped from under me. I felt like lying down for the Socratic "supreme pleasure" of "a dreamless sleep." And it was so with all our war correspondents. Even John Bass, most war-seasoned of us, was worthless. Charles Dennis, our editor-in-chief, cabled me in London: "What is the matter with our foreign staff? Our correspondents to a man seem to be news-hunters emeritus." I got a little laugh out of that and cabled back to Mr. Dennis: "As for myself, I want to come home. When I took this job I promised to hold it, if not sooner fired, for five years only. I've held it for twenty. I'm all in. When do I sail?"

Quick from Mr. Dennis came this reply: "You don't sail. Wake up and wake up your men. The fight for world peace lies ahead."

Electric to me was that cable. My spirits revived as if they had received some magic touch. The fight for world peace! So the war was not over. It had been begun only. The sword had done its part (and a puissant part it was) in the age-old fight for peace; now the pen must deploy its power on the illimitable battle-line. John Maynard Keynes[3] said to me in his London home: "Reaction from toil, dread, pain, and grief has us on our backs. No anticipation can be so fearful or hideous now as to move us." True. No danger, no threat, moved one then. But I said to Keynes: "How about the fight for peace?" He sat erect. "Let it start now!" he cried. "Let the writers of the world *change opinion*!" And I was inspired and comforted.

---

1. By late 1918, the Hermann line was Germany's last line of defense in France.

2. November 11, 1918.

3. John Maynard Keynes was an English economist. In contrast to laissez-faire economics, Keynesian economics advocated a mixed economy (with both private and public involvement) and argued that economic growth was driven by demand, not supply, as many classical economists believed. Keynes joined Prime Minister Lloyd George at the Versailles Peace Conference after World War I, but soon left the conference, distressed over the regressive reparations policy that he feared would devastate Europe. See Harrod, *Keynes*.

All our men responded to our appeal for a re-awakening. In our political dispatches without exception ran the note of international education, understanding, sympathy, compromise, tolerance, cooperation, justice, peace. Mr. Lawson's instructions were: "Avoid censoriousness. You are not there for hypercriticism. It is not your business to run the country in which you may be located. It is your business to get the news of world importance and to try with diligence and honesty to understand and faithfully report why races and nations feel as they feel and do as they do. You will serve our readers, and therefore ourselves and the cause of peace, by preferring the sympathetic and expository to the antagonistic and captious. We cannot cast other peoples into our own mold; we must do our best to understand theirs and to respect it."

I do not think any publisher in any land ever issued to his foreign correspondents more high-minded or wiser instructions than those. And we followed them; it was not at all safe for us *not* to follow them; Mr. Lawson sat there in his pigeon-hole above Wells Street, Chicago, to see that what he said went. So I had four more happy years in London, working with happy, conscientious, and productive men scattered throughout the world. We did our best to create that world sentiment without which world statesmen (as President Herbert Hoover was to say to me impressively some years later) are unable to build structures of common benefit, or to bring peace, to the nations. Our efforts, however far they may have fallen short of important or enduring results, pleased Mr. Lawson and Mr. Dennis and filled their mails, as they filled mine, with letters of enthusiastic, even deeply grateful, appreciation from our readers. Let no man tell me our common humanity does not want the statesmanship which brings peace!

My most affecting hour or so in London was when President Woodrow Wilson came there during the trouble-enshrining peace-fabrication in Paris. He was without question the most-adored statesman of the world at that moment of fateful history. And why? Because mankind regarded him as the embodiment of their hopes for political freedom and permanent redemption from war. He was a god. His car scarcely could move through the London streets for men, women, and children wild to see him and lay the tips of their fingers on his passing motor. Dearly as the Londoners love their king and queen and all their royalty, I never saw them lovingly impinge upon royalty with quite the facial marks of homage and hope which one saw over the whole multitude as Wilson passed slowly through it.

So the people, the "democracy."

How about the aristocracy?

Its emotions were strikingly visible in its demeanor as Wilson spoke in the crowded Guildhall, long, narrow, high-vaulted, historic. Years before, as I have reported, I sat there by the side of Balfour and observed his delighted nods and murmurings as Teddy Roosevelt spoke from the red-carpeted dais to a packed assemblage of the mighty. Now Woodrow Wilson stood on that dais, and again the mighty were there, and in soberer mood than when Teddy spoke. Not a smile to be seen on the expanse of upturned faces reaching to the dim far end of the great corporation hall of the City of London. As Wilson stepped to the edge of the platform, close about him Britain's first elect, he looked very tall, very gaunt, and his face was unwontedly white. But his whole mien was one of self-assurance and self-command.

He had no notes, spoke extempore and fluently, though with studied emphasis and deliberation. It was a brief speech, but one of the best of his life. It came from a great and honest heart and from a mind as deeply convinced and sincere as it was brilliant and powerful. The audience to the last man understood and yielded to the full: one could see that with half an eye. Woodrow Wilson, that audience unmistakably said, *is* a great man; he *does* love humanity; he *will* accomplish new and splendid things. God bless him! Then the Peace of Versailles. What a gulf is fixed between idealism and practicality! What a difference there is between *a priori* dreams and the attainable! What a pity that Wilson's magnificent political air-liner crashed on the mountain-side of reality!

Time wore on in London, and I did not get home till four years later, on the eve of Thanksgiving Day, 1922. I had seen America a few times since leaving it, but one of my intervals of absence was unbroken for eight years. My wife gave seventeen years on end to her work and pleasure in England and Continental Europe. America seemed to her not so much like an actual country as like a great and interesting and beautiful place she had seen in her dreams. My children, English-educated and French-educated (in the schools and the University of Lausanne, Switzerland), were leaping to womanhood and manhood, and were whole-souled Americans, but they knew America as only a pleasant-sounding name. They wanted, like their mother and myself, to go home. I put some pressure on Mr. Lawson, my big Chief, and Ambassador George Harvey supplemented that pressure a bit. Mr. Lawson said, "Come!"

"When you first suggested to me that I try to get you back to Chicago," said Harvey at the American Embassy shortly prior to our leaving England, "I was reluctant. It seemed to me dead-wrong for you to leave this capital, where your name has come to signify so much in relation to Anglo-American good feeling and world cooperation. I so wrote Victor Lawson but in the same letter told him I had changed my mind; I had reached the conclusion from further thought that his London manager and correspondent, henceforth, could transfer his base of operations with all-round advantage from the Thames to the Lake. You know Lawson and I are anciently fairly close to each other. Your paper was my journalistic Alma Mater. I worked as a reporter for Lawson when he was man-of-all-work on the *Daily News*. I'm not sure he didn't open up and sweep out. I know he went personally to the bank every Saturday and brought back a canvas bag with the money in it for the pay-roll. He locked himself with the money in a brass cage before the pay-window, outside of which was a good-sized crowd of males and females queued up hungrily for the 'necessary,' I one of them."

The Ambassador was grinning.

"Lawson paid me thirteen dollars and a half a week. One Saturday the idea was knocking about in my head that I ought to have more salary. How should I speak of it to the sandy-whiskered, blue-eyed, dignified though jovial fellow gazing at me through that window? A bright thought came to me.

"'Mr. Lawson,' I said, 'I don't like odd numbers. Can't you raise my salary from thirteen and a half to fourteen?'

"'Well, George,' replied Lawson with one of his ringing laughs, 'Since you don't like odd numbers, let us make it twelve.'

"I was put aback so visibly and so painfully that Lawson handed out fourteen to me with the low, kindly remark, 'My boy, it will be fourteen hereafter.'"

"What made you change your mind about me?" I asked Harvey.

"It gradually came more clearly to me that your great cycle here was probably, for the time being anyhow, finished. Your orbit has been a shining one by general acknowledgment, and you know I'm not at home as a flatterer. We're at the end of a well-defined epoch, the most notable in history. I believe you should go home and try to do, with the backing of Lawson and Dennis, further work on your familiar lines of endeavor toward international education and peace. By long odds Northcliffe was your most powerful co-worker in London. He threw the columns of *The Times* wide to you and said to his editor, Geoffrey Dawson,[4] 'Publish what Edward Price Bell writes whether you believe him right or wrong.'" Dawson was a very able editor. He naturally did not relish such peremptoriousness from even the Chief. For one reason or another, doubtless for a combination of reasons, Dawson quit in 1919, and Wick Steed succeeded him. Steed believed in me, but he was gone now as editor, and

4. Geoffrey Dawson was twice editor of *The Times*, from 1912 to 1919 and again from 1923 to 1941.

Northcliffe was dead. Said the Ambassador, "I'm afraid *The Times,* which gave you your initial chance to affect world opinion, is closed to you for at least the period of Dawson's second editorship. In these circumstances, I believe Chicago, not London, is your best *point d'appui.*" Some weeks before Christmas, 1922, my family and I, with all we possessed, were back in America.

From war trail to peace trail was my course. And I was little short of fatally despondent; I really wanted to go back to the land in Indiana near where I was born and forget politics and men's cruelty and blundering forever. Impossible. I was held to my task as if by chains, moral chains, material chains. Sir Henry Hughes Wilson's memorable forecast of Versailles, as we dined behind the Vimy lines in 1918 (his prophecy that the ignorant and revengeful peacemakers would pave the way to another world war instead of to a lasting world peace), seemed to me not only to have been verified but verified with a bitter comprehensiveness beyond anyone's gloomiest forebodings.

Just this minute I have been reading Chancellor Hitler's speech to the Reichstag April 28, 1939.[5] He calls the dominant Allied leaders at Versailles "criminals" and "madmen." He is stung to the quick by President Roosevelt's staggeringly inept peace overtures and doubtless is bearing in mind the harsh and ill-mannered and buffle-headed language the President has been using about the so-called "dictators" for many months: fishing in troubled world waters as no other President has done in the history of the Republic. Herr Hitler, to boil down his long and passionate speech to a few words, declared that the men at Versailles had forced at the point of the bayonet not a treaty of prosperity and peace but a treaty of economic world disaster and of potential world war. *"And it must be changed."*

As I read this address by one of the greatest figures in international politics since the Great War, I seem to be sitting again at dinner with Field Marshal Sir Henry Wilson and listening to his clairvoyant despair. And I think of several other men, particularly Dr. E. J. Dillon[6] *(The Eclipse of Russia),* who was one

5. In this speech, Hitler officially renounced both the British-German naval treaty (which reduced the size of the German navy to one-third the size of the British navy) and the German-Polish non-aggression pact. Hitler passionately defended Germany's aggressive foreign policy, sarcastically answering President Franklin Delano Roosevelt's request for German assurance of peace. The speech, writes Hitler's biographer, "was a remarkable display of mental gymnastics . . . [Hitler] took up the President's message point by point, demolishing each [point] like a schoolmaster." See Toland, *Hitler,* 528–30.

6. Emile Joseph Dillon was a special correspondent for the *Daily Telegraph.* Dillon, who could speak some twenty-five languages, was well known for his high connections and intimate knowledge of foreign affairs.

of the most distinguished correspondents at the Peace Conference, and John Maynard Keynes, C.B., who went to the conference with the British delegation as one of its two ablest economic advisers and in a little time came back to Cambridge disgusted with the ignorance and folly which, as he himself said to me at the time, "are going to make Versailles the worst mess in the history of international relations." He added: "They will ruin both European and world economy and suspend a sword above the heads of all humanity."

Dr. Dillon was equally impetuous and categoric. Ethically, socially, and politically, "the Conference was awful." It would "wreck manufacture and trade, impoverish victors and vanquished alike, set class against mass, create internal strife and external hostility, give a new lease of life to imperialism and militarism, breed anarchy all over the shop, and make a future world war certain." Dr. Dillon shook with ironic merriment when he talked to me of Versailles. "Get it straight," he admonished in his high-pitched voice. "We have killed and maimed and driven mad millions of the best men on earth in order to destroy Prussianism only to embrace it ourselves. We shall set half the world psychologically against the other half now, and the physical collision between the two will come later."

Some men *saw* from the first!

"But," I said to myself shortly after I returned from London, as I sat alone in my small glazed-in study stuck on the back end of my house in Evanston, "the second world war is not here yet. I don't think it ever will come; the *possibility* is manifest of course, but the *probability* is not. The heavy factors of the situation are, it strikes me, dead against it. Peoples are against it. Leaders of paramount influence know it means all-reaching suicide. Economic and financial and material urgencies all are against it. *It cannot happen.* Who shall sound, so that the world may hear, the note of reason and peace?"

As a juvenile journalist, you will remember, I was caught by the fascination and the potentiality of the great interview as a force for the general good. The idea was confirmed in my mind by the "interview" which Ingersoll wrote for me in 1890 and by my somewhat rich experience along that line in subsequent years in Europe. I walked out of that study into the finest, the thickest, snowstorm I had seen in nearly a quarter of a century, and as I reveled in it in the open I was repeating aloud to nobody but myself: "I'll see if we can do anything."

29. Peace-Seeking on Three Continents

Seated in a straight-lined high chair (specially made for him and always standing by a wide window also specially made and commanding a spacious view of Lake Michigan), Victor Fremont Lawson sat with legs crossed, right arm caught over the back of the chair, hands clasped, thoughtfully looking at the lake. So I found him in his Lake Shore Drive home, with its beautiful little Grecian sanctuary hidden from outside eyes at the center of the top of the building, on a bright mid-winter morning in 1924. His expression was uncommonly serious, and I asked if I might inquire as to what was on his mind.

"I am thinking of Europe," said he.

"Of the chaos there?"

"Yes. Apparently it is chaos, mental and material. I can make out no coherence of thought anywhere. Unless the leaders pull themselves together, I am afraid the consequences of the war are going to be even worse than the war itself."

Two days later, in a written communication, I proposed to Mr. Lawson that we attempt to get from each of the most responsible officials of Europe a carefully reasoned statement designed to correct existing misunderstanding, allay inflammation, point the way to reconstruction, and define the principles of an established international accord. I suggested that such statements, published throughout the world, might prove of real service toward a restoration of constructive mental processes.

Again I found the great publisher and editor (the supreme journalist of America, in my opinion) in his high chair by the big window looking at the lake. It was another bright and frosty morning, and Mr. Lawson was fresher and less preoccupied. He greeted me with especial cordiality, I thought, and said at once:

"Your idea, Bell, is most interesting and suggests large possibilities. But whom should you see in Europe?"

I replied that I should try to see Chancellor Wilhelm Marx of Germany, Premier Benito Mussolini of Italy, Premier Raymond Poincaré of France, and Premier Ramsay MacDonald of Great Britain. Mr. Lawson listened smilingly but, I thought, with pleasant incredulity. I asked him if he thought me visionary.

"Well," he answered, "I can't help feeling you're audacious. You already, however, have interviewed at length, and with a success familiar to the world, Grey and Haldane and others, the outstanding feats in that line in the history of our profession. Do you really *feel* you can induce Marx, Mussolini, Poincaré, and MacDonald to talk with care and fullness for publication?"

"I can't say I have any definite presentiment on the point," I replied, "but I strongly desire to try. It was many years before I could prevail upon Grey and Haldane to give me interviews. I rather think I could land the present chief European premiers in a few months."

"Very good," said Mr. Lawson with the sheer definitiveness of tone which marked all his decisions. "Go and try. Let me say this before you leave: You're tackling a hard and precarious job. Don't get discouraged because you're spending a lot of the paper's money. If you land *one* of those men, the expense will be justified. If you land none, I still shall not quarrel with you. I don't quarrel with men who have big and rational ideas and the courage to put them to the test."

Could a man have set forth on an uncertain mission with his spirits more nobly sustained? I went to sea with a light heart, no drag upon me in the shape of obstinate lack of confidence or niggardliness at home. It was Mr. Lawson's inestimable contribution to the promise of what he termed our "Great Adventure."

Reaching Berlin early in March, 1924, I eventually (after patient tactical maneuvering) found myself seated in the library of the Chancellery in the Wilhelmstrasse at a round table with Chancellor Marx, gray, high and wide of brow, round-faced, be-spectacled, and benign. Between us on the Chancellor's right sat Dr. Otto Carl Kiep, legal counselor of the Chancellery, an ex-soldier of cavalry, smooth-faced and bright-eyed, his velvet jacket buttoned to the chin. Nearly everyone in Washington and New York knows Dr. Kiep and his excellent English. He was with us as interpreter. We looked out upon the wooded gardens of the Chancellery, a paradise in summer, already flooded with the melody of the thrush. Above us was the coat of arms of Bismarck.

Judge Marx talked in a low, rapid voice, pausing attentively for Kiep's rendering in English. We parted and met in the same place again. For a fortnight we repeated these meetings, seizing scraps of time early and late between Cabinets, administrative duties, and the demands of an electoral campaign, then at its height. Our talks occupied a total of twenty-four hours, followed by days and nights of translating, re-translating, revising, and revising again. The Chancellor made his final study of my finished manuscript as he traveled between Berlin and Frankfort in the course of a speaking tour, and in a few days' time I received his written approval and *imprimatur*. The interview ran to about 7,000 words and covered the entire German situation, domestic and foreign, as Judge Marx saw it at that time.

At my specific request, the Chancellor gave the following as "Republican Germany's message to other states and peoples":

> We appeal for justice in judgment, fair treatment, mutuality of forbearance and respect. Let us leave on one side the controversy regarding who caused the war. But let me say that no one at all acquainted with the German people could imagine them capable of deliberately and wantonly setting out to slay and conquer. The world's need of needs is that of international education. Nations do not know one another. Even the highest-placed statesmen lack the international knowledge indispensable to peace-building diplomacy. Germany yearns for eternal peace. She is deeply concerned to ensue it in company with her powerful neighbors. Give us concentration of effort, internationally organized, to uncover the only physical and psycholog-bases of world peace. It cannot rest on conflicting ideologies. It can rest on realities alone. Let governments and the Press and all persons of light and leading in every country strive to learn what those realities are and to force the accommodation of states' policies to them.

In May I was in Rome and hot on the track of Signor Mussolini, transcendent human dynamo and constructive influence in modern Italy. Interviewing Il Duce then was not the comparatively facile achievement it later became. I do not think he ever had been interviewed, not at least formally and lengthily, when I turned up at the Quirinal. Our Rome correspondent, Hiram K. Motherwell, stood high among Italian officials as a correspondent of competence, sympathy, and rigid honor. He helped me greatly, and one lovely morning, the beautiful city of the Seven Hills matchless in a gown of sunshine and shadow, we were with Mussolini in his resplendent room at the Chigi Palace (that was before he moved into a yet more gorgeous room at Palazzo Venezia), Hi as interpreter (Mussolini spoke only a few words of English in those days), I as interrogator. We got our interview, 6,000 words, and Mussolini incorporated in his written *imprimatur* happily-worded praise of our "diligence" and our "most commendable objective." Hiram wrote a vivid and charming description of the scene.

Then an amusing thing happened. I was talking with our consul-general and told him in confidence of our touch-down at Chigi Palace. He was tickled. His hilarity, as I soon learned, had nothing to do with the interview itself.

"What on earth are you interviewing *him* for?"

The question set me back rather rudely.

"Why," I said, "he's the head of the Italian state, and I'm out to talk with a few such men."

"Good enough," was the penetrating consul-general's reply, "but *he*'ll be out before you get to Paris."

Such was the obtuseness of many foreigners in Rome at that time. They were bat-blind, swamped in bias, dead to all the marvelous things going forward about them from end to end of the peninsula, wholly unappreciative of the manifest genius of Mussolini. Such stupidity I never had seen before with reference to any national situation or racial and political leader. I was back in Rome on an economic mission two years later (1926), and the same consul-general said to me:

"He's stronger today than he was when you saw him."

I talked with Mussolini eleven years after he was to be out before I reached Paris. And he was still the firmly-seated head of re-born Italy, with Italian postage stamps bearing the symbols XIII, signifying that his national ascendency and leadership had lasted for thirteen years.

Premier Mussolini, in that first interview of 1924, told me how Fascism was born (not as a philosophy issuing in a movement but as a movement producing a philosophy which even yet was only in its exploratory and formative state). Fascism was Italy's "national and spontaneous child." It was "Italianity become tangible, a living organism, in the form of government." "It has no dictator but itself. It never will or can have any other. I do not control or bend the national destiny; it controls and bends me. Read Roman history. Mix and talk with Italians from the Alps to the sea. The experience will aid you to grasp the inevitability of Fascism to the salvation of Rome."

War talk and peace talk had been bursting alternately from Mussolini's lips until the world was befogged, bewildered, as to what he meant. He had said that "it is blood which moves the wheels of history." And he also had said that "mankind's one all-overshadowing need is the need of peace." I asked him in 1924 to clarify his attitude. He did so with pains and with precision and eloquence.

"Blood has been the necessary historical wheel-mover," he declared, "because only blood could clear the road to human existence. The road of history is the road to food and the possibility of a decent life for men, women, and children. That road perpetually has led expanding peoples into trouble, for it was obstructed by what we designate the *status quo*. Human beings, usually savages, barbarians, or disorganized and feeble peoples of some civilization, already were there. They could not use effectively or thoroughly what they esteemed their patrimonies, their lands and natural resources, and peoples more numerous and stronger slaughtered them or shoved them out of the way. There was no ethics about it. There was no forbearance or pity about it. And all the imperialists were precisely alike, each feeling righteous and damning the others as unrighteous. You gentlemen of the *Chicago Daily News* desire from statesmen light on the peace problem. My humble contribution to your search is this: Make governments and the millions they represent or misrepresent understand the impossibility of maintaining today, any more than in the past, a *status quo* which would block humanity's road to food."

"Then Fascism," I said, "is for those international re-adjustments which it feels to be necessary to peace."

"That is right. It can be for nothing less; it wants nothing more. There is plenty of room in the world for us all. Earth's varied capacities and contents are practically inexhaustible. Only arbitrary and unjust interference with the natural, proper, and resistless evolution of society as a whole can cast us into the bottomless pit of another world war."

Our reception by Signor Mussolini was highly and impressively formal. We walked to the tall double-doors admitting us to the corridor leading to Il Duce's room with a great company of admirals and generals and diplomats and provincial Italian politicians on either hand. They were waiting to see the Chief, and Motherwell and I wondered how it was, in such circumstances, that the Chief would or could take sufficient time to talk for more than an hour to newspaper men. Perhaps it was because of his essentially journalistic nature and his long service as the brilliant and influential editor of *Popolo d'Italia*.[1] This individualist son of a Socialist father believed in the Press, though none more than he knew its shortcomings and its not infrequent sins. Formal the approach and formal the approached. Signor Mussolini was smart and decorous

---

1. While a leader of Italy's Socialist Party, Mussolini was editor of *Avanti!*, the Socialist daily. When internal disagreements led Mussolini to leave *Avanti!*, he started his own *Il Popolo d'Italia* (*The People of Italy*), which eventually became the Fascist Party organ. For Mussolini as a journalist, see Smith, *Mussolini*; and Bosworth, *Mussolini*.

in a handsome morning suit. I will tell you presently how different I found things in Paris.

Supporting me in Paris in my effort to persuade Premier Poincaré to line up with Marx and Mussolini in our peace enterprise was Paul Scott Mowrer, the *Daily News*'s Paris correspondent, now the chief editorial writer of that great Chicago afternoon newspaper. Paul went with me to the Quai d'Orsay on receipt of word from the Premier that he would receive us at 11 o'clock one morning. No admirals or generals or diplomats or provincial politicians in Poincaré's reception room. None in the great corridor leading to his office door. Paul knew the door and applied the iron knocker. It was opened not by a livery-servant nor yet by a secretary. It was opened by a heavy man, short, scraggily-bearded and mustached, bald on the top of the large head, clad in a wrinkled, rather worn jacket-suit, decidedly a commoner in appearance, though one of a strength of character and mind affecting the observer instantly.

It was Poincaré himself, smiling and giving us welcome by softly-spoken French words and a firm hand-clasp. It was France, post-war France, in the shape of a man. All the national emotion, conviction, and purpose were wrapped up snugly in him. France, before and during and after the Great War, had been utterly innocent of error of policy or of wrong to anyone. The Allies had fought a Holy War. A monster of infamous and unpitying aggression had been laid forever in the dust at an awful cost of blood and treasure. There that monster should lie till we witnessed the miracle of the leopard changing his spots. It was grim stuff which poured in burning French from the lips of that scraggily-bearded man with his awesome air of mental concentration and moral pertinacity. Germany never had had, never could have, an atom of abatement for what she and her coalition had done to France and all mankind.

A great Frenchman, Poincaré, perhaps the greatest of the post-war period. But not a great internationalist, not a comprehensive viewer of history. It was his attitude and that of men like him which gave birth to and implemented a policy fraught with the certain provocation of epoch-making changes in Germany: in a phrase, the German Renaissance or supersession, with Adolf Hitler as Führer, and with Germany re-armed for another major war. France had only one real internationalist after the war, Aristide Briand;[2] and he was bound hand and foot by official association and uninstructed public opinion.

2. Aristide Briand, eleven-time premier of France, was known for his international diplomatic efforts. He was a great proponent of the League of Nations and engineer of the Kellogg-Briand pact, a post–World War I multilateral agreement to settle international disputes through peaceful means, which despite its wide approval and acceptance turned out to be largely ineffective.

Our interview with the great Frenchman (Paul Scott Mowrer, in a searching character sketch of the Premier written to go with my report of the talk,
described it as "perhaps M. Poincaré's most important interview in a long life
of statesmanship") ran to upward of 6,000 words and was an honest and ago-
nizing summing-up of what France had lost and suffered in the Great War. She
had fought for her own and the world's liberties. She would fight so, if necessary, again. Neither individual nor national life was tolerable without liberty;
far better that one should die in battle. Peace could come to the nations only
through a sacred fidelity to the processes of law and reason and negotiation.
The big guns must not intrude themselves into the discussion. Aggression
must cease. The powerful democracies had fought side by side. They never
must part company, France, Britain, and the United States.

Despondency I could not resist as I traveled from Paris to London. Marx
and Poincaré were diametrically at odds; Marx could not endure the thought
of international policy and action on the assumption of exclusive German
war-guilt; he really was as convinced of Germany's innocence as Poincaré was
of the innocence of France. Little hope of Franco-German mutual trust and
friendship and cordial cooperation for peace while those antagonistic sentiments and opinions held the field. And likewise as regards Mussolini. He saw
the national Haves, such countries as France and England, blocking the road
of the Have-nots to food and consequently to peace. Poincaré saw the Have-
nots, the opponents of the *status quo,* as presumptive warlike aggressors who
must be held in check by superiority of arms.

Premier Ramsay MacDonald I had known for many years personally and
politically and considered him the most profound and practical Socialist of the
day. He discussed Socialism intelligibly to the most hard-boiled realist, and realist he himself was; he showed it in his first, second, and third premierships.
He was no Socialist bull rushing at a gate. He saw national and international
externalities not in a rosy mist but in a dry light. The Socialist ideal was never
absent from his vision nor from his resolute aim, but he would move toward
its realization with a full understanding of circumstances and of the necessity
of a gradual transmutation of them to Socialist ends. Thus he lost the confidence of the extremists of his party and died with them calling him a "traitor."[3]

My first meeting with him was early one winter morning when (a black-
haired, muscular, fresh-complexioned young Scot) he was living in very

---

3. When MacDonald formed a coalition government with Conservatives during Great Britain's
Great Depression, the Labour Party expelled him from its ranks.

humble quarters with his greatly-loved wife in Lincoln's Inn Fields. He was just a budding politician then, the whole of his tumultuous and illustrious career an unsuspected potentiality. His wife apparently was not with him that morning; at least he himself answered the knocker, and I saw no one else in the house. He was coatless and his shirt-sleeves were rolled up, and he had an awful-looking butcher-knife in his brawny right hand. I thought he might be disposed to whittle down the journalistic nuisance a little that day, but he was quite peaceful and charming; he only was getting his own breakfast. He gave me the first interview I ever had had with an exponent of what he styled "a religion of popular service, Socialism."

To brief it, he answered my request for a full-dress interview as Marx, Mussolini, and Poincaré had answered it, and within a few days of my arrival in London he and I were in deep colloquy in the Prime Minister's private room at the House of Commons, while the members of the body humdrummed in the shaded light of their lofty chamber not many yards distant. In its complete and authorized form, and bearing MacDonald's written *imprimatur,* the interview ran to more than 5,000 words; and Hal O'Flaherty, then foreign editor (now managing editor) of the *Chicago Daily News,* in a critical study of it, wrote: "The genius of Ramsay MacDonald is revealed more fully in the interview he has granted Edward Price Bell than in any of his speeches or printed works." And Hal wrote out of a close personal knowledge of MacDonald and all his public utterances.

What did he say about peace?

"Peace is a creature of sympathy, war a creature of blind savagery. Sympathy opens the human mind; war closes it. And it is the closed human mind which, cut off from vitally relevant facts and holding fast to its own preconceptions and prejudices, will not see international problems in all their crucial relations and therefore will not know justice even if disposed to do justice. That posture is hopeless, for until the powers know and do justice there can be no universal contentment, no international friendship, no restoration of world economy, no peace. If the Press can inspire statesmanship with the sympathy and the courage of the poet, it will inspire governments to find peace-breeding solutions of every great problem, and humanity will cry rejoicingly, 'Amen!'"

It amounted to the old counsel of international education as the *sine qua non* of peace. International politics must be made not emotional but scientific; not intuitive but empiric. It must seek definite knowledge as the biologist, physicist, and chemist seek it. And, having found knowledge, it must bow to it, to the hard objective facts, as physical scientists bow to such facts. Obsti-

30. I Push On to the Far East, Economics, and Latin America

After the successful *finis* of our great adventure in 1924, my mind began to turn to other issues of international concern—the situation in the Pacific foremost among them. Japano-American relations were getting very bad. The news pouring out from the Far East and from Washington and New York looked growingly ominous. Our legislators were hell-bent on shutting the Japanese out of America as the Chinese had been shut out. We were planning great maneuvers in the Premier Ocean. We were going to make Hawaii into a mighty fortress and base of naval power. One American politician was howling for "a white League of Nations in the Pacific."[1]

Japan, by no means unnaturally, was uncomfortable, fearful.

I set out again, this time in search of an answer to the question of Occidental-Oriental peace, traveling to Canada, the Pacific slope of the United States, to Hawaii, Japan, China, and the Philippine Archipelago. The interviews produced from that journalistic mission were published by the *Chicago Daily News*.

Mr. Lawson was unable to read them all. He died late that year. I was on my way back home from the Philippines, sailing by the *Madison*, struck with dengue. At Victoria, Vancouver Island, where we touched before dawn on a September morning, a journalist I had met in that ultra-English city of many

1. By the mid-1920s, Japanese-American relations had already been strained for decades. In the background were questions about China, naval disarmament, and racial equality. In 1924, the U.S. Congress passed the National Origins Act, which limited immigration from countries that had not had large populations in the United States as of 1890. This targeted Italians, Russians, Poles, and especially Japanese. The passage of this act, also known as the Exclusion Act, was opposed by many prominent Americans and influential government leaders. See LaFeber, *The Clash*, 128–59.

delights knocked hard on my stateroom door at 5 o'clock. He entered with apologies and said: "Thought you'd like to have the news, though it's sad. Victor Lawson died at his home in Chicago yesterday."

It *was* a shock. It had its peculiarly deplorable aspect. Mr. Lawson, without whose international neighborliness and financial backing our "Great Adventure" could not have been carried out, did not live to see with his own eyes the completed work. But he knew by cable that our efforts in the Far East had been as successful as our efforts of 1924 in Europe. And he had cabled me:

"The end crowns the work, and a great work it has been."

In 1926, the work was yet unfinished.

One great and grievous thing about international affairs had nonplussed and disturbed me for many years: the general ignorance, especially in the highest quarters of leadership and authority, respecting the fundamentals of economics. I myself was no economist, but I was born, I venture to think, with a modest degree of horse sense. Visiting Chicago in 1919 for the first time since 1913 (the year before the Great War), I was invited to address the Chicago Association of Commerce on the War Debts. I told an audience of a thousand hard-headed businessmen that I was convinced those debts, including the appalling reparations demanded of Germany, never would be, never could be, paid. At the conclusion of my speech, the whole assembly rose and clapped with extraordinary vigor. I took that demonstration to mean that the unpayability of the debts soon would be appreciated by governments and peoples.

Nothing of the kind. Old stupidities and passions pretty well held the lay field from the top to the bottom of society except in England; there statesmanship was calling for cancellation and actually itself canceling. It occurred to me that an explanation and exposition of the minds of the foremost economists in Europe and America might do something to lift the fog and disclose the reefs. Mr. Lawson was gone, but in his place was another open-minded and imaginative publisher, Walter Strong, and we still had at the editorial helm of the *Chicago Daily News* the broad sympathies and the journalist genius of Charles Henry Dennis. These men, when I suggested a tour of Europe and America for interviewing men really versed in economics, men who had given their lives to it, replied: "Go!"

I went. I spent ten months on the assignment and interviewed more than fifty European and American economists, selecting the admittedly superior if not unrivaled, some of the extremely abstract and intellectual, some experienced and in regular work as industrialists, traders, financiers, and engineers. We at last made a book of the interviews and articles, *Europe's Economic Sun-*

rise, and it was "dedicated to the proposition that in all departments of human affairs the Big Idea is better than the Big Stick."

My first whole year in America for more than a quarter of a century was 1927. It seemed thoroughly good to me. I did a lot to reacquaint myself with the land of *The Old Swimmin' Hole* and *Pipes o' Pan.*[2] I actually visited the ole swimming hole again and dived and swam in it not only in luxuriating fancy but in dripping fact. And I also sat for many a delicious hour listening to the god of woods and hills and flocks and streams piping, I suggest, more or less as he piped to my old boyhood friend, James Whitcomb Riley.

But 1927 was not all reminiscence and relaxation and sweet idling for me. I dug like a navvy at the old job of newspapering. I became a columnist, a humble atom in a proud if sometimes boring company. I wrote *The Marching World* for the editorial page of my paper, pouring forth my opinions in bacchanalian abandon and having my column adorned regularly with a half-column cut of my physical facade. I received thousands of letters of eulogy and not a few blistering me with abuse. I put my bitter critics down as jealous, but possibly they were right.

I wrote other things for the editorial page. I called them historical, literary, and philosophical; my wife called them "editorial gems." Mr. Dennis came to my cubicle one day and said of this stuff, "It's great." That bucked me. There was a fine fellow at Northwestern University (he is there yet) named Robert Harvey Gault, a professor of psychology and criminology. He had a highly intelligent wife, I thought. One evening in Evanston I ran upon Prof. Gault in the street, and he stopped me to say, "My wife and I regard your editorial-page matter as the best writing, both in substance and in form, we ever have seen in a newspaper." I went home rejoicing. My wife handed me a bunch of letters. It was a bad catch. Several anonymous chaps (and anonymity is usually another name for spontaneity and honesty) called my stuff "ignorant," "presumptuous," "lousy." It was "bunk." It was "utter boloney." "Why don't you follow Osler and chloroform yourself?"

And I also flowered as a lecturer and radio barker. My platform audiences were angelically kind and tolerant, and I had a great time with them. I made such a hit often that I could not escape for an hour after the lecture, and I wrote autographs till I was limp. What the minorities in those audiences thought I dare not guess. Indeed a lecturer never knows really what any part

2. Both works were written by one of Bell's childhood heroes, Midwest author James Whitcomb Riley, who wrote under the penname Benjamin F. Johnson of Boone.

of his audience thinks. Audiences seem to me to be habitually more compassionate than critical. I have seen them applaud when they ought to have committed murder.

In upon my varied preoccupations beat from time to time the deplorable fact that Anglo-American relations, which seemed established rationally forever by the arms-comradeship of the Great War, were again going dangerously awry. Britain was disgusted with us for "letting civilization down," as she put it, over the League of Nations. We had been guilty of a "Great Betrayal."[3] And, instead of piping low and hiding our heads with shame, we were chesty, claimed we had "won the war," and never ceased to bully the Allies about the war debts. As for ourselves, we accused Britain and our other debtors of "welshing" and went steadily on demanding that they "crack down." I suggested to my superiors that I go to England and see if something could not be done to swing the British Press against diabolically silly bickering.

I was instructed to go after the National Election of 1928. Our publisher had received a number of requests from men of influence that I be released from the paper to deliver a series of lectures in the Middle West in impartial analysis of the leading candidates for the presidency, Hoover, Al Smith, and the Socialist Thomas.[4] The thesis of these gentlemen was that the independent vote was growing in America, that the *Daily News* has a long and unsullied record of political discrimination and objectivity, that Edward Price Bell had "won international fame as an astute and fair writer upon all sorts of men and things," and that the independent voter would like to hear him on the platform as well as to read him in the paper. So I went lecturing on the candidates. I liked them all. What guidance I gave to anyone I do not know. I do know that when I finished speaking of Hoover there were audible whispers in the audience, "He's a Republican." And after Smith, "He's a Democrat and Catholic." After Thomas, "Damned if he isn't a Socialist!"

And all I had done was to describe personalities, define principles, and leave the choice of candidates wholly to my auditors!

3. Although President Woodrow Wilson had strongly supported the proposed League of Nations after World War I, the U.S. Congress did not ratify the Treaty of Versailles, which contained the pledge of membership in the League. This seriously weakened the League, which proved ineffective and fell apart during the Second World War.

4. Herbert Hoover won the election of 1928. Al Smith was four-time Democratic governor of New York. When he ran as the Democratic nominee against Hoover in 1928, he became the first U.S. Catholic to seek that office. Norman Thomas was an American Socialist and pacifist leader who frequently sought public office in New York and ran for president six times.

In that year 1928, in June, Northwestern University, at the instance of its president, Walter Dill Scott, conferred a dual honor upon me, made me an honorary LL.D., and asked me to deliver the commencement address to an audience of students and parents packing the great Patten Museum, on the Evanston Campus, to the doors. I spoke on *ego* and tried to glorify beyond all else in women and men the principle of self-dependence. The address was published and widely distributed by the *Daily News* in brochure form, and I venture to quote three men on it as they are quoted in that brochure. Scott himself: "One of the very finest commencement addresses I have ever heard." Rev. J. Hastie Ogders, A.B.: "An effective appeal to initiative and self-reliance." Judge Martin M. Gridley: "An inspiring statement of the first principles of success."

In my Evanston home after dinner one evening in November, 1928, I was cogitating upon my forthcoming trip to England to attempt a little more peace-building. The national election was over, and Herbert Hoover was President-elect. The telephone rang, and Walter Strong, our publisher, said to me: "Ed, it's a hurry-up job. We've decided to send you with Hoover on what he calls his 'Good Will Tour' to Central and South America.[5] He sails on the battleship *Maryland* from San Pedro very soon. You'll have to leave Chicago tonight for San Francisco in order to catch Hoover before he leaves Palo Alto for San Pedro. You can go?"

"Yes," I said. "I'll come down and touch you for some dough and get out on the Northwestern in good time."

So it befell that I was ensconced in a cramped private room in one of the great masts of the *Maryland* when she put to sea on a brilliant November morning with all the naval and merchant craft in San Pedro harbor making a mighty fuss over her. We were off on a 20,000-mile journey to visit most of the capitals of the Latin Americas from Honduras right round to Rio and to see the Bolivians at the Chilean port of Antofagasta, since they had no port of their own. The President-elect and Mrs. Hoover, with their personal party (including Press-boss George Barr Baker),[6] had swell quarters in the stern

5. In late 1928, then President-elect Hoover took a trip of "good will" to ten Latin American countries for almost two months to tout his "good neighbor" policy toward Latin America. Good neighbors, Hoover said in a speech at Amapala, Honduras, "call upon each other as evidence of solicitude for the common welfare and to learn of the circumstances and point of view of each that there may come both understanding and respect." Hoover also said good neighbors allow each other to "work out their own salvation," signaling his determination to end American over-interference in Latin American affairs. See Burner, *Hoover,* 285–8.

6. George Barr Baker was an American journalist who supported Hoover for the presidency in the 1928 campaign. He was Hoover's press secretary on the Good Will Tour.

of the battleship, and twenty correspondents and cameramen were distributed over the huge vessel as its accommodations allowed. Mixed up with the *Maryland*'s complement of cultured and friendly officers, and with 900 tanned and brawny doughboys, we had an interesting and jolly time.

Those were Prohibition days, and to be in Latin America under the restraint of loyalty to Prohibition laws is to be pitiably out of luck. The Latin-Americans, when they are not cutting off one another's heads, are princes of good-fellowship, hospitable till one's eyes are large, rolling, and staring. Unexpected graces they have to match those of even the elect of China. At Amapala, Honduras, for example (our first stop), the stairway into the large reception hall near the sea was strewn with aromatic plants in order that our favored feet might fill the air with a pungent fragrance. Champagne sparkled among us everywhere, borne by smiling waiters, in native costumes, on beautifully figured trays. The President-elect and his wife of course were served first. They barely touched their lips to the dry and dancing beverage. I observed no such abstention on the part of any correspondent or cameraman, and I cannot take oath that a single member of the presidential *entourage* labored under the full meticulosity of its chief's constraint.

At Guayaquil, Ecuador, forty miles up the tumbling Guayas River from the Gulf of the same name, we were welcomed in a manner to suggest that the whole country, gorgeous panama hats and all, was ours for nothing at all but the delight we gave the Ecuadoreans by coming. Great dance. Thousands there, handsome men, and exquisitely piquant and fascinating ladies, many hardly more than flappers, others not so young but quite as beautiful. One long bar where champagne was free. Help yourself! Any wonder a certain budding New York journalist, our most callow and symmetrical member, fell in love with a marvelous *señorita* and led her to the moonlit veranda (above the city's principal street) for breathless adoration?

President Dr. Isidro Ayora of Ecuador presented each man of the whole of the American group with a velvety panama hat, the finest his country produced. Were we proud and thankful! And mine was stolen between Guayaquil and Antofagasta! More than a year later, I walked into the office of George Akerson, Secretary to President Hoover (who had been with us in Latin-America), and he said to me:

"I've a great surprise for you. You were so sad over losing your panama that I wrote Dr. Ayora about it. Here is another, even finer, he says, than the one you lost. He begs you to accept it with his kindest remembrances."

I bow low and lift my panama to Dr. Ayora!

Barren coasts, bald and broken against a gray sky, were about all we could see as the *Maryland* dropped anchor six miles off Antofagasta, Chile, in deep water. We were gazing at the famed port of the Province of Antofagasta and the still more famed nitrate deserts of that rainless and plantless region, with not so much as a blade of grass for hundreds of mirage-carpeted miles: enchanting lakes which turned to mocking dust as one drew eagerly near them. Two of my newspaper companions stood near me as we gazed from the rail of the quarter-deck, one Phil Simms, foreign editor of the Scripps-Howard chain, the other big, good-looking, young (27) Rodney Dutcher of another branch of the same organization. We could not see the city. It all appeared of a single desert pattern. There was shore-leave, and Phil and Rodney and I elected to see Antofagasta, while Hoover held his talks with the Bolivians, who had descended from La Paz, sunk deep in the cliff-flanked valley of La Paz River, to honor the peripatetic chief executive of the "Colossus of the North" and try to find out what the Good Will Tour was all about.

That sour old captain of the *Maryland*, appearing to regard journalists as a nuisance at the best, put Simms, Dutcher, and me in an awful hole. He said he would sail for Santiago at 3 p.m. that day. We lunched with a crowd of celebrants at the British-American Club, the supervisor of the port in the party. He kept saying to us: "Have a good time now, and don't worry about the *Maryland*. She sails at 3. I'll take you in my own launch and have you alongside the battleship not later than 2:30." At 2:30 we were there, but the battleship was gone. The Bolivians and the President-elect had finished their conference earlier than was anticipated, and the Captain, although well knowing we were ashore, said, "What the hell?"

Some time we had after that! Our gear consisted of the white flimsies we had on our backs. At the Hotel de Londres we ran into an angel anthropomorphically designed: David E. Kaufman, American Minister to La Paz, who had journeyed to Antofagasta with the Bolivians. He had money to burn, and we had only a few wretched shekels in our cotton breeks. He dined us and wined us, bought us pyjamas and razors and razor-blades, put us up in good rooms at the hotel, sent radiograms to Hoover and telegrams to the President of Chile, forced upon us a wash-basketful of Chilean paper money, and said:

"Good night boys, I'll stay over here a while. In the morning I'll take you and what you need in my two cars, and you will catch a mountain train at Baquedano, sixty miles up the Andes, putting you in Santiago in time to rejoin Hoover. Sleep well and don't worry."

We slept well and did not worry, and Minister Kaufman did all he said he would do, rushed us up the Andes and through the mirages and saw us on that funny little train, in that funny little mud-town of Baquedano, Chile, with an enormous hamper filled with roast chicken, deviled eggs, rolls and butter, and bottles of still white wine. We waved the angel good-by from the car windows, and looked long after his cars winding seaward through the desert valleys. At 7 the next morning our train stopped at Pueblo Hundido, another Chilean mud-village, and a dwarfish Anglo-Chilean whom I had met the night before came to me and said: "This train stops here all day." "Holy Jesus!" I cried. "When do we get to Santiago?"

"Don't know," was the answer. "Auto-rail out here waiting for you and your friends. Sent by the President of Chile to run you to Copiapo."

Off we piled with our hamper of food and into that auto-rail, an old Dodge car fitted with railway wheels, driven by a grinning little Chilean to whom English was a joke. We scarcely were seated when the chauffeur put his odd buggy into violent motion, and we shot ahead on the most hair-raising flight any of us ever had known. It was a hurricane. Narrow-gauge, winding, tunnel-piercing, the road itself was terrifying. But not to that swarthy, wizened mad hatter at the wheel, under orders from the President! At last he turned to us, frozen in our seats, grinned some more, and pointed. Blades of green were appearing: delightful! And there actually, at the foot of the hills, was Copiapo, bowered in pepper-trees, paradise.

And who could that gorgeous gentleman be, standing by the side of the narrow-gauge under the eaves of the little wooden station, plumes in his hat, epaulettes on his shoulders, ribbons wreathing his body? It was another angel, Señor Rafael Ruiz, Intendente of Chile's province of Atacama, dispatched by the President to receive us, look after us, feed us, treat us to excellent wine, and see that we got aboard two military planes for a quick hop to Santiago. He did it all.

By and by, we returned to the Hoover Party's hotel in Santiago, where men wildly agitated over our return beat us half to death and pressed upon us more wine than was good for us.

Great was our railway journey to Buenos Aires, dark, stupendous mountains; thrilling waterfalls; dashing, whirling snow-storms; bright-eyed, wonder-smitten villagers crowding the tiny stations for a glimpse of the President-elect of the United States and his menagerie of officials and pressmen. At the mountain-top line between Chile and Argentina we saw that deeply impressive monument, "Christ the Redeemer," symbol and sentry of Christianity and peace unbreakable between Chile and her great sister of the Atlantic.

That monument, they said, had tears to shed; if the Chilean-Argentinian peace there dedicated ever were broken, that statue would weep.

Over the pampas (600 miles of fertile lowlands between the Andean foothills and the Atlantic, with thousands of farmers waving to us from their furrows and their hay-wagons) and, at sunset, into the great city, seat of the Argentine government. Crowded, noisy, throbbing station. My feet barely had touched the platform when a man rushed along calling out, "Is Edward Price Bell in this party?" It was my old friend, Count Kiehl of The Hague, who had helped me beat the world nearly thirty years before on the wedding of Queen Wilhelmina. He was "it" there. He left word about my baggage, nodded and winked at police and soldiers, and led me out of that station in advance of every other soul. A rousing, reverberant cheer arose from the people massed outside.

"They think you're Hoover!" said Kiehl, concealing his spasmic mirth.

All sorts of fun-provoking things happened in Buenos Aires. "I've been sober all the way," said a responsible New York correspondent. "I may get drunk in this town tonight; I feel that way now. If I do, I want one of you chaps to send a thousand words to my paper at the full rate, dollar a word." Early in the evening a colleague saw that the man was making good, jumped into a taxi, sped to the telegraph office, and filed a thousand words as directed. Later another obliging colleague did the same. And about midnight a third functioned for the happy delinquent. The next morning this delinquent said to me: "I'm ruined. Three damned fools did it. Three stories from this mad burg with my name signed to them!"

"Never mind," I said. "Your paper simply scoops things in anyhow. It will think merely that you've been especially speedy on the home-stretch."

Beautiful time in that city, in Montevideo, and in matchless ocean-side Rio, last stopping place of the Good Will Tour. In the Brazilian capital we were received with profusions of flowers, entertained magnificently, and sent on our way past the renowned Sugar Loaf[7] with the decks of the battleship *Utah* flashing and coloring with parti-hued fireworks bursting far and near and seeming, from the Sugar Loaf's summit, to break against the over-arching night-sky.

Did the Good Will Tour do good? I think so. It surely was led with tact, friendliness, and wisdom by Herbert Hoover, perhaps the best-informed and most intelligent internationalist the White House has known. Not to say our

7. The Sugar Loaf is a peak on the Atlantic Ocean in Rio de Janeiro, Brazil, that overlooks that city's Guanabara Bay.

Latin-American neighbors were made wholly to trust us. They will be a long time in doing that. Will you show me any nation on earth which implicitly and always trusts another? I know of none. But I think Hoover did some good, in the snail-paced work of advancing international good will, on that arduous Latin-American Tour.

31. I Bring MacDonald to America

Two things memorable to me came to pass shortly before we landed in a drenching rain at Hampton Roads, Virginia, on January 6, 1929, at the end of the Good Will Tour to Central and South America. The first of these things was meteorologic, a mid-night storm of great violence off Cape Hatteras, North Carolina, during which the general alarm of the battleship was sounded and immense excitement reigned for more than an hour. The second was political, a private talk with President-elect Hoover respecting the international situation and his coming foreign policy.

My talk with Hoover took place on the *Utah,* forward, where the President-elect, strolling the deck, found me seated alone on the perforated wooden cover of a hatch, sunning myself. He stopped and asked me what I thought of the state of Anglo-American relations. I told him I thought it was shockingly bad, and he said: "So do I." Then he inquired whether I had questioned myself at all concerning the problem of making it better. At that I related how I was on the point of sailing for England on a little Good Will Tour of my own when I was ordered to join him at Palo Alto for San Pedro and the *Maryland.*

"I wish you would carry out that intended mission," said Hoover with every appearance of uncommon sincerity and earnestness.

"Have you some idea of what can be done?" I asked.

His answer was "No." It was a problem for the Press. Sentiment between Britain and America must be sweetened, the atmosphere of the English-speaking world must be cleared and purified, before statesmen could do anything to put the peace of that world on a definite and firm foundation. Sentiment-creation, atmosphere building, between and among nations called for the powers of journalism, particularly of the daily Press. I requested the President-elect (soon to go for a rest in Florida) to invite Walter Strong, our new publisher, to pay him a visit.

"I should like you to say to Mr. Strong," I explained, "just what you have said to me."

Promptly, after our landing, that invitation was extended and accepted, and Mr. and Mrs. Strong visited Mr. and Mrs. Hoover in their holiday retreat. Mr. Strong returned to Chicago and instructed me to go to England at once. I asked him for suggestions. He had none. Said: "You know Great Britain; I don't. It's up to you." Charles Dennis, editor-in-chief, heartily for the undertaking, merely gave me *carte blanche*. I hopped to Ottawa, Canada, and told my old friend, Premier Mackenzie King, ever eager for good feeling among the English-speakers, what I was about. He said he would help all he could, and I knew something of his influence in Downing Street. Just how I should proceed he left to me. By that time Hoover was in the White House, and I ran down from Ottawa to see him for any final word he might have to offer. He was more anxious than ever for a radical change in the sentiment which was growing worse, not better, between the British and ourselves. But he still had no specific suggestions of methods to effect that change.

After consultations in Washington with Secretary of State Stimson, Ambassador Hugh Gibson, British Ambassador Sir Esme Howard, and Canadian Minister Vincent Massey, I sailed on the *Île de France* for Plymouth, England.[1]

"A job for the newspapers," Hoover had said on the *Utah*. Who was the most individual, the freest, the most brilliant and powerful editorial writer in England? Garvin! J. L. Garvin of *The Observer*. Garvin, editor-in-chief of the fourteenth edition of the *Encyclopaedia Britannica*. Garvin so much my friend that he long before had said to me: "I'm going to call you Edward; I want you to call me Garve." And ever afterward it was Edward and Garve between us. At the Garrick Club within twenty-four hours of my arrival in London, Garvin had me to lunch with him alone. I told him all about my purpose. Like many of his fellow-countrymen, he imagined Hoover was none too friendly to the British and was a man to whom economics meant more than human feelings, flesh, and blood. I told him that was a lot of nonsense, a silly caricature of the

---

1. Henry L. Stimson was an influential U.S. foreign policy adviser who served in five presidential administrations between 1911 and 1945. Hugh Gibson was an American diplomat who at various times served as U.S. minister to Poland, Switzerland, Luxembourg, and Belgium. Hoover made him his "Ambassador at Large." Esme Howard was British ambassador to the United States from 1924 to 1930. Canadian statesman Charles Vincent Massey became Canada's first official diplomatic envoy to the United States in 1926, a post he held until 1930.

new president; that Hoover was fond of the British, though dubious of the entire beneficence of their social order; and that his international economics were as enlightened as those of any man I knew. Delighted with this assurance (it was in his dramatic eyes), and characteristically impetuous, Garvin exclaimed:

"Splendid news! You own *The Observer* for the purposes of your mission."

"Do you recommend that I see *The Times*?" I asked.

"Emphatically. Go straight to Dawson."

I went to Geoffrey Dawson, then editor of *The Times* of London, and found him courteous enough but not in the least inflammable with reference to my enterprise. He considered my incipient Good Will Tour ill-timed and of decidedly doubtful promise. Too much already had been said about Anglo-American relations. Their delicacy was such that only silence on the part of both statesmanship and journalism was advisable. My fervor was dashed for a time by the coldness and stiffness of the reverenced editor. And then I got a bit of steam up.

"I'm quick to admit, Mr. Dawson," I said, "that too much foolishness already has been uttered touching Anglo-American relations. It strikes me as urgent that something sensible, something wise, be said in this connection, and said without needless delay. That is what I am here for, and that is what I believe I can accomplish."

At that I got on my legs.

"Mind you, Price Bell," said Dawson, "I'm in the warmest sympathy with your object. I will give you any help I can in any quarter; make any inquiries you suggest. But I cannot open the columns of *The Times* to you."

My first gun, which I tried to make a good-sized one, was fired on the foreign page of *The Observer,* and blending with it was the report of a much more powerful piece of artillery than I commanded: a great editorial by Garvin entitled "Hoover and Hope." I said, to sum up my article in a few words, that the new administration in Washington, contrary to the opinion of many, was "genuinely friendly to the whole British family of nations" and desired to make English-speaking solidarity the starting-point for the reconciliation and rationalization of the world. I declared that Hoover was *not* ultra-economic; that he understood as well as any man living that man was not made for economics but economics for man.

Glorious use did Garvin make of this text, which he endorsed one hundred percent. Editorial after editorial, all flaming with the familiar Garvin fire, demanded that British-American "petty and perilous bickering" should cease and "measures of sanity and reconstruction" begin. He swept not only the British but the European Press with his logic and his intensity, and the American Press from ocean to ocean responded with enthusiasm to his point of view.

Meanwhile I was giving interviews (instead of begging for them), writing articles for numerous British papers and magazines, having a fling on the platform, and talking with the leaders of all parties. Letters from rank-and-file Britishers poured in on me at my hotel, forwarded by various editors. Vastly in the majority were the letters of congratulation and commendation: the heart of Britain speaking. But I had my sharp questioners and critics. "Hoover sent you over here to lull us into a false sense of security." "Your country boasts she won the war." "America wants to push England under and usurp her place in the sun." "You Yanks want to tell us what sort of navy we should have." "You made the League of Nations, dragged us into it, and then let us down: a crime against the world." "How about the debt?" "How about the service rendered America by the millions of boys who died on European battlefields to stop the Huns?"

With all good feeling, and with such dialectic skill as lay in me, I patiently answered those critical letters in *The Observer;* they were too numerous to be dealt with epistolarily. And not only my protagonist, Garvin, but editorial writers in every part of Great Britain stood by me for an end, complete and permanent, of the mutual bitterness and slanging which were injuring and threatening Britain and America and correspondingly weakening their joint influence in world diplomacy. The dissentients and intractables became a zephyr-murmur in a gale. British common sense asserted sovereignty.

And just at the right moment, President Hoover startled and enchanted the peace-loving nations with a ringing call at Geneva (through the voice of Ambassador Hugh Gibson) for "drastic naval reductions" and "for an organization of humanity in a spirit of friendship and trust."[2] That indeed was a mill-race on my wheel. It revealed Hoover as the man I had been telling the British he was. It clinched all I had done, and all Garvin and the British Press in general had done. Talk of trouble between Britain and America became tongue-tied. Good will and bayhorse sense took over.

What else?

What great dramatic stroke might one use to finish the business?

2. Hugh Gibson was head of the American delegation to the 1932 conference on disarmament in Geneva. Hoover tells in his memoir that he drafted a bold plan for naval disarmament, which he instructed Gibson to deliver at the conference. Britain and France opposed the plan, while Germany, Italy, and 38 other nations supported it. See Hoover, *Memoirs,* 352–7.

I sat down in my room at the Carlton Hotel and wrote a brief note to Premier Stanley Baldwin. Would he see me for a few words? Under-Secretary of State Sir Robert Vansittart said "Yes." Within a day or two, I talked with the Premier in his room at the House of Commons. He had been "deeply troubled" about British-American relations. Suddenly taking his beloved pipe from his mouth, he leaned toward me and said:

"I'd do *anything* to put those relations right."

That "anything," with its arresting emphasis, was a spark which fired a little mine which had been forming in my brain for several days.

"Come to Washington!" I urged. "See Hoover! Talk everything over frankly with him! Personal intercourse among the heads of states has saved European civilization since the Great War. I call that intercourse 'Primary Diplomacy'; it short-circuits secondary diplomats and gets things done. Why not apply it in straightening out British-American affairs?"

"If the President invites me, I will go, provided I am Premier again after the pending General Election. I'd love to go and have all cards laid face-up on the table."

"And won't you travel on to Chicago and deliver one of your incomparable speeches on democracy?"

"I will, thank you."

And the humane, stocky, typically English premier wore the look of a very happy man.

"You have Prohibition in America," he said slyly as we parted. "I like something with my meals!"

"Trust us!" I said.

In my diary that night I wrote:

"This has been probably my greatest day in international affairs; the matter is so big."

First meeting in history of the official chief of Great Britain, and the ranking Premier of the British Commonwealth of Nations, with the President of the United States! Surely that would get the headlines, capture the editorial pages, and magnetize the public mind of every continent and island knowing the printed word. I cabled Hoover and waited. I also re-invaded the British Press, hinting at "possible developments at an early date of historical moment to the English-speaking world."

Then came the General Election and the shattering of the arrangement with Premier Baldwin. He was no longer premier. Ramsay MacDonald took his place. Instantly I went after the Socialist-Labor statesman, told him of

Baldwin's promise, and asked if he would do what the defeated Conservative had promised to do, adding that it seemed to me there would be wisdom in asking Premier Mackenzie King of Canada to make it a "Council of Three" at the White House. MacDonald assented without hesitation, and I cabled the fact to the President.

About that time General Dawes[3] arrived in London as President Hoover's ambassador. Hardly had he well warmed his official chair in Grosvenor Gardens when I went to see him and related what Hoover had said to me on the *Utah,* what he had repeated to Walter Strong in Florida, and what I had done to mobilize the Press for a house-cleaning in respect of the behavior of Britain and America toward each other. I also told the Ambassador that Baldwin first and MacDonald afterward had given me a promise to go to Washington to see Hoover about British-American naval affairs and all other questions before the two countries. Dawes astounded me with his obvious displeasure. He was of course quite as anxious as anyone for an improvement in British-American relations, but he was thumbs down on my scheme absolutely.

"We don't want MacDonald over there now," he said in his positive way. "We have other steps in mind relative to sea power and the general problem of British-American relations."

"Well, Mr. Ambassador," I replied, "I'm sorry. I was asked by the President, and directed by my superiors in Chicago, to visit England on a peace mission. I've done my best, and I say to you frankly I think I've done pretty well. The Press over here is for my proposal almost to the last sheet in the country, and we've had here reflections of nothing but approval in the American Press. The thing's gone too far now for any reversal. I've reported to Hoover, and Mac-Donald awaits his invitation."

"We don't want him," reiterated Dawes.

Rudeness, even out of ambassadors, I never did like.

"Mr. Ambassador," I said, rising to go, "I give it you as my opinion that anyone who gets in the way of this movement, at the height it has gained, will be run over."

Working as a rather nifty borer in Washington at that time was a young correspondent by the name of Robert Barry. The White House and the State Department were in his beat. In some way unknown to me (I never had seen

3. Charles G. Dawes, who had lived most of his adult life in Evanston, Illinois, served as U.S. ambassador to Great Britain from 1929 to 1932 and also was vice president under Calvin Coolidge.

Barry, now a public relations man in a big job in New York City, since those stirring days) he tapped the wires, so to speak. He got the whole yarn about my mission abroad, including the fact of belated official opposition to the idea of bringing MacDonald to America, and spilled it under a big head on the first page of the *New York Evening World*. He stated that Edward Price Bell had "backed the statesmen into a corner and made them do what he told them to do." MacDonald would "come to America." There was a resounding "follow" of interviews with prominent senators and representatives, all of whom declared the British premier would receive a grand and sincere welcome in America. It was "a great idea."

Back to London came the news of favorable reactions, journalistic, official, and popular, all over America. I saw Sir Austen Chamberlain, Secretary of State for Foreign Affairs; David Lloyd George, former premier; Aime Joseph de Fleuriau, French Ambassador to London; and Tsuneo Matsudaira, Japanese Ambassador to London. All these men except one gave hearty expression of their happiness that MacDonald was to visit Hoover and that the visit held out some hope of relief for the world from its excessive armaments. Lloyd George said British-American relations "hardly could be worse short of war," but he feared that an "ostentatious getting together" of Britain and America "might alarm the rest of the world and start an anti-British-American *bloc* in Europe and elsewhere." I cited to him the cordial words of the French and Japanese ambassadors.

"Very good," he said. "We shall see."

I felt my work was finished. I was finding respiration somewhat difficult under my load of laudatory efflorescence. The *Daily Express* (London), for instance, wrote: "One who has labored for years in the cause of Anglo-American accord and from whose brain sprang the suggestion for a Tripartite Conference in Washington: that man is Edward Price Bell, a great journalist, a great patriot, and a true lover of this country." The *Evening Transcript* (Boston): "The personal meeting between MacDonald and Hoover will be the result of intimate negotiations with British leaders conducted by an American journalist, Edward Price Bell." To the *Cork Examiner* I had shown myself to be "a distinguished publicist as well as foreign correspondent." *World's Press News* (London): "Edward Price Bell, now sailing for home, is the journalistic Ambassador of the century." *Variety* (London): "Edward Price Bell, the great American journalist, is the real creator of the Anglo-American situation which will make it possible for Hoover and MacDonald to meet." *Editor & Publisher* (New York): "In the brain of an American newspaper man, for more than a quarter of a century a good-will envoy between Britain and America, this great idea was born." And from far-off China, in *Peiping and Tientsin Times:* "Edward Price Bell, whose great work in bettering Anglo-American relations long has been famous, initiated the idea and conducted the preliminaries of this proposed dramatic meeting in Washington." Even *The Times* (London), while reserving personal acknowledgments, swam gracefully and helpfully with the overwhelming news stream.

But I was not thoroughly easy in my mind about it all. The proverbial fly was in the ointment. Had Hoover actually said to MacDonald "Come!"? Universally the British Press thought so. It leapt to the conclusion that Dawes had brought from the President "a cordial invitation" to visit him at the White House. I did not believe it; indeed I knew from Dawes's own lips it was not true. Whether the President had cabled MacDonald direct I did not know; the Premier was silent, and I did not raise the question with him. I called early in the morning of June 26, 1929, to bid the Scottish statesman good-by in his reception room at 10 Downing Street, and the following memorandum I ventured to place in his hands:

I. Why that Washington Conference is urged: In order to get acquainted, to examine in the intimacy of direct conference the fundamentals of British-American relations, to try to find the broad basis of an accepted and permanent British-American peace, and to fortify the favorable sentimental position built up within the last three months on both sides of the Atlantic.

II. Unless this big thing is done now, many complications may intervene and possibly nothing unique and conclusive will be done for years. Meanwhile disaster might overtake us. Until we establish the principle that in no situation will war occur between us, we and the rest of the world are in greater or less peril. Anything like a great war tomorrow would bring us instantly face to face with the problem of getting our Fleets, passively if not actively, on the same side or taking terrible chances of collision. That is what we want: no war if we can prevent it, our Fleets passively or actively on the same side if we cannot. Obviate the possibility of British-American maritime opposition, and you place a virtually indestructible foundation beneath the general peace of the world.

III. It sometimes is suggested that a dramatic departure in British-American relations would alarm other nations. I do not think so; I think political education is too far advanced for such apprehensions to amount to anything appreciable. And anyway we cannot let our affairs drift simply because we may arouse a certain anxiety in others. We should show the world that no matter what others may have in mind we at any rate have turned our backs forever upon war between ourselves.

IV. What I have roughly in mind is that the Canadian-American theory and practice of a bilateral and conciliatory approach to every British-American question shall
have formal and final acceptance as between the whole British world and the United
States of America. In other words, "The North American Method," as Mackenzie
King has called it, shall be universalized in the English-speaking political sphere.

Half-engulfed in the leather of a huge sofa, Premier MacDonald, rather lan-
guid and worn in look, read the memorandum carefully with hard-converging
brows. At the end, his features brightened, and he stood up. There was a noise
of feet and voices below.

"They're arriving," he said, meaning his Cabinet ministers. "Many thanks,"
folding the memorandum and putting it in his coat pocket.

At the foot of the stairway, walking side by side on the yielding carpet, we
were surrounded by the foremost men of British labor, jovially assembling for
council with their chief. MacDonald, laying a strong hand on my shoulder and
looking me in the eyes in the way of a man who wished each word to be noted
unforgettably, said:

"Tell Hoover I am in complete sympathy with him in the matter of reducing armaments and will do everything in my power to attain the end we both
have in view. Tell him I am ready and eager to visit Washington at a moment
mutually deemed auspicious. Tell him I trust him absolutely and want him to
trust me in the same way."

"Mr. Prime Minister," I said, holding his hand, "let nothing keep you from
visiting Washington. Put on your hat and come. Hoover, all Washington, all
America will welcome you with unprecedented warmth, pleasure, and hope. I
don't know what Ambassador Dawes may be counseling in this great matter. But,
whatever he may say, *come*! Dawes, after all, is a technician, not a statesman."

"I will come," said MacDonald, turning from me.

All of which I related to President Hoover at the White House within
twenty-four hours of my landing in New York. He had me to lunch with him,
no one else present, in the dining-room of the presidential home. I felt we
were oddly infinitesimal in our loneliness in that big room. We had a most
excellent luncheon, fit indeed for monarchs. Before we touched the soup, the
President said with what struck me as singular formality:

"Concerning what you have done in Great Britain, I have just one word to
speak. That word is *gratitude*."

And truly he spoke no other. We talked of many aspects of the international situation, but Mr. Hoover gave a wide berth to Dawes and to the enigma

of that "invitation." Did he *ever* send it? Your guess is as good as mine.[4] But we all know the courageous and wise British Premier came. We know the President radioed him the finest of welcomes as he neared our shores. We know the historic meeting amid the blushing sumac on the Rapidan River and the epoch-marking Hoover-MacDonald Declaration of an unbreakable peace in the English-speaking world. We know all America acclaimed the visit and the Declaration, and we know that Declaration holds as firmly today as when it was announced in Washington in October a decade ago. Even General Dawes came round handsomely, publicly affirming that the fruits of the meetings represented "one of the greatest diplomatic feats of history."

I think the General was well within the mark. For the achievement, with its effects all over the world of English-speakers, did not rest in that world. Its lineaments appeared as clear as noonday at Munich in 1939, when Premier Neville Chamberlain of Great Britain, daring as most politicians never will dare, joined with Chancellor Hitler of Nazi Germany in a Declaration of a "British-German War Never Again." Nor does that tell it all. Premier Daladier of France followed in Chamberlain's footsteps along the sharply-defined path of the Hoover-MacDonald Declaration.[5] Daladier and Hitler sealed the bilateral pledge: "A Franco-German War Never Again."

Are those European declarations worthless?

I think they are worth a very great deal. They are emphatically on the right side. If less firm and dependable than the British-American pronouncement, they have far greater meaning and solidity, as I view them, than feather-heads and cynics lightly suppose. Can you see Britain attacking Germany in any situation reasonably conjecturable? Or Germany Britain? Or France Germany? Or Germany France? Such a thing of course is not impossible, but I am persuaded to the point of perfect tranquillity of mind that the youngest of you never will live to see it. Our war-mongers undoubtedly we shall have, and our ever-recurring luridities of the yellow-dog Press, and our congenital croakers and pessimists. We shall have too bilateral wars, frontier conflicts. We shall have

4. Hoover's recollection in his memoir is that he did send an invitation: "My immediate purpose in extending an invitation to Prime Minister MacDonald to visit the United States was of course to settle the remaining questions as to the naval limitations" (Hoover, *Memoirs,* 342).

5. Edouard Daladier was a French Socialist statesman who served three terms as prime minister. The first term was about a month long, the second about nine months, and the third, at the beginning of the Second World War, lasted for two years. His signature on the Munich Pact with Nazi Germany in 1938, along with Neville Chamberlain's of Great Britain, enabled Germany to invade a region of Czechoslovakia without fear of French interference.

little fires to spare, but I cannot think we are likely in our maddest moment to start a big fire in order to put out a little one. I pay governments and peoples that compliment, and my confidence in governments is not too great either.

Was my original idea respecting the British-American difficulty realized fully? In form, no. In essence, yes. I wanted Mackenzie King to sit in at Rapidan and Washington as symbolic of Dominion approval and participation. For one reason or another, he was not called in the flesh; but he and all his Dominion colleagues were there in understanding and determination that the British-American peace movement should not fail through any fault of theirs. Constant intercommunication prevailed between Homeland and Dominions, and MacDonald finally reported to Mackenzie King in Ottawa. From that Ottawa Conference went out the good word to all Britain, and the ideal of bringing the primary statecraft of the whole English-speaking world into conference and agreement for the first time in its long annals was an historical fact.

Of the glad and beautiful honors paid MacDonald and his daughter Ishbel in Washington, I was a journalist observer on the side-lines; no longer a "diplomat," famous or obscure; no longer even a "publicist"; just a practitioner at my old trade of seeking the news. Not one invitation of a social nature came to me from the Administration during the entire visit of our notable British friends. I was "the man who had done it," but who cared? I was ten thousand times more than satisfied. And when, to my great surprise, Sir Esme Howard, British Ambassador, invited me to attend his public reception of the visitors, I was happy to go only to shake hands with them, and to say to MacDonald:

"I'll see you at the Naval Conference in London next year."

32. My Final Interviews for Peace

I went to the Five-Power Naval Conference in 1930[1] and did all I could at my keyboard (little enough undoubtedly) to bring out clearly and positively, in both the British and the American newspapers open to me, the propitious as opposed to the hurtful facts and forces of the great interracial and international meeting to accommodate differing standpoints relative to sea power and to make progress toward the distant goal of armaments reduction and limitation. Japan, let me say at once, strove with all her strength at the conference to bring the British and the Americans together and so to shape her own sea policy. That this success was not gained must be charged not to any one of the foremost sea powers but to Franco-Italian dissonance and other Continental circumstances.

France, one is compelled to say, was the most captious and least helpful power at the conference. Italy, led by Benito Mussolini and Dino Grandi[2] (the latter, 33, the youngest delegate at the conference), was distinctly more flexible and inclined to accommodation than her great Latin sister. France was granite. One understands. She had her memories. She was out of all conceit

1. The purpose of the Five-Power Naval Conference between the United States, Great Britain, Japan, France, and Italy in 1930 was to continue the post–World War I goal of decreasing naval armaments. While the United States, Great Britain, and Japan increased their set allowances for battleships, all five countries agreed to tighten regulations for submarines, aircraft carriers, and their heaviest and most important warships.

2. Dino Grandi was an Italian Fascist who served in Mussolini's government as minister of foreign affairs and later as ambassador to Great Britain. Grandi opposed Italy's involvement in World War II. Although he had helped bring Mussolini to power in 1922, he helped bring about Mussolini's downfall in 1943.

with the acts of the Washington Conference of 1921[3] and had growing naval ambitions. All the time her eyes were on the temporarily prostrate power east of the Rhine. She did not want that power to rise again. She would see to it, navally as well as militarily, that the Teutonic specter were laid to rest for good and all.

One Frenchman at the conference, Aristide Briand the internationalist, had his twinges of conscience and intellect with reference to the hardness and arrogance of France against Germany and to France's comparative indifference to Italian feelings and ideas. The old statesman, as a fact, did not like these things in the least; they figured in his internationally comprehending mind as heavy with trouble in the future. But French opinion and dominant leadership overrode him. Premier Tardieu,[4] who himself came to London to safeguard what he deemed French interests, displayed no grasp of international potentialities, no concern for the European situation which French intransigence probably would produce.

In sharp lines come back to me a dinner and dinner-talk in the main dining-room of the Carlton Hotel one evening when the French attitude was endangering a Five-Power achievement. At the dinner were Premier Tardieu, his lieutenant and secretary, M. Louis Aubert, of the Quay d'Orsay,[5] editor J. L. Garvin of *The Observer,* and myself. In *The Observer* the day before I had had a long article, splashed on the foreign page, sounding an alarm in respect of the conference outlook. The substance of the article was that France appeared to be driving the Five-Power possibility on the rocks. Garvin asked Tardieu if he had read the article.

"Yes," said the Premier curtly.

"What will you say about the burden of it?"

"France must do all she can to make herself secure."

"You think she can hold Germany down indefinitely?" asked Garvin.

"France will take no further risk. *We have the power.*"

Tardieu shrugged his shoulders with an air of such complacence and disdain that the great British editor was nettled.

---

3. The Washington Naval Conference brought nine nations together with the purpose of multilateral agreement for naval disarmament.

4. Andre Tardieu was a three-time French premier who consistently refused to relax post–World War I reparations demands on Germany.

5. The French Ministry of Foreign Affairs is located on the Quai d'Orsay, a street that borders Paris's Seine River. "Quai d'Orsay" can refer to the bank of the river, the street, or the ministry itself.

"You know well, Monsieur Tardieu," he said with barest dash of asperity, "that I and my paper, and our whole Empire likewise, are solicitous that no interest of France shall suffer at this conference or elsewhere. Now I'm bound to tell you neither Britain nor America can go with you in a policy of unremitting enmity to Germany and of European hegemony. As a genuine friend, I entreat you to hold fast to British-American confidence. If you lose it, I can't help saying, you'll lose your international sheet-anchor. I'll go a step further. I give it to you as my deep sense of truth that without British-American support your defenses of whatever sort will be ultimately inadequate to your needs."

M. Tardieu looked over the rim of his champagne glass, smiled, and the talk flowed into a different channel. I had a feeling then, and the feeling hardened into conviction later, that Garvin's plain and sensible words left Tardieu and Aubert utterly cold. These gentlemen played some poker at that conference, though I say so without disparagement; diplomats are appointed to serve their countries as best they can. From American Secretary of State Henry Stimson they tried to extract a gesture which they hoped at the proper moment (if such a moment came) to interpret as a definite commitment of America to take up the cudgels for France.

What they said, in effect, was this:

"Mr. Secretary Stimson, if we reduce and limit our naval armament as you urge we must assume that in the event of such reduction and limitation imperiling our national existence the United States of America will come to our aid effectively."

That suggestion made Mr. Stimson think. One of his great friends in England was Lord Edward Grey of Fallodon. Grey had had a deal of experience of French diplomacy, and of French interpretations of international conversations, and he paid a visit to Stimson's sumptuous drawing-room in the Ritz Hotel overlooking London's Piccadilly Street. He counseled our chief delegate to make himself familiar with the operations of the French diplomatic mind, recalling how the Quay d'Orsay, prior to the Great War, read into "purely tentative and exploratory interchanges of military facts and opinions a formal pledge on Britain's part to send on the instant an expeditionary force to France if Germany attacked Belgium or France or both."

When Mr. Stimson next saw M. Tardieu, he said to the chief French delegate:

"You are asking us explicitly for the assurance, in circumstances not yet foreseeable, of a *quid pro quo*. We can enter into no such contract, however tacit and vague and nonstatutory it might be. Our bedrock international principle is that of non-entanglement and entire freedom to meet every specific international crisis as it arises. What France or any other power does at this conference, or any conference, must be done, so far as America is concerned, *unconditionally*."

Right there the Five-Power naval project passed from the 1930 picture.

I broadcast these facts from London (my first and only over-the-Atlantic talk) and returned to Chicago to renew my work as a columnist, interviewer, and lecturer. My forty-one-year association with the *Daily News* (eight years as a country correspondent and feature writer and thirty-three years as a staff man) had reached the lengthening shadows. Victor Fremont Lawson and Walter A. Strong, with their life-long traditions and ideas and ideals, were dead. We had a new management with notions and purposes of its own.[6] The time clearly seemed to have come for the removal of my provocative features from the editorial page of the *Daily News* and for my own removal into the aroma of the pines, where the sunsets make merry with art, where the wildflowers are as varied and shy as they are beautiful, and where the silence yields hardly ever except to music. But I did do one more foreign assignment for the new fashioners of the newspaper which a lone man, Victor Lawson, had made great: I reported *a là* side-light the politico-economic-financial crisis in England in the fall of 1931, when my old friend Ramsay MacDonald, Socialist-Labor, was made Premier in a Conservative national government.

Retirement then for a time, I thought for all time. But the blood of a journalist is mercurial. World events will not let one alone in one's solitude. Just how it chanced I scarcely know, but on a summer-like morning in April, 1934, I found myself in a Pullman car bound for New York with a document in my pocket: a memorandum describing how I believed the world's Press might be mobilized for peace. It was in reality an expansion to inter-continental proportions of my scheme for setting British-American affairs in order. I proposed to interview all the principal premiers and foreign ministers of the world on the question: "What is *your* magician's wand for waving evil out and good in as regards humanity's common welfare?"

New York's editors, but for one man, were unknown to me or nearly so. This one man was Arthur Draper, editor of the *Literary Digest*. Long before, he had been a colleague of mine in London, succeeding my veteran pal I. N. Ford, London correspondent of the *New York Herald-Tribune;* and later he had been assistant editor of that great daily. I went to his office not to try to sell him my dream but to explain it to him and to ask his opinion as to what New York

---

6. Colonel Frank Knox bought the *Daily News* in 1931. For this change, see pp. xxxv–xxxvii.

editor might be interested in it. Arthur took my memorandum, smoked his pipe almost as industriously as Stanley Baldwin or Charlie Dawes, and read with care all I had set down. Then eyeing me humorously (as I felt) through the smoke, he said:

"Ed, you speak of mobilizing the Press of the world. That's a mouthful. How'll that happen?"

"It'll happen, I hope, because the proposed interviews will be so interesting and important that virtually all newspapers, and other publications of news and opinion, will give greater or less attention to them. The various standpoints and arguments, in other words, ought to see the light in some form and to some extent in all the literary languages. Would that not be, essentially, a mobilization of the Press of the world for international understanding and its correlative, peace?"

Draper smiled and smoked.

"Is there in New York," I insisted, "an editor who would take any stock in my idea?"

"Why not let *us* have it?" asked the editor.

I indeed was surprised; I did not have a magazine in mind at all; I was a newspaperman through and through. But I was nonetheless delighted, and particularly so because my scheme commended itself to a man whom I long had known and for whose native appreciation of what struck me as the finest journalism I had the greatest admiration. So I pitted such talent and experience as I had against the big round world for the *Literary Digest*. I was a solid year on the task, spent a lot of money, traveled 39,000 miles, interviewed all the premiers and foreign ministers of the chief powers except Russia (Josef Stalin would not pledge himself in advance to talk for publication, and I omitted Moscow from my itinerary) and also the Supreme Pontiff of Rome, Pius XI, introduced to his Holiness by the great Prelate who now holds his exalted and most important place, Pius XII.

Once more (April, 1935) among the pines and the colors and the melodies of the Mississippi Coast, I asked myself:

"Did I do it? Did I mobilize the Press of the world? Did the interview, a great series certainly, have any molding effect whatever on world events?"

No answer comes readily to me. Arthur Draper was the soul of kindness and fraternal encouragement all through the long-drawn ordeal (and ordeal it was) and after. He wrote me a letter at the conclusion praising the work in the highest terms and declaring that the results "far exceeded" his "first-blush expectations." Reproductions of the interviews in part appeared in many languages, scores of editorials were written about them, countless letters reached the *Digest* and myself commenting upon and eulogizing them, and there could be no doubt they had released moral and intellectual forces (the men interviewed were great men, mind you) which had stirred world emotion and opinion as these rarely are stirred by any such influences.

But does history, does human evolution, have any heed for such things? Does it care in the least what vocalisms ripple round the world from any source or through any medium? I wonder. I dare not so much as guess. I know the human mind cannot measure the influence of intangibilities bearing upon political and social progress. And I think I know this: if thinkers and policy-makers throw themselves athwart the road of natural world advance, the developments inherent in human necessity, they will be crushed or brushed remorselessly aside. The very first thing for would-be world ameliators to realize, in my judgment, is that the laws of the unfolding of man on this planet (his moral, mental, and physical unfolding) are inexorable. If you want peace, do not block the road which nations needs must follow.

"Good sense is the sole remedy for war," Premier Ramsay MacDonald told me. "And good sense means more frequent and closer interracial and international consultation, more candor, a fuller revelation of realities (things irreducible), great forbearance, better tempers, increased readiness to weigh and to respect one another's susceptibilities and necessities. We've too much ogre-superstition now."

In like vein spoke Foreign Minister Sir John Simon[7] as I talked with him in his quiet, beautiful, memory-steeped room at the west end of Downing Street above St. James's Park. Like MacDonald, he set great store by the League of Nations and said the one thing which more than any other operated as a stabilizer of world peace was "Anglo-Saxon solidarity."

On to Paris, early in 1935, and to interviews with Pierre-Etienne Flandin and Pierre Laval[8] (respectively Premier and Foreign Minister), with both of whom

---

7. John Allsebrook Simon was Britain's foreign secretary from 1931 to 1935. Simon supported Prime Minister Neville Chamberlain's policy of appeasement toward Hitler and Nazi Germany in the 1930s.

8. Pierre-Etienne Flandin was a Conservative French statesman who was premier in late 1934 and early 1935. Pierre Laval was a French statesman who served as foreign minister and premier in the years leading up to World War II. During the war, Laval became convinced that Germany would emerge the victor. He led the Vichy government to corroborate with Germany, hoping to secure France a prominent place in Europe's future. Laval was accused of treason and executed in 1945.

naturally enough the watchword of watchwords was, "Vive la République!" But each was strong for international understanding and peace. Premier Flandin, I thought, voiced a sort of international Sermon on the Mount in these passages:

"'Peace' is an expansive term. Civilization organized to safeguard frontiers against war-makers is only the first step. After that, social, economic, and monetary peace; an intelligent and friendly international social atmosphere; economic reciprocity according to Cordell Hull;[9] international monetary stabilization; artificial meddling of every sort in the natural course of world economic development renounced: that's the prerequisite of enmities neutralized, unemployment drastically reduced, prosperity restored, and peace made secure because just."

On to Rome to Palazzo Venezia, for the view of Premier Mussolini, and to the Vatican, for Pope Pius XI. "I will not break the peace of civilization." Signor Mussolini, speaking to me at his desk in his vast room in the slow English which had become his since I first talked with him (1924), said that. And he repeated it twice as the interview progressed. "And," someone says truly, "in a little while his Fascist legions were battering Ethiopian independence to dust."[10] "Yes," Il Duce and his Fascist nation will reply. "But peace with Ethiopia was not *the peace of civilization*. In warring upon refractory and insufferable savagery, and in establishing for Italy an outlet for her genius and people in Northeast Africa, we were extending the boundaries of civilization and conferring a boon upon mankind, not excluding the Ethiopians themselves."

Take it or leave it, that is the Italian attitude, and behind the attitude is the armed might of a great nation morally and materially re-born. Mussolini said to me: "We must expand. We've an indefeasible right to expand, the same right others before us have had. We have indeed a national and international duty to expand, for this earth belongs to the best, not the worst, to be found in it. *Civilization cannot be arrested*. Savagery and barbarism have no right to exist. Let us alone, and we'll settle peacefully with Ethiopia; our expansion will be accepted as good for the Ethiopians as well as for ourselves and others. Encourage the Ethiopians to mount a high horse, and there may be war."

9. Cordell Hull is still remembered today for his principle of economic reciprocity, whereby nations agree bilaterally or multilaterally to lower tariffs on imports, increasing trade between the countries to mutual benefit. Hull's principles and ideas about free trade were the basis for the Reciprocal Trade Act of 1934.

10. The reference here is to the Italian-Ethiopian War of 1935–1936, in which Italy invaded Ethiopia. Benito Mussolini claimed Italy had a right to build an empire, similar to Britain and France, which also held colonies in Africa.

Trouble on a world scale I do not think it will bring. Mussolini does not want war. Hitler does not. Japan certainly is abundantly preoccupied with her principle of Japanese primacy in the Far East. We all know Britain and France, despite their "encircling" policy (which is not an encircling policy for anything but defense), want peace; Chamberlain's behavior, culminating in Munich and the Daladier-Hitler Declaration, is the most splendid performance for peace which blazes across the general darkness of diplomacy since the Great War. Hitler knows Chamberlain wants peace, and Mussolini knows it. It is for this reason that any warlike outbreak against the "encircling" policy is most unlikely. Central Europe is saner and more realistic today than it was in 1914. But let negotiation not move too lamely! Hitler and Mussolini, both soldiers who know what shrapnel and mustard gas mean, are mortal. Will their successors esteem peace as they esteem it?

And Russia? Does Josef Stalin want war? I think not. Complications for him on a European battlefield would make him frightfully anxious about possibilities along the Amur River.[11] I think he will play his cards cautiously. Eager he may be to see the breakers of Soviet ideology rolling over the "capitalist" world; have we not high and very recent authority for supposing America wants the breakers of *her* conception of political economy to roll over the "dictatorial" world? But one scarcely can believe we shall try to universalize our theories by *force*. No more, in my view, will Stalin try to blanket the world with Bolshevism by force.

Sitting at the feet of Pope Pius XI, who was old, ruddy, full of life and the fascination of an all-embracing humanity, I had strange reflective feelings. We were in Vatican City, in the Vatican itself, in its Consistorial Hall. The Pope, commanding and at ease in a high chair on a dais at the east end of the hall, was in white gown and skull-cap and ermine-trimmed scarlet cape. His emerald ring was on the third finger of the right hand. He smiled through circular rimless spectacles, a shade of deep concern occasionally showing in his face. I thought: "Millions upon millions of people hang upon this man's words. His personal authority is without parallel in Christendom. And yet here sit I, a man of the secular Press, privileged to listen to his Holiness and to transmit his message to the world!" What a span of life and change broke before me! Far back yonder, I saw a sun-browned farm boy in Indiana on the bank of the old Raccoon River holding converse with the ripples. And here was the same

11. The Amur River forms a natural border between the Russian Far East and Manchuria in China.

boy, in full evening dress on a fine Sunday morning in Consistorial Hall, the Vatican, hearing the words of the Pope!

What was his message? *"Join charity to justice; even make charity prevail over justice."* That was his admonition to the sovereigns of economics. And that is the admonition also of Pius XII. In both men individualism Christianized is the fundamental ideal.

On to the Wilhelmstrasse, Berlin, and a long talk with Adolf Hitler in company with Dr. Hans Thomsen, interpreter, now charge d'affaires of the German Embassy in Washington. "They who say I want war lie!" It issued from Hitler's lips almost like lava. "We're *anti*-imperialistic in an imperialistic world. Grasp that!" "Colonies, economic equality, of course we want them. We're told they're no good to anyone. Then why do the colossal empires hug them so tightly? Economic equality among the great manufacturing and trading nations is heavy with the fate of peace. Nazi politics has much to ask, political and territorial, but will ask nothing unjust and will look to negotiation, not war, for the fulfillment of its inescapable duties to the German race and nation. My advice is: 'Fit negotiation with nimble feet.' Negotiation hitherto not only has dallied fatally but has reversed the current of good-fellowship and wisdom."

Those words Adolf Hitler spoke to me in the spring of 1935. I was convinced then, and I am convinced yet, that he was sincere. I so wrote to *The Times* (London) a few days later, and my letter was published conspicuously under the heading, "A Plea for Sympathy." I have had no reason to regret that letter; and many level-headed Englishmen, Lord Lothian[12] among them, after inquiries of their own in Germany, including heart-to-heart talks with Herr Hitler, reached similar conclusions and stated their views *in extenso* in *The Times*.

Very weighty indeed was the body of British opinion which appreciated Germany's post-Versailles position and held that concessions to her were essential to European peace. But this opinion, important as it was and persuasively as it found public utterance, failed to hasten negotiation sufficiently to forestall German action on her eastern frontier inimical to peace. What was deemed ruthless Hitlerian aggression (and, more, a dark-looming menace to the British and French Empires) blew up such a fury of popular resentment in Britain and France that pacific statesmanship became a pitiful derelict in the storm.

---

12. Philip Kerr, Marquess of Lothian, was Prime Minister David Lloyd George's private secretary during World War I and was active in the peace conference after the war.

33. War Again after Twenty Years

Britain's declaration of war on the Central Powers in 1914 found me in my London office at the head of the Special Foreign News Service of the *Chicago Daily News*. Adolf Hitler's Reichstag speech announcing his irrevocable purpose to move against Poland found me at the approach of day at my radio on the Mississippi Coast. In London I moved swiftly to throw our great staff into the most difficult and dangerous and momentous task history ever had assigned to newspaper men. In Mississippi I rose from my radio and said to my wife:

"Peace-seeking and peace hopes, I fear, are somewhat ironic again."

"Well," was the reply, "if Europe is going to fight again America must be neutral."

Hitler having done what his speech portended, and Britain and France having declared war upon Germany, I set myself to do what little might lie in me for the principle of American neutrality not only in the British-French-German-Polish war but in every future foreign war whatsoever. The new war seemed to me merely a resumption of the World War of painful retrospect. And I could foresee no end of war until a radical change should come over the minds of the world's dominant men.

My heart as well as what brain I had was with the Allies in 1914–1918. I thought they were fighting with clean hands defensively. I knew of not one word to be said for the Central Powers, more especially Germany. I saw the struggle as indubitably one of autocracy bent upon conquest against democracy resolute to live. This was my view long before German ruthlessness brought America into the war. So one-sided and implacable was I that I very nearly lost my job and got within a hair's-breadth of assassination. I was a "paid minion of the British." I cannot tell you how many foreign governments have bought me up at one time or another!

Ignorance was my trouble. I had not traveled enough. I had not studied the pertinent and vital points of view with adequate care and impartiality. I had seen British and French diplomacy forging a ring of steel round Germany and Austria-Hungary, but I knew it was not for aggression. I knew, or thought I knew, it was solely and purely to safeguard the great nations of the ring against a very formidable and a very wicked enemy. Time and reflection, aided by travel and inquiry, convinced me that the Central Powers really had become alarmed for *their* security, not to mention their legitimate world aspirations, and had struck, as they believed, for what was not only right but holy.

No historian of recognized worth today, I think, will say that the war-guilt of a quarter of a century ago was exclusively on one side. Even French historians hardly will say that. And the time for the balanced point of view respecting the present war well might be considered now rather than two or three decades later. I at all events see two distinct sides to the case. I see Germany fighting against what she looks upon as an intolerable *status quo,* and I see Britain and France resisting her as a treaty-breaker and a would-be destroyer of other sovereignties and of the individual liberty which long has been the objective of Anglo-Saxon and of Gallic civilization. Thus confronted abroad, our proper course, in my judgment, is neither to buttress those who are fighting a *status quo* war nor to align ourselves with their opponents.

Faithlessness to his word is the gravamen of British and French statesmen when they oppose any negotiated agreement with Adolf Hitler as the chief of the German state. Germans are angered profoundly by this charge. Their retort is that pledge-breaking after the Great War began not with the conquered but with the conquerors; that it was born in the deliberate and sustained failure of the Allies to fulfil their self-assumed obligation to follow Germany on the way to her enforced disarmament. And the Germans renounce fierily the whole idea of the binding nature of their signature on the Treaty of Versailles, a signature obtained at the point of the bayonet.

On this point, for many years, the cogency of the German argument has been acknowledged in Great Britain by both newspapers and men of high public standing. *The Times* of London (April 18, 1935), for example, indignantly deplored the treatment of the German delegates at Versailles: "The facts of the conclusion of the Treaty of Versailles, however little that are remembered by most governments today, are not only familiar to Germans but burnt into their minds. Hitlerism is largely a revolt against Versailles; and until this fundamental truth is taken fully into account there will be no real peace in Europe."

It was not "taken fully into account," and there is "no real peace in Europe." Instead there is a *status quo war*. And there will be another, another, and yet another until the *status quo* answers to the principle of a square deal politically and economically for all the Great Powers. Whoever may win this time, there will be no victory for settled peace unless the new peace treaty recognizes inalienable rights alike for the so-called victors and for the so-called vanquished. Races and nations virile and self-respecting will live peaceably in no steel jacket "made abroad."

Actuated by President Roosevelt's broadcast,[1] still ringing in my ears, I wired him at the White House on September 8, 1939:

> Every sane American, I think, has heard with satisfaction your "assurance and reassurance" that you will do all in your power to safeguard American neutrality in Europe's latest war. To "destroy Hitlerism," we hear officially, is the purpose of Britain and France. Precisely. That was their real purpose when they declared war on Germany. Not Poland but their own world hegemony moved them primarily. *Tout comprendre c'est tout pardonner* is imperishably true. With malice toward none, with charity for all, let us keep our neutrality effectual and impregnable against whatever may assail it: pretension, argument, flattery, bullying.

That was the opening gun in my own poor little fight for American neutrality, at least so far as high-ranking leaders were concerned. I followed it at once with appeals to Secretary of State Cordell Hull[2] to uphold afresh and forcibly the neutrality principles to which he already was committed. Similarly I addressed Herbert Hoover and a score of United States senators and representatives along with numerous Americans distinguished in religion, scholarship, literature, business, and journalism. True, I could speak for myself only; the objects of my urgency may have put me down as an amazing egotist and busybody. If so, *voilà*! These importunities were meant in no spirit of forward-

1. Bell is probably referring to Franklin Roosevelt's September 3, 1939, radio broadcast after Germany invaded Poland, in which Roosevelt assured listeners that America would remain neutral, although he could not "ask that every American remain neutral in thought."

2. Cordell Hull, mentioned earlier for his principle of economic reciprocity, was U.S. secretary of state from 1933 to 1944. Hull was a proponent of international trade and worked to build friendship between the United States and Latin America, as well as China. He won the Nobel Peace Prize for his involvement in engineering the United Nations. After the outbreak of World War II, Hull sided with President Franklin Delano Roosevelt in believing that the United States could not long remain neutral and must side with the Allies.

ness; only in a spirit of patriotism at a time of manifest national danger. An American, however mean, is reckoned a democrat; sometimes I almost think he is one. Well, is there much difference between a *mute* democrat and a *dead* democrat?

To all these leaders, "in order to make the Monroe Doctrine[3] a logical and symmetrical whole," I suggested the formal declaration by the President of the United States of the following addenda as Indestructible Principles of American Foreign and Domestic policy:

> 1. We shall stand invincibly against embroilment in any foreign war. If men abroad elect to fight, they must fight without us. We shall hallow our resources of every kind to peace.
> 2. We shall prepare to the limit of our power to defend the Western Hemisphere against either war from without or any foreign intervention fraught, as we think, with the threat of such a war.

And I went on to argue the proposition:

> So long as the Monroe Doctrine stops where it stops now, the peace of the Americas (the core-ideal of the doctrine) is not secure. The United States particularly is in constant jeopardy of involvement when great nations go to war. Such nations go to war, if and when they feel they must, with keen and hopeful eyes upon America, upon the possibility of drawing her in, upon her vast emporium of the things men need when they fight. Let us say to them in advance: "No! We will not help you in any way to submerge humanity with grief and disaster." And let this message to them all be unmistakably implicit in *what we have done:* "Our Principles of Peace are backed by our utmost defensive strength. Call us yellow if you like; you have had some practice at that. *But keep your hands off us!*"

To Senator Arthur H. Vandenberg,[4] in Washington for the special session of the Congress to deal with our Neutrality law, I sent the following telegram on September 19, 1939:

---

3. The Monroe Doctrine was a bedrock principle of U.S. foreign policy, proclaimed by President James Monroe in 1823. Its purpose was to keep Europe out of the affairs of the Western Hemisphere and the United States out of the affairs of Europe.

4. Arthur Vandenberg was a Republican U.S. senator from 1928 until his death in 1951. Vandenberg, whose primary interest was foreign relations, was an isolationist and critic of President Franklin Delano Roosevelt's foreign policy. His views came closer in line with Roosevelt's, however, after Japan attacked Pearl Harbor in December of 1941.

As you suggested in your Grand Rapids speech, our Neutrality Code was fair notice to the world. Roosevelt, however, by his berating of certain foreign leaders and systems and his fight for a revision of the Code, led Britain and France to expect an American neutrality which would favor the maritime Powers. Nevertheless, I believe the best character and thought of America are for the retention of the war with the implements of mass slaughter, and no man can tell what the Nemesis of that policy may be.

On the next day (September 20) I filed this telegram to President Roosevelt:

You had an opportunity to lead this country away from the immemorial abomination of the manufacture for profit of the means of the mass slaughter of the world's youth. That leadership would have given you immortality. Such leadership will appear just as certainly as civilization endures and evolves. As an American, I wish it might come to us. But I long for it to come, and to come quickly, no matter what race or nation or individual may have the incomparable distinction.

Two days later (on September 22) I resumed action with the following dispatch to Stephen Fowler Chadwick, then commander of the American Legion assembling in Chicago:

Respectfully submit for your consideration apropos of your National Convention that President Roosevelt's neutrality speech is fatally defective. Its standpoint is quintessentially unneutral. Effectively, it names the aggressor in this war and marks that alleged aggressor as America's potential enemy. Is that neutral? Is it not a categoric abnegation of neutrality? This war's embryo was placed in the Versailles Treaty, and that Treaty was not made by Germany. This is a *status quo* war, and in no instance has the President recognized the slightest validity in the point of view of the Revisionist Powers. He has stood stoutly and outstandingly with those whom Lord Lothian has called "the beneficiaries of Versailles" and of whom he has said (in no less a newspaper than the London *Times*) "they have behaved none too well." In the World War the Allies were out to crush Kaiserism. They crushed, with our vital aid, the Old Germany and incubated this war. Now they say they are out to crush Hitlerism. If they succeed they will crush the New Germany and incubate another war. World peace never will be safe till the *status quo* exemplifies the principle of the approximate political and economic equality of the Great Powers. And President Roosevelt throws no light on the road to that goal.

Presuming upon services I had tried to render to the cause of British-American friendship and cooperation, and also upon old personal associations and affections, I decided early in October to approach Britons about the war, my first initiative in that direction. On October 4 I cabled as follows to J. L. Garvin, editorial chief of the *London Observer*, whom I esteem the greatest newspaper writer in the world today:

> If peace were made now (Hitler and Stalin had established their armed arbitrament in the Near East and were proposing a truce and an international conference), and faithlessness to it issued in an attack upon Britain and France, nothing could keep America out, just as nothing in existing circumstances can draw her in. Urge that every care be taken not to break the defensive solidarity of the democracies. This solidarity I consider in great jeopardy at the moment.

On the same day (October 4) I wrote to Lord Lothian at the British Embassy in Washington:

> It gives me the keenest pleasure to risk expecting that Britain and France will go just as far as they feel honor and safety will allow to negotiate a stoppage of hostilities in the hope of reaching a settled peace without further bloodshed. If they do this, and if the trust they place in the enemy prove misplaced, America's attitude to the new situation will be very different from its attitude to the existing situation. Overwhelmingly, Americans are determined to stay out of this war. They are determined indeed to stay out of all foreign wars. But if any Power or coalition of Powers directly attacked Britain and France, with what seemed clearly to be purposes of world conquest, I have not the slightest doubt this country would say, virtually as one man, "This is not, from the American point of view, a foreign war." It would be just as hard, in other words, to keep us out of that war as it is to get us into this one.

I also sent a few lines to Lloyd George and to Colonel Robert R. McCormick, editor of the *Chicago Tribune*. The Colonel kindly admitted to his editorial page a brief statement of my notion of a useful extension of the Monroe Doctrine. That statement swelled my mail quite a lot, some correspondents approving, some criticizing sharply what they supposed was "lack of sympathy with the Allies." Admitted again to the editorial page of the *Tribune*, I explained that my sympathies were with "all peoples under the blight and misery of war."

Now if an honest and an effectual neutrality in foreign wars is to be an indestructible principle of American policy (a principle as fundamental as anything we have in the Constitution, the Declaration of Independence, or the Monroe Doctrine), how can we best fortify it? By not suffering ourselves to be misled in international quarrels by any sort of propaganda or *ex parteism*. We must not list in these heavy seas. We must do our own steering and do it on an even keel. We must not be frightened into paroxysms and choking sensations by a cry from any crow's-nest, *"Periscope!"*

We lately have had such cries in over-plenty. And they have not reached us from foreign observation posts only. These cries, whether from foreign or from domestic sources, have embodied a common purpose, to break down our will to neutrality and lead us on political and military wild-goose chases unspeakably dangerous not only to our liberty but to every natural immunity and every paramount interest we have as individuals and as a nation.

Epilogue
Where Are Our Plans Built?

Finally, I presume, I should touch in philosophic vein upon the profession of my choice. Certainly I am among the old-timers of the trade, bearing the marks of about all its activities from reportorial work on bare-knuckle prizefights to ponderings on problems of politics and economics in a world still far from equal to their rational solution.

Then what of it?

Well, if my brother Will and I once more were casting our horoscopes as we cast them more than sixty years ago on a moonlit night in Indiana I suspect he would stand where he stood at that time, for surgery. I know I should reaffirm my choice of journalism. Not that it rejoices me in all its aspects. It has, as practiced, its odious faults.

But it is a grand game if you play it right. Played right, it is grand for you, grand for everyone; big and liberal enough for all emotions, talents, interests; all shades of political, literary, historical, and philosophical opinion. And it serves only one master: the *people,* whose labor and money enable it to exist. No special interest, however rich and strong, can sway newspapers at their best. Editorial and news columns alike in such journals belong to the commonwealth.

Not all newspapers unhappily are always, or even usually, at the peak of journalistic idealism. I speak of the great journalism. The vision of it was seen and cherished by such pioneers of the profession as Victor Fremont Lawson of the United States and Charles Prestwich Scott of England, the first the founder, builder, and autocrat of the *Chicago Daily News,* the second the serene, broad, handsome, honest, fair, and unflinching genius of the *Manchester Guardian.* If journalism had no other glory than the tradition of these two exponents of it, it would be in that respect not too badly off. Very brightly shine these personalities against some men and some things in the world of newspapering!

Fanaticisms were unknown to Lawson and Scott. They were not haters of persons who differed from them or did what they deplored; they were students of such persons and such acts. They strove to serve the public. Neither of them, as I have most excellent reason to know, ever sent a reporter on his way at home or abroad with any instructions except to seek the truth and to tell it, never remembering for a moment that the home office *had* a point of view.

That is what I call journalism worthy of the name.

For my own part, my long association at close quarters with newspaper publishers, editors, and writers is all but wholly free from unpleasant recollection. Only once in nearly sixty years of daily journalism, and this very late in my experience, did a superior suggest that I color the news.[1] And on only one occasion, in all that time and in so many different situations throughout the world, a colleague acted dishonorably with me.

To do justice to the man above me who ordered a coloring of the news to suit his point of view, I must say this: Quick as thought, he was ashamed of himself. "Mind you," he said sharply (accusing as he excused), "nobody more than I hates propaganda in a newspaper. But—." I went on his assignment. I did *not* color the news.

The scoundrelly act by a colleague was done in the flooded gun-room where nine of us lived and wrote on the battleship *Utah* as we returned from the Hoover Latin-American Tour. A long radiogram was stolen from my bag. I reported the theft to George Barr Baker, who handled the correspondents' copy on the ship. After a search, Baker said to me: "You'd not believe me if I told you who stole your story." I asked him to keep the secret and he has it yet.

On meditative review, may I ask:

"Did my work have any lasting effect upon leaders or events?"

If it did, it had that effect, I am sure, purely because it chanced to move with the unsearchable force of history. This force, call it what you will, seems

---

1. Although we cannot know for sure to whom Bell is referring here, there is good reason to suspect it is Frank Knox, owner and publisher of the *Daily News* after Walter Strong. First, Bell says this event occurred late in his career, which points to Knox. Second, he says the man was a superior, and during the later stage of Bell's career, he had few superiors save the publisher and editor-in-chief. Third, Bell writes earlier in this memoir that neither Lawson nor Dennis ever asked him to color the news. Whether the statement that Knox asked him to color the news (if indeed the reference is to Knox) is true or merely a result of Bell's disillusionment with having to cut ties with the *Daily News* during Knox's tenure is, of course, difficult to know.

to me to brook no interference. Some have called it "blind." On the contrary, it is, I think, the only thing in our universe that *sees*. Japanese Premier Okada Keisuke (by no means a mysticist) said to me in Tokyo: "We are going some place." Aye; and all our ignorance and folly, I conjecture, cannot keep us from getting there!

Only a little while ago, immediately before I saw the dreams of European peace fade again as they so often have faded through the centuries, I went back to the gorgeous sands of Dymchurch, England, where my kiddies used to build thatched cottages, castles, fortresses, and moats for the tides to reduce to the level from which they came. It was the same beautiful and sweetly tranquil place of the old days; the holiday world where the Italian anarchist Malatesta (moved, I suppose, by the daemon of destruction within him) jumped with his hard bare heels upon a fortress the children had made and caused a domestic commotion of the most painful kind.

As I sat again viewing those wide and wonderful sands and the white-capped waters sparkling beyond, I ran back in mind over what I had tried to do for world peace. Particularly I recalled those things which prompted two great universities, Northwestern and the University of Chicago, following a recommendation of J. L. Garvin of England, to propose my name statutorily for the Nobel Peace Prize for 1929, the MacDonald-Hoover year, the year of the declaration in Washington of an unbreakable British-American *rapprochement*. Then, in imagination, I saw the war-clouds ever-thickening about Europe.

I wrote:

> My plans are built on a shelving beach
> By the hands of a boy grown gray;
> By the soundless wash of a waveless tide
> They are broken and borne away.

THE END

Appendix
"What, in Your Opinion, Is the Matter with the Service?"

The struggle to decide how to run the *Chicago Daily News* foreign service and cover foreign news was ceaseless. Changing personalities and circumstances, as well as the vagaries of the news itself, were always in play. Below are two letters, by Bell and Paul Scott Mowrer, that illustrate this. They both are in the Edward Price Bell Papers at the Newberry Library. Many more like them can be found in the papers of the *Daily News* and of its staff.

Letter No. 1
August 28, 1918

Dear Mr. Dennis,

Perhaps you will allow me to put your recent letter relative to our work abroad into this form: "What, in your opinion, is the matter with the service?"

All things considered, I really regard the service as "carrying on" pretty well. Of course, nearly everyone among us is "fed up" with the war, and consequently far less keen than we were in writing about it. Doubtless, as you intimate, some new blood in the foreign field would help. I ought to have an assistant in London. I wish you or Mr. Lawson would talk with [James] Keeley on this point. He has got well into the situation here. One or two fresh writers of the solid sort would strengthen us immensely in France. As regards Switzerland, Holland and such places we never shall get a decent service out of them until we put our own men on the job. Our long experience has proved this to the hilt and I have written to this effect on many previous occasions. I hope you will succeed in returning [Louis Edgar] Browne to Russia. Obviously we need a vigorous level-headed man there more than in any other part of the theater of war.

These general observations I would offer:

I. We need a more effectual devolution of authority. Our executive is in a semi-paralytic state and the fact is reflected more or less seriously throughout the service. Our men have come to look upon Mr. Lawson as the only real source of authority in our service. This makes them less responsive than they ought to be either to what you say or to what I say. In such circumstances men inevitably tend to await the voice of the master. If Mr. Lawson, happily, were in good health and always at the office, he could transmit his authority quickly and effectively. Unfortunately this has not been the case invariably and we have suffered more or less as a consequence. Ours is the only service I know of that has lacked strong executive authority in Europe. Neef, Chamberlain, Ford, Vandercook—all were supreme over their European men. Their authority was definite and their responsibility definite. It goes without saying that responsibility cannot be placed rightly upon those from whom authority is withheld. At this moment the London heads of American services have the power they need to give instant effect to their wills.

II. We need, and very greatly need, periodic visits from our chiefs at home—yourself or Mr. Lawson. Every other service has the benefit of such visits. On no account should the interval between them be longer than two years; they *should* take place yearly. I can think of nothing else at this moment that would do us all so much good, and so powerfully stimulate the service, as would an intimate visit from yourself. (I assume that Mr. Lawson would not feel able to undertake the journey.)

III. Your London man should personally confer with all our main correspondents at least twice a year. Nobody really can keep tab on the service without visiting the men regularly and closely inquiring into what they are doing and what is their reputation in their several capitals. In no other way can one either understand their difficulties or estimate their opportunities. I never have known an organization of any kind that would run itself or that could be run altogether satisfactorily by means solely of letters and telegrams. The personal touch, with all it means, is absolutely essential to the best results. In this respect also we have been at a disadvantage as compared with other services. These visits are advisable not only from the point of view of a service of uniform life and strength but in order that due check may be had upon expenditure. We should know whether our men are spending the paper's money wisely or not.

In conclusion I will say this: If Mr. Lawson will devolve upon you the necessary authority to command proper respect from our men, and will agree to the scheme of visits I have suggested, I shall be willing to guarantee that the service will be almost doubled in respect of constant value. In suggesting your coming regularly to Europe and the London man going regularly among the men of the service I do not forget our old plan of triennial visits to the home office. I think these should take place. By this system we could maintain an organism full of life and force and moving sharply on the lines of our known interests.

I have read Paul Mowrer's long letters to you?[sic] They seem to me erratic, contradictory, almost incoherent. Clearly, he needs a break with his arduous war duties. This war has killed a lot of men who never have seen a battlefield. Paul's idea of doing most of the first-rate assignments in France himself and still being the active executive head in Paris strikes me as bordering on lunacy. My recommendations regarding the service in France (dispatched to you at length early in the present year) I adhere to still. But Paul either should give up the idea of chiefship in France or should give up the notion of going away on long assignments. His proposal suggests that of a news editor who aspires to do most of the star reporting while leaving the rest of the staff to shift for itself.

With every friendly sentiment, I am,

Yours sincerely,

E. P. Bell (signed)

Charles Henry Dennis, Esq.

Letter No. 2

SUGGESTIONS FOR REORGANIZING THE FOREIGN SERVICE

Paris, May 6th, 1920

In view of the present confusion in the minds of our foreign correspondents as to what they should send, I venture to submit the following suggestions, which are the result of years of study and experience, and of much careful thought:

1. There is no reason why complete harmony between Europe and Chicago should not prevail as to the amount of cable transmitted. Chicago should keep

London, our head foreign office, constantly informed of the fluctuations of space available for the European service. London should allot this space to our various offices according to its judgment, varying the allotment to suit circumstances. This is perfectly practical, as there is far more material available than can be printed, and for the correspondent the question is simply one of selection and compression. Of course under exceptional circumstances, exceptional quantities may be filed, but ordinarily there is no reason why the daily European service should run over the limits set.

2. The basic aim of our service should be to inform the American people regarding all important *social, political, economic* and psychological developments in Europe.

    a. The United States is governed by public opinion. If public opinion is to conduct our foreign affairs wisely, it must be rightly informed, by expert observers. This responsibility should be accepted by leading newspapers.

    b. The Daily News, to remain true to its ideal of serving the public interest, ought to undertake to supply the American public with careful, serious information. The community, as I was able to observe when in America, is hungering for such service. Note the development of serious weeklies, and the growing circulation of the Literary Digest.

    c. In giving this kind of a service, The Daily News will perhaps interest only such readers as are public spirited; but these are perhaps more numerous than is generally imagined. It is, I believe, an illusion to hope that any foreign service can reach *everybody*. It is better to give a first-class service to those who can appreciate it than to aim to please all, and succeed in pleasing none. Nevertheless, the prestige which would be gradually acquired by a fine service would doubtless suffice to win many supplementary readers who are content to follow the leadership of others.

3. What are the modalities of such a service? The relation of events, of simple "news," is monopolized by the three big American agencies, with whom we are in no way organized to compete. Indirect relation, by interviews with European personalities, has many inconveniences. The agencies can obtain such interviews with much greater facility than we, because the person interviewed is flattered by the thought that through the agencies he will reach every part of the United States. Again, such interviews are apt to be mere propaganda, and not to give the essential facts to which the American people have a right. Our service should of course aim at interviews from time to time, as the occasion presents itself. But the three questions which I imagine the public-spirited

American reader wants answered, and which we are better equipped to answer than anyone else, are:

  a. What are the essential facts of the situation?

  b. What is the relative importance of these facts?

  c. What does the correspondent, who is trained, who is on the spot, think of the situation?

Only by a service which answers these questions can we obtain, in my opinion, the full value of our experienced, highly-trained men, for this is work which none but a highly trained, experienced man can do.

4. When any event of world-wide interest occurs, we should immediately get an eye-witness to the spot, to write descriptive matter, and generally "cover" the story. The London office should exercise an immediate initiative in such matters, in order that no time should be lost.

5. Finally, by way of interesting a larger public (the mass of women readers, and people generally who take small account of big issues), we could exploit the picturesque sides of European life far more than we have ever done in the past. Such matter, depending more on the charm of the style and the manner of presentation than on timelines or the analytical faculties, should be carefully written, and should be transmitted by mail. The length of the stories should be strictly limited. The subjects should be travel, local customs,—anything which strikes the fancy of the trained correspondent. If I were to imagine an ideal "foreign page," I should see one such story, a little less than a column in length, placed right beside the cable dispatches, in every issue.

In conclusion, may I point out that the principles now almost universally applied to ordinary business are equally applicable to the newspaper business. A man who has merchandise for sale, which he knows to be unique and of good value, but to which the public is perhaps as yet not entirely accustomed, by advertising his merchandise, educates the public and creates a market. In undertaking to furnish a sounder, finer service than has yet been seen in America, we should perhaps at first have to explain our aims to our readers. I believe that the public reaction to such an explanation would be a generous response.

The thing which our service at present needs more than anything else is an ideal. Our men are simply itching to do their best, provided they are given a high aim, and a feeling of mutual support and encouragement.

If Chicago, after due reflection, approves these ideas, and will say the word, I think we can undertake to furnish the most valuable service in America.

Paul Scott Mowrer

Sources

The story of the *Chicago Daily News* deserves to be told in full. In addition, elements of its history offer rich, unrealized opportunities for case studies of the evolution of modern journalism.

Only one published history of the *Daily News* has been written, *Victor Lawson: His Time and His Work* (1935), which as its title suggests ends the story with the death of its owner. The author is Victor Lawson's editor, Charles Dennis. It is full of useful detail, but verges on memoir. Several doctoral studies have been written about the *Daily News,* but none of these have been published as books. The raw material for study, however, is abundant.

The *Daily News* had a well-deserved reputation for recruiting excellent writers. Eugene Field, who joined seven years after the newspaper's founding, wrote the first popular American newspaper column, whose title—"Sharps and Flats"—was borrowed from the title of a popular play written by Slason Thompson, also of the news staff. Later came columnists Finley Peter Dunne, creator of the homespun, nationally famous philosopher "Mr. Dooley," and playwright George Ade. Legendary editor Henry Justin Smith, who wrote two novels about "a certain famous and fascinating newsroom," hired poet Carl Sandburg even though he was not sure what to do with him. The original idea to hire Sandburg came from Ben Hecht, who went on to plays and movie scripts (including *Front Page*). Others who became famous included Ray Stannard Baker, chief of President Wilson's Paris press office and his biographer; Robert Hardy Andrews, author of the Jack Armstrong radio serials; and theater critic Lloyd Lewis, who doubled as a Civil War historian and co-authored a play with Sinclair Lewis. When the *Daily News* disappeared in 1978, it had one of the country's best columnists, Mike Royko, the conscience of Chicago.

Many of these talented editors and reporters wrote memoirs that give facts and texture to the history of the newspaper. Many also left behind their personal papers. Most of these are found at the Newberry Library. It is a pity that they have not received more attention. The best of these collections are those of Victor Lawson and Charles Dennis, as well as the general file for the *Chicago Daily News*. Bell's papers are described in the article "The Private Papers of a Foreign Correspondent," *Newberry Library Bulletin* 1 (1948): 1–11. A few *Chicago Daily News* staffers left collections at other institutions.

The references below are divided into two categories.

The first group is a general resource list for materials that fill in the history of the *Chicago Daily News*. These include the memoirs by correspondents (but not their other books). This list is by no means complete and is weighted toward foreign reporting. One of the best sources for history of the *Daily News* is the *Daily News*. Proud of its accomplishments and relentless in advertising them, it wrote many stories about itself. The grand finale, written when the newspaper folded, was M. W. Newman's lead article of the final edition, "So Long, Chicago," *Chicago Daily News*, March 4, 1978.

Following this bibliography is a list of sources used in assembling the footnotes for Bell's memoir.

SOURCES FOR THE HISTORY OF THE *CHICAGO DAILY NEWS*

Manuscript Collections

Arizona State University Library, Tempe
A. T. Steele Papers.

Library of Congress, Washington, D.C., Manuscript Division
Edgar Ansel Mowrer and Lilian T. Mowrer Papers.
Frank Knox Papers.

Michigan Historical Collections, University of Michigan, Ann Arbor
William H. Stoneman Papers.

Newberry Library, Chicago
George Ade Papers.
Edward Price Bell Papers.
Carroll Binder Papers.

Luther Daniels Bradley Papers.

Robert Casey Papers.

Chicago Daily News, Inc., Records.

Charles H. Dennis Papers.

John Drury Papers.

Robert Gruenberg Papers.

Harry Hansen Papers.

Ben Hecht Papers.

Victor Lawson Papers.

Lloyd Lewis Papers.

Paul Scott Mower Papers.

Richard S. Mowrer Papers.

Howard Vincent O'Brien Papers.

Mike Royko Collection.

Henry Justin Smith Papers.

Melville E. Stone Papers. (Related materials are in the Associated Press Archives in New York.)

Leland Stowe Papers.

Eunice Tietjens Papers.

University of Chicago Library, Chicago, Special Collections

John Gunther Papers.

Wisconsin Historical Society, Madison

Leland Stowe Papers.

Clifford Utley Papers.

Dissertations and Theses

Abramoske, Donald J. "The *Chicago Daily News:* A Business History, 1875–1901." Ph.D. dissertation, University of Chicago, August 1963.

Powell, Stacy M. "The Chicago Daily News Foreign Service During World War Two and the Men Who Made It Great." Honors' thesis, University of Michigan, April 7, 1984.

Tree, Robert Lloyd. "Victor Freemont Lawson and His Newspapers, 1890–1900: A Study of the Chicago *Daily News* and the Chicago *Record.*" Ph.D. dissertation, Northwestern University, June 1959.

Zobrist, Benedict Karl. "Edward Price Bell and the Development of the Foreign News Service of the Chicago *Daily News.*" Ph.D. dissertation, Northwestern University, June 1953.

Articles

Abramoske, Donald J. "The Founding of the *Chicago Daily News*." *Journal of the Illinois State Historical Society* 59 (Winter, 1966): 341–53.

Cumming, Gary. "The *Daily News* Looks Homeward." *Columbia Journalism Review* 15 (March/April 1977): 60–61.

Garvin, James Louis. "Edward Price Bell." *The Landmark* 12 (April, 1930): 217–20.

Gunther, John. "Funneling the European News." *Harper's Magazine* 160 (May, 1930): 635–47.

"How the *Chicago Daily News* Covers the War." *Editor and Publisher,* September 2, 1916, 5–7.

Shanor, Donald R. "CDN: What We'll Miss about the *Chicago Daily News*." *Columbia Journalism Review* 17 (May/June 1978): 35–37.

Zobrist, Benedict Karl. "How Victor Lawson's Newspapers Covered the Cuban War of 1898." *Journalism Quarterly* 38 (Summer, 1961): 323–31.

Books and Pamphlets

1940 A.D.: Cartoons by Vaughn Shoemaker. Chicago: Chicago Daily News, 1941.

Beasley, Norman. *Frank Knox, American: A Short Biography.* Garden City, N.Y.: Doubleday, Doran and Co., 1936.

Becker, Stephen. *Marshall Field III: A Biography.* New York: Simon and Schuster, 1964.

Brown, Constantine. *The Coming of the Whirlwind.* Chicago: Regnery, 1964.

Casey, Robert J. *More Interesting People.* Indianapolis: Bobbs-Merrill, 1947.

———. *Such Interesting People.* Garden City, N.Y.: Garden City Publishing, 1945.

Dennis, Charles H. *Victor Lawson: His Time and His Work.* Chicago: University of Chicago Press, 1935.

Farson, Negley. *A Mirror for Narcissus.* Garden City, N.Y.: Doubleday and Co., 1957.

———. *The Way of a Transgressor.* New York: Literary Guild of America, 1936.

Geyer, Georgie Anne. *Buying the Night Flight: The Autobiography of a Woman Foreign Correspondent.* New York: Delacorte Press, 1983.

Griffin, Dick, and Rob Warden, eds. *Done in a Day: 100 Years of Great Writing from the "Chicago Daily News."* Chicago: Swallow Press, 1977.

Heald, Morrell. *Transatlantic Vistas: American Journalists in Europe, 1900–1940.* Kent, Ohio: Kent State University Press, 1988.

Hecht, Ben. *A Child of the Century.* New York: Simon and Schuster, 1954.

Mower, Edgar Ansel. *Triumph and Turmoil: A Personal History of Our Time.* New York: Weybright and Talley, 1968.

Mowrer, Lilian T. *Journalist's Wife.* New York: William Morrow, 1937.

Mowrer, Paul Scott. *The House of Europe.* Boston: Houghton Mifflin, 1945.

Starrt, James D. *Journalism's Unofficial Ambassador: A Biography of Edward Price Bell, 1869–1943.* Athens, Ohio: Ohio University Press, 1979.

Stone, Melville E. *Fifty Years a Journalist.* Garden City, N.Y.: Doubleday, Page and Co., 1921.

Swing, Raymond. *"Good Evening!": A Professional Memoir.* New York: Harcourt, Brace and World, 1964.

Tietjens, Eunice. *The World at My Shoulder.* New York: Macmillan, 1938.

Walters, James H. *Scoop: How the Ciano Diary Was Smuggled from Rome to Chicago Where It Made Worldwide News* (self-published, 2006). Pamphlet.

Wile, Frederic William. *News Is Where You Find It: Forty Years' Reporting at Home and Abroad.* Indianapolis: Bobbs-Merrill, 1939.

SOURCES USED IN ASSEMBLING FOOTNOTES

Adams, R. J. Q. *Bonar Law.* Stanford, Calif.: Stanford University Press, 1999.

Aston, George Grey. *The Biography of the Late Marshal Foch.* New York: Macmillan, 1929.

Ayerst, David. *Garvin of "The Observer."* London: Croom Helm, 1985.

———. *The Manchester Guardian: Biography of a Newspaper.* Ithaca, N.Y.: Cornell University Press, 1971.

Bosworth, R. J. B. *Mussolini.* London: Arnold, 2002.

Brittain, Harry. *Pilgrims and Pioneers.* London: Hutchinson and Co., 1946.

Burner, David. *Herbert Hoover: A Public Life.* New York: Knopf, 1979.

Cahm, Caroline. *Kropotkin and the Rise of Revolutionary Anarchism, 1872–1886.* Cambridge, Eng.: Cambridge University Press, 1989.

Callwell, Charles Edward. *Field-Marshal Sir Henry Wilson: His Life and Diaries.* London: Cassell, 1927.

Campbell, John. *F. E. Smith, First Earl of Birkenhead.* London: Jonathan Cape, 1983.

Cassar, George H. *Kitchener's War: British Strategy from 1914 to 1916.* Washington, D.C.: Brassey's, 2004.

———. *The Tragedy of Sir John French.* Newark: University of Delaware Press, 1985.

Castle, H. G. *Fire over England: The German Air Raids of World War I.* London: Secker and Warburg, 1982.

Cecelski, David S., and Timothy B. Tyson, eds. *Democracy Betrayed: The Wilmington Race Riot of 1898 and Its Legacy.* Chapel Hill: University of North Carolina Press, 1998.

Clayton, Charles C. *Little Mack: Joseph B. McCullagh of the "St. Louis Globe-Democrat."* Carbondale, Ill.: Southern Illinois University Press, 1969.

Collier, Basil. *Brasshat: A Biography of Field-Marshal Sir Henry Wilson.* London: Secker and Warburg, 1961.

Collin, Richard H. *Theodore Roosevelt, Culture, Diplomacy, and Expansion: A New View of American Imperialism.* Baton Rouge: Louisiana State University Press, 1985.

Cooper, John Milton. *Walter Hines Page: The Southerner as American, 1855–1918*. Chapel Hill: University of North Carolina Press, 1977.

Cross, Colin. *The Liberals in Power, 1905–1914*. London: Barrie and Rockliff, 1963.

Dobson, John M. *Reticent Expansionism: The Foreign Policy of William McKinley*. Pittsburgh, Pa.: Duquesne University Press, 1988.

Duncan, Bingham. *Whitelaw Reid: Journalist, Politician, Diplomat*. Athens, Ga.: University of Georgia Press, 1975.

Farwell, Byron. *The Great Anglo-Boer War*. New York: Harper and Row, 1976.

Finnan, Joseph P. *John Redmond and Irish Unity, 1912–1918*. Syracuse, N.Y.: Syracuse University Press, 2004.

Gallo, Max. *Mussolini's Italy: Twenty Years of the Fascist Era*. Translated by Charles Lam Markmann. New York: Macmillan, 1973.

George, W. R. P. *Lloyd George, Backbencher*. Llandysul, Dyfed: Gomer, 1983.

Gilbert, Bentley B. *David Lloyd George: A Political Life*. Vol. 1. Columbus: Ohio State University Press, 1987.

Gilbert, Martin. *Churchill: A Life*. New York: Henry Holt and Company, 1991.

Giles, Frank. *A Prince of Journalists: The Life and Times of Henri Stefan Opper de Blowitz*. London: Faber and Faber, 1962.

Gollin, A. M. *"The Observer" and J. L. Garvin, 1908–1914: A Study in a Great Editorship*. London: Oxford University Press, 1960.

Grey, Sir Edward. *Speeches on Foreign Affairs, 1904–1914*. London: George Allen and Unwin, 1931.

Griffiths, Dennis, ed. *The Encyclopedia of the British Press, 1422–1992*. New York: St. Martin's Press, 1992.

Hammond, J. L. *C. P. Scott of the Manchester Guardian*. London: G. Bell and Sons, 1934.

Harrod, Roy Forbes. *The Life of John Maynard Keynes*. New York: Harcourt and Brace, 1951.

Heckscher, August. *Woodrow Wilson*. New York: Scribner, 1991.

Hendrick, Burton Jesse. *The Life and Letters of Walter H. Page*. Garden City, N.Y.: Doubleday, Page and Co., 1925.

Hibbert, Christopher. *Queen Victoria: A Personal History*. New York: Basic Books, 2000.

Hoover, Herbert. *Memoirs*. New York: Macmillan, 1951–52.

Howard, Robert P. *Illinois: A History of the Prairie State*. Grand Rapids, Mich.: W. B. Eerdmans, 1972.

Hughes, Michael. *British Foreign Secretaries in an Uncertain World, 1919–1939*. London: Routledge, 2006.

Huss, Richard E. *The Development of Printers' Mechanical Typesetting Methods, 1822–1925*. Charlottesville: University Press of Virginia, 1973.

Ingham, Kenneth. *Jan Christian Smuts: The Conscience of a South African*. New York: St. Martin's Press, 1986.

Jenkins, T. A. *Sir Robert Peel*. New York: St. Martin's Press, 1999.

Johnson, Willis Fletcher. *George Harvey, "A Passionate Patriot."* Boston: Houghton Mifflin, 1929.

Kamen, Henry. *The Duke of Alba*. New Haven, Conn.: Yale University Press, 2004.

Keiger, John F. V. *Raymond Poincaré*. Cambridge: Cambridge University Press, 1997.

Kent, William. *John Burns, Labour's Lost Leader: A Biography*. London: Williams and Norgate, 1950.

Kinsley, Philip. *The Chicago Tribune, Its First Hundred Years*. Vol. 3, *1880–1900*. New York: A.A. Knopf, 1946.

Koss, Stephen E. *The Rise and Fall of the Political Press in Britain*. Chapel Hill: University of North Carolina Press, 1981–1984.

LaFeber, Walter. *The Clash: A History of U.S.-Japan Relations*. New York: W. W. Norton and Co., 1997.

Leach, William. *Land of Desire: Merchants, Power, and the Rise of a New American Culture*. New York: Vintage Books, 1993.

Lee, Alan J. *The Origins of the Popular Press in England, 1855–1914*. London: Croom Helm, 1976.

Link, Arthur Stanley. *Wilson*. Princeton: Princeton University Press, 1947.

Lorenz, Alfred Lawrence. "The Whitechapel Club: Defining Chicago's Newspapermen in the 1890s." *American Journalism* 15 (Winter 1998): 83–102.

Ludwig, Emil. *Wilhelm Hohenzollern, the Last of the Kaisers*. Translated by Ethel Colburn Mayne. New York: G. P. Putnam's Sons, 1928.

MacDonogh, Giles. *The Last Kaiser: The Life of Wilhelm II*. New York: St. Martin's Press, 2001.

Mace, Rodney. *Trafalgar Square: Emblem of Empire*. London: Lawrence and Wishart, 1976.

Manchester, William. *The Last Lion, Winston Spencer Churchill*. Vol. 1, *Visions of Glory, 1874–1932*. Boston: Little, Brown and Co., 1983.

Marquand, David. *Ramsay MacDonald*. London: Jonathan Cape, 1977.

Marsh, Peter T. *Joseph Chamberlain: Entrepreneur in Politics*. New Haven, Conn.: Yale University Press, 1994.

Massie, Robert K. *Castles of Steel: Britain, Germany, and the Winning of the Great War at Sea*. New York: Random House, 2003.

Maurice, Frederick. *Haldane: The Life of Viscount Haldane of Cloan, K.T., O.M.* London: Faber and Faber, 1937–39.

McCartney, Paul T. *Power and Progress: American National Identity, the War of 1898, and the Rise of American Imperialism*. Baton Rouge: Louisiana State University Press, 2006.

Middlemas, Keith, and John Barnes. *Baldwin: A Biography*. New York: Macmillan, 1969.

Miller, James Edward. *From Elite to Mass Politics: Italian Socialism in the Giolittian Era, 1900–1914*. Kent, Ohio: Kent State University Press, 1990.

Moran, James. *The Composition of Reading Matter: A History from Case to Computer*. London: Wace, 1965.

Mowrer, Paul Scott. *The House of Europe*. Boston: Houghton Mifflin Co., 1945.

Nomad, Max. *Rebels and Renegades: A Series of Portraits of Outstanding Representatives of Contemporary Revolutionary Tendencies*. New York: Macmillan, 1932.

Pakenham, Thomas. *The Boer War*. New York: Random House, 1979.

Petrie, Charles. *The Chamberlain Tradition*. New York: Frederick A. Stokes Co., 1938.

Pound, Reginald. *Selfridge: A Biography*. London: Heinemann, 1960.

Pound, Reginald, and Geoffrey Harmsworth. *Northcliffe*. London: Cassell, 1959.

Powell, Geoffrey. *Plumer, the Soldiers' General: A Biography of Field-Marshal Viscount Plumer of Messines*. London: Leo Cooper, 1990.

Roberts, Frederick Sleigh. *Forty-One Years in India: From Subaltern to Commander-in-Chief*. New York: Longmans, Green and Co., 1900.

Roberts, Sidney I. "The Municipal Voters' League and Chicago's Boodlers." *Journal of the Illinois State Historical Society* 53 (Summer 1960): 117–48.

Rock, William R. *Chamberlain and Roosevelt: British Foreign Policy and the United States, 1937–1940*. Columbus: Ohio State University Press, 1988.

Roddis, Louis H. *The Indian Wars of Minnesota*. Cedar Rapids, Iowa: Torch Press, 1956.

Roll, Charles. *Colonel Dick Thompson, the Persistent Whig*. Indianapolis: Indiana Historical Bureau, 1948.

Sanders, Michael, and Philip M. Taylor. *British Propaganda during the First World War, 1914–18*. London: Macmillan, 1982.

Schults, Raymond L. *Crusader in Babylon: W. T. Stead and the Pall Mall Gazette*. Lincoln: University of Nebraska Press, 1972.

Scott, J. W. Robertson. *The Story of the Pall Mall Gazette, of Its First Editor Frederick Greenwood and of Its Founder George Murray Smith*. London: Oxford University Press, 1950.

Selfridge, Harry Gordon. *The Romance of Commerce*. London: John Lane, 1923.

Seton-Watson, Christopher. *Italy from Liberalism to Fascism, 1870–1925*. London: Methuen, 1967.

Smith, Daniel Maloy. *Robert Lansing and American Neutrality, 1914–1917*. Berkeley: University of California Press, 1958.

Smith, Frank. *Robert G. Ingersoll: A Life*. Buffalo, N.Y.: Prometheus Books, 1990.

Smith, Henry Justin. *Deadlines*. Chicago: Covici-McGee, 1922.

———. *Josslyn: The Story of an Incorrigible Dreamer*. Chicago: Covici-McGee, 1924.

Smith, Mack. *Mussolini*. New York: Knopf, 1981.

Steevens, G. W. *With Kitchener to Khartum*. London: Greenhill Books, 1990.

Strachey, John St. Loe. *The Adventure of Living: A Subjective Autobiography, 1860–1922*. New York: G. P. Putnam's Sons, 1922.

Strauss, William Louis. *Joseph Chamberlain and the Theory of Imperialism*. Washington, D.C.: American Council on Public Affairs, 1942.

Swartz, Marvin. *The Politics of British Foreign Policy in the Era of Disraeli and Gladstone*. New York: St. Martin's Press, 1985.

Swettenham, John Alexander. *To Seize the Victory: The Canadian Corps in World War I.* Toronto: Ryerson Press, 1965.

Tebbel, John William. *An American Dynasty.* Garden City, N.Y.: Doubleday and Co., 1947.

Thorpe, D. R. *The Uncrowned Prime Ministers.* London: Darkhorse, 1980.

Tilchin, William N. *Artists of Power: Theodore Roosevelt, Woodrow Wilson, and Their Enduring Impact on U.S. Foreign Policy.* Westport, Conn.: Praeger Security International, 2006.

———. *Theodore Roosevelt and the British Empire: A Study in Presidential Statecraft.* New York: St. Martin's Press, 1997.

Toland, John. *Adolf Hitler.* Garden City, N.Y.: Doubleday and Co., 1976.

Tomes, Jason. *Balfour and Foreign Policy: The International Thought of a Conservative Statesman.* Cambridge: Cambridge University Press, 1997.

Traxel, David. *Crusader Nation: The United States in Peace and the Great War, 1898–1920.* New York: Alfred A. Knopf, 2006.

Trevelyan, George Macaulay. *Grey of Fallodon: The Life and Letters of Sir Edward Grey, Afterwards Viscount Grey of Fallodon.* Boston: Houghton Mifflin, 1937.

Tuchman, Barbara Wertheim. *The Zimmermann Telegram.* New York: Viking Press, 1958.

Van Allen, Elizabeth J. *James Whitcomb Riley: A Life.* Bloomington: Indiana University Press, 1999.

Wall, Joseph Frazier. *Henry Watterson, Reconstructed Rebel.* New York: Oxford University Press, 1956.

Warner, Philip. *Kitchener: The Man Behind the Legend.* New York: Atheneum, 1985.

Wheeler-Bennett, John Wheeler. *Munich: Prologue to Tragedy.* New York: Duell, Sloan and Pearce, 1948.

Wiener, Joel H. *Papers for the Millions: The New Journalism in Britain, 1850s to 1914.* New York: Greenwood Press, 1988.

Willson, Beckles. *America's Ambassadors to England (1785–1928): A Narrative of Anglo-American Diplomatic Relations.* London: J. Muray, 1928.

———. *The Life of Lord Strathcona and Mount Royal, G.C.M.G., G.C.V.O.* Boston: Houghton, 1915.

Wintour, Charles. *The Rise and Fall of Fleet Street.* London: Hutchinson, 1989.

Woodcock, George, and Ivan Avakumovic. *The Anarchist Prince: A Biographical Study of Peter Kropotkin.* London: T. V. Boardman, 1950.

Index

Ade, George, 331

Advertising, x, xvii, xxxiii–xxxiv

African Americans. *See* Blacks

Akerson, George, 290

Alba (or Alva), Duke of, 238, 238*n*1

Allen, George, 63–66

American Legion, 319

Andrews, Robert Hardy, 331

AP. *See* Associated Press

Archer, Alice M., 153, 210–11, 219, 220

Arnold, Mather, 155*n*2

Asquith, Herbert Henry: and Bell's interview with Grey, 194, 198, 199; and Bell's interview with Haldane, 195; and Burns, 122–23; and Churchill, 142; as contributor to World War I book, 201; and journalists, 140; and Law, 139, 139*n*20; political career of, 122*n*11, 123*n*13, 131*n*2, 139*n*20; and World War I, 134*n*11

Associated Press, ix, xviii–xx, xix*n*, xxiv–xxv, 78, 112, 145–47, 186, 189

Astor, Waldorf, 160, 160*n*9

Atlantic Monthly, xxxviii–xxxix, 202*n*1

Atter, Robert, 149

Aubert, Louis, 307, 308

Australia and Australians, xviii, 161–62, 161*n*11, 173, 173*n*15, 256–58, 256*n*1, 261, 265

Avanti!, 127, 128*n*26, 128*n*28, 280*n*1

Aviation: during World War I, 225–35; flying competition, 166, 166*n*3; R-38 airship, 225–26; record flight between London and Paris, 233–35; seaplane observational cruise over North Sea by Bell, 229–33

Ayora, Isidro, 290

Bacon, General, 73–75, 77, 78, 262

Baker, George Barr, 289, 289*n*6

Baker, Ray Stannard, 331

Baldwin, Stanley, 160, 160*n*10, 299–300, 310

Balfour, Lord Arthur James: and "Balfour Note" on war debts, 136–38, 136*n*13; Bell's meetings with, 133–34; and Boer War, 131–32; and Chinese workers in African gold mines, 132*n*6; as contributor to World War I book, 201; on newspapers, 177; resignation of, as prime minister, 131*n*6; and T. Roosevelt, 135–36; and Wilson's "Peace Note," 207, 210; and World War I, 134, 134*n*11

"Balfour Note," 136–38, 136*n*13

Ball, Spencer F., 9–17

Ball, William C., 9

Barnett, Canon, 57–58

Barrès, Maurice, 201, 201*n*10

Barry, Robert, 300–301

Baseball, 64–66

Bass, John, 269–70

Battles, World War I. *See* World War I

Beatty, David, 134, 134*n*11, 183, 233

Beaverbrook, Baron, 154, 154*n*1, 156

Belgium, 194–95*nn*4–5, 195, 196, 208, 232, 246, 246*n*1, 247*n*4, 308

Bell, Edward Price: accomplishments of, xv, xxv, xxxiv, xxxix, 136*n*14, 137, 163–64, 218, 301; and Anglo-American relations after World War I, 288, 295–305; as Anglophile, xxxvii, 202*n*1; biographical monograph (1979) on, xvi; brother of, 5–6, 14–16, 16*n*9, 321; children of, 129, 166, 272, 324; death of, xxxix; and Debs, 35–36, 38; editorial-page writing by, 287; education of, xxi, 53–60; at *Evansville Standard*, 47–53; father of, 36*n*1, 38, 39, 41, 43, 45; and Five-Power Naval Conference, 306–9; homes of, xiii, xxxvii, xxxviii, 63–64, 70, 96, 176, 220, 275; honors for, 163, 289, 324; and Hoover's Good Will Tour to Latin America, 200–201, 289–94; at *Indianapolis Democrat*, xxi, 18–26; on journalism generally, 322–24; as lecturer, 286, 288–89; marriage of, xxii, 59–60, 63, 112; memoir and diaries of, xvi, xxxix, 3; and pageantry, 185–91; papers of, in Newberry Library, xxix, 332; personality of, xxii, 192; photographs of, xxiii, xxxv; poetry and reading interests of, 6, 10, 25–26, 25*n*2, 36–38, 57, 287, 287*n*2, 324; at *Raccoon Valley Independent*, 38–45; retirement of, ix, xiii, xxxvi, xxxvii, xxxviii–xxxix, 309, 323*n*1; and return to U.S. from England, 270, 272–74; salaries of, xxii, 63, 66, 70; servants of, in England, 220, 221; shorthand skills of, ix, 14, 14*n*6, 20; and spelling, 6, 9, 17, 20; at *St. Louis Globe-Democrat*, 27–34, 27*n*1; and telegraphy, ix, 14–16, 31, 65; at *Terre Haute Daily News*, 45–47, 56; at *Terre Haute Evening Gazette*, xxi, 9–17, 26, 45, 185–86; at *Terre Haute Express*, 63–69; travels to Far East by, 285–86; and trip across Canada, 121; typesetting by, ix, 11–12, 11*n*1; and World War II, xxxix, 315–21; writing by, in later life, xxxviii–xxxix; youth of, on farm, xxi, 5–6, 36, 36*n*1. See also *Chicago Daily News; Chicago Daily News* foreign news service; *Chicago Daily News* London bureau; Interviewing; Peace

Bell, Mary Alice Mills: and Bell's newspaper assignments, xxii, 72, 112; children of, 129, 166, 272, 324; and conflict at *Terre Haute Express*, 66–67; in England, xxii, 129, 162, 166, 186–89; homes of, 63–64, 70, 96, 176, 220, 275; and jury bribing in Chicago, 99–100; meeting between Bell and, 59–60; and return to U.S. from England, 272, 274; and trip across Canada, 121; wedding of, 59

Bell, Moberly, 129, 129*n*30

Bell, Will, 5–6, 14–16, 16*n*9, 321

Bennett, James Gordon, xx, 177, 178*n*1

Bernard, William H., 82

Bethmann-Hollweg, Theobald von, 194–95, 195*n*5

Biegler, George, 32

Bigsworth, A. W., 232, 232*n*6

Billings, Josh, 151

Birkenhead, Lord, 140

Bismarck, Otto von, 181

Blacks, xxii, 80–89, 80*n*1, 101–2

Blaine, James, 14, 14*n*5

Blatchford, Montagu John, 155*n*1

Blatchford, Robert Peel Glanville, 154, 155*n*1, 162

Blériot, Louis, 166, 166*n*3, 225

Blumenfeld, Ralph David, xxx, 154, 155*n*1, 156

Boer War, 130–33, 130–31*nn*1–8, 144, 156, 180*n*5, 184*n*8

Bonham Carter, Mr., 195

Boudinot, Frank, 15

Boxer Rebellion, xix*n*

Brazleton, Mr., 70–71

Briand, Aristide, 281, 281*n*2, 307

Bribery, 90–100, 103–4

Britain. *See* England

Brittain, Harry, 139–40, 139*n*19

Brown, Constantin, 152

Browne, Louis Edgar, 152, 325–26

Bryce, James, 200, 200*n*9, 201

Burke, John, 247

Burnham, Lord, xxxiv, 154, 154*n*1, 161–64

Burns, John, 122–23, 122–23*nn*11–13, 131, 131*n*5

Burroughs, Dr., 55, 192

Butts, Jimmy, 152

Cabot, Sebastian, 56

Campbell-Bannerman, Henry, 122*n*11, 123*n*13, 130, 131*n*2, 131*n*6, 132–33, 139

Campbell-Orde, A. C., 234

Canada and Canadians, 82, 121, 237, 247, 247*n*3, 254, 254*n*9, 261, 296, 296*n*1, 303

Carlyle, Thomas, 177, 177*n*1

Carrier pigeons during World War I, 232–33

Carson, Sir Edward, 141

Casey, Mont, 43–45

Censorship of the press, 140–41, 140–41*n*21, 171, 171*nn*11–12, 184

Chadwick, Stephen Fowler, 319

Chamberlain, Joseph: Bell's friendship with, 123, 129; and Boer War, 130*n*1, 131; and British Empire, 123–25, 123*n*15; communication style of, 139; compared with F. E. Smith, 140; compared with T. Roosevelt, 135; and Disraeli, 124, 124*n*17; and popular education, 170; sons of, 123–26, 123*n*15

Chamberlain, Joseph Austen, 123–25, 123*n*15, 124*n*16, 301

Chamberlain, Neville, 123–26, 123*n*15, 126*n*22, 304, 304*n*5, 311*n*7, 313

Chamberlin, Henry Barrett, 70, 96–98, 102, 109–11, 119, 186

Chapman, Sir Samuel, 203

Chicago, Ill.: jury bribing in Cook County, 90–100

Chicago Daily News: advertisements in, xvii; and Anglo-American relations after World War I, 288, 295–305; beginnings of, under Lawson, xvi–xvii; and Bell's articles from first trip to England, 57, 58; Bell's first meeting with Lawson at, 111–12; and Bell's interviews with European leaders after World War I, 276–84; and Bell's travels to Far East, 285–86; Bell's waiting for first meeting with Lawson at, 91, 110–11; on Chippewa in Minnesota, xx, 71–79; circulation of, xvii, xix; conflict between Bell and Brazleton at, 70–71; on corruption in Illinois politics, 90–107; on Darrow's labor trial, xxii; on economy after World War I, 286–87; editorial-page writing by Bell, 287;

editorial policy of, xvii, xxix, xxxiv, xl*n*6; end of, x, xvi; finances of, xi; and Five-Power Naval Conference, 306–9, 306*n*1; hiring of Bell at, 70; and Hoover's Good Will Tour to Latin America, 200–201, 289–94; and Indiana coal miners' strike, 31, 33, 36; on jury bribing in Cook County, 90–100; Knox's purchase of, xxxi, xxxiii, xxxv–xxxvi; Marshall Field family's purchase of, xxxiii; organization of, xx; problems of, in 1960s, xxxiii–xxxiv; profitability of, xi, xvii, xxxiv; publications on, 331; resignation of Bell from, xxxvi, 323*n*1; Strong's purchase of, xxxiii, xxxv; on Wilmington race riots, xxii, 80–89; writers for generally, xvi–xvii, 331–32; and Yerkes investigation, 93–95, 97, 98, 100–107. *See also* Bell, Edward Price; *Chicago Daily News* foreign news service; *Chicago Daily News* London office; Dennis, Charles H.; Lawson, Victor

Chicago Daily News foreign news service: and Associated Press, ix, xix–xx, xix*n*, xxiv, xxv, 112, 145–47; Bell as general manager of, 148–53, 236; Bell on, 325–27; Bell's advice to reporters, 150–52; Berlin bureau of, xxiv, 120, 144; and cable versus mail service for news stories, xxvi–xxvii; characteristics and principles of, ix, xix–xx, xxi, xxiv–xxv, xxx, xxxiv, 122; during cold war, 32; communication within, xxviii–xxix; cost of, xx, xxv–xxviii, xxxii; coverage question for, xxii–xxv, 144–53; decline of, x; diplomatic role of reporters in, xxix–xxxi; editorial policy of, xxix; education of foreign staff of, 148–52; egotism of reporters for, 150–51; and end of World War I, 269–70; foreign staff of, 148–50; hiring of Bell for, 112; hiring of correspondents for, xxi; and Knox, xxxiii, xxxv–xxxvi; Lawson's development of and directives to, ix, xviii–xxi, xxx, 111–12, 144, 271; list of reporters working for, 152–53; Mowrer on reorganization of, 327–29; offices and furnishings for, xxvii, xxviii, 117–20, 120*n*5; organization of, 149, 325–29; Paris bureau of, xxiv, xxviii, xxix, xxxi,

Chicago Daily News foreign news service *(cont.)*:
119–20, 120*n*5, 327; prestige of, xxviii; and
reporters "going native," xxix–xxxi, xxxvi;
salaries in, xxii, xxv–xxvii; significance
and excellence of, x, xv, xxv, xxix; stringers
for, xxi, xxiii; and Strong, xxxiii; syndication of, xx; women reporters working for,
152–53; during World War I, xv, xxv, xxx,
133–34, 161–62, 164, 179–80, 225–65. *See
also* Bell, Edward Price; *Chicago Daily
News* London bureau

Chicago Daily News London bureau: and
Associated Press, 145–47; and Bapaume
battle, 258–65; Bell as general manager of
foreign news service, 148–53, 236; Bell's arrival at, xxii, 112; Bell's leaving, and return
to U.S., 272–74; and Bell's lectures to public
schools, 204–5; and Bell's letters to the
Times, 136–37, 207–15, 217–19; and Bell's
tea with royalty, 181–83; and Bell's travels
in Europe, 148; and Boer War, 130–32, 144,
156; and British journalists, 154–76; and
British politicians and statesmen, 123–26,
130–43, 147–48; and coronation of King
George V and Queen Mary, 189–91; and
coverage question, 144–53; criticisms of
Bell at, xxx, 218, 219; and end of World War I,
269–70; expenses of Bell at, xxv–xxvi;
Farson's resignation from, xxxi; and flying
privileges for Bell during World War I, 134,
225–35; Haldane-Grey interviews by Bell,
xxx, 3, 3*n*, 190, 192–201, 205; hiring of Bell
for, 112; honors for Bell at, 163; Lawson's
directives to, 144, 271; and Mont St. Quentin battle, 256–58; and Northcliffe, 165–76;
office of and furnishings for, xxvii, xxviii,
117–20; and Page, 202–11, 214–15, 217, 236;
photograph of, xxvii; positive comments
on Bell at, xxxix, 136*n*14, 137, 163–64, 218;
salary of Bell at, xxii; and Sinn Féin's threat
against Bell, 219–21; and stringers, xxvi;
and Vimy Ridge battle, 247–55, 247*nn*2–3;
visitors to, 121–29; and wedding of Queen
Wilhelmina, 186–89; Wile in, 144–45; and
Wilson's "Peace Note," xxx, 207–13, 207*n*3;

during World War I, xv, xxv, xxx, 133–34,
161–62, 164, 179–80, 225–65; and Ypres Salient, 236–47; and Zimmermann telegram,
215–17, 215*n*2. See also *Chicago Daily News*
foreign office; England

Chicago Record: on Chinese laundryman/dip-
lomat, 108–13; Curtis as Washington correspondent for, xviii, 71*n*1; and Dennis, 57;
and jury bribing in Cooke County, 99–100;
and Lawson, xvi, xix, 31; sale of, by Lawson, xix, xxii; on Tanner, 107; on Yerkes
investigation, 102, 104

Chicago Tribune, xviii, xxx, 73, 99–100, 118–
19, 118*n*3, 162*n*12, 320

China, xix*n*, 108–13, 112, 112*n*2, 285*n*1, 302, 317*n*2

Chinese laundryman/diplomat, 108–13

Chippewa Indians, xx, 71–79, 72*n*2, 79*n*4

Churchill, Lord Randall, 142

Churchill, Winston, 140*n*21, 141–43, 141*n*23,
142*n*24, 173*n*15

Circulation of newspapers, x, xvii, xix

Civil War, 27*n*1, 83*n*2, 84*n*3, 94, 145*n*1, 196

Clarke, Arthur, 73, 78

Clemenceau, George, 248*n*5

Cleveland, Grover, 21–24, 26, 66, 66*n*1

Clinton Clarion, 43–45

Cold war, 32

Cole, George E., 91, 91*n*2, 94–95, 97, 98

Collins, Robert M., 186, 189

Comstock, Mr., 19–27

Connelly, James, 221

Connerly, Lafe, 39, 41

Coolidge, Calvin, xxxiv, 300*n*3

Cork Examiner, 301

The Cornhill, 158

Coughlin, Bath-House John, 94

Cuba, xviii, 66–67, 66*n*1, 67*n*2, 73

Cullerton, Foxy Ed, 94

Currie, Sir Arthur, 254, 254*n*9

Curtis, William Eleroy, xviii, 70–71, 71*n*1

Czechoslovakia, 126*n*22, 304*n*5

Daily Mail (London): on Bell, 218; on Conservative Party meeting, 175; founding of, 166;
job offer for Bell from, 165; journalists at,

154–55*n*1, 186; on Kitchener, 171–72*n*13, 172; office of, 171*n*10; ownership of, 129*n*30; on record flight between London and Paris, 233–34

Daladier, Edouard, 304, 304*n*5

Dana, Charles, 177, 177–78*n*1

Daniels, Josephus, 226

Darrow, Clarence, xxii

Dawes, Charles G., xxxvi, 300, 300*n*3, 303–4, 310

Dawson, Geoffrey, 154, 154*n*1, 273–74, 297

De Blowitz, Henri, 148, 148*n*3, 205

Debs, Eugene, 35–36, 38, 118*n*3

Delane, John Thadeus, 178, 178*n*3

Deneen, Charles S., 90, 97–99

Dennis, Charles H.: and Bell's articles from first trip to England, 57, 58; and Bell's position in London bureau, 112; Bell's positive comments on, 152; and Bell's trip to England for improved Anglo-American relations, 296; and cable versus mail service for news stories, xxvi; and Chippewa in Minnesota, 71–72, 80; and coal miners' strike, 31, 33, 36; and coverage question for foreign news service, xxii–xxv, 144; editorial policy of, xxix; and end of World War I, 270; on foreign correspondent as unofficial envoy, xxx; hiring of Bell by, 70; and Judge Wing, 92; and jury bribing in Cooke County, 92, 98–99; Lawson's biography by, 331; and Northcliffe, 167–68; and recreational interests, 168; on salaries for stringers, xxvi; and Versailles Peace Conference, xxviii; and Wile, 144–45; and Wilmington race riots, 80–81; on world peace, 270; and Yerkes, 102

Dewey, Harriet, 152–53

Dickens, Charles, 6, 10, 155*n*1

Dillon, Emile Joseph, 274–75, 274*n*6

Disraeli, Benjamin, 124, 124–26*n*17–19, 125, 158

Dockery, Oliver H., 84, 84*n*3

Donald, Sir Robert, 154, 154*n*1

Doyle, Sir Arthur Conan, xv

Draper, Arthur, 309–10

Drummond, Eric, 194, 197, 198, 200

Dunne, Finley Peter, 331

Dutcher, Rodney, 291

Economy, after World War I, 286–87

Editor & Publisher, xxv, 301–2

Education, in England, 169–70

Edward VII, 120

Edward VIII, 181–82

England: Bell and Anglo-American relations after World War I, 288, 295–305; Bell's first trip to, 56–58; education in, 169–70; imperialism of, 125, 125*n*18; Lake District in, 57, 57*n*2; Lord Mayor's day in, 121, 121*n*8; "Siege of Sidney Street" in, 142, 142*n*24; St. James's Park in London, 133; Toynbee Hall in, 56, 56*n*1, 57–58; Trafalgar Square in, 117, 117*n*1, 133–34; and World War II, 315–16, 319–20. *See also* Boer War; *Chicago Daily News* London bureau; World War I; specific politicians and newspapers

Ethiopia, 312, 312*n*10

Europe's Economic Sunrise, xxxiv, 286–87

Evansville Standard, 47–53

Fagin, Jack, 6

Farson, Negley, xxxi, 152

Fascism, 128, 279, 280, 280*n*1, 312

Faye, Charles, xviii–xix, xxii, xxiii

Field, Eugene, 331

Fiske, Minnie Maddern, 64

Five-Power Naval Conference, 306–9, 306*n*1

Flandin, Pierre-Etienne, 311–12, 311*n*8

Fleet Street, 155, 155*n*3, 169–70

Fleuriau, Aime Joseph de, 301

Foch, Ferdinand, 166, 166*n*4, 248, 248*n*5

Ford, I. N., 119, 186, 187, 190, 309

Foreign news services. See *Chicago Daily News* foreign news service; *Chicago Daily News* London bureau; and other newspapers

France: Paris bureau of *Chicago Daily News*, xxiv, xxviii, xxix, xxxi, 119–20, 120*n*5, 327; Vichy government, 311*n*8; in World War I, 161–62, 164; and World War II, 315–16, 320. *See also* specific politicians

French, John, 183–84, 184n8, 228, 237, 242
Friedrich Wilhelm, Kaiser, 251, 251n7

Gardiner, Alfred George, 154, 155n1, 160–61, 169
Garrick Club, 159, 159n7
Garvin, J. L.: and "Balfour Note," 136; on Bell, xxxiv; and Bell's trip to England after World War I, 296–98; at dinner honoring Bell, 162–63; as editor of *The Observer*, 136n15, 154, 154n1, 160–61, 160nn8–9, 169; and Five-Power Naval Conference, 307–8; nominates Bell for the Nobel Peace Prize, 324; and Northcliffe, 160n9; and World War II, 320
Gault, Robert Harvey, 287
George V, 120, 158, 181–83, 189–91
Germany: appeasement policy toward, 126n22, 304, 311n7, 313; Berlin bureau of *Chicago Daily News*, xxiv, 120, 144; foreign correspondents in, 149; Haldane's diplomatic visit to, 194–95, 195n5; invasion of Poland by, 315, 317n1; and Munich Agreement, 126n22; navy of, 274n5; Nazism in, 125, 125n21, 126, 314; propaganda by, during World War I, 208–9, 208n4; and Versailles treaty, 286, 307n4, 316–17, 319; and Zimmermann telegram, 215–17, 215n2. *See also* Hitler, Adolf; World War I
Gibson, Hugh, 296, 296n1, 298, 298n2
Gladstone, William Ewert, 125, 125n19, 131n2, 158, 158–59n6, 170, 193n1
Goethe, Johann Wolfgang von, 151
Goode, Sir William, 145–46
Grandi, Dino, 306, 306n2
Graves, E. P., 229–33, 235
Grayson, Richard, 124n16
Great Britain. *See* England
Greeley, Horace, 145n1, 177, 177n1
Greenwood, Frederick, 154, 154n1, 158–60, 158–59n6, 169
Greist, Howard, 55
Grey, Sir Edward: interview of, by Bell, xxx, xxxvii, 3, 3n, 190, 193–94, 197–201, 205; political career of, 131n2; speech on World War I by, 194, 194n4; and Stimson, 308

Gridley, Martin M., 289
Grigg, Joe, 247
Gunther, John, 152

Hadfield, Sir Robert, 162, 162n12
Haig, Douglas, 184, 184n8, 237, 242, 242n7, 245, 259, 260, 269
Haldane, Richard Burdon: German diplomatic visit by, 194–95, 195n5; interview of, by Bell, xxx, 3, 3n, 194–201, 205; political career of, 131n2, 197n6
Hall, Sir William Reginald, 214–16
Hanover College, 53–54
Hansen, Harry, 152
Hard, Bill, 152
Hardy, Tom, 40, 41–42
Harrison, Benjamin, 145n1
Harvey, George, 137–38, 137nn17–18, 181, 272–73
Hawaii, 285
Hayes, Rutherford B., 15
Hecht, Ben, 331
Heider, Albert, 234, 235
Hendrick, Burton J., 204
Hill, William, 154, 154n1
Hindenburg line, 258, 258n4, 269–70
Hindenburg, Paul von, 251, 251n7, 258n4
Hitler, Adolf: appeasement policy toward, 126n22, 304, 311n7, 313; Bell on Hitler and war, xxxvii, 313; Bell's interview with, xi, 314; invasion of Poland by, 315, 317n1; and Nazism, 314; and Poincaré, 281; on Roosevelt, 274, 274n5; and World War II, 320. *See also* Germany
Hobhouse, Emily, 131n2
Hoge, James F., Jr., ix–xi
Holden, Bob, 110
Hoover, Herbert: and Anglo-American relations after World War I, 295–97, 299–304; and Geneva disarmament conference, 298, 298n2; and Good Will Tour to Latin America, 200–201, 289–94, 289n5; and MacDonald's visit to U.S., 125, 299–305, 304n4; on peace, 271; presidential election of, 288, 288n4, 289n6

Hoover, Lieutenant, 75

Hornaday, Jim, 30–34

House, Edward M., 137, 137*n*16

Howard, Esme, 296, 296*n*1

Howitzers, 239–40, 239*nn*2–3

Hughes, Billy, 162

Hughes, Charles Evans, 34

Hughes, Michael, 124*n*16

Hull, Cordell, 312, 312*n*9, 317, 317*n*2

Hymans, Paul, 201, 201*n*10

Illinois politics, 92–105

Il Popolo d'Italia, 280, 280*n*1

India, 135*n*12, 173*n*16

Indiana militia, 28–33

Indianapolis Democrat, xxi, 18–26

Indianapolis Journal, 26, 37

Indianapolis News, 30–34

Ingersoll, Robert Green, 49–53, 49*n*1, 141, 192, 275

Insley, Mr., 16

Internet, x

Interviewing: Bell's skills and interest in, xxii, xxxvii–xxxviii, 192, 275; of economists in Europe and America, 286–87; in England after World War I, 298; of European leaders by Bell after World War I, 277–84, 309–14; of Flandin, 311–12; "great man" vision of, xi, xxxvii, 192; of Grey, xxx, xxxvii, 3, 3*n*, 190, 193–94, 197–201, 205; of Haldane, xxx, 3, 3*n*, 194–201, 205; of Hitler, xi, 314; of Ingersoll, 49–52, 192, 275; of Laval, 311–12; of MacDonald, 282–84, 311; of W. Marx in Germany, 277–78; of Mussolini, xxxvii, 278–80, 312–13; of Poincaré, 281–82; of Pope Pius XI, 313–14; of F. E. Smith, 141–42; of Stalin, 313; of world leaders by Bell for *Literary Digest*, 309–14

Ireland, 141, 141*n*22, 147, 147*n*2, 219–21, 221*n*4, 248

Irwin, Will, xxxiv

Italian-Ethiopian War, 312, 312*n*10

Italy, 125–28, 125–26*nn*21–22, 127–28*nn*26–28, 278–80, 306–9, 306*n*1, 312, 312*n*10. *See also* Mussolini, Benito

James, Frank, 70, 71*n*1

James, Jesse, 70, 71*n*1

Japan: Bell's trip to, 285; British policy toward, 124–26; and Five-Power Naval Conference, 306–9, 306*n*1; and force of history, 324; and Pearl Harbor attack, 318*n*4; primacy of, in Far East, 313; relations between U.S. and, 285, 285*n*1; and Zimmermann telegram, 215–17

Japanese Americans, 82

Jealous, George, 170*n*8

Jellicoe, John Rushworth, 134, 134*n*11, 183, 233

Jews in Palestine, 138

Johnson, Mr., 101–2, 104

Jones, Evan R., 196

Jones, Herby, 47–48

Journalists: Bell on generally, 322–24; bylines for, 13, 13*n*2; education of, for foreign news services, 148–52; egotism and prophecy to be avoided by, 150–51; in England, 154–76; ethics of, 13; and Fleet Street, 155, 155*n*3, 169–70; foreign language abilities of, 150; hiring of foreigners for foreign news services, xxi, 148–50; new journalism, 129*nn*29–30, 136*n*15, 154*n*1, 155*n*2, 169*n*6, 264*n*8; poker playing by, 47, 64; salaries of, xxii, xxv–xxvii, 63, 66, 70, 273; social position of and public opinion on, 177–84; and stringers for foreign news services, xi, xxi, xxiii. *See also Chicago Daily News; Chicago Daily News* foreign news service; *Chicago Daily News* London bureau; Yellow journalism; and specific journalists and newspapers

Joyce, Jack, 16–17

Jury bribing. *See* Chicago, Ill.

Kaufman, David E., 291–92

Keeley, James, 162, 162*n*12, 163, 325

Kellogg-Briand pact, 281*n*2

Kenly, J. R., 82

Kenna, Hinky Dink, 94

Kennedy, John Russell, 152

Keynes, John Maynard, 270, 270*n*3, 275

Kiehl, August F. J., xxvi, 187–89, 293

Kiep, Otto Carl, 277

King, Mackenzie, 296, 300, 303, 305

Kingsbury, Dr., 82

Kipling, Rudyard, 52

Kitchener, Herbert, xxx, 140*n*21, 171–73, 171*n*9, 171–72*nn*11–15, 179–80, 184, 184*n*8

Knight, John, xxxiii

Knox, Frank, xxxi, xxxiii, xxxv–xxxvi, 323*n*1

Koss, Stephen, 160*n*8

Kropotkin, Prince, 126–27, 126–27*nn*23–24

Kruger, Paul, 132, 132*n*8

Ku Klux Klan, 71

Labor movement. *See* Strikes

Lansdowne, Lord, 198, 198*n*7

Lansing, Robert, 210, 210*n*5

Latin America, xviii, 200–201, 289–94, 289*n*5, 317*n*2

Laval, Pierre, 311–12, 311*n*8

Law, Bonar, 139–40, 139–40*n*20, 173

Lawson, Victor: and beginnings of *Chicago Daily News*, xvi–xvii; and Bell's interviews with European leaders after World War I, 277–78, 284; and Bell's lectures to public schools in England, 204–5; Bell's positive comments on, 152, 177, 321–22; Bell's relationship with, xxxv; and Bell's return to U.S. from England, 270, 272–73; Bell's wait to meet, 91, 110–11; biography of, 331; and *Chicago Record*, xvi, xix, 31; on Chinese laundryman/diplomat, 110–11; competitors' views of, 117–19, 118*n*2; and cost of foreign news service, xx, xxv–xxviii; and coverage question for foreign news, xxii–xxv, 144; death of, xvii, xxxiii, xxxv, 285–86, 309; editorial policy of, xvii, xxix, xl*n*6; on end of World War I, 271; European tours by, xxviii; first meeting between Bell and, 111–12; and foreign news service, ix, xviii–xxv, xxx, 111–12, 117–19, 144; and Grey-Haldane interviews, 201; home of, 276; and Judge Wing, 91, 92; and Municipal Voters' League, 91*n*2; nervous breakdown of, xxxv; and offices and furnishings for foreign news service,

117–20, 120*n*5, 122; papers of, in Newberry Library, xix; personality of, 111; physical appearance of, 111; and profitability of *Chicago Daily News*, xi, xvii, xxxiv; and salaries for reporters and stringers, xxii, xxv–xxvi; sale of *Chicago Record* by, xix, xxii; secretary for, 111; and syndication of foreign news, xx; and Tanner, 107; and Yerkes, 102. *See also Chicago Daily News*

League of Nations, 137*n*17, 194, 281*n*2, 288

Lee, D. Campbell, 163

Leroy, Albert, 54–55, 58–60

Lewis, J. H., 234

Lewis, Sinclair, 331

Lincoln, Abraham, 15, 109, 217

Literary Digest, 309–11

Lloyd George, David: and Boer War, 131, 131*n*3, 131*n*5; and Churchill, 141*n*23; as contributor to World War I book, 201; and Foch, 248*n*5; and Kitchener, 171*n*9; Lothian as secretary of, 314*n*12; and MacDonald's trip to U.S., 301; as munitions minister during World War I, 173*n*14; political career of, 131*nn*2–3, 139*n*20; public opinion on, 143; and F. E. Smith, 140; and Versailles Peace Conference, 270*n*3; H. H. Wilson as military adviser to, 221*n*4; and World War II, 320

Loew, Lloyd, 331

London. *See Chicago Daily News* London bureau; England

London Daily Chronicle, xv, 154–55*n*1

London Daily Express, 154–55*n*1, 264*n*8, 301

London Daily Telegraph, xxxiv, 129*n*30, 154*n*1

London Evening News, 129*n*30, 154*n*1, 172

London Evening Transcript, 301

London Standard, xx, 139*n*19, 154*n*1, 264*n*8

Longfellow, Henry Wadsworth, 130

Lorimer, William, 94, 94*n*4, 104

Lothian, Marquess of, 314, 314*n*12, 320

Louisville Courier-Journal, 14*n*3

Ludendorff, Erich, 251, 251*n*7, 257*n*2, 269–70

Lusitania, 213, 213*n*1

Lynching, 89

MacDonald, Ramsey: Bell's interviews of, 282–84, 311; and Boer War, 131, 131*n*4; as prime minister, 131*n*4, 299–300, 309; trip to U.S. by, 125, 299–305, 304*n*4

Mahjigabo, 78–79

Malatesta, Enrico, 127–29, 127*n*26, 128*n*28, 324

Manchester Guardian, 154, 154*n*1, 157, 157*n*4, 158, 321

Marlowe, Thomas, 154, 155*n*1

Martyn, Henry, 173, 173*n*16

Marx, Karl, 35

Marx, Wilhelm, 277–78, 282

Mary, Queen, 181–83, 189–91

Massey, Vincent, 296, 296*n*1

Massingham, Henry William, 154, 154–55*n*1

Matsudaira, Tsuneo, 216–17, 301

Mazzini, Giuseppe, 109, 109*n*1

McCormick, Robert R., 320

McCoy, W. D., 82

McCullough, Joseph B., 27–34, 27*n*1, 36, 48

McEnnis, John T., 48, 49, 51–53

McKee, Will J., 29–33

McKeen, Bill, 66–69

McKinley, William, 14, 14*n*5, 66–68, 66*n*1, 78

McRae, High, 82

Mecklenburg-Schwerin, Duke, 186

Medill, Joseph, 118*n*3

Metternich, Prince, 137

Mexico, 15, 215–17, 215*n*2

Milford, Arthur Bartlett, 54–55, 57

Mills, Mary Alice. *See* Bell, Mary Alice Mills

Milner, Alfred, 130*n*1

Miners' strike, 28–33, 36

Mjelde, Mons Monsen, 149–50

Monash, John, 161, 161*n*11, 256–59, 256–57*nn*1–2, 261

Mond, Sir Alfred, 162, 162*n*12, 163

Monroe Doctrine, 318, 318*n*3, 320

Morgan, Tom, 66, 67, 68

Morley, John, 129, 129*n*30, 154, 154*n*1

Motherwell, Hiram K., 152, 278–80

Mowrer, Edgar Ansel, xxix, xxxvii, 152

Mowrer, Paul Scott: and Bell's interview of Poincaré, 281, 282; and Bell's resignation from *Chicago Daily News*, xxxvi; and coverage question, xxiv; as Francophile, xxxi; on furnishings of foreign bureaus, xxviii, 120*n*5; and Haldane interview, 196; on Lawson, 118*n*2; in Paris bureau of *Chicago Daily News*, xxiv, xxxi, 152, 327; on reorganization of *Chicago Daily News* foreign news service, 327–29; resignation of, xxxiii

Moy, Sam, 108–13

Munich Agreement, 123*n*15, 126, 126*n*22, 304*n*5

Municipal Voters' League, Chicago, 91, 91*n*2, 94, 98

Murdoch, Keith, 174–75

Murphy, Theresa, 153

Murray, Gilbert, 201, 201*n*10

Mussolini, Benito: on airplanes, 245; and Ancona riots, 128, 128*n*28; as *Avanti!* editor, 127, 128*n*26, 128*n*28, 280*n*1; Bell's interviews of, xi, xxxvii, 152, 277, 278–80, 282, 312–13; and Fascism, 128, 279, 280, 280*n*1, 312; and Five-Power Naval Conference, 306; and Italian-Ethiopian War, 312, 312*n*10; and *Il Popolo d'Italia*, 280, 280*n*1; and Socialist Party, 127–28*n*26; during World War I, 128*n*26, 128*n*28; and World War II, 306*n*2

Napoleon, 142, 159, 205

Napoleon III, 159

Native Americans. *See* Chippewa Indians; Ojibwe Indians

Naval conferences, 306–9, 306*n*1, 307*n*3

Nazism, 125, 125*n*21, 126, 314. *See also* Hitler, Adolf

Nelson, Horatio, 117*n*1

Nelson, Thomas Henry, 15–16, 15*n*8

Nenni, Pietro, 128*n*28

Neutrality during World War II, 317–21

New York Evening World, xviii, 301

New York Herald, xviii, xx, 119, 129*n*30, 178*n*1

New York Herald Tribune, xv, xvi, 309

New York Journal, xviii

New York Sun, xviii, 119, 178*n*2, 186

New York Times, x, xv, xvii, xx, xxi, xxxi, xxxii, xxxv, 118*n*3, 247

New York Tribune, xx–xxi, 11*n*1, 119, 145*n*1, 177*n*1, 186, 187, 190

New York World, xviii, 137*n*17, 247

Newberry Library, Chicago, xvi, xix, xxxix, 332

Newlove, Thomas E., 14, 20

Newspapers. See *Chicago Daily News; Chicago Daily News* foreign news service; *Chicago Daily News* London bureau; Journalists; Yellow journalism; and specific newspapers and journalists

Noel, Edmond Percy, xxvii, 152, 196

Norfolk, Duke of, 190–91

Northcliffe, Lady, 166, 167

Northcliffe, Lord: on absolute ruler for England, 168–69; accomplishments of, 165, 165*n*1, 178; and aviation competition, 166, 166*n*3; Bell's first meeting with, 166*n*2; and Bell's letters to the *Times*, 136, 209, 214; Bell's relationship with, xxxix, 129, 136, 154, 165–76, 273; and Blériot, 225; and British Empire, 175; and censorship of press, 171, 171*nn*11–12, 184; characteristics of, as journalist, 156–57, 165–76; death of, 166, 167*n*5, 274; and Dennis, 167–68; dinner for employees of, 166–67; and dinner honoring Bell, 163; on "diseased" reading and viewing materials, 174–75; on food for body and for brain, 173–75; and Garvin, 160*n*9; home of, 166, 167; illness of, 167–68, 167*n*5; job offers for Bell from, 165–66; and Kitchener, 171–73, 171–72*n*13; lottery scheme of, 173–74; and new journalism, 129*n*30, 136*n*15, 154*n*1, 155*n*2, 169*n*6; newspapers owned by, 129*n*30, 136*n*15, 154*n*1, 165–66, 169, 169*n*6; and party politics, 175; physical appearance of, 170; on travel, 168–69; and U.S. entry into World War I, 176; wealth of, 156; and Wile, 145; and Wilson's "Peace Note," 209–10; youth of, 170, 170*n*8

Northwestern University, xxxix, 59, 287, 289, 324

O'Brien, James, 221

The Observer (London), 136, 136*n*15, 154*n*1, 160, 160*n*9, 203, 296–98, 307, 320

Ochs, Adolph, xvii, xx

O'Connor, T. P., 129, 129*n*30

O'Flaherty, Hal, 152, 283

Ogders, Rev. J. Hastie, 289

Ojibwe Indians, xx, 71–79, 72*n*2, 79*n*4

O'Neill, Aeneas, 205–6

Oxford, Earl of. *See* Asquith, Herbert Henry

Page, Walter Hines, 202–11, 202*n*1, 214–15, 217, 218, 236

Palestine, 138

Pall Mall Gazette, 129*nn*29–30, 154*n*1, 158, 158*n*6, 160*n*9, 180*n*5

Parker, Sir Gilbert, 122, 122*n*10

Parks, Frank, 32

Patent medicine, 43–45

Patterson, Robert Wilson, 118–19, 118*nn*2–3

Peace: and Anglo-American relations after World War I, 288, 295–305; Bell on horrors of war and desire for, 251–52; and Bell's interviews of European leaders after World War I, 277–84, 309–14; and Bell's interviews of world leaders for *Literary Digest*, 309–14; Bell's reaction to end of World War I, 270; and Bell's travels to Far East, 285–86; Flandin on, 311–12; and Geneva disarmament conference, 298, 298*n*2; Hitler on, 314; and Hoover's Good Will Tour to Latin America, 200–201, 289–94, 289*n*5; Keynes on, 270, 270*n*3; Laval on, 311–12; Lawson's directives on, to foreign correspondents, 271; MacDonald on, 283–84, 311; and MacDonald's trip to U.S., 299–305; W. Marx on, 278; Mussolini on, 279–80, 312–13; Poincaré on, 282; Pope Pius XI on, 313–14; recommendation of Bell for Nobel Peace Prize, 324; Simon on, 311; and U.S. neutrality during World War II, 317–21; Versailles Treaty, xxviii, 270*n*3, 274–75, 288*n*3, 316–17; H. H. Wilson on, 249–50, 274; Woodrow Wilson's speech on, in London, 271–72

Pearson, Sir C. Arthur, 264–65, 264*n*8

Peel, Sir Robert, 117, 117*n*1

Petrie, Sir Charles, 124*n*16

Philippines, xviii, 135*n*12

Pitman, Sir Isaac, 14, 14n6

Pius XI, Pope, 312, 313–14

Pius XII, Pope, 314

Plumer, Herbert, 242–43, 242nn6–7, 245–47

Poetry, 10, 25–26, 25n2, 36–38, 57, 287, 287n2, 324

Poincaré, Raymond, 157–58, 157n5, 163, 277, 281–82

Poland, 315, 317n1

Powell, G. B., 234, 235

Powers, Johnny, 94

Prohibition, 290, 299

Pulitzer, Joseph, 137n17, 177, 178n1

R-38 airship, 225–26

Raccoon Valley Independent, 38–45

Race riots in Wilmington, N.C., xxii, 80–89, 80n1

Ralph, Julian, 186

Red Cross, 259–61

Redmond, John Edward, 147, 147n2, 148

Reid, Whitelaw, 145, 145n1

Religion, 58–60, 87–88, 117

Riley, James Whitcomb, 10, 25–26, 25n2, 36–37, 287, 287n2

Robb, Walter, 152

Roberts, Colonel, 228, 264–65

Roberts, Frederick Sleigh, 120, 120n6, 132, 132n8, 180

Roosevelt, Franklin Delano, 274, 274n5, 317–19, 317nn1–2, 318n4

Roosevelt, Theodore, 73n3, 135–36, 135n12, 138, 145n1, 272

Rose, Mr., 104–5

Rosebery, Earl of, 193, 193n2

Rosedale, Ind., 38–45

Roseman, Lizzie, 49, 52

Rosencranz, Major, 47, 48, 52

Rothermere, Lord, 173

Rountree, George, 82

Royko, Mike, 331

Ruskin, John, 57

Russia, xviii, 313

Ryan, Little Mike, 94

Salaries of reporters, xxii, xxv–xxvii, 63, 66, 70, 273

Salisbury, Harrison, xxxv

Salvini, Alessandro, 14, 14n4, 24–25

Salvini, Tommaso, 14n4, 24, 24n1

Sandburg, Carl, 331

Scandinavia, xviii, 149–50

Schuettler, Chief of Police, 94, 96–97

Schults, Raymond, 129n29

Scotland Yard, 220–21

The Scotsman, 203

Scott, Charles Prestwich, 154, 154n1, 157–58, 157n4, 169, 321–22

Scott, Walter Dill, 289

Selfridge, H. Gordon, 123, 123n14, 141, 162, 163

Shakespeare, William, 186

Shanklin brothers, 48, 49

Shanor, Donald, 32

Shidehara, Baron, 216

Shipping News (London), 196

Shorthand skills, ix, 14, 14n6, 20

Simms, Phil, 291

Simon, Sir John Allsebrook, 311, 311n7

Sims, William Sowden, 183, 183n7

Sinn Féin, 219–21, 248

Smalley, George, xx–xxi

Smallwood, Will, 56–58

Smith, Al, 288, 288n4

Smith, C. V., 55

Smith, Donald Alexander, 121–22, 121n9, 126

Smith, Doug, 16, 45–51, 53, 63

Smith, F. E., 140–42, 140n21

Smith, Henry Justin, 152, 152n4, 331

Smuts, Jan Christian, 132n7

Snyder, Milton V., 119

Socialist Party, 35, 127n24, 128nn26–27, 155n1, 280n1, 282, 288, 288n4, 304n5

Southey, Robert, 57

Spain, 238, 238n1

Spanish-American War, xvii–xx, 66–67, 66n1, 67n2, 73, 73n3, 130

The Spectator (London), 136, 136n14, 140, 154n1, 161, 218

Spender, Hugh F., 154n1

Spender, John Alfred, 154, 154n1

St. James's Gazette, 158, 159*n*6

St. Louis Globe-Democrat, 27–34, 27*n*1, 48

Stalin, Josef, 313, 320

Stanley, Henry, xx

Stanton, Theodore, xix–xx

Starrt, James D., xxxvi

Stead, W. T., 129, 129*n*29, 154, 155*n*2, 187

Steed, Wickham, 154, 154*n*1, 273

Steevens, George Warrington, 180, 180*n*5

Stiles, Gordon, 228

Stimson, Henry L., 296, 296*n*1, 308–9

Stone, Melville, xvi–xvii, xix

Strachey, John St. Loe, 136, 136*n*14, 140, 154, 154*n*1, 161, 218

Strathcona, Lord, 121–22, 121*n*9, 126

Strikes, 28–33, 36, 122*n*12, 142, 142*n*24

Stringers, xi, xxi, xxiii

Strong, Walter, xxxiii, xxxv, 286, 289, 296, 300, 309

Suez Canal, 159

Sullivan, Yank, 39, 41

Swing, Raymond, xxiv, 152

Tanner, John R., 94–95, 102, 104–7

Tardieu, Andre, 307–9, 307*n*3

Taylor, J. E., 86–88

Tcherkesoff, Prince, 126–27, 127*n*25, 129

Telegraphy, ix, 14–16, 31, 65

Television, x, xi, xxxi, xxxiii

Terre Haute Daily News, 45–47, 56

Terre Haute Evening Gazette, xxi, 9–17, 26, 45, 185–86

Terre Haute Express, 63–69

Thackeray, William Makepeace, 158

Thomas, Norman, 288, 288*n*4

Thompson, Henry Yates, 158*n*6

Thompson, Richard, 15, 15*n*7

Thompson, Slason, 331

Thomsen, Hans, 314

Thomson, Sir Basil, 220–21

Tillett, Ben, 122, 122*n*12

Times (London): Bell's job offer from, 165–66; Bell's letter on "Balfour Note" in, 136–37; Bell's letter on Hitler, 314; Bell's letters foretelling U.S. entry into World War I

in, xxx, 207–15, 217–19; and Bell's support for Page, 203; and Bell's trip to England after World War I, 297; Dane as editor of, 178*n*3; and dinner honoring Bell, 163; on Germany and Versailles Treaty, 316–17, 319; journalists at, 129, 129*n*30, 143*n*3, 154*n*1; on Kitchener, 171–72*n*13, 172; and MacDonald's trip to U.S., 302; office of, 171*n*10; O'Neill as correspondent for, 205–6; ownership of, 264*n*8; Plumer on Bell's writing in, 243; Walter as founder of, 178*n*3; and Wilson's "Peace Note," xxx, 207–13

Tirpitz, Alfred von, 251, 251*n*7

Titanic, 129, 157

Toynbee Hall, 56, 56*n*1, 57–58

Trevelyan, George Macaulay, 200, 200*n*8, 201

Typesetting, ix, 11–12, 11*n*1

University of Chicago, 324

Vandenberg, Arthur H., 318–19, 318*n*4

Vansittart, Sir Robert, 299

Variety (London), 301

Versailles Treaty, xxviii, 270*n*3, 274–75, 288*n*3, 316–17, 319

Victoria, Queen, 120, 120*n*7, 178*n*3

Voorhees, Daniel, 14, 14*n*5

Wabash College, xxi, 54–56, 58–60

Waddell, Alfred Moore, 83–84, 83*n*2

Waller, Judith, 153

Walter, John, 177–78, 178*n*3

Walters, Basil "Stuffy," xxxiii

Walton, Izaak, 193, 193*n*2

Warneford, Reginald, 232, 232*n*7

Washington Naval Conference, 307, 307*n*3

Washington Post, x, xxxii

Watterson, Henry, 14, 14*n*3

Wehrner, Miss, 111

Weyler, Valeriano, 67, 67*n*2

Whitechapel Club, Chicago, 90, 90*n*1, 92

Wile, Frederic William, xxii, xxvi, 99, 118*n*2, 144–45, 148, 162–64, 162*n*12, 218

Wilhelm, Kaiser, 194–95

Wilhelm II, Kaiser, 120, 120*n*7

Wilhelmina, Queen, 186–89, 293

Williams, Wythe, xxi

Wilmington, N.C., race riots, xxii, 80–89, 80*n*1

Wilmington Star, 82

Wilson, Arthur, 142*n*24

Wilson, Henry Hughes, 221, 221*n*4, 247–50, 247*n*4, 274

Wilson, Woodrow: and Bell's letters to the *Times* foretelling U.S. entry into World War I, 207–15, 217–19; Harvey's criticism of, 137*n*17; House as adviser to, 137*n*16; and League of Nations, 288*n*3; *New Freedom* by, 217–18, 218*n*3; and Page, 217, 218; "Peace Note" by, xxx, 207–13, 207*n*3; speech by, in London after World War I, 271–72; and Zimmermann telegram, 216

Wing, Judge, 90–94, 96–98

Wood, Junius, xxx, xxxvii

Wordsworth, William, 57

World Chancelleries (Bell), xxxiv

World War I: air war during, 133–34, 225–35; Bell on Central Powers in, 206; Bell's flying privileges during, 134, 225–35; Bell's letters to the *Times* foretelling U.S. entry into, xxx, 207–15, 217–19; and Boers, 132, 132*n*7; Britain's declaration of war in, 205–6, 315; British bombing of submarines during, 232; British on West Front of, 173, 173*n*14, 179–80, 179*n*4, 237, 269–70; British war propaganda during, xxx; carrier pigeons used during, 232–33; and *Chicago Daily News* London bureau, xv, xxv, xxx, 133–34, 161–62, 164, 179–80, 225–65; conscription in England during, 173; end of, 269–70; event precipitating, 120*n*7; in France, 161–62, 164; and Gallipoli, 173, 173*n*15; gas emission by Germans during, 237; gas-filled balloons during, 227–28, 227*n*2; German bombing of London during, 133–34, 133–34*n*10;

German occupation of Belgium during, 163, 163*n*13; German propaganda in U.S. during, 208–9, 208*n*4; German sinking of *Lusitania* during, 213, 213*n*1; Grey's speech on, 194, 194*n*4; Haldane-Grey interviews by Bell during, xxx, 3, 3*n*, 190, 192–201, 205; and Hermann line, 270, 270*n*1; and Hindenburg line, 258, 258*n*4, 269–70; howitzers used during, 239–40, 239*nn*2–3; and journalists' status, 178–81, 183–84; and Kitchener, 171–73, 171*n*9, 171–72*nn*11–15, 179–80, 184, 184*n*8; mines during, 264; naval blockade of Germany during, 139–40, 139–40*n*20; sharpshooting by Germans during, 252–54; trench architecture during, 260–61; U.S. entry in, xxx, 137, 137*n*18, 176, 206; U.S. neutrality during, 205, 207, 207*n*3; Wilson's "Peace Note" during, xxx, 207–13, 207*n*3, 210*n*5; and Zimmermann telegram, 215–17, 215*n*2. *See also* Versailles Treaty; and specific generals and politicians

—battles: Bapaume, 258–65; Liège, 246, 246*n*1; Mametz, 261, 261*n*6; Messines Hill, 242–47, 242*nn*6–7; Mont St. Quentin, 256–58, 256*n*1; naval battles, 134, 134*n*11, 183, 183*n*7; Second Battle of the Somme, 161–62, 161*n*11, 257, 257*n*2; Vimy Ridge, 247–55, 247*nn*2–3, 254*n*9; Ypres Salient, 183–84, 184*n*8, 228–29, 236–47

World War II, xxxix, 126*n*22, 306*n*2, 315–21

World's Press News (London), 301

Wright, Orville, 225

Wright, Wilbur, 225

Yellow journalism, xvii, xviii, 67, 178*n*1, 304

Yerkes, Charles T., 93–95, 93*n*3, 97, 98, 100–107

Ypres Salient, 183–84, 184*n*8, 228–29, 236–47

Zeppelins, 133, 133*n*10, 226, 232

Zimmermann, Arthur, 215–17, 215*n*2